Leveraging Services for Development: Prospects and Policies

Edited by

Matthias Helble and Ben Shepherd

Asian Development Bank Institute
Kasumigaseki Building 8F
3-2-5, Kasumigaseki, Chiyoda-ku
Tokyo 100-6008, Japan
www.adbi.org

Contents

Tables, Figures, and Boxes

Figures

Boxes

List of Contributors

Christine Ablaza is a PhD candidate at the Institute for Social Science Research, University of Queensland.

Marcio Cruz is a senior economist in the Finance, Competitiveness and Innovation Global Practice, World Bank.

Matteo Fiorini is a research fellow at the Robert Schuman Centre for Advanced Studies, European University Institute.

John Paul Flaminiano is a graduate student in economics at the University of Ottawa and a former ERCD consultant.

Matthias Helble is an economist in the Economic Research and Regional Cooperation Department, Asian Development Bank.

Bernard Hoekman is a professor and director at the Global Economics at the Robert Schuman Centre for Advanced Studies, European University Institute, and research fellow at CEPR.

Sameer Khatiwada is an economist in the Economic Research and Regional Cooperation Department, ADB.

Justine Lan is an economic affairs officer at the World Trade Organization.

Trang T. Le is a research associate at the Asian Development Bank Institute.

Trinh Q. Long is a project consultant at the Asian Development Bank Institute.

Valerie Mercer-Blackman is a senior economist in the Economic Research and Regional Cooperation Department, Asian Development Bank.

Sébastien Miroudot is senior trade policy analyst in the Trade in Services Division, Organisation for Economic Co-operation and Development, Trade and Agriculture Directorate.

Gaurav Nayyar is a senior economist in the Finance, Competitiveness and Innovation Global Practice, World Bank.

Ben Shepherd is the principal of Developing Trade Consultants.

Erik van der Marel is a senior economist at the European Centre for International Political Economy and associate professor at the Université Libre de Bruxelles.

Deborah Winkler is the principal of Global Economic Policy, LLC.

Acknowledgments

The publication of this book is the outcome of efforts by many. The editors of this book would like to thank Dean Yoshino of the Asian Development Bank Institute (ADBI) and Chief Economist Yasuyuki Sawada of the Asian Development Bank (ADB) sincerely for supporting this book project since its inception in December 2017. The editors also owe a debt of gratitude to the chapter writers of this book. They all delivered exceptional content on schedule and were highly responsive to our comments, which made the editing of this book a very smooth process. A special thanks goes to ADBI, which financed the entire project and generously hosted two workshops in Tokyo in December 2017 and June 2018. We also owe our thanks to the editing team composed of Tiffany Chezum and Adam Majoe and led by Ainslie Smith for their high-quality and speedy work. Finally, we would like to thank the communications teams of ADBI and ADB, especially David Hendrickson and Grant Stillman, for coordinating the publication and promotion of this book.

1

Introduction

Matthias Helble and Ben Shepherd

Economies around the world are shifting toward services. Today, it is estimated that about two-thirds of economic activity worldwide consists of services. In high-income countries, services have accounted for more than two-thirds of gross domestic product since the turn of the millennium, but this share has been increasing slowly. Meanwhile, in low- and middle-income countries the transformation toward services is happening rapidly, with services as a share of the economy increasing from 48.5% in 2007 to 54.3% in 2017 (World Bank).

Services are not only increasingly responsible for value added, but also for jobs created. Today, about half of the world's workforce is active in the services sector. This share has increased most rapidly in low- and middle-income countries. Figure 1.1 illustrates how the employment shares in agriculture, manufacturing, and services have changed in high-, low-, and middle-income countries over time, with this figure increasing from 28.5% in 1995 to 44.8% in 2015 in low- and middle-income countries. This rise occurred at the same time as did a fall in employment in agriculture. As agriculture has become more capital-intensive and less labor-intensive, workers are moving almost directly into the services sector, skipping the manufacturing sector.

This relatively rapid shift toward services has been received with a certain skepticism. The main concern is whether services can be a source of sustained economic growth comparable to the manufacturing sector. Many experts cite the work of Kaldor (1967), who in his seminal book postulated that productivity increases in the manufacturing sector were the main driving force of overall economic growth. He argued that other sectors, such as agriculture and services, are hampered by low productivity. Kaldor (1967) did not provide an elaborate analysis of why services would be low in productivity. His main argument was that the demand for services would be constrained by the domestic market and thus limited, whereas the manufacturing sector enjoyed an unlimited demand thanks to export opportunities. His hypothesis was mainly based on observations of the post-war economic development of the United Kingdom.

Figure 1.1 Employment Shares of Macro Sectors (1995–2015)

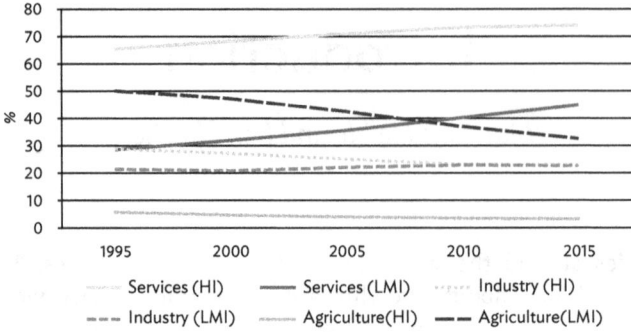

HI = high-income countries, LMI = low- to middle-income countries.
Source: World Bank. World Development Indicators: Economy. http://datatopics.worldbank.org/world-development-indicators/themes/economy.html (accessed 10 April 2019); based on International Labour Organization estimates.

The literature on the structural transformation of economies has recently regained popularity in the field of economics. This renewed interest was mainly triggered by Piketty's influential book on long-term trends in inequality and factor rewards (Piketty 2014), as well as by a several seminal papers studying the sudden fall in manufacturing employment and rise in inequality in the United States (US) (e.g. Autor, Dorn, and Hanson 2016). In the development context, Rodrik's concept of premature deindustrialization has received considerable attention from scholars as well as policy makers. Rodrik's main hypothesis is that developing countries are seeing their employment share of manufacturing decline at a lower level and at an earlier stage of economic development than currently advanced economies. Building on Kaldor's work, Rodrik concludes that developing countries should actively seek to increase the employment share in manufacturing, or risk limiting long-term growth prospects (Rodrik 2016).

Parallel to, and possibly inspired by, these debates in the field of economics, several countries have taken active measures to reinvigorate their manufacturing sectors. In 2014, the Government of India launched the "Make in India" initiative with the explicit objective to transform the country into a global manufacturing hub. A year later in 2015, the Government of the People's Republic of China (PRC) announced the strategy "Made in China 2025." The upgrading of traditional and advanced manufacturing industries is one of the main targets of this strategy. In 2018, the Government of the US under President Donald Trump began imposing tariffs on a wide range of industrial goods from various trading partners, but mainly from the PRC, with the stated goal of bringing manufacturing jobs back to the US.

With regard to the long-term dynamics of economic development, these policy measures are highly questionable. The shift of employment and value creation from agriculture toward manufacturing and more recently toward services are transformations driven by demand and supply factors. As economies develop, demand first increases for manufactured goods and later for services, such as health and recreational services. In terms of supply, the manufacturing sector is becoming more capital-intensive and less labor-intensive, mainly due to technological progress. The manufacturing sector is thus no longer absorbing large amounts of labor. Instead, the services sector has become the sector of current and future employment. Policies to engineer an increase in employment in the manufacturing sector artificially are thus ill-suited to create sustained growth and will be very costly. The policy challenge is not to reverse the long-term trends toward services, but to ensure that it delivers inclusive growth and sustainable development.

The objective of this book is to provide an up-to-date understanding of the services sector as an engine of growth. Despite the significance of the services sector, it has still not received the attention it deserves from both scholars and policy makers. Recent advances in information technology (IT) and global connectivity have drastically changed how services can be provided and consumed, both within countries and across borders. In addition, technological advances have opened up new areas for service providers. The growth potential for services is very promising and its limits are still unknown.

This book therefore constitutes a timely read for all interested in services and services trade. We hope that policy makers and academics alike enjoy the book. Each chapter contains proposals that are highly relevant for policy. Some chapters use econometric analysis to answer a specific research question. However, the authors also provide a nontechnical summary of the main findings at the beginning of each chapter and derive concrete policy proposals.

The book is divided into four parts addressing four main themes: The first theme is the role of the services sector in generating economic growth and sustainable development. To address this, we first examine whether the services sector has been successful in improving its productivity and how its productivity compares to that of manufacturing. Part 1 also studies how a less restrictive services trade policy can improve access to services that support sustainable development. Part 2 aims to shed new light on the question of how manufacturing and services are related. It presents new evidence as to how closely intertwined the two sectors are and discusses the statistical challenges arising from this. Furthermore, Part 2 highlights the potential for pro-competitive reforms in services to boost manufacturing performance. Part 3 comprises a detailed analysis of what drives productivity growth in the services sector. The use of technology and skills combined with open markets are strong predictors of productivity growth and spillovers of services firms. The last theme of this book is the potential of services to offer decent and more gender-balanced jobs.

Several facts about services are well established. First, the services sector is highly heterogenous in many respects. While some services sectors are highly technology-intensive, such as banking or other financial industries, technology is used much less frequently in other sectors, such as legal services. In terms of competition, some business services are open to market competition, whereas other services, such as education and health, predominantly fall under the domain of governments. The size of services companies can also vary significantly. Compared to the manufacturing industry, services often require less physical capital. Service providers thus have lower fixed costs and can remain small in size.

Another stylized fact is that manufacturing increasingly uses inputs from services in its production processes. One main reason for the so-called "servicification" of manufacturing is the fragmentation of manufacturing production into tasks, such as research, marketing, and logistics. Manufacturing firms increasingly outsource tasks in the value chain and thus increase the demand for service providers. Advances in information and communications technology (ICT) as well as lower trade costs have made it possible to spread tasks across countries. Services are becoming an integral part of regional and global value chains (GVCs), implying that the sector is no longer constrained by domestic demand and can thus expand. Furthermore, being exposed to international competition helps to increase the sector's productivity.

Services that enjoy relatively high productivity tend to make intensive use of ICT. These services sectors also employ a high share of skilled workers. Although future growth in labor productivity might be constrained by the availability of skilled workers, this does not imply that the manufacturing sector could absorb them. Due to more capital-intensive production, manufacturing is requiring increasingly fewer low-skilled workers. Thus, the manufacturing and services sectors are both in need of a skilled workforce and skill upgrading. The potential of the services sector to lead productivity growth depends crucially on these factors.

A common feature of the services sector across countries is the fact that trade opening in services has been slow and lagged behind trade liberalization efforts with respect to goods. Trade in services only entered the multilateral trading system with the creation of the World Trade Organization in 1995. Preferential trade agreements increasingly incorporate commitments on trade in services. Despite these efforts the barriers to trade in services remain relatively high, and the Organisation for Economic Co-operation and Development (2018) has estimated that they constitute a much higher barrier to trade than do tariffs.

Trade in services thus remains subject to high trade barriers. Yet, as a result of technological progress, almost all services across all modes can now be traded across borders and are increasingly being exchanged. Before the advent of new ICT, it was unthinkable that a surgeon could operate on a patient physically located in another country. Another trend that would have been hard to imagine previously is that every day millions of students attend online classes in other countries. Furthermore, a drop in the cost of cross-border transportation has increased the number of people moving internationally and providing or consuming services abroad. Even a haircut, a widely referenced example of an allegedly non-tradable service, can now be traded across borders, with famous hair stylists traveling across countries to provide their services and some clients willing to do the same. While this market is certainly very small, these examples illustrate that it is becoming increasingly difficult to find a service that is not being traded internationally.

Services can be provided in four modes of supply as defined in the General Agreement on Trade in Services. Today, companies typically use several of these modes when interacting with a customer. In Mode 1, services can be sold across borders without requiring the service provider or the consumer to move. However, if, for example, an information technology (IT) company in the US purchases a new IT application developed in Mexico and sends its employees to Mexico to be trained in the new IT application, then the service delivery falls under Mode 2 trade (consumption abroad). If the application finds success in the US, the Mexican company might decide to open a branch in the US, a transaction that would be classified as Mode 3 trade (commercial presence abroad). Finally, if, to secure a smooth business collaboration, the Mexican IT company begins to dispatch specialists regularly to travel to the US to explain their products to its customers, this temporary movement of professionals across countries to provide a service is categorized as Mode 4 trade.

The fact that services are increasingly being traded internationally has had an impact on their productivity. For the manufacturing industry, we have well-established evidence that countries tend to move toward the international productivity frontier. In contrast, it was long believed that services would not follow the same dynamic and would be constrained by domestic productivity frontiers. However, we now have increasing evidence that services have also begun to converge toward an international productivity frontier (International Monetary Fund 2018). There are two main reasons for this. First, while the demand for services was initially limited to the domestic market, the increased tradability of services has opened up the global market for service providers and thus offers previously unknown opportunities. Second, technological progress and the rapid propagation of knowledge has allowed service providers in less advanced economies to upgrade their operations and move closer to the frontier.

Asia

Several chapters in this book focus on the Asian region. We consider Asia one of the most interesting regions to study with regard to the question of services-led development. The structural transformation has been particularly fast in many developing countries in Asia. For example, in the PRC, the share of agricultural employment fell from 49.4% in 1995 to 17.5% in 2017, while services employment increased from 21.6% to 55.9% during the same period. In India and Indonesia, the other two most populous countries in Asia, the share of people employed in services has now reached 47.1% (in India) and 33.5% (in Indonesia). Today, services account for about 60% of the region's economic activity and employ 45.5% of its labor (World Bank, World Development Indicators).

In Asia, trade in services has also increased rapidly in recent decades. Asia's efforts to open trade combined with technological advances have propelled trade in services. Figure 1.2 depicts the growth of nominal exports of manufacturing, commercial services, and travel in Asia. The value of exports of commercial services increased from $515 billion in 2005 to $1,325 billion in 2017, clearly outpacing the growth of merchandise exports. One reason for the strong growth in services is the fact that manufacturing is increasingly relying on services. As described above, more and more services are entering the manufacturing process as intermediate goods. As production is organized in regional and GVCs, services are increasingly being traded. Yet, services still represent only 17.2% of total exports (merchandise and services), implying a high untapped potential.

The move toward services is also reflected in the rise of foreign direct investment (FDI) in services in Asia. Historically, FDI in Asia mainly took the form of greenfield investment in the manufacturing sector, building up regional and GVCs for the production of goods.

Figure 1.2 Asia's Exports of Commercial Services, Merchandise, and Travel to the World (indexed 2005 = 100)

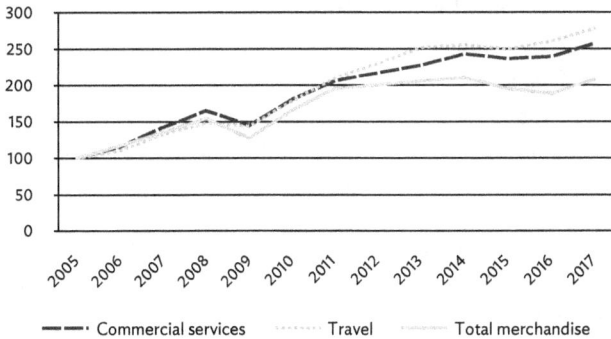

Sources: Authors' calculation; World Trade Organization. 2018. Statistics on Trade in Commercial Services. https://www.wto.org/english/res_e/statis_e/tradeserv_stat_e.htm (accessed 12 December 2018).

However, more recently we have observed a rise in mergers and acquisitions in the services sector. As a consequence, FDI in services is accounting for an increasing share of total FDI (see Figure 1.3). In 2015, FDI in services accounted for 53.1% of total FDI in Asia.

Figure 1.3 Total Inward Foreign Direct Investment (Greenfield and Mergers and Acquisitions) to Asia, by Sector ($ billion)

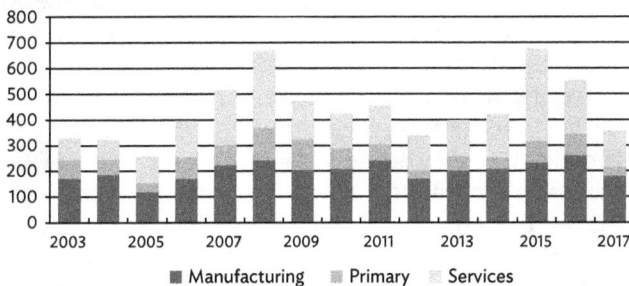

Source: Asian Development Bank. 2018. *Asian Economic Integration Report*. October. Manila: Asian Development Bank; authors' calculation.

Overall, Asia's rapid structural transformation toward services makes it crucial to gain a better understanding of this sector of the economy and the opportunities it offers. We hope that this book can make a valuable contribution to this end.

Chapter Overview

The first part of the book examines how services promote economic growth and how barriers to trade in services impede access to services, thereby hindering development.

The first chapter, by Gaurav Nayyar and Marcio Cruz, explores the prospects for services-led development compared to the traditional export-led manufacturing model. The authors find that determinants of productivity growth previously thought unique to manufacturing are increasingly shared by some services sectors. These sectors can thus become engines of economic growth without requiring a manufacturing core. However, the authors highlight that these sectors typically require high-skilled workers. The main challenge is to find opportunities for low-skilled labor in the services industry where productivity gains can be achieved equally. New technologies can help to raise substantially the productivity of notoriously low-productivity services sectors, such as construction and hotels. The authors also point out that there is a high level of resource misallocation within the services sector. Reducing this could be another way to boost aggregate output.

Chapter 3, entitled "Restrictiveness of Services Trade Policy and the Sustainable Development Goals" by Matteo Fiorini and Bernard Hoekman, first maps out the role of trade in services in achieving the sustainable development goals (SDGs). The authors explain that more trade in services is associated with economic growth and increased income, which is critical for realizing many of the SDGs. They then show how opening trade in services can help realize the SDGs by improving access to services. Using an econometric approach, the authors demonstrate that reducing the level of services trade and investment restrictiveness enhances the performance of the domestic services sectors and increases access to services. An important policy recommendation that they derive is that the pursuit of the SDGs should include a focus on facilitating trade and investment in services.

Part II of the book is dedicated to the question of how the manufacturing and services sectors are becoming increasingly interdependent and mutually reinforcing for each other. In the chapter entitled "Services and Manufacturing in Global Value Chains," Sebastien Miroudot first challenges the belief that the current statistical frameworks accurately capture the activities of manufacturing and services firms. He shows that, in the age of GVCs, it has become increasingly difficult to disentangle manufacturing from services activities. Goods are produced with services, services are produced with goods, some manufacturing firms do not have factories, and companies tend to sell solutions to customers by bundling goods with services. The chapter then introduces a taxonomy of services activities in GVCs and describes the main statistical challenges in assessing the contribution of manufacturing and services to output, value added, and trade. Finally, the chapter reviews three approaches that GVCs take into account in analyzing income, comparative advantage, and productivity to address these challenges.

Chapter 5, by Valerie Mercer-Blackman and Cristina Ablaza, studies the rise of 'servicification' of manufacturing in Asia. The authors exploit an updated global dataset to estimate the contribution of services to the production of both traded and non-traded manufacturing goods, as well as the link with labor productivity. The authors distinguish between direct and indirect contribution: direct components are services directly used as inputs in manufacturing sectors for arms-length transactions, while indirect components are defined as services incorporated in inputs that are used by a particular sector. For example, an automobile manufacturer may require basic metals, which are produced using leased equipment; thus, rent is an indirect input to the manufacture of a vehicle. The estimates show that the direct contribution of services to manufacturing's value added stayed broadly constant between 2000 and 2017, while the indirect contribution grew by more than 15%. Together, the direct and indirect contribution of services to a $1.00 value added in manufacturing has increased from $0.55 in 2000 to $0.62 in 2017.

Chapter 6, by Ben Shepherd, uses a structural gravity model to compare the effects of liberalizing services versus lowering tariffs on manufacturing exports. His results show that the effects on trade and output are greater in the former scenario than in the latter. Discriminatory barriers to services trade thus have a significant negative effect on manufacturing exports. The intuition behind these results is that exporters of manufactured goods typically source a substantial amount of their inputs from world services markets. Liberalizing services policies allows these exporters to access services inputs on global markets at competitive prices, leading to a positive productivity shock and greater exports. The chapter underscores the important finding that the development of manufacturing cannot be divorced from the development of services, and that policies that bring about more competitive and integrated services markets are perfectly aligned with the goal of promoting manufacturing.

Part III examines the prospects for developing countries to achieve productivity growth in services. Chapter 7, by Deborah Winkler, assesses whether spillovers from services firms to manufacturing firms occur in low- and middle-income countries. Using cross-sectional data from the World Bank's Enterprise Surveys on more than 38,000 manufacturing firms and 24,000 services firms in 105 low- and middle-income countries, the chapter finds positive spillovers as long as the services firms enjoy high productivity and technological intensity. Furthermore, the magnitude of the spillovers depends on a country's income status and the manufacturing firm's absorptive capacity, including its services intensity, firm size, foreign ownership status, and exporting behavior. Finally, using the World Bank's Services Trade Restrictions database, the author shows that services liberalization increases productivity spillovers from services firms to manufacturing firms.

Chapter 8, by Ben Shepherd, first presents the evolution of services in Asia from 1995 to 2011 and shows that services exports have grown nearly as rapidly as manufacturing exports. The author concludes that services are thus an integral part of "Factory Asia." Building on this trade data, the author uses a recently developed Ricardian model of trade to predict patterns of relative comparative advantage in manufacturing and services across countries. The results show that the revealed productivity measures differ markedly across sectors and countries, but are often comparable between manufacturing and services. Over time, the author observes a rapid increase in revealed productivity in some services subsectors, comparable to what has been seen in manufacturing. These findings also suggest that it is important to look at performance at a disaggregated level to better understand the development potential of the services sector.

In chapter 9, Erik van der Marel studies the role of new technologies in promoting productivity in manufacturing and services. He first shows that digital-intensive services sectors have experienced significant productivity increases in recent years, comparable to or larger than in the overall manufacturing sector. Digital-intensive services can therefore become a primary driver of overall economic growth. Next, the chapter shows that larger amounts of ICT services used in the manufacturing and service sectors are strongly associated with a larger contribution of value added to the economy across countries. Finally, the author assesses empirically the effect of regulatory restrictions on data services on productivity. His findings reveal that restrictive digital policies, especially on data, hinder productivity growth. The author concludes that policies regulating data and the internet should be developed with great care to avoid inhibiting prospective productivity developments in services.

The last part of the book focuses on the topic of labor markets in services. Chapter 10, by Sameer Khatiwada, asks how the services sector can provide decent and gainful employment in developing Asia. He first observes that recent developments in ICT have greatly expanded business opportunities for developing economies through the global outsourcing of tradeable labor. To make the modern services industry the backbone of inclusive growth, workers must be moved from low- to high-productivity sectors. The chapter identifies two primary challenges to this strategy: first, further training and upskilling of workers in the traditional services sectors are needed to generate a more skilled workforce while mitigating informal employment and unemployment. Second, developing economies must expand their investments in infrastructure, including electric power, road and rail connectivity, telecommunications, air transport, and efficient ports, to increase their capacity to provide modern and highly productive services.

Chapter 11, by Matthias Helble, Trinh Long and Trang Le, first provides new evidence on the labor productivity of the services sector in developing Asia. Using data from the Asian Productivity Organization as well as the World Input–Output data and applying a decomposition approach, the authors show that in many Asian economies the services sector has made the largest contribution to labor productivity growth in recent years. Furthermore, they draw attention to the major reallocation of labor from agriculture to services, bypassing the manufacturing sector. This finding challenges the traditional view that, to develop economically, economies must see their workforces employed first in manufacturing before switching to services. Lastly, the chapter examines how different skill levels contribute to productivity growth. The chapter suggests that medium- to high-skilled workers have been contributing the most to overall labor productivity growth in developing Asia. In particular, medium- and high-skilled workers have been driving productivity in services, indicating that upskilling and training are instrumental for services-led development.

The final chapter, by Justine Lan and Ben Shepherd, is dedicated to the topic of women in the services sector in developing Asia. The chapter first uses country-level data to show that the distribution of female employment has continuously shifted away from agriculture and manufacturing toward services in all regions of the world. Women have been absorbed into the services sector relatively quickly, which can be explained by the increasing relative importance of services, the comparative advantage that women enjoy in services, the inadequate demand for female labor in industry, and sometimes gender-based legal restrictions excluding women from certain jobs in heavy industries. In the second part of the chapter, the authors use firm-level data to analyze the role of female management in firms' success. They find that the share of female-managed firms is, on average, higher in services than in manufacturing in all regions of the world. Furthermore, an econometric analysis reveals that more productive firms in the services sector are more likely to have a female senior manager. Overall, the authors conclude that services can serve as a powerful avenue toward achieving gender equality, if the proper policies are in place.

References

Asian Development Bank. 2018. *Asian Economic Integration Report*. October. Manila: Asian Development Bank.

Autor, D., D. Dorn, and G. Hanson. 2016. The China Shock: Learning from Labor Market Adjustment to Large Changes in Trade. *Annual Review of Economics* 8: 205–240.

International Monetary Fund (IMF). 2018. Manufacturing Jobs: Implications for Productivity and Inequality. *IMF World Economic Outlook 2018* Ch. 3. April. Washington, DC: IMF.

Kaldor, N. 1967. *Strategic Factors in Economic Development*. Ithaca: New York State School of Industrial and Labor Relations, Cornell University.

Organisation for Economic Co-operation and Development (OECD). 2018. OECD Services Trade Restrictiveness Index. Trade Policy Note, March. Paris: OECD.

Piketty, T. 2014. *Capital in the Twenty-First Century*. Cambridge, MA: The Belknap Press of Harvard University Press.

Rodrik, D. 2016. Premature Deindustrialization. *Journal of Economic Growth* 21: 1–33.

World Bank. World Development Indicators: Economy. http://datatopics .worldbank.org/world-development-indicators/ (accessed 11 December 2018).

PART I
Services, Development, and Trade

2

Developing Countries and Services in the New Industrial Paradigm

Gaurav Nayyar and Marcio Cruz

2.1 Introduction

Some of the biggest development gains in history have been associated with industrialization. Technological advances from the late 1700s to the mid-1800s spurred a manufacturing-based, fossil-energy-fueled Industrial Revolution, leading to a significant boost in growth among early industrializers. During 1820–1870, average annual per capita income growth reached 1.0% in the earliest industrializing countries in Western Europe and 1.3% in the United States (US). In contrast, growth remained close to zero in other regions such as East Asia and Latin America (Bolt and Van Zanden 2014). Other countries began to catch up to the early industrializers by industrializing themselves, a process that began in the late 19th century with Japan, before spreading to other parts of East Asia during the 1960s and more recently the People's Republic of China (PRC) (Leipziger 1997; Rodrik 1994; Stiglitz and Yusuf 2001; World Bank 1993). The few countries that have reached high income levels through other means have done so by extracting natural resources or exploiting specific locational or other advantages.

However, between 1950 and 2012 the peak shares of manufacturing in value added and employment across a range of developing economies were both lower and occurred at lower levels of per capita income compared to their high-income, early industrializer precursors. This premature deindustrialization suggests that not all countries have benefited equally from the manufacturing sector as a central driver of development. Looking ahead, there is concern that new technologies and resulting shifts in patterns of globalization may make it even harder for lower income countries to play a significant role in manufacturing.

To the degree that new technologies associated with Industry 4.0—such as robotics, the internet of things, and three-dimensional (3D) printing— may be labor-saving, they are potentially making it more difficult for less developed countries to industrialize.

At the same time, features of manufacturing once thought of as uniquely favorable for productivity growth might be increasingly shared by the services sector. Technologies associated with the information and communications technology (ICT) revolution have made it possible to trade various professional services internationally. At the same time, the deregulation of services markets has coincided with a marked increase in foreign direct investment inflows for some services activities. The increased integration of trade and investment means that services increasingly yield the benefits of scale, greater competition, and technology diffusion. Innovation has also been growing rapidly in certain segments of the services sector. These productivity-enhancing characteristics associated with different services sectors are reflected in those sectors' levels of productivity and contribution to economic growth. So, can services-led development offer an alternative to the traditional export-led manufacturing model? To answer this question, it is also necessary to consider its potential for widespread job creation, particularly for unskilled labor, and to determine whether the services sector can grow in the absence of a manufacturing core.

2.2 Premature Deindustrialization

The literature on structural change during the 1960s documented canonical shifts of output and labor—from agriculture to industry, and then from industry to services—in the structural transformation of today's advanced economies (Kaldor 1963; Kuznets 1971). However, recent trends show that the share of manufacturing in employment and value added appears to be peaking at lower levels and at earlier levels of per capita gross domestic product (GDP) than in the past (Figure 2.1). Controlling for population size and per capita GDP in a sample of 42 economies between 1950 and 2012, Rodrik (2016) finds a lower share of manufacturing in employment and value added over time, as reflected in the coefficients of decadal time dummy variables, which are negative and larger over time. Therefore, if industrialization is defined as an increase in the share of manufacturing in employment and value added, these results are indicative of "premature deindustrialization" (Dasgupta and Singh 2007).

The following should be noted: first, the trend of "premature deindustrialization" is not uniform across manufacturing subsectors. For example, in low- and lower middle-income countries in sub-Saharan

Figure 2.1 Peak Manufacturing Share of Total Employment (1950–2012)

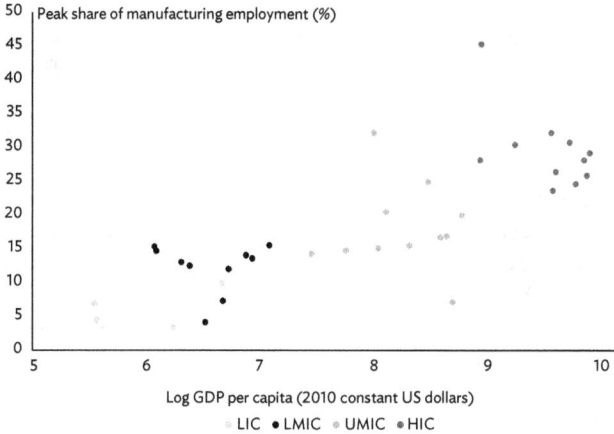

GDP = gross domestic product, HIC = high-income country, LIC = low-income country, LMIC = lower middle-income country, UMIC = upper middle-income country, US = United States.
Note: The sample covers the period 1950–2012.
Source: Groningen Growth and Development Center, 10-Sector Database.

Africa (e.g., Tanzania) where the manufacturing share of GDP declined between 1994 and 2015, the share of commodity-based processing manufacturing, such as that of food, beverages, and tobacco, typically expanded. Among upper middle-income countries in Latin America where the manufacturing share of GDP declined between 1994 and 2015, Peru and Ecuador saw an increase in the GDP share of commodity-based processing manufactures, while Brazil, Colombia, Mexico, and Uruguay saw an increase in the GDP share of industries such as computing, electronics, and optical equipment and pharmaceutical products over the same period (albeit from a low base) (Hallward-Driemeier and Nayyar 2017).

Second, defining deindustrialization as declining *shares* does not necessarily mean that manufacturing employment or value added has declined in *absolute* terms over time. In fact, these relative declines of the manufacturing sector's share of GDP and/or employment translate into absolute declines in very few instances. Of a large cross-section of countries, an absolute decline in real manufacturing value added over the past 20 years was seen in 12 countries, many of which were enduring conflict situations. Although some high-income countries have seen only marginal increases over the past 20 years (such as Italy, the United Kingdom, and the US), many other countries have seen significant growth, more than doubling or tripling their real manufacturing value added. As for employment, a somewhat larger share of countries experienced an absolute decline in jobs.[1] Seven countries stand out for having lost close to 1 million or more manufacturing jobs from 1994 to 2011 (Hallward-Driemeier and Nayyar 2017).[2]

Third, premature deindustrialization may be attributable, at least in part, to the fact that activities previously classified as "manufacturing" are now "services." This reflects a statistical artifice, whereby activities previously subsumed in manufacturing value added are now accounted for as services sector contributions to GDP. Due to a larger scale and the application of new technologies that have made production more complex, firms in the manufacturing sector may find it more profitable to "contract out" service activities to specialist providers than to produce them in-house, a process that Bhagwati (1984) refers to as "splintering." Estimates suggest that such "contracting out" can explain about 10% of annual average services sector growth in large developing economies such as Brazil, the PRC, India, and the Russian Federation between 2000 and 2014 (Nayyar, Cruz, and Zhu 2018). It is worth noting that these estimates are based on input–output tables and therefore do not reflect the increased services intensity of manufacturers within firm boundaries.

2.3 Industry 4.0 and the Changing Feasibility of Manufacturing-Led Development

The potential for low- and middle-income economies to boost their manufacturing exports and leverage them for growth in the future will be further influenced by how emerging labor-saving technologies transform production processes. Greater digitalization through the internet of things, advanced robotics, and 3D printing—some of the most emphasized technologies in the Industry 4.0 literature (Cirera et al. 2017)—may challenge established patterns of comparative advantage if it becomes more efficient to rebundle activities in "smart" factories. By reducing the relative importance of wage competitiveness, increased automation under Industry 4.0 may induce some leading firms to reshore labor-intensive activities back to high-income economies and closer to final consumers.

---

[1] Comparable data for employment across sectors are only available from 66 countries.

[2] These countries are the Russian Federation, Japan, the US, Ukraine, Germany, the United Kingdom, and France.

Although the available evidence suggests that reports about the advent of reshoring and subsequent changes in globally fragmented production are exaggerated (De Backer et al. 2016), there are signs of a beginning. In 2016, Citigroup and the University of Oxford's Oxford Martin School reported that 70% of surveyed Citi institutional clients believe that automation will encourage companies to move their manufacturing closer to home. North America was seen as having the most to gain from this trend, while the PRC, Association of Southeast Asian Nations member countries, and Latin America were seen as having the most to lose (Citigroup 2016). For example, 3D printing can dramatically shorten the design-to-production cycle of footwear manufacturing from 18 months to less than a week (*Economist* 2017). Adidas, the German sporting goods company, has established "speedfactories" in Ansbach, Germany and Atlanta, GA that produce athletic footwear through the almost exclusive use of computerized knitting, robotic cutting, and 3D printing.

At the same time, the PRC stands out as a middle-income country that is rapidly automating production through robotization to address declining wage competitiveness. Standard Chartered Global Research (2016) found that 48% of 290 surveyed manufacturers in the Pearl River Delta would consider automation or streamlining processes in response to labor shortages, while less than one-third would consider moving capacity either inland or out of the PRC. However, some high-profile firms are already replacing a substantial number of workers with industrial robots. For example, Foxconn—the firm known for producing Apple and Samsung products in the PRC's Jiangsu province—recently replaced 60,000 factory workers with industrial robots (*South China Morning Post* 2016). Nationally, with more than 400,000 industrial robots in 2018 (Figure 2.2), the PRC is estimated to have the largest operational stock in the world, accounting for about one-fourth of industrial robots installed globally.

If high-income economies are reshoring production, this could affect current manufacturing exporters and stifle the potential entry of newcomers. The case of the PRC is potentially even more important given recent expectations of a migration en masse of light manufacturing activities to poorer economies with lower labor costs, such as those in sub-Saharan Africa. This could lead to manufacturing-led development strategies becoming less feasible. If low wages are no longer sufficient to keep a country competitive, producers may need to meet more demanding ecosystem requirements in terms of infrastructure, logistics and other backbone services, regulatory requirements, and supplier bases, among others. Firms in countries with a less established manufacturing base will face greater challenges

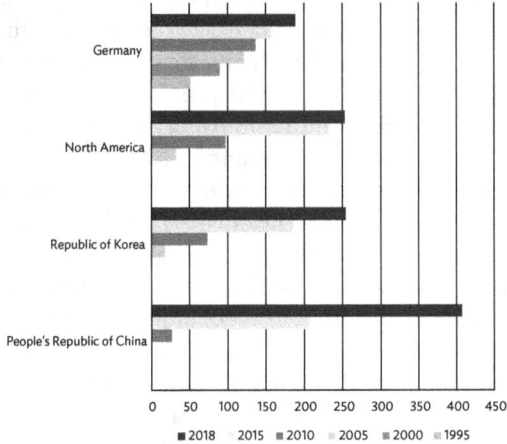

Figure 2.2 Operational Stock of Industrial Robots in the Manufacturing Sector, 1995–2018
('000)

Source: International Federation of Robotics.

in leapfrogging into using new technologies if they have not already established certain processes, skills, and networks using more accessible technologies.

2.4 Why Manufacturing was Special in the Past

The empirical evidence documents a robust association between the growth of manufacturing activity and overall economic growth. "Kaldor's growth laws," which are based on data from high-income economies in the 1960s, proposed that economic growth is related to positive associations between three different pairs of factors: (i) growth of manufacturing output and average GDP growth, (ii) growth of manufacturing output and manufacturing productivity, and (iii) growth of manufacturing output and the overall productivity of the economy (Kaldor 1966). More recent evidence based on data from low- and middle-income countries (LMICs) also reveals a positive relationship between the growth of manufacturing output and overall GDP growth (Fagerberg and Verspagen 1999; Szirmai and Verspagen 2015). Between

Figure 2.3 Share of Manufacturing in Value Added and Employment and Per Capita Income Growth, 1970–2010 (percentage points)

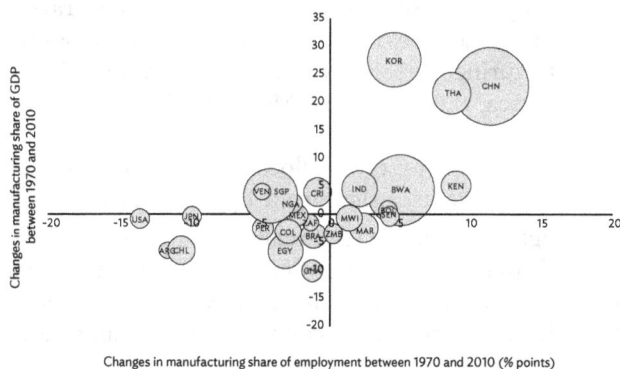

Changes in manufacturing share of employment between 1970 and 2010 (% points)

Note: The size of the circle corresponds to differences in per capita income growth rates across countries.

Source: Groningen Growth and Development Center, 10-Sector Database.

1970 and 2010, the PRC, the Republic of Korea, and Thailand saw significant increases in the share of manufacturing in employment and value added, as well as some of the highest per capita income growth rates in the world (Figure 2.3).

However, these relationships in the data represent correlations not causality, which is hard to establish. In fact, the potential impact on development of how a good is produced is just as important—if not more so—as that of what is produced. Baldwin (1969), de Ferranti et al. (2002), Lederman and Maloney (2010), and Rodríguez-Clare (2007) caution that expanding a sector with potential positive spillovers does not necessarily imply that the spillovers will automatically occur if the sector is not organized appropriately. For example, although both the Republic of Korea and Mexico began assembling electronics in the early 1980s, only the Republic of Korea has produced a truly indigenous electronic device: the Samsung Galaxy smartphone line.

Production processes in the manufacturing sector have typically absorbed large numbers of relatively unskilled workers from other sectors, particularly agriculture, at a substantial productivity premium. Large and systematic differences in labor productivity between the agricultural and manufacturing sectors are well documented, with these intersectoral gaps being widest in the poorest countries (Caselli 2005; Herrendorf, Rogerson, and Valentinyi 2013; Restuccia, Yang, and Zhu 2008). Across developing countries, the typical worker in manufacturing produces four times more output on average than the typical worker in agriculture. There is some variation across regions: the average manufacturing–agriculture productivity ratio is 2.3 in Africa, 2.8 in Latin America, and 3.9 in Asia (McMillan, Rodrik, and Verduzco-Gallo 2014).

Given these differences, the reallocation of labor from agriculture to manufacturing presents a significant opportunity for productivity-enhancing structural change. This relates to the literature on dual-economy models that placed the movement of surplus labor from (rural) agriculture to (urban) manufacturing along with capital accumulation in manufacturing at the center of economic development (Lewis 1954). Evidence suggests that the bulk of the difference between productivity performance in Asian countries and that in most countries in sub-Saharan Africa and Latin America was accounted for by differences in the pattern of structural change, with labor moving from low- to high-productivity sectors in Asia, but in the opposite direction in Latin America and Africa (McMillan, Rodrik, and Verduzco-Gallo 2014).[3] Over time, if productivity growth is higher in manufacturing than in agriculture, the benefits from resource reallocation accrue dynamically.

In contrast, the mining sector—the productivity of which is also significantly higher than that of agriculture (16.8 times higher among a sample of 11 countries in sub-Saharan Africa [McMillan and Rodrik 2011])—is capital-intensive and thus cannot absorb as much of the unskilled labor supply as the manufacturing sector. The education, health, and professional services sectors (where high value-added, high-productivity services are typically skill-intensive) may be skill-biased, whereas many low-end services that *could* absorb surplus labor from agriculture typically provide little productivity growth. The latter illustrates Baumol's (1967) "cost disease" hypothesis, which emphasized that productivity in labor-intensive services cannot be readily increased through capital accumulation, innovation, or economies of scale.

Furthermore, in contrast to evidence on per capita income levels or aggregate labor productivity, Rodrik (2011) shows that labor productivity in (formal) manufacturing exhibits "unconditional convergence" across countries. Therefore, labor productivity in lagging manufacturing

---

3   Since 2000, structural change has contributed positively to Africa's overall productivity growth, accounting for about 40% of the total, on average, across the 19 countries in the sample.

sectors, such as those in low- and middle-income economies, tends to rise over time and eventually converges with the global technological frontier, regardless of policy and institutional determinants. More recent evidence suggests that high productivity growth in the manufacturing sector explains about 50% of the catch-up in relative aggregate productivity across countries (Duarte and Restuccia 2010). This convergence may be attributable to the manufacturing sector's production of tradable goods. International trade provides firms with the opportunity to access a larger market, thereby facilitating scale economies. Such integration also expands the scope for "learning-by-doing" and technology diffusion. Even if they produce solely for the domestic market, manufacturing firms must boost their productivity to compete with efficient suppliers from abroad.

Although agricultural products are also traded internationally, they typically face price volatility in export markets, and productivity improvements have been closely linked to labor-saving technologies. Demand-side dynamics also play a role: as per capita incomes rise, the share of agricultural products in total expenditure declines, while the share of manufactured goods increases in accordance with a hierarchy of needs. As a result, countries specializing in agricultural production do not benefit from the global expansion of markets for manufactured goods (Szirmai 2012). As for the services sector, as noted above, high-end services have typically been skill-intensive and were largely not tradable in the past.

Other spillover effects associated with the manufacturing sector were manifested in its contribution to innovation and linkages with other sectors in the economy. Based on a sample of the 2,000 companies that spend the most on research and development (R&D), it has been observed that about 90% of the patents published in 2014 were related to manufactured goods and almost 80% of all R&D came from manufacturing firms (Daiko et al. 2017). Beyond R&D, the manufacturing sector has also long benefited from product and process innovation—about 22% of all manufacturers introduced a new product or service between 2006 and 2008, compared to 8% of non-manufacturing firms. Furthermore, direct backward and forward linkages within and between sectors are typically regarded as stronger in manufacturing than in agriculture or services (Su and Yao 2017). For example, advances in ICT hardware technologies produced in the manufacturing sector (e.g., silicon chips and glass fiber cables) fuel technological change in service sectors that produce and use software (Szirmai 2012).

The fact that all economies did not benefit equally from industrialization demonstrates that growth outcomes are influenced by how an economy produces and not just what it produces. The contrast between export-oriented industrialization in East Asia and import-substitution industrialization in Latin America is often highlighted in this regard.[4] The success of East Asian economies is often attributed to export-oriented industrialization, which integrated the economies with world markets, enabling them to achieve scale, face competition, and acquire foreign technology (Agénor and Canuto 2015). In contrast, import-substitution industrialization in Latin American countries—an inward-oriented strategy that used trade barriers to strengthen local producers in sectors that did not conform to the countries' comparative advantages—did not deliver similar growth benefits (Gereffi and Wyman 2014). Similarly, the adoption of capital-intensive production techniques in heavy industries did not result in the large-scale absorption of unskilled labor.

In sum, more so than the agriculture and services sectors, manufacturing combined trade in international markets and other productivity-enhancing characteristics with large-scale job creation for the relatively unskilled. Specifically, manufacturing absorbed a substantial part of an economy's low-skilled labor and placed its employees on a productivity path up to the global frontier.

2.5 Prospects for Services-Led Development

The unique desirability of manufacturing-led development in terms of the twin wins of productivity and jobs may be eroding. The number of current jobs put at risk by labor-saving technologies is at the heart of these concerns. "Potential jobs" could also be lost in LMICs as high-income countries adopt new technologies and keep more manufacturing within their own borders. Further, if the only way LMICs can compete in manufacturing global value chains is by adopting labor-saving processes, this too will eliminate an additional set of potential jobs. For example, the adoption of robotics in the manufacturing of motor vehicles will reduce the labor intensity of production. The international trade dimension and its associated spillover effects may change too. If advanced robotics enables the PRC to retain low-value-added manufacturing segments as they move up the value chain, global value chains might

---

[4]   Between 1965 and 1986, manufacturing output in the Republic of Korea and Taipei,China grew twice as much as in the fastest growing Latin American economies (Jenkins 1991). At the same time, between the 1960s and the 1990s, Asian economies such as Indonesia; Malaysia; the Republic of Korea; Singapore; Taipei,China; and Thailand began leaping past Latin American countries in terms of growth (Devlin and Moguillansky 2011). These Asian economies also sharply and sustainably reduced poverty, while Latin America did not (Devlin, Estevadeordal, and Rodríguez-Clare 2006).

shorten. Moreover, if 3D printing reduces the need for physical parts and components to be moved across borders, the productivity benefits associated with international trade in manufactured goods will likely diminish as well.

Therefore, while manufacturing held out the promise of both more productivity and job creation in the past, more trade-offs may occur going forward. At the same time, some services are beginning to share many of the pro-development characteristics traditionally associated with manufacturing, that is, they are becoming increasingly tradable in addition to being sources of innovation and technology diffusion. The use of automation technologies in the services sector, relative to manufacturing, is also currently low.

2.5.1 Services as an Alternative Source of Productivity and Jobs

The Blurring Lines Between Manufacturing and Services

The boundaries between the manufacturing and service sectors are becoming blurrier. The assertion that productivity improvements are harder to achieve in services than in manufacturing is traditionally explained by the labor-intensive character of services, as per Baumol's cost disease hypothesis. However, certain categories of services are increasingly being produced according to manufacturing methods, including capital- and energy-intensive production processes, scale economies, strong use of technology, and engagement in international trade. Due to changes in trade and technology, the features of manufacturing once thought of as uniquely favorable for productivity growth might be increasingly shared by the services sector in several ways. This would expand the range of activities with likely positive spillovers for development.

International Tradability Through Information and Communications Technology Advances

Dramatic changes in ICT have given rise to a category of "modern" services—financial, telecommunications, and business services—that can be digitally stored, codified, and more easily traded internationally (Ghani and Kharas 2010). Such "modern" services can therefore yield the benefits of greater competition, technology diffusion, and access to demand beyond the domestic market. Regulatory barriers continue to drive a wedge between tradability and actual trade in these services, although deregulation has coincided with a marked increase in foreign direct investment inflows.

Increasing Benefits of Scale

ICT development also means that scale economies have become important in ICT-enabled services sectors as the marginal cost of providing an additional unit approaches zero. For example, data centers, search engines, and cloud platforms all require high levels of fixed assets, and their costs rapidly decrease with scale (Fontagné, Mohnen, and Wolff 2014).

Contribution to Technology Development

R&D expenditure in services increased from an annual average of 6.7% of total business R&D during 1990–1995 to nearly 17% during 2005–2010 (World Trade Organization 2013). This may reflect growing R&D investments in certain services sectors, the outsourcing of R&D to specialized laboratories classified in the services sector, and better measurement of R&D in services (Lopez-Bassols and Millot 2013). When innovation is defined as taking forms other than R&D—marketing and organizational innovation, for instance—the share of innovating firms is relatively similar across manufacturing and services in most countries (Pires, Sarkar, and Carvalho 2008).

Growing Linkages with Other Sectors

Services are increasingly being used as intermediate inputs in manufacturing production. On average, cross Organisation for Economic Co-operation and Development (OECD) countries, around 40% of gross output produced by service industries is used as intermediate inputs by other industries (Pilat and Wölfl 2005). Further, manufacturing exports increasingly include more inputs from service industries; 30%–40% of manufacturing exports in OECD economies are actually value added created within (domestic and foreign) service industries. The largest value-added contributions come from distribution and business services. The evidence also indicates that services are improving the productivity of manufacturing (Arnold, Javorcik and Mattoo 2011; Goldar, Renganathan, and Banga 2004).

2.5.2 Productivity Growth and Catch-Up

That the expanding opportunities for productivity gains have been realized is reflected in the sizable overlap between productivity growth among the services and manufacturing sectors. While the manufacturing sector as a whole has typically experienced faster productivity gains than the services sector, the differential has shrunk across most developed and developing economies since the year 2000. In many developing economies, including India, the PRC, and some sub-Saharan African countries, average productivity growth in services recently exceeded that of manufacturing (International Monetary Fund [IMF] 2018).

Furthermore, disaggregated labor productivity data show that some service industries register growth in output per worker that is as fast as that in the top-performing manufacturing industries. For example, across a sample of 19 advanced and 43 developing economies, labor productivity in two out of four market service industries—transport and communications, and financial intermediation and business activities—is either comparable to or higher than labor productivity in manufacturing (IMF 2018). This is reinforced by the evidence that knowledge-, ICT-, and trade-intensive services such as telecommunications, finance, and distribution have recorded higher rates of productivity growth than manufacturing (Jorgenson and Timmer 2011). Evidence from the US suggests that some services are also making a larger contribution than manufacturing to aggregate total factor productivity (TFP) growth (Caliendo et al. 2017).[5]

The reallocation of resources from agriculture to market service industries has featured prominently in the contribution of structural change to aggregate productivity growth in developing economies, which has been positive in all regions since 2000 (IMF 2018). In Africa for example, where the positive contribution of structural change since 2000 has been particularly large, the bulk of this contribution was attributable to the movement from agriculture into services (Enache, Ghani, and O'Connell 2016; McMillan, Rodrik, and Sepulveda 2017). Meanwhile, in India, the positive contribution of structural change to economic growth after the 1990s was largely attributable to the expansion of high-productivity service activities: finance, information technology (IT), business process outsourcing (BPO), and other business services (McMillan, Rodrik, and Sepulveda 2017).

Further, there is evidence of unconditional convergence of productivity to the frontier: countries starting from lower labor productivity in the services sector grew faster than those with higher initial labor productivity in that sector (Enache, Ghani, and O'Connell 2016; Kinfemichael and Morshed 2016). This relates to the fact that new ICT technologies, international tradability, and increased competition, especially since the 1990s, no longer fell within the exclusive domain of manufacturing. There are differences across subsectors. For instance, the IMF (2018) finds significant convergence in three of the four market services sectors: trade and accommodation, transport and communications, and financial and business services. The dispersion of productivity across countries,

---

[5] Productivity shocks across different sectors can lead to heterogeneous effects on TFP.

another indicator of convergence, also declined over time in each of these sectors after having accelerated since the mid-1990s or early 2000s, at which time the tradability of services increased considerably (Heuser and Mattoo 2017). The evidence of convergence in services productivity notwithstanding, the level of productivity in services may be further away from the technological frontier compared to manufacturing. This would reduce the prospect of narrowing the gap in income per worker as labor shifts from goods-producing sectors to services, at least in the short term. However, for most developing countries, the productivity gap vis-à-vis the US in 2005 was larger for goods-producing sectors than for the services sector (IMF 2018).

2.5.3 Trade-Off Between Productivity Growth and Job Creation

Therefore, some service industries have the potential to boost the growth of aggregate productivity and facilitate the convergence of labor productivity across countries. Yet, these dynamic service industries may not necessarily account for a large share of employment and thus may play a limited role in driving aggregate productivity. Ancillary evidence, however, suggests that service industries with favorable productivity dynamics account for a meaningful share of employment and can play a key role in driving aggregate productivity growth. For instance, the service industries that ranked in the top one-third of the labor-productivity growth distribution between 2000 and 2010 accounted for, on average, about 30% of total services employment, and close to 20% of overall employment (IMF 2018). Some service industries simultaneously registered above-average labor productivity growth and rising employment shares during the 2000s, thanks to strong demand (for example, financial intermediation in Hungary, the Russian Federation, and Slovenia; and telecommunications in the Republic of Korea and Lithuania).

Yet, most services sectors that exhibit "productivity-enhancing" characteristics are less likely to be associated with large-scale employment creation for unskilled labor. For example, based on World Bank Enterprise Survey data across the manufacturing and services sectors from a sample of six LMICs, IT services are classified as "high" or "medium" across a range of learning-by-doing characteristics, such as potential for scale economies and formal worker training programs, exports, and innovation as measured by new products, new processes, and R&D spending. At the same time, they also belong to the group that is "high" in skill intensity. Communication services are also classified as "medium" or "high" regarding not only (indirect) international trade, the use of foreign technology, and on-the-job learning programs, but also skill intensity (Nayyar, Cruz, and Zhu 2018). Therefore, without sufficient human capital, there are limits as to how much labor can be absorbed by highly skill-intensive service sectors; for example, it is easier to turn a rice farmer into a garment factory worker than into a software engineer.

At the same time, services that create jobs for unskilled labor are less likely to provide much in the way of productivity gains. Services such as construction and hotels and restaurants are characterized by both "low" skill intensity and "low" or "medium" productivity-enhancing traits: formal worker training programs, use of foreign technology, exports (direct and indirect), the introduction of new products and new processes, and R&D spending (Nayyar, Cruz, and Zhu 2018). Such non-traded services sectors could also be constrained by the pace of expansion in domestic demand. For example, while the productivity-enhancing structural change in Africa has been attributed to an expansion in low-end services, this expansion may be unsustainable due to limited demand beyond the domestic market (McMillan, Rodrik, and Sepulveda 2017). Nevertheless, recent studies suggest that the domestic demand for services exhibiting strong productivity growth may increase in relative terms over time as they become more affordable (IMF 2018).

Of the various services sectors, tourism and retail trade are perhaps exceptions in that they are both tradable and create jobs for unskilled labor. For example, based on World Bank Enterprise Survey data across the manufacturing and services sectors from a sample of six LMICs, wholesale and retail trade is not skill-intensive and is classified as "medium" in tradability, linkage effects, use of foreign technology, and on-the-job learning programs (Nayyar, Cruz, and Zhu 2018). Similarly, many low-income countries have used tourism services to help diversify their exports away from volatile primary sectors. In Uganda, for instance, services account for just over half of total exports, and tourism accounts for 45% of this figure. Furthermore, technology has the potential to transform some low-productivity services such as construction and tourism services (for example, through e-commerce platforms) because it allows services to be produced and traded just like goods and hence generate greater employment opportunities. Since barriers to international trade are higher for services than for goods (Miroudot, Sauvage, and Shepherd 2013), exports of these services could gather speed if appropriate policy actions are taken.

The issue of the *quality* of employment among lower-end service activities, which are large employment creators for unskilled labor, deserves emphasis. Evidence suggests that labor compensation is somewhat higher in the industrial sector than in services for comparable workers. In a sample of 20 advanced economies, for example, the median difference in labor earnings between industry and services is about 6 percentage points for high-skilled workers and 9 percentage points for low-skilled workers (IMF 2018). Similarly, in the US, lower-wage workers earn about 11% more in manufacturing than in other sectors, while high-wage workers earn just 4% more (Helper, Krueger, and Wial 2012). Using data from India, Nayyar (2011) finds that similar workers earn less in wholesale and retail trade, hotels and restaurants, transport services, and community and personal services than they do in manufacturing.

However, shifts in employment shares between industry and services accounted for, as an upper bound, less than one-fourth of the rise in economy-wide income inequality in a sample of 20 advanced economies from the 1980s to the 2000s (IMF 2018).[6] Instead, changes in aggregate labor income inequality were predominantly explained by rising labor income inequality within sectors, with the skill premium taking center stage; the gap between earnings for middle- versus low-skilled workers within a sector was about twice as large as the gap between low-skilled workers in industry and services.

Yet, some valuable nonwage attributes of manufacturing jobs appear less widespread in other sectors. Manufacturing jobs tend to be characterized by formal employment arrangements with associated benefits for workers, such as access to minimum wages, labor codes, retirement plans, paid holidays and sick leave, and health and life insurance (Söderbom and Teal 2004; Verhoogen 2008). They also tend to provide relatively stable arrangements, relying less on part-time or temporary contracts than other sectors, and may offer collective bargaining via unions (Jaumotte and Osorio Buitron 2015). Recent experimental evidence from Ethiopia also indicates that not all manufacturing jobs are better than self-employment in services: in the studied factories, there is no evidence of a significant industrial wage premium, and there are significant concerns about worker health and the safety of working conditions (Blattman and Dercon 2016).

2.6 Services-Led Development Without a Manufacturing Base

It is unclear whether service sectors with productivity-enhancing characteristics "need" a manufacturing core to develop. To the extent that final demand contributes substantially to the growth of a given

---

[6]   The dispersion and relative level of earnings were kept constant at their initial values.

services subsector, opportunities can be created independent of a country's manufacturing base.

A range of professional, scientific, and technical services—including software services, BPO and other IT services, accounting, legal services, education, and health care—are "stand-alone," with transactions taking place directly between a service provider and the final consumer. Numerous LMICs have sought to diversify their export baskets through offshore professional services. Many countries began with BPO services, such as contact and call centers, which laid the foundation for higher value services such as finance and accounting. India was at the forefront of diversifying into these operations (Nayyar 2012), where final demand and (net) exports accounted for about 90% and 60%, respectively, of the growth in professional, scientific, and technical services (Figure 2.4). Other countries that have successfully entered the market are Costa Rica and the Philippines (Bamber et al. 2017). Medical tourism is also on the rise, such as in sub-Saharan African countries where many hospitals are treating foreign patients (Dihel and Goswami 2016).

In addition, a range of professional services are either embedded in, or added to, goods and often bundled together in a single product, including applications for personal electronic devices, after-sales maintenance

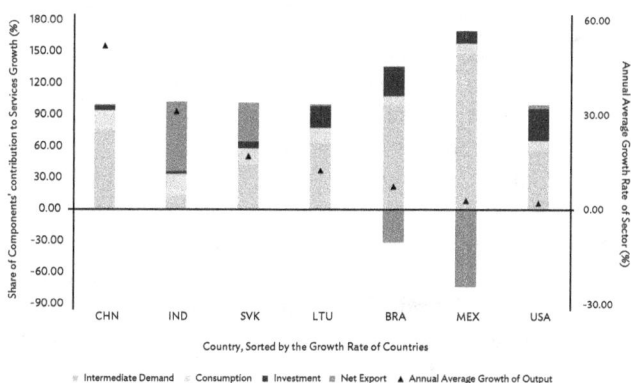

Figure 2.4 Decomposition of Output Growth in Professional, Scientific, and Technical Services, 2000–2014

BRA = Brazil, CHN = People's Republic of China, IND = India, LTU = Lithuania, MEX = Mexico, SVK = Slovak Republic, USA = United States, VA = value added.
Source: World Input-Output Database.

services for consumer durables, and "smart" solutions for "smart" factories. These services could be developed without the involvement of firms in the complementary manufacturing process. In fact, the development of content that tailors global business and technology solutions to local needs is essential to penetrate the market in these services, thus providing an advantage to domestic firms. For example, local language and cultural considerations have to be taken into account in the design and marketing of mobile phone applications. Adequate technological solutions must also be adapted. In areas with low communication coverage, for instance, lower technology solutions must be designed, for example, by using narrowband instead of broadband, or mobile money instead of bank transfers. This market for startups and the development of applications is booming worldwide, including in Africa, where several incubators and accelerators have emerged and are supporting the development of local technological solutions and startups. Financial and agriculture technology, e-health, and distance learning are just some of the areas where the digital revolution is taking place and where the potential of embedded services for economic growth and development can be seen (Bamber et al. 2017).

Opportunities for high-productivity services to grow in the absence of a manufacturing core might be reinforced if intermediate demand for a given services subsector largely comes from sectors other than manufacturing. For example, in the PRC the contribution of final demand to the growth of professional, scientific, and technical services between 2000 and 2014 was 24%, while (net) exports accounted for only 1%. Therefore, the contribution of intermediate demand in the growth of these services was paramount. Yet, this was not limited to links with the manufacturing sector, and the input of professional scientific and technical services into agriculture, mining, utilities and construction, and other services made sizeable contributions to the growth of the sector (Nayyar, Cruz, and Zhu 2018).

Other services sectors characterized by a range of productivity-enhancing characteristics—such as transportation and communication services and wholesale and retail trade—also serve consumers directly and are linked to intermediate demand from other sectors. For example, in India and the PRC, final demand accounted for 50% of the growth of wholesale and retail trade between 2000 and 2014. In the case of transportation and storage services, final demand mattered less, accounting for approximately 31% of the sector's growth in the PRC, for instance. In terms of providing input to other sectors, the contribution of wholesale and retail trade and transportation services into manufacturing activity matters greatly. Between 2000 and 2014, input into the manufacturing sector accounted for 62% of the annual average growth of wholesale and retail services in the PRC, and 38% in India. The growth of transportation services presents a similar picture (Nayyar, Cruz, and Zhu 2018). This suggests that the growth of these services sectors might depend, at least in part, on a manufacturing core.

That services may "need" a manufacturing core to develop does not diminish the fact that many services such as design, marketing, and distribution are in turn vital inputs into the production of manufactured goods. Other services, such as logistics and e-commerce platforms, enable trade to take place. Hence, to the extent that services are embodied in manufacturing, there will likely be a symbiotic relationship between the two sectors. The increasing servicification of manufacturing underscores the growing interdependence of the two sectors. For example, in the PRC, which experienced high rates of growth in services value added between 2000 and 2014, services input into manufacturing accounted for 38% of the annual average growth in the services sector between 2000 and 2014, while manufacturing input into services accounted for 30% (Figure 2.5).

2.7 Conclusion

The features of manufacturing once thought uniquely favorable for productivity growth are increasingly shared by some services sectors

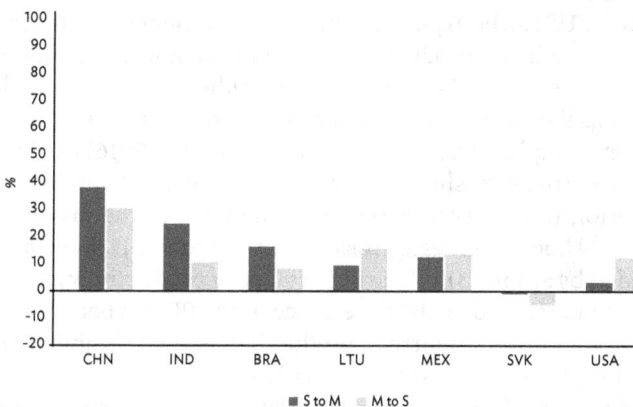

Figure 2.5 Contribution of Intermediate Demand from Manufacturing to Services and Vice Versa to Growth in Services Output, 2000–2014

BRA = Brazil, CHN = People's Republic of China, IND = India, LTU = Lithuania, M = manufacturing sector, MEX = Mexico, S = services sector, SVK = Slovak Republic, USA = United States.
Source: World Input-Output Database.

that are internationally tradable through ICT advances, yield the benefits of scale, and contribute to technology development. A range of these professional, scientific, and technical services can provide growth opportunities without a manufacturing core in that they are, at least in part, "stand-alone" or provide inputs to other sectors. Yet, without sufficient human capital, there are limits on how much labor can be absorbed in these productivity-enhancing services sectors (such as finance, telecommunication services, IT, accounting, and legal services), which are also highly skill-intensive.

On the other hand, low-end services that create jobs for unskilled labor are less likely to provide much in the way of productivity gains. Therefore, a given services subsector is unlikely to provide opportunities for productivity growth and job creation for unskilled people simultaneously. Wholesale and retail trade and tourism somewhat oppose this trend in that they are both tradable and create jobs for unskilled labor. Furthermore, there is the possibility that technology will enable low-productivity services such as construction and hotels and restaurants to be traded internationally while continuing to generate greater employment opportunities for unskilled labor.

In exploring the prospects for services-led development compared to the traditional export-led manufacturing model, it is worth emphasizing the following. First, productivity gains from resource reallocation will also happen within sectors, and there is evidence of large heterogeneity in productivity across firms (Caballero, Engel, and Micco 2004; McMillan and Rodrik 2011; Bloom et al. 2010). Hsieh and Klenow (2009), for example, find that between one-third and half of the differences in manufacturing TFP that can be observed among India, the PRC, and the US can be explained by the large number of inefficient firms. This dispersion in the productivity distribution of firms applies equally, if not more, to services. Recent empirical studies report a higher level of resource misallocation in the services sector than in the manufacturing sector. For example, Dias, Marques, and Richmond (2016) use firm-level data from Portugal to show that closing the sectoral gap by reducing misallocation in the services sector to the level in the manufacturing sector would boost aggregate gross output by around 12% and aggregate value added by around 31%. The importance of productivity gains within sectors is underscored by the experience of the PRC, where reallocation accounted for only one-fourth of productivity growth from 1980 to 2010 (Herrendorf, Rogerson, and Valentinyi 2013).

Furthermore, firms are increasingly structured around the close interaction of manufacturing and services, making it difficult to assign them exclusively to one sector. Manufacturing companies increasingly no longer sell only physical goods, but instead sell bundles including design, development, marketing, warranties, and after-sales care, among other things. Xerox, for example, has restructured itself as a "document solution" company, offering not only technologically advanced printing systems but also services like document management and consulting. Services now represent around 40% of Xerox's turnover and are expected to represent more than 50% soon (Benedettini et al. 2010). Similarly, many services firms are becoming more like manufacturing firms as outputs are mass produced, and they have even introduced new goods, such as Google in the tablet market and Amazon with its Kindle (Lopez-Bassols and Millot 2013).

References

Agénor, P-R., and O. Canuto. 2015. Middle-Income Growth Traps. *Research in Economics* 69(4): 641–660.

Arnold, J. M., B. S. Javorcik, and A. Mattoo. 2011. Does Services Liberalization Benefit Manufacturing Firms? Evidence from the Czech Republic. *Journal of International Economics* 85(1): 136–146.

Baldwin, R. E. 1969. The Case Against Infant-Industry Tariff Protection. *Journal of Political Economy* 77(3): 295–305.

Bamber, P., O. Cattaneo, K. Fernandez-Stark, G. Gereffi, E. van der Marel, and B. Shepherd. 2017. Diversification through Servicification. Unpublished manuscript. Washington, DC: World Bank.

Baumol, W. J. 1967. Macroeconomics of Unbalanced Growth: The Anatomy of Urban Crisis. *American Economic Review* 57(3): 415–426.

Benedettini, O., B. Clegg, M. Kafouros, and A. Neely. 2010. *The Ten Myths of Manufacturing: What Does the Future Hold for UK Manufacturing?* London: Advanced Institute of Management Research.

Bhagwati, J. N. 1984. Splintering and Disembodiment of Services and Developing Nations. *The World Economy* 7(2): 133–144.

Blattman, C., and S. Dercon. 2016. Occupational Choice in Early Industrializing Societies: Experimental Evidence on the Income and Health Effects of Industrial and Entrepreneurial Work. National Bureau of Economic Research (NBER) Working Paper 22683. Cambridge, MA: NBER.

Bloom, N., A. Mahajan, D. McKenzie, and J. Roberts. 2010. Why Do Firms in Developing Countries Have Low Productivity? *American Economic Review* 100(2): 619–623.

Caballero, G., G. R. E. Engel, and A. Micco. 2004. Microeconomic Flexibility in Latin America. *Journal Economía Chilena* (The Chilean Economy), Central Bank of Chile 7(2): 5–26.

Caliendo, L., F. Parro, E. Rossi-Hansberg, and P-D. Sarte. 2017. The Impact of Regional and Sectoral Productivity Changes on the U.S. Economy. *The Review of Economic Studies* 85(4): 2042–2096.

Caselli, F. 2005. Accounting for Cross-Country Income Differences. In P. Aghion and S. Durlauf (eds), *Handbook of Economic Growth, Vol. 1*, pp.679–741. Amsterdam: Elsevier.

Citigroup. 2016. *Technology at Work v2.0: The Future Is Not What It Used to Be.* Citi GPS: Global Perspectives & Solutions. Joint Report with Oxford Martin School.

Daiko T., H. Dernis, M. Dosso, P. Gkotsis, M. Squicciarini, and A. Vezzani. 2017. *World Corporate Top R&D Investors: Industrial Property Strategies in the Digital Economy.* A Joint Research Centre and Organisation for

Economic Co-operation and Development (OECD) common report. Luxembourg: Publications Office of the European Union.

Dasgupta, S., and A. Singh. 2007. Manufacturing, Services and Premature Deindustrialization in Developing Countries: A Kaldorian Analysis. In G. Mavrotas and A. Shorrocks (eds), *Advancing Development: Core Themes in Global Economics*, pp.435–454. London: Palgrave Macmillan UK.

De Backer, K., C. Menon, I. Desnoyers-James, and L. Moussiegt. 2016. Reshoring: Myth or Reality? OECD Science, Technology, and Industry Policy Paper 27. Paris: OECD.

De Ferranti, D., G. E. Perry, D. Lederman, and W. E. Maloney. 2002. *From Natural Resources to the Knowledge Economy: Trade and Job Quality*. Washington, DC: World Bank.

Devlin, R., A. Estevadeordal, and A. Rodríguez-Clare, eds. 2006. *The Emergence of China: Opportunities and Challenges for Latin America and the Caribbean*. Washington, DC: Inter-American Development Bank.

Devlin, R., and G. Moguillansky. 2011. *Breeding Latin American Tigers: Operational Principles for Rehabilitating Industrial Policies in the Region*. Washington, DC: World Bank.

Dias, D. A., C. R. Marques, and C. Richmond. 2016. Misallocation and Productivity in the Lead up to the Eurozone Crisis. *Journal of Macroeconomics* 49: 46–70.

Dihel, N., and A. G. Goswami, eds. 2016. The Unexplored Potential of Trade in Services in Africa. Working Paper 107185. Washington, DC: World Bank.

Duarte, M., and D. Restuccia. 2010. The Role of the Structural Transformation in Aggregate Productivity. *The Quarterly Journal of Economics* 125(1): 129–173.

Economist. 2017. 3D Printers Will Change Manufacturing. June 29.

Enache, M., E. Ghani, and S. O'Connell. 2016. Structural Transformation in Africa: A Historical View. Policy Research Working Paper 7743. Washington, DC: World Bank.

Fagerberg, J., and B. Verspagen. 1999. 'Modern Capitalism' in the 1970s and 1980s. In *Growth, Employment and Inflation: Essays in Honour of John Cornwall*, edited by M. Setterfield, pp.113–126. London: Palgrave Macmillan UK.

Fontagné, L., P. Mohnen, and G. Wolff. 2014. No Industry, No Future? Economic Analysis Notes 13. Paris: French Council of Economic Analysis.

Gereffi, G., and D. L. Wyman, eds. 2014. *Manufacturing Miracles: Paths of Industrialization in Latin America and East Asia*. Princeton, NJ: Princeton University Press.

Ghani, E., and H. Kharas. 2010. An Overview. In E. Ghani (ed), *The Service Revolution in South Asia*, pp.13–37. New York, Oxford: Oxford University Press.

Goldar, B., V. S. Renganathan, and R. Banga. 2004. Ownership and Efficiency in Engineering Firms: 1990–91 to 1999–2000. *Economic and Political Weekly*: 441–447.

Hallward-Driemeier, M., and G. Nayyar. 2017. *Trouble in the Making? The Future of Manufacturing-Led Development*. Washington, DC: World Bank.

Helper, S., T. Krueger, and H. Wial. 2012. Why Does Manufacturing Matter? Which Manufacturing Matters? A Policy Framework. Report, Advanced Industries Series, Metropolitan Policy Program at the Brookings Institution, Washington, DC.

Herrendorf, B., R. Rogerson, and A. Valentinyi. 2013. Growth and Structural Transformation. NBER Working Paper 18996. Cambridge, MA: NBER.

Heuser, C., and A. Mattoo. 2017. Services Trade and Global Value Chains (English). Policy Research Working Paper WPS 8126. Washington, DC: World Bank Group.

Hsieh, C.-T., and P. J. Klenow. 2009. Misallocation and Manufacturing TFP in China and India. *Quarterly Journal of Economics* 124(4): 1403–48.

International Monetary Fund (IMF). 2018. *World Economic Outlook April 2018: Cyclical Upswing, Structural Change*. Washington, DC: International Monetary Fund.

Jaumotte, F., and C. Osorio Buitron. 2015. Inequality and Labor Market Institutions. International Monetary Fund Staff Discussion Note No. 15/14. Washington, DC: International Monetary Fund.

Jenkins, R. 1991. The Political Economy of Industrialization: A Comparison of Latin American and East Asian Newly Industrializing Countries. *Development and Change* 22(2): 197–231.

Jorgenson, D. W., and M. P. Timmer. 2011. Structural Change in Advanced Nations: A New Set of Stylised Facts. *Scandinavian Journal of Economics* 113(1): 1–29.

Kaldor, N. 1966. Causes of the Slow Rate of Economic Growth in the United Kingdom: Inaugural Lecture at the University of Cambridge. Cambridge: Cambridge University Press.

Kaldor, N. 1963. *Capital Accumulation and Economic Growth*. London: MacMillan.

Kinfemichael, B., and A. K. M. Morshed. 2015. Unconditional Convergence of Labor Productivity in the Service Sector. Discussion Paper Series. Carbondale, IL: Southern Illinois University.

Kuznets, S. S. 1971. *Economic Growth of Nations*. Cambridge, MA: Harvard University Press.

Lederman, D., and W. Maloney. 2010. *Does It Matter What LAC Produces and Exports? Semiannual Report of the Office of the Regional Chief Economist, Latin America and the Caribbean Region*. Washington, DC: World Bank.

Leipziger, D. M., ed. 1997. *Lessons from East Asia*. Ann Arbor: University of Michigan Press.

Lewis, W. A. 1954. Economic Development with Unlimited Supplies of Labour. *The Manchester School* 22(2): 139–191.

Lopez-Bassols, V., and V. Millot. 2013. Measuring R&D and Innovation in Services: Key Findings from the OECD INNOSERV Project. Paper prepared for the Working Party of National Experts on Science and Technology Indicators and the Working Party on Innovation and Technology Policy. Paris: OECD.

McMillan, M. S., and D. Rodrik. 2011. Globalization, Structural Change and Productivity Growth. NBER Working Paper 17143. Cambridge, MA: NBER.

McMillan, M., D. Rodrik, and Í. Verduzco-Gallo. 2014. Globalization, Structural Change, and Productivity Growth, with an Update on Africa. *World Development* 63: 11–32.

McMillan, M., D. Rodrik, and C. Sepulveda. 2017. Structural Change, Fundamentals, and Growth: A Framework and Country Studies. Policy Research Working Paper 8041. Washington, DC: World Bank.

Miroudot, S., J. Sauvage, and B. Shepherd. 2013. Measuring the Cost of International Trade in Services. *World Trade Review* 12(4): 719–735.

Nayyar, G. 2011. The Quality of Employment in India's Services Sector: Exploring the Heterogeneity. *Applied Economics* 44(36): 4701–4719.

Nayyar, G. 2012. *The Service Sector in India's Development*. New York: Cambridge University Press.

Nayyar, G. 2013. Inside the Black Box of Services: Evidence from India. *Cambridge Journal of Economics* 37(1): 143–170.

Nayyar, G., M. Cruz, and L. Zhu. 2018. Does Premature Deindustrialization Matter? The Role of Manufacturing versus Services in Development. World Bank Policy Research Working Paper Series 8596. Washington, DC: World Bank Group.

Pilat, D., and A. Wölfl. 2005. Measuring the Interaction Between Manufacturing and Services. OECD Science, Technology and Industry Working Paper 2005/5. Paris: OECD Publishing.

Pires, C. P., S. Sarkar, and L. Carvalho. 2008. Innovation in Services— How Different from Manufacturing? *Service Industries Journal* 28(10): 1339–1356.

Restuccia, D., D. T. Yang, and X. Zhu. 2008. Agriculture and Aggregate Productivity: A Quantitative Cross-Country Analysis. *Journal of Monetary Economics* 55(2): 234–50.

Rodríguez-Clare, A. 2007. Clusters and Comparative Advantage: Implications for Industrial Policy. *Journal of Development Economics* 82(1): 43–57.

Rodrik, D. 1994. King Kong Meets Godzilla: The World Bank and the East Asian Miracle. Discussion Paper 944. London: Centre for Economic Policy Research.

Rodrik, D. 2011. The Future of Economic Convergence. NBER Working Paper 17400. Cambridge, MA: NBER.

Rodrik, D. 2016. Premature Deindustrialization. *Journal of Economic Growth* 21(1): 1–33.

Söderbom, M., and F. Teal. 2004. Size and Efficiency in African Manufacturing Firms: Evidence from Firm-Level Panel Data. *Journal of Development Economics* 73(1): 369–394.

South China Morning Post. 2015. Rise of the Robots: 60,000 Workers Culled from Just One Factory as China's Struggling Electronics Hub Turns to Artificial Intelligence. September 21.

Stiglitz, J. E., and S. Yusuf, eds. 2001. *Rethinking the East Asian Miracle.* New York: Oxford University Press.

Su, D., and Y. Yao 2017. Manufacturing as the Key Engine of Economic Growth for Middle Income Economies. *Journal of the Asia Pacific Economy* 22(1): 47–70.

Szirmai, A. 2012. Industrialisation as an Engine of Growth in Developing Countries, 1950–2005. *Structural Change and Economic Dynamics* 23(4): 406–20.

Szirmai, A., and B. Verspagen. 2015. Manufacturing and Economic Growth in Developing Countries, 1950–2005. *Structural Change and Economic Dynamics* 34(C): 46–59.

Timmer, M. P., and G. J. de Vries. 2009. Structural Change and Growth Accelerations in Asia and Latin America: A New Sectoral Data Set. *Cliometrica* 3(2): 165–190.

Verhoogen, E. 2008. Trade, Quality Upgrading and Wage Inequality in the Mexican Manufacturing Sector. *Quarterly Journal of Economics* 123(2): 489–530.

World Bank. 1993. *The East Asian Miracle: Economic Growth and Public Policy.* New York: Oxford University Press.

World Trade Organization. 2013. *World Trade Report 2013: Factors Shaping the Future of World Trade.* Geneva: World Trade Organization.

3

Restrictiveness of Services Trade Policy and the Sustainable Development Goals

Matteo Fiorini and Bernard Hoekman

3.1 Introduction

The United Nations (UN) Sustainable Development Goals (SDGs) are a major focal point for international efforts to promote global welfare over the next decade (UN 2015). The SDGs span 17 broad objectives, ranging from poverty reduction to improving public health and protecting the environment.[1] One route to implementing the SDGs is through international trade and trade policy. A number of goals explicitly reference trade-related measures as instruments that can help in attaining the objective concerned. For example, Goal 2 (ending hunger) includes a call to correct and prevent distortions in world agricultural markets by eliminating all forms of agricultural export subsidies and measures with equivalent effect. Goal 8 (decent work and economic growth) recognizes the role of Aid for Trade's support for developing countries, especially for the least developed countries (LDCs). Goal 9 (resilient infrastructure and inclusive industrialization) notes the need for trans-border connectivity and greater integration of small-scale industrial and other enterprises into international value chains. Goal 10 (reducing inequality) emphasizes the importance of special and differential treatment for trade in developing countries, in accordance with World Trade Organization (WTO) agreements. Goal 14 (conservation of maritime resources) highlights the need to reduce fishery subsidies for rich countries.

---

[1] The SDGs are listed in Appendix A.

The main link between the SDGs and trade policy is made in Goal 17 (strengthening the global partnership for sustainable development). This stresses the importance of a multilateral trading system that is universal, rules-based, open, non-discriminatory, and equitable; the timely implementation of duty- and quota-free market access on a lasting basis for all LDCs, supported by transparent, simple rules of origin that facilitate market access; and respect for national policy space and leadership to establish and implement policies to realize the goals.

The trade policies referenced in the text of the SDGs center on actions that importing countries could or should take to facilitate market access for export firms in developing countries, along with policy space for developing countries and technical and financial assistance to bolster productive supply capacity and address infrastructure weaknesses. Preferential market access, removing policies that distort global markets and create incentives for the excessive exploitation of non-renewable natural resources, and aid to enhance capacity to use trade for sustainable development can contribute significantly to achieving a number of the SDGs. However, it is important to note how the role of trade is conceptualized in the wording of the SDGs. Measures to facilitate merchandise exports in developing countries are emphasized implicitly if not explicitly. Low-income countries may have a comparative advantage in services such as transport, travel and tourism-related activities, or business process outsourcing. Due to technological advancements, services of all types are becoming easier to trade, thus creating opportunities for firms in developing countries to expand trade in nontraditional products, including services as well as goods. Approximately one-quarter of all LDCs are net exporters of services, and during the 2000s services exports grew more rapidly for the LDCs as a group than for the world as a whole. LDCs increased their share of global trade in services from 0.4% in 2005 to 0.8% in 2015, with commercial services exports growing by 14 percentage points over this period, more than twice the rate of other countries. Services exports as a whole represented some 20% of total LDC exports of goods and services in 2015 (WTO 2016).

Services matter for the realization of the SDGs, not just because they are a potential source of foreign exchange revenue and associated employment and household income, but also because the realization of many of the SDGs is conditional on enhancing the performance of a range of specific services sectors in developing countries. Attaining the SDGs is, to a significant extent, a services agenda. Eliminating poverty and hunger, improving health and educational outcomes, and reducing regional inequalities will require increased services capacity and the productivity of a range of services activities, including transport, distribution, logistics, information and communications technology (ICT), vocational training, and medical services.

This chapter provides a conceptual framework for considering the role of trade in services in the effort to attain the SDGs. We make a case for devoting greater efforts to identify, at the country level, whether and how actions to promote trade in services can support the achievement of some of the SDGs. We focus on two dimensions of the role that services trade policy can play in the attainment of the SDGs. The first is the link between services sector performance and economic growth and incomes. Increasing per capita income is critical to realize many SDGs, both directly (e.g., by reducing the incidence of poverty and hunger) and indirectly (e.g., by generating additional domestic resources that can be allocated to measures targeting specific SDGs). Given that services account for a significant share of employment and gross domestic product (GDP) in all countries, improving services sector productivity is one avenue to increasing real incomes and fostering economic growth. Greater trade in services, in turn, is a potential instrument for generating higher growth rates. Second, services trade policy could help realize the SDGs by bolstering access to specific types of services that are either important "inputs" for some of the SDGs, or "outputs" that are highly correlated with achieving a specific goal. Many of the SDGs require better access to higher quality services while others call for improving connectivity-providing service networks.[2]

Whether and how changes to services trade and investment policy can enhance overall economic growth performance (i.e., per capita incomes) and access to services that matter for specific SDGs is an empirical question. This chapter provides an illustrative analysis with the aim of discussing the potential role that trade in services can play in achieving the SDGs. We also undertake an initial empirical assessment of the salience of alternative channels through which services trade policies can impact the SDGs. The feasibility of a rigorous cross-country quantitative study of these channels is limited by data constraints. Further, the absence of comparable time series information on services trade policies severely impedes an empirical analysis that can appropriately consider endogeneity and identification issues. We are therefore limited to an exploratory investigation using available data on services trade policy to assess the extent to which such policies are associated with outcomes that matter from an SDG perspective.

The findings suggest that services trade and investment policy may matter more for enhancing access to services than for increasing overall

---

[2]   This part of the chapter draws on Fiorini and Hoekman (2018).

economic growth, although more liberal trade policies toward transport services are positively associated with per capita income levels. Services trade policies appear more strongly associated with measures of the availability of, and access to, a number of services (i.e., financial, ICT, and transport services) that figure prominently in the text of several SDGs. We also find that the relationship between services trade policy regimes and access to (and performance of) the services sectors is affected by the quality of prevailing regulatory institutions. One policy implication of the analysis is that international efforts to attain the SDGs should pay more attention to services trade policies and related regulatory and economic governance institutions. Which types of services matter more for different SDGs requires a country-specific analysis, which is likely to be less affected by the data limitations constraining a cross-country analysis of the impact of services trade policy on SDGs. We hope that our findings will motivate such research and more generally stimulate greater consideration of services trade policies in country-level efforts to identify and implement measures that will help in attaining the SDGs.

3.2 Services and the Sustainable Development Goals

The performance of services sectors in an economy can impact the prospects of attaining the SDGs through two main channels, both indirect and direct. The first (indirect) channel is the impact on per capita income. More efficient and productive services sectors can increase economic growth, which in turn is important for the overall achievement of the SDGs. The second (direct) channel consists of improving access to, and the quality of, specific types of services, which is central to a number of the SDGs.

3.2.1 Services and Economic Development

One of the stylized facts of economic development is that the share of services in GDP and employment rises as per capita income increases.[3] In the lowest income countries, services generate 35%–40% of GDP. This rises to over 75% of national income and employment in many Organisation for Economic Co-operation and Development (OECD) countries. The increasing share of services in GDP and employment is part of economic development. This expansion in the services-intensity of economies

---

[3]   Buera and Kaboski (2009) suggest that the relationship between services as a share of GDP and log per capita income is linear.

as they become wealthier is driven by a number of factors.[4] Standard explanations involve both demand- and supply-side factors. Growth in the share of services as countries grow richer is in part a function of changes in final demand patterns and higher average income elasticities of demand for services than for goods. It also reflects differential labor productivity growth across sectors, technological changes that support greater specialization by firms through the outsourcing of services tasks, and an associated growth in demand for coordination and intermediation services (Backer, Desnoyers-James, and Moussiegt 2015; Francois and Hoekman 2010; Schettkat and Yocarini 2006).

While an expanding share of services in total output and employment is nothing new for the world as a whole (see, e.g., Kravis, Heston, and Summers 1983), for any level of economic development or per capita income, the role of services in the economy is more important today than in the past due to advances in ICT and transport. Growth in the share of services in GDP is part of the process of structural transformation associated with rising per capita income levels. In part it reflects the inter-sectoral reallocation of factors of production from low-productivity agriculture and informal services to higher productivity activities in the formal sector (i.e., industry and services). Shifts within sectors, including increasing demand for intermediate services, are equally salient (Berlingieri 2015). Resource allocation shifts are a driver of productivity growth within services sectors just as in goods-producing sectors (Young 2014).

Efficient services are critical for economic development because they are determinants of the productivity of capital and labor. Financial services intermediaries are critical for providing firms with funds that have been generated by households seeking to invest their savings. Health and education services are key "inputs" that help determine workers' skills and quality of life. Other services form the backbone of connectivity by facilitating the physical movement of goods and people (transport services) and the exchange of knowledge and information (communications services).[5] Telecommunications are crucial to the dissemination and diffusion of knowledge, including through the internet. ICT services are a transport mechanism for information services and other products that can be digitized. Similarly, transport services affect the cost of shipping goods and the movement of workers within and between countries. Business services such as accounting,

---

[4]   See, e.g., Baumol (1967) and Fuchs (1968).

[5]   For an excellent discussion of the role of services and services trade for connectivity, see OECD and WTO (2017).

engineering, consulting, and legal services reduce the transaction costs associated with the operation of financial markets and enforcement of contracts, and are a channel through which process innovations are transmitted across firms in an industry and across industries. Health and education services are key inputs into, and determinants of, the stock and growth of human capital. In short, the performance of the services sector matters for economic growth and the overall productivity of the economy as a whole. From an SDG perspective, this implies that income is the first channel through which services performance matters.

3.2.2 Services and Sustainable Development

The indirect link between services and economic development visible in the effect of services sector performance on economy-wide productivity and real income growth is just one channel through which services are relevant to the SDGs. While this is important (e.g., per capita income growth can help achieve the poverty reduction SDG), the performance of the services sector is also highly salient for many "non-income" dimensions of the SDGs and their associated specific targets.[6] Some SDGs depend directly on the performance of specific services sectors (e.g., health services in SDG 3 and education services in SDG 4). Of the 17 SDGs, 11 either explicitly refer to or indicate at least one distinct service sector as a means of attaining the goal in question. This generally spans one or more of the following three elements:

    (i) access to services, that is, expanding access to or improving the affordability of a given services activity, output, or product;

    (ii) quality of services, that is, enhancing the quality, efficiency, capacity, or resilience of a service sector; and

    (iii) environmental services, that is, reducing the environmental footprint (negative spillover effects) of an economic activity.

Table 3.1 illustrates some of the connections between services and SDGs. It reports the services sectors to which various SDGs refer based on a text search of the keywords embodied in the description of the SDGs as well as the focal point for action implied by, and needed to attain, the respective goals.

This text-based mapping exercise illustrates that the intersection between the SDGs and the performance of services sectors is substantial.

---

[6] The 17 main SDGs are listed in Annex 1. For more detailed targets for each SDG, see United Nations (2015). In this chapter, we consider both the SDGs and the more detailed targets associated with the respective SDGs insofar as they involve specific services activities.

Table 3.1 Services Referenced in the Sustainable Development Goals

Services Sector	SDG	Activity Given in the Respective SDG	Focal Point
Health services	1	Basic services	A
	3	Health services; sexual and reproductive health services	A and Q
Education services	1	Basic services	A
	4	Pre-primary, primary, secondary, vocational, and tertiary education	A and Q
Sanitation services	1	Basic services	A
	6	Sanitation	A, Q, and EF
ICT services	1	New technology	A
Financial services	1	Financial services; microfinance	A
	2	Financial services	A
	3	Financial risk protection	A
	8	Financial services	A
	9	Financial services	A
R&D services	2	Seeds; climate resistance	A and Q
	3	R&D of vaccines and medicines	Q
	8	Technological innovation	Q
	9	Scientific research; technological capabilities; innovation; R&D workers	Q
Water services	6	Drinking water; water quality; water use and management	A, Q, and EF
Energy services	7	Distribution of energy	A, Q, and EF
Tourism	8	Sustainable tourism	Q and EF
Transport services	9	Infrastructure	A, Q, and EF
	10	Transport systems; public transport	A, Q, and EF
Construction services	9	Infrastructure	Q and EF
Waste management services	11	Waste management	Q
	12	Recycling; reuse	Q and EF

A = access, EF = environmental footprint, ICT = information and communications technology, R&D = research and development, Q = quality, SDG = sustainable development goal.

Source: Authors' elaboration based on the text of the SDGs in United Nations. 2015. *Transforming Our World: The 2030 Agenda for Sustainable Development*. New York: United Nations.

Services matter for attaining specific SDGs. Beyond access to basic services in the areas of health, education, sanitation, water, and energy, access to financial services is identified in five SDGs, making itthe most frequently referenced factor across the services subsectors. Other services mentioned include ICT services; improved quality, efficiency, capacity, and resilience of R&D services; and tourism, transport, construction, and waste management services. SDGs that aim to reduce the negative environmental footprint of economic activity also identify specific services sectors, including sanitation, water- and energy-related distribution services, transport, construction, and waste management services.

Services are also relevant for SDGs that do not explicitly refer to services (and for that reason are not listed in Table 3.1). This is the case for SDG 5 (gender equality) and SDGs addressing environmental sustainability (13, 14, and 15). In general, services are not energy intensive, with the notable exception of transport.[7] This makes services activities relevant for the sustainability of development strategies; an increase in the services share or intensity of economic activity will be associated with a lower carbon footprint. Moreover, services are also relevant for improving environmental sustainability and the implementation of green development strategies because achieving these goals will require technological progress and innovation. Lowering the environmental footprints of production and consumption processes calls for basic research, engineering and R&D services, and so-called environmental services,[8] such as the elimination of exhaust gases, noise abatement services, nature and landscape protection services, and so on. Other services sectors such as finance and insurance are important "facilitators", helping to mobilize and channel the resources needed to fund the investments required to reduce environmental footprints across economic sectors more generally.

The services sector plays an important role in gender equality, as it offers significant opportunities for women's employment and empowerment. Ngai and Petrongolo (2017) document the evolution of what they call the comparative advantage of women in the services sector. In the early 20th century, services involved safer, cleaner working conditions and shorter working hours than jobs in factories (Goldin 2006). While these factors may have become less relevant over time, many services sector activities require a greater use of communication skills than required in manufacturing, and do not involve heavy manual labor (Galor and Weil 1996; Rendall 2010).

---

[7] Technically, mining and the production of electricity are not mapped to the services sector in national accounts.

[8] See Dihel (2010) for a detailed discussion of environmental services and trade in environmental services.

Table 3.2 Female Employment Share by Sector (International Standard Industrial Classification Revision 3 Categories)

Country	Year	Total	A	D	F	G	H	I	J	K	M	N
Burundi	1998	55.6	58.3	24.3	0.0	28.0		4.0	45.8	26.1	13.1	
Bangladesh	2005	23.8	34.6	24.8	6.8	5.7	7.2	1.7	22.7	4.6	26.3	33.7
Bhutan	2012	51.0	61.6	59.8	12.5	54.2	58.6	12.3	35.5	34.8	38.4	32.3
Ethiopia	2006	50.1	32.1	50.4	13.9	48.4	80.2	7.1	29.7	31.6	44.3	
Cambodia	2001	51.7	53.3	69.0	11.8	72.6	56.6	3.7	45.0	40.1	37.3	37.3
Lao PDR	1995	51.8	54.1	54.2	9.2	63.0	54.5	5.4	40.2	25.9	42.1	58.0
Lesotho	1999	43.9	39.3	63.5	35.8	61.7	79.4	12.8	43.8	37.4	61.2	58.3
Madagascar	2005	49.4	50.0	23.3	6.9	63.0	52.4	6.3	34.1		58.4	48.5
Mali	2006	45.1	45.3		2.6	67.2		6.9	34.5		31.9	
Nepal	2001	43.4	48.1	47.6	17.8	39.6	34.5	3.6	14.5	13.7	26.0	29.4
Senegal	2006	35.0	35.9	17.0	3.7	50.6	57.5	4.1	29.4			
Sierra Leone	2004	48.9	51.4	21.4	27.7	62.1	46.9	8.0	42.4	49.2	32.8	50.3
United States	2008	46.7	23.9	29.3	9.7	45.0	53.1	23.8	58.0	43.1	69.7	79.1

Lao PDR = Lao People's Democratic Republic.
Source: International Labour Organization. 2016. Key Indicators of the Labour Market database. https://www.ilo.org/ilostat (accessed 15 March 2017).

Connections between the development of services sectors and female labor force participation have been empirically supported in the context of mature services economies.[9] Data for LDCs suggest that the potential of services is particularly high in regions where female participation in primary and secondary sectors appears "inefficiently" high. In LDCs for which data are available, women account for more than 50% of total employment in agriculture and manufacturing. Table 3.2 reports employment shares across sectors[10] for a number of

---

[9] Ngai and Petrongolo (2017) discuss the case of the US and provide a review of the literature.

[10] Sectors are given according to the International Standard Industrial Classification Revision 3 1-digit categories. A corresponds to agriculture, hunting, and forestry; D to manufacturing; F to construction; G to wholesale and retail trade, and the repair of motor vehicles, motorcycles, and personal and household goods; H to hotels and restaurants; I to transport, storage, and communications; J to financial intermediation; K to real estate, renting, and business activities; M to education; and N to health and social work. Data are from the International Labour Organization. 2016. Key Indicators of the Labour Market database. https://www.ilo.org/ilostat (accessed 15 March 2017).

LDCs and the United States (US) for the latest available year. The US has lower employment shares for women in both agriculture (International Standard Industrial Classification Sector A) and manufacturing (D), and generally higher shares in services sectors. The highest shares of female employment in services sectors in LDCs are in the wholesale and retail trade (G) and hotel and restaurants (H). For other services sectors, the differences compared to employment shares observed in the US are significant.

3.3 Services Trade Policy and the Sustainable Development Goals

Given the presumption that services performance matters for the attainment of many SDGs, the policy challenge is to encourage improvement in services sector performance. This is a multifaceted issue that will be inherently sector specific, in practice. National specialist agencies responsible for the operation and regulation of health, education, transport, finance, and other services sectors will need to undertake diagnostic analyses and identify binding constraints and priorities for action. This sector-level engagement constitutes a major dimension of the activities of governments and the support provided by development agencies (see, e.g., Abbott, Sapsford, and Binagwaho 2017; Joshi, Hughes, and Sisk 2015; Koehler, Thomson, and Hope 2015; Ssozi and Amlani 2015). Below, we focus on the supportive role that services trade and investment policy can play in complementing sector-specific interventions and policy reforms to improve the productivity performance of services sectors and enhance access to services.

Historically many services were characterized as non-tradable, reflecting their non-storable and intangible nature. The implication was that international trade in services often required the cross-border movement of providers or consumers, in turn involving the movement of capital and labor. The need for such factor movement has been declining as technical change has allowed services to be digitized and exchanged cross-border through ICT networks and air transportation and information services that facilitate the identification of market opportunities. Information and telecommunications advances have increased direct exports of services by allowing the sale or provision of services over ICT networks, and enabling suppliers and/or customers to move physically and thereby overcome the proximity constraint that frequently still impedes cross-border services transactions. While developments in areas such as software and applications, business process outsourcing, and the like attract much attention, these activities depend on a variety of services inputs that determine the ability of entrepreneurs to participate in international value chains or to sell products directly to clients through business-to-business or business-to-customer e-commerce platforms. The quality, price, and availability of such inputs is determined in part by a country's services trade and investment policies.

Trade costs for services remain much higher than trade costs for goods, and the rate of decline in such costs has been much less than for goods (Miroudot and Shepherd 2016). This consequently reduces the volume of trade in services by compromising the ability of firms to exploit their competitive advantages on world markets. High services trade costs imply that many services tend to be traded indirectly. Recent initiatives such as the OECD and WTO project to measure trade in value added have demonstrated that services account for a significant share of the value added in all sectors in the economy. As this value added is embedded in traded goods, services play a much larger role in international exchange than is measured by a nation's balance of payments. At least 50% of global trade on a value-added basis comprises services, that is, the sum of the value of services output that is traded directly and is captured in balance of payments statistics (20%–25% of total exports), plus the value of services embedded in traded goods (another 25%–35%). Some of these embedded services are provided by foreign-owned firms. Often the most efficient way for foreign firms to provide services in a market is to establish a commercial presence, and to engage in foreign direct investment (FDI).[11]

There is substantial empirical evidence that services FDI has positive effects on productivity by inducing greater competition and providing access to higher quality, more varied, and cheaper services (Francois and Hoekman 2010). Many studies and reports have analyzed the role of services trade and related policies from an economic development perspective (see, e.g., Balchin et al. 2016; Cali, Ellis, and te Velde 2008; Dihel and Goswami 2016; Mattoo and Payton 2007; Saez et al. 2015; World Bank 2010), complementing research on developed economies (see, e.g., Breinlich and Criscuolo 2011; Wagner 2012). This literature demonstrates that firm heterogeneity plays an important role in shaping patterns of services trade, much as is the case for trade

---

[11]   The importance of FDI as a "mode of supply" implies that the adjustment costs of trade in services may differ from those when trade comprises goods. Because the services are produced locally, greater foreign competition through FDI will generally involve less reallocation of employment across sectors than in the case of liberalization of trade in goods (Konan and Maskus 2006).

in goods. A robust finding is that an important determinant of services sector performance, and thus economy-wide productivity, is the role that many services play as an input into the production of both goods and other services.

In the remainder of this chapter we explore empirically whether services trade policy can be a tool to support achievement of the SDGs. Consistent with the discussion above, we start by assessing the relationship between services trade policy regimes and economic development (per capita income growth) using a cross-section regression framework. We then go on to investigate the empirical relationship between services trade policy and access to a subset of the services highlighted in the various SDGs. In particular, we look at access to financial, ICT, and transport services. These three services are frequently referenced in the text of the SDGs and associated targets (Table 3.1).

3.3.1 Services Trade Policy and Per Capita Income Growth

We construct a cross-section growth regression framework to estimate the connections between services trade policy and economic growth. The main database used in this exercise is the World Bank's Services Trade Restrictions Database (STRD), which covers 103 countries and provides information on services trade policy for many services sectors including finance, telecommunications, transport, and professional services. The indexes in the STRD capture the trade policy regime prevailing in a given country from 2007 to 2010.[12]

The dependent variable is the average growth rate of per capita GDP (purchasing power parity) for the 6-year period between 2008 and 2013. We use a standard growth empirical model with the initial level of economic development, education, and investment share of GDP plus a number of additional variables (see Mattoo, Rathindran, and Subramanian 2006). In particular, we control for the degree of political stability, the level of government consumption, the share of tropical land within the country's territory,[13] and sub-Saharan Africa (SSA) and Latin America (LAC) regional dummy variables. We also add a dummy control variable taking the value of one if the country has experienced

---

[12] For a detailed description of the STRD see Borchert, Gootiiz, and Mattoo (2014).

[13] We are grateful to Ulrich Sperling for providing the climate data. In particular, the shares of tropical land within the country territory were computed by the Geographical Institute of the University of Bern using the Köppen-Geiger climate classification data.

a systemic financial crisis as measured by the Laeven-Valencia Systemic Banking Crisis Database in the 2007–2011 period.[14]

The estimation sample contains 92 countries spanning all income categories and geographical regions. The countries are listed in Table B1, and Table B2 contains summary statistics, definitions, and sources for all of the variables used in the estimation. The results are presented in Table 3.3. In the first five columns, the services trade restrictiveness

Table 3.3 Services Trade Policy and Economic Growth

	Dependent Variable: Per Capita GDP Growth					
	(1)	(2)	(3)	(4)	(5)	(6)
STRI overall	0.013					
	(0.015)					
STRI finance		0.010				0.009
		(0.012)				(0.014)
STRI telecommunications			0.011			0.013
			(0.009)			(0.009)
STRI transport				−0.017		−0.028***
				(0.011)		(0.010)
STRI professional					0.012	0.020
					(0.011)	(0.012)
Log initial pc GDP	−0.938***	−0.916***	−0.914***	−0.855***	−0.973***	−1.023***
	(0.192)	(0.197)	(0.196)	(0.188)	(0.183)	(0.186)
Education	0.025**	0.025**	0.028***	0.026***	0.025**	0.032***
	(0.010)	(0.010)	(0.010)	(0.010)	(0.010)	(0.009)
Investment	0.121***	0.122***	0.119***	0.133***	0.124***	0.127***
	(0.028)	(0.028)	(0.029)	(0.026)	(0.027)	(0.025)
Crisis	−0.303	−0.302	−0.238	−0.505	−0.289	0.034
	(0.458)	(0.457)	(0.458)	(0.416)	(0.443)	(0.453)

continued on next page

---

[14] The findings presented below are stable if only data for the 2010–2013 period are used so as to reduce the potential effects of the global financial crisis. Results remain qualitatively robust when eliminating high-income countries from the estimation sample. Regression results are available upon request.

Table 3.3 *continued*

	Dependent Variable: Per Capita GDP Growth					
	(1)	(2)	(3)	(4)	(5)	(6)
Political stability	0.636**	0.630**	0.529*	0.407	0.670**	0.598**
	(0.313)	(0.305)	(0.267)	(0.306)	(0.290)	(0.291)
GVT consumption	−0.048	−0.046	−0.041	−0.051	−0.050	−0.041
	(0.035)	(0.038)	(0.036)	(0.038)	(0.036)	(0.039)
Share of tropical land	0.007	0.008	0.007	0.008	0.006	0.006
	(0.006)	(0.005)	(0.005)	(0.006)	(0.006)	(0.006)
SSA dummy	−0.437	−0.429	−0.481	−0.463	−0.429	−0.611
	(0.463)	(0.458)	(0.489)	(0.438)	(0.453)	(0.506)
LAC dummy	0.684	0.579	0.622	0.267	0.776	0.753
	(0.604)	(0.529)	(0.538)	(0.604)	(0.601)	(0.638)
Constant	5.868***	5.743***	5.509**	5.786***	5.888***	5.721***
	(2.193)	(2.176)	(2.116)	(2.170)	(2.192)	(2.108)
Observations	92	92	92	92	92	92
Adjusted Rsq	0.603	0.604	0.609	0.613	0.606	0.635

GDP = gross domestic product, GVT = government, LAC = Latin America and Caribbean, pc = per capita, Rsq = R-squared, SSA = sub-Saharan Africa, STRI = services trade restrictiveness index.

Notes: Robust standard errors in parentheses. * 0.1, ** 0.05, *** 0.01.

Source: The sources of all variables used in the regressions are provided in Table B2.

indices (STRIs) are introduced one at a time, starting with the STRI that aggregates trade policy information across the four services sectors used for the analysis; the last column includes all the sector-specific STRIs jointly. The estimated coefficients for the initial level of economic development, education, and investment share of GDP have the expected signs and are statistically significant across all of the specifications in Table 3.3.[15] The other growth controls (except for share of tropical land and the LAC dummy) all have the expected signs; however, neither of these is statistically significant.

Turning to the services trade policy coefficient estimates, the overall STRI does not appear to have any effect on growth performance. The same is true when sector-specific STRIs are included separately: coefficients are never statistically significant. Only the sign of the

---

[15] Levine and Renelt (1992) identified the initial level of economic development, education, and investment share of GDP as empirically robust determinants of growth.

coefficient estimate for transport services suggests that less restrictive trade policy regimes are associated with higher economic growth (Column 4); however, the estimate is not statistically different from zero. These patterns remain robust when we include all of the sector-specific STRIs in the growth equation (Column 6), with the exception of the coefficient for the STRI for transport, which becomes statistically significant and doubles in magnitude. The estimate implies that reducing restrictions on trade in transport services by the equivalent of half of one standard deviation is associated with an increase of 0.25 percentage points in the average growth rate. Analogous results are obtained if we replicate the estimation using only data for STRIs pertaining to the establishment of a commercial presence (i.e., restrictions on inward FDI or Mode 3 of the General Agreement on Trade in Services) (Table 3.4). This reveals that the finding is mostly due to barriers to establishment.[16]

Table 3.4 Mode 3 Services Trade Policy and Economic Growth

Dependent Variable: Per Capita GDP Growth					
	(1)	(2)	(3)	(4)	(5)
STRI overall	0.012				
	(0.013)				
STRI finance		0.010			0.007
		(0.011)			(0.013)
STRI telecommunications					0.012
					(0.010)
STRI transport			-0.012		-0.020**
			(0.009)		(0.009)
STRI professional				0.006	0.009
				(0.007)	(0.008)
Log initial pc GDP	-0.955***	-0.924***	-0.830***	-0.965***	-0.963***
	(0.195)	(0.198)	(0.193)	(0.189)	(0.195)
Education	0.025**	0.025**	0.026***	0.024**	0.031***
	(0.010)	(0.010)	(0.010)	(0.010)	(0.009)

continued on next page

[16] Since the STRI score for telecommunications in Table 3.3 reflects only Mode 3 policy measures, the results of the model when STRI telecommunications is introduced in isolation (Column 3 of Table 3.3) are not replicated in Table 3.4.

Table 3.4 *continued*

	Dependent Variable: Per Capita GDP Growth				
	(1)	(2)	(3)	(4)	(5)
Investment	0.122***	0.123***	0.129***	0.124***	0.122***
	(0.028)	(0.028)	(0.026)	(0.027)	(0.026)
Crisis	−0.287	−0.302	−0.527	−0.305	−0.082
	(0.458)	(0.454)	(0.425)	(0.435)	(0.462)
Political stability	0.645**	0.637**	0.435	0.645**	0.591**
	(0.314)	(0.305)	(0.303)	(0.293)	(0.285)
GVT consumption	−0.048	−0.047	−0.049	−0.048	−0.036
	(0.036)	(0.038)	(0.037)	(0.036)	(0.038)
Share of tropical land	0.006	0.007	0.008	0.007	0.007
	(0.006)	(0.005)	(0.006)	(0.006)	(0.006)
SSA dummy	−0.458	−0.448	−0.505	−0.493	−0.771
	(0.462)	(0.458)	(0.439)	(0.440)	(0.487)
LAC dummy	0.700	0.616	0.309	0.691	0.682
	(0.611)	(0.538)	(0.605)	(0.596)	(0.633)
Constant	6.053***	5.789***	5.496**	6.169***	5.731**
	(2.205)	(2.177)	(2.229)	(2.177)	(2.174)
Observations	92	92	92	92	92
Adjusted Rsq	0.604	0.604	0.610	0.603	0.622

GDP = gross domestic product, GVT = government, LAC = Latin America and Caribbean, pc = per capita, Rsq = R-squared, SSA = sub-Saharan Africa, STRI = services trade restrictiveness indices.

Notes: Robust standard errors in parentheses. * 0.1, ** 0.05, *** 0.01.

Source: The sources of all variables used in the regressions are provided in Table B2.

Tables C1 and C2 in Appendix C replicate the regression results for a sample limited to the 61 non-high-income countries covered in the dataset. The transport result and other findings remain very similar. Thus, these results are not driven by differences in economic development.

Overall, the regression results suggest that, as far as raising per capita incomes is concerned, most services trade policies are not particularly salient; however, this is not necessarily the case. One explanation for the finding that, apart from the transport sector, services trade policy does not appear to be a determinant of the cross-country variation in average economic growth, is that STRIs by themselves may not fully capture the policy factors that constrain services trade and investment.

In practice, a variety of product market regulation measures and the quality of a country's investment climate and economic governance may have a greater impact on services trade and investment than do the discriminatory policies that make up the STRIs. Recent research concludes that the effect of STRIs may be conditional on the incidence of other policies that affect the business environment, especially the quality of domestic institutions and economic governance (see, e.g., Beverelli, Fiorini, and Hoekman 2017; van der Marel 2012).

3.3.2 Services Trade Policy and Access to Services

In this section we investigate the effects of STRIs on the indicators of access to services relevant to various SDGs. In particular, we focus on access to financial, ICT, and transport services, three sectors for which STRI data are available and which appear frequently in the texts of the different SDGs. We use a simple bivariate regression model to estimate the conditional expectation function of a services-related SDG outcome given the prevailing services trade policy regime for the respective services sectors. As discussed previously, it is assumed that less restrictive trade policies will be associated with better services performance (i.e., access to or availability of services), which in turn supports the realization of the relevant SDGs.[17] We take into account particular features of the economic environment that are likely to affect the relationship between access to services that matter for SDG outcomes and services trade policy.

The following sector-specific interaction model is estimated:

$$\text{SDG-outcome}_i = \alpha + \beta \text{STRI}_i + \gamma \text{Moderator}_i + \delta(\text{STRI}_i \times \text{Moderator}_i) + \epsilon_i \qquad (1)$$

Two moderator variables are used. The first is the level of economic development (GDP per capita). For many SDGs, increasing per capita income is important for the achievement of the goal, suggesting a need to test whether the relationship between services trade policy and services access-related performance indicators are moderated by the initial level of income. A stronger relationship between STRIs and the realization of SDG performance indicators is expected when the process of achieving the latter is less constrained by income levels. The second moderator variable is the quality of economic institutions in a country. This second exercise follows Beverelli, Fiorini, and Hoekman (2017), who identified economic governance as a key shaping factor for the effect of services

---

[17]   See, e.g., D'Amelio, Garrone, and Piscitello (2016).

trade restrictiveness on the productivity of downstream manufacturing industries, controlling for the intensity of use of services inputs into production. The focus here is on access to services as a function of services trade policy, which will be affected by the same type of institutional interdependence relationships that Beverelli, Fiorini and Hoekman (2017) found to be important.

The non-storability and intangibility of most services gives rise to a proximity burden (Francois and Hoekman 2010): the agent providing a service must be in the same location as the buyer or consumer. As a consequence, exporters of services often must perform some stages of their economic activity in the importing country, and are thus affected by local regulations and the prevailing business environment, that is, the quality of economic governance and related institutions. Accordingly, better institutions should attract more productive services providers and support higher levels of services performance. We therefore expect a stronger positive relationship between services trade openness and access to services in countries with higher quality regulatory institutions.

Data on access to financial services were obtained from the Global Financial Development Database of the World Bank. As a proxy for access we use the share of the population that is at least 15 years of age and has an account at a formal financial institution.[18] In the case of access to ICT services, we consider the number of individuals per 100 people who have used the internet in the last 12 months (from any location and via any device). These data are collected by the International Telecommunication Union and reported in the World Bank's Millennium Development Goals database. Finally, we measure access to transport services using the World Bank Logistics Performance Index. This index reflects the perceptions that professionals (freight forwarders) have of a country's logistics situation, based on the efficiency of the customs clearance process, the quality of trade and transport-related infrastructure, ease of arranging competitively priced shipments, and the quality of services (e.g., the ability to track and trace consignments, and the frequency with which shipments reach the consignee within the scheduled time). The index ranges from 1 to 5, with a higher score representing better performance.

Information on services trade policy is again taken from the STRD described in Section 3.1. For each access variable introduced above we use the corresponding sector-specific STRI. Specifically, we take the

---

[18]   The results reported below are robust to using other measures of consumer access to basic financial services. The results also hold for proxies for firm access to financial services, which is an important determinant of firm performance (Chauvet and Jacolin 2017).

overall-modes STRI, which, in the case of communication services, corresponds to the Mode 3 STRI. As the STRI data is for policies prevailing from 2007 to 2010, for each access variable we use the average of the available values for 2010–2012.[19] By merging the services access and quality indicators and the trade policy data by sector, we end up with three cross-section datasets where the number of countries (observations) is determined by the intersection of the country coverage of the source databases.

Finally, we use data on institutional regimes from the Worldwide Governance Indicators database. We also use the Worldwide Governance Indicators measure of regulatory quality as a proxy for the prevailing institutional framework.[20] The dependent variable is constructed as an average for the 3-year period from 2010 to 2012. Table B3 presents the summary statistics by sector.

Table 3.5 reports the estimation results. The negative signs of the estimated coefficients in the bivariate models (Columns 1, 4, and 7) indicate that, *ceteris paribus*, a lower level of trade restrictiveness for a sector is associated with better access to the services concerned,

Table 3.5 Services Trade Policy and Services Components of the Sustainable Development Goals

Sector	Finance			ICT			Transport		
	(1)	(2)	(3)	(4)	(5)	(6)	(7)	(8)	(9)
STRI s	-0.432**	1.921***	0.142	-0.342***	0.280*	-0.008	-0.005*	0.028***	0.002
	(0.191)	(0.448)	(0.128)	(0.109)	(0.150)	(0.083)	(0.003)	(0.007)	(0.002)
Log pc GDP		21.274***			16.563***			0.388***	
		(1.490)			(0.953)			(0.033)	
STRI s x log pc GDP		-0.226***			-0.039**			-0.004***	
		(0.045)			(0.017)			(0.001)	
Institutions		37.302***			26.631***			0.586***	
		(2.890)			(2.650)			(0.068)	

continued on next page

---

[19] Detailed information on the years covered for each variable is given in Table B3. The results reported below are robust to modifications of the average time period, especially taking into account the years 2008, 2009, and 2013 when these are available.

[20] Our results are robust to using other indicators such as the rule of law, control of corruption, and political stability.

Table 3.5 *continued*

Sector	Finance			ICT			Transport		
	(1)	(2)	(3)	(4)	(5)	(6)	(7)	(8)	(9)
STRI s x institutions			-0.539***			-0.111			-0.004**
			(0.083)			(0.079)			(0.002)
Observations	100	100	100	103	103	103	102	102	102
Rsq	0.066	0.753	0.638	0.105	0.849	0.651	0.025	0.734	0.641

GDP = gross domestic product, ICT = information and communications technology, pc = per capita, Rsq = r-squared, STRI = services trade restrictiveness index.

Notes: Institutions are proxied with the World Governance Indicators measure of regulatory quality. Robust standard errors in parentheses. * 0.1, ** 0.05, *** 0.01.

Source: The sources of all variables used in the regressions are provided in Table B3.

and a higher level of performance in supporting the attainment of the respective SDGs. This relationship is statistically significant for all three services sectors, with levels of significance ranging from the 1% (ICT) to the 10% (transport) level of statistical significance. These results are consistent with the hypothesized positive role of international trade in improving access to services.

In the interaction models, the coefficient estimates for the direct effects of GDP per capita and regulatory quality are positive and strongly significant, meaning that higher levels of economic development and a better quality of institutions are positively associated with services access indicators. More interestingly, the coefficient for the interaction term is always negative. When statistically significant, this reflects a moderating role—of either economic development (per capita income) or quality of institutions—in shaping the relationship between services trade policy and measures of access to services relevant to the SDGs. In particular, the negative sign implies that the positive association between trade openness and services performance (an input into SDG progress) is stronger for higher values of the moderator variable. The interaction term between GDP per capita and the sectoral STRI is statistically different from 0 for all three sectors, while the interaction between the STRI and the quality of domestic institutions is significant for both finance and transport.[21]

To get a sense of the behavior of the STRI–services access relationship as a function of the moderator variable, we calculate the estimated

---

[21] The moderating role of institutions suggested by our estimates is consistent with the literature on the complementarities between trade and trade policy, and institutions (Ahsan 2013; see also, e.g., Beverelli, Fiorini, and Hoekman 2017; Freund and Bolaky 2008; Rodriguez and Rodrik 2014).

partial derivative of Equation (1) with respect to the STRI, which is given by. Consider for example the link between financial services trade restrictiveness and access to financial services.[22] Figures 3.1 and 3.2 plot this relationship at two different levels of per capita GDP (Figure 3.1) and institutional quality (Figure 3.2).[23]

Figure 3.1 Access to Financial Services and Services Trade Restrictiveness Indices Finance—The Role of Initial Conditions

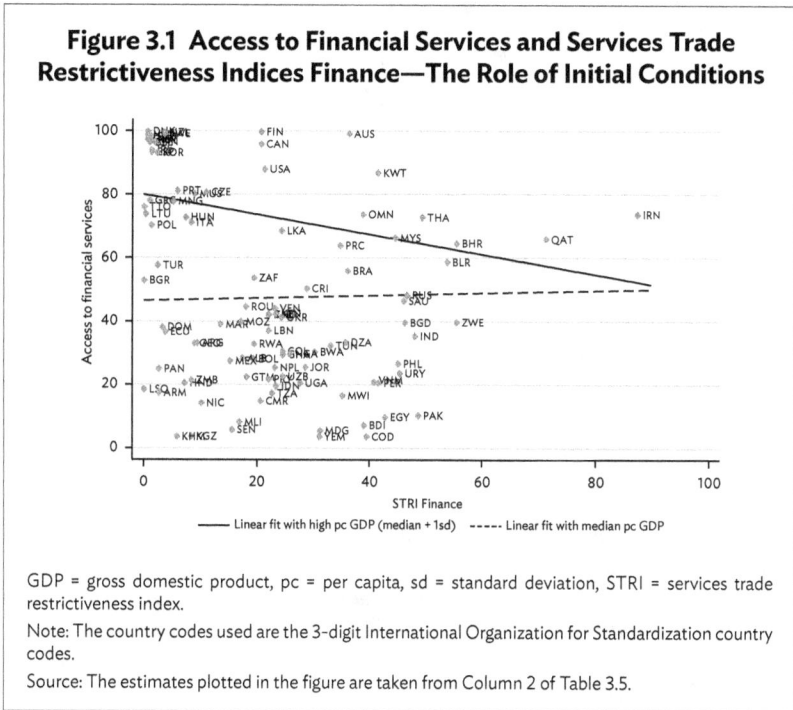

GDP = gross domestic product, pc = per capita, sd = standard deviation, STRI = services trade restrictiveness index.

Note: The country codes used are the 3-digit International Organization for Standardization country codes.

Source: The estimates plotted in the figure are taken from Column 2 of Table 3.5.

The solid line in both figures represents the fitted linear relationship when the level of economic development (quality of institutions) is at its median value plus one standard deviation. In that case, lower services trade restrictiveness is associated with better access indicators. More

---

[22] The same patterns emerge for ICT and transport but are not reported for space considerations.

[23] The regression line in Figures 3.1 and 3.2 is obtained by fitting the interaction model for per capita GDP (the institutional variables) using the estimation from Table 3.5, Column 2 (for Figure 3.1) and Column 3 (for Figure 3.2).

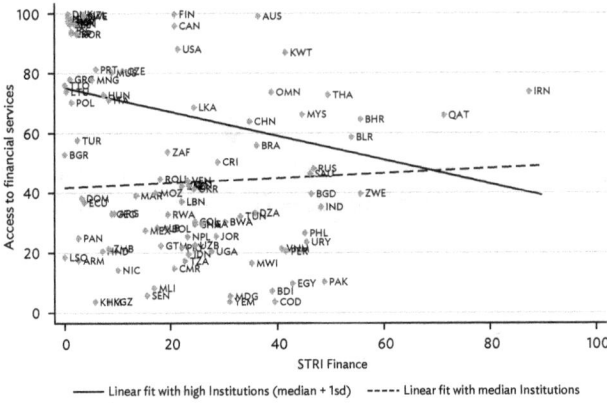

Figure 3.2 Access to Financial Services and Services Trade Restrictiveness Indices Finance—The Role of Institutions

sd = standard deviation, STRI = services trade restrictiveness index.

Note: The country codes used are the 3-digit International Organization for Standardization country codes.

Source: The estimates plotted in the figure are taken from Column 3 of Table 3.5.

precisely, when per capita GDP (quality of institutions) is used as the moderator, a reduction in the sectoral STRI of half of one standard deviation is associated with an increase in access of 2.8 (3.6) units.[24] In contrast, when the level of per capita GDP or the quality of institutions are at their median levels, such a positive relationship between lower services trade restrictiveness and better access might not exist. Indeed, the estimated slope of the dashed line in both figures is not statistically different from 0.[25]

3.4 Conclusion

Achieving many of the SDGs depends in part on bolstering the performance of services sectors and improving access to specific

[24] The estimated slope coefficient and the robust standard error for the solid line are −0.315 and 0.086 in Figure 3.1, and −0.4 and 0.159 in Figure 3.2.

[25] The estimated slope coefficient and its robust standard error for the dashed line are 0.04 and 0.105 in Figure 3.1, and 0.081 and 0.130 in Figure 3.2.

services in developing countries. Conceptually, services trade policy can contribute to the SDGs by helping to increase the productivity performance of services sectors and thus impact economic growth, an important necessary condition for realizing many of the SDGs. Services trade policy can also affect the availability and quality of a variety of services that will determine the attainment of specific SDGs. We have shown that prevailing services trade and investment policies are associated with indicators of access to services that matter for the realization of a number of SDGs, and our data suggest that, with the exception of transport-related trade policies, their association with per capita income growth is weak. The available data suggest that reducing levels of services trade and investment restrictiveness is a potential primary instrument to enhance access to services sectors that are important to the SDGs. One implication of this is that policy research should focus on the direct channels between services trade policy and services performance, as opposed to the indirect channels between trade openness and growth.

Other policies (most obviously sector-specific policies and sector-specific regulatory regimes) will undoubtedly be more important in affecting the performance of services. These, appropriately, are the focus of SDG-related analysis and projects around the developing world. On the trade front, attention is focused on measures to facilitate trade in goods with developing countries and enhance productive capacity. This is also appropriate and important, and this chapter does not argue the contrary. Instead, our goal is simply to highlight that trade policies for services can contribute to the attainment of the SDGs, and that analysis of the potential role of services trade policies should be part of country-level diagnostics and prioritization efforts. Most discussion on the leveraging of trade's potential to support the achievement of the SDGs is restricted to merchandise trade. This is exemplified in the Agenda 2030 document incorporating the SDGs, that highlights measures to increase merchandise exports from developing countries through duty-free, quota-free access and liberal rules of origin, and by giving countries space to pursue industrial policies (UN 2015). The main policy implication of this chapter is that the focus on trade policies should span services trade and investment regimes, and not just (or primarily) merchandise trade.

Reducing services trade costs is a neglected dimension of the challenge of realizing the SDGs. Lowering services trade costs will involve more than reducing formal or explicit barriers to trade, as captured in the STRIs. It is important to recognize that the STRIs used for the empirical analysis are just one element of the set of policies that impact the level of competition on services markets and thus the prices and availability of services. When it comes to services trade, the quality of economic governance institutions is likely to be particularly important, since FDI is a major vehicle for foreign suppliers to provide services. Attention must also focus on improving regulatory regimes and lowering costs for firms to demonstrate compliance with applicable regulatory policies, that is, services trade facilitation.

The identification of trade policy-related priorities from the perspective of specific SDGs clearly requires a country-level analysis and detailed investigation of the services performance measures that are most salient to a given country context. In this respect, the results reported in this chapter are intended to be illustrative, and suggest that such analysis is worth undertaking as part of the broader effort to pursue the SDGs.

References

Abbott, P., R. Sapsford, and A. Binagwaho. 2017. Learning from Success: How Rwanda Achieved the Millennium Development Goals for Health. *World Development* 92: 103–116. http://dx.doi.org/10.1016 /j.worlddev.2016.11.013 (accessed 31 October 2018).

Ahsan, R. N. 2013. Input Tariffs, Speed of Contract Enforcement, and the Productivity of Firms in India. *Journal of International Economics* 90(1): 181–192. http://dx.doi.org/10.1016/j.jinteco.2012.11.006 (accessed 31 October 2018).

Backer, K. D., I. Desnoyers-James, and L. Moussiegt. 2015. Manufacturing or Services—That Is (Not) the Question: The Role of Manufacturing and Services in OECD Economies. Organisation for Economic Co-operation and Development (OECD) Science, Technology and Industry Policy Papers 19. Paris: OECD Publishing. https://doi .org/10.1787/5js64ks09dmn-en (accessed 31 October 2018).

Balchin, N., B. Hoekman, H. Martin, M. Mendez-Parra, P. Papadavid, D. Primack, and D. W. te Velde. 2016. *Trade in Services and Economic Transformation*. London: Overseas Development Institute (ODI).

Baumol, W. J. 1967. Macroeconomics of Unbalanced Growth: The Anatomy of Urban Crisis. *American Economic Review* 57(3): 415–426.

Berlingieri, G. 2015. Managing Export Complexity: the Role of Service Outsourcing. Mimeo. London: London School of Economics, Center for Economic Performance.

Beverelli, C., M. Fiorini, and B. Hoekman. 2017. Services Trade Policy and Manufacturing Productivity: The Role of Institutions. *Journal of International Economics* 104: 166–182. http://dx.doi.org/10.1016 /j.jinteco.2016.11.001 (accessed 31 October 2018).

Borchert, I., B. Gootiiz, and A. Mattoo. 2014. Policy Barriers to International Trade in Services: Evidence from a New Database. *The World Bank Economic Review* 28(1): 162–188. https://doi .org/10.1093/wber/lht017 (accessed 31 October 2018).

Breinlich, H., and C. Criscuolo. 2011. International Trade in Services: A Portrait of Importers and Exporters. *Journal of International Economics* 84(2), 188–206. https://doi.org/10.1016 /j.jinteco.2011.03.006 (accessed 31 October 2018).

Buera, F. J., and J. P. Kaboski. 2009. Can Traditional Theories of Structural Change Fit The Data? *Journal of the European Economic Association* 7(2–3): 469–477.

Cali, M., K. Ellis, and D. W. te Velde. 2008. The Contribution of Services to Development and the Role of Trade Liberalisation and Regulation. ODI Working Paper 298. London: ODI.

Chauvet, L., and L. Jacolin. 2017. Financial Inclusion, Bank Concentration, and Firm Performance. *World Development* 97: 1–13. http://dx.doi.org/10.1016/j.worlddev.2017.03.018 (accessed 31 October 2018).

D'Amelio, M., P. Garrone, and L. Piscitello. 2016. Can Multinational Enterprises Light up Developing Countries? *World Development* 88: 12–32. http://dx.doi.org/10.1016/j.worlddev.2016.06.018 (accessed 31 October 2018).

Dihel, N. C. 2010. Understanding Trade in Environmental Services: Key Issues and Prospects. In *International Trade in Services. New Trends and Opportunities for Developing Countries*, edited by O. Cattaneo, M. Engman, S. Sáez, and R. M. Stern. Washington, DC: World Bank.

Dihel, N., and A. G. Goswami. 2016. *The Unexplored Potential of Trade in Services in Africa: From Hair Stylists and Teachers to Accountants and Doctors*. Washington, DC: World Bank.

Fiorini, M., and B. Hoekman. 2018. Services Trade Policy and Sustainable Development. *World Development* 112: 1–12. https://doi.org/10.1016/j.worlddev.2018.07.015 (accessed 31 October 2018).

Francois, J., and B. Hoekman. 2010. Services Trade and Policy. *Journal of Economic Literature* 48(3): 642–692.

Freund, C., and B. Bolaky. 2008. Trade, Regulations, and Income. *Journal of Development Economics* 87(2): 309–321.

Fuchs, V. R. 1968. *The Service Economy*. New York: National Bureau of Economic Research.

Galor, O., and D. Weil. 1996. The Gender Gap, Fertility, and Growth. *American Economic Review* 86(3): 374–387.

Goldin, C. 2006. The Quiet Revolution That Transformed Women's Employment, Education, and Family. *American Economic Review, Papers and Proceedings* 96: 1–21.

International Labour Organization. 2016. *Key Indicators of the Labour Market, Ninth Edition*. Geneva, International Labour Office.

Joshi, D. K., B. B. Hughes, and T. D. Sisk. 2015. Improving Governance for the Post-2015 Sustainable Development Goals: Scenario Forecasting the Next 50 Years. *World Development* 70: 286–302. http://dx.doi.org/10.1016/j.worlddev.2015.01.013 (accessed 31 October 2018).

Koehler, J., P. Thomson, and R. Hope. 2015. Pump-Priming Payments for Sustainable Water Services in Rural Africa. *World Development* 74: 397–411. http://dx.doi.org/10.1016/j.worlddev.2015.05.020 (accessed 31 October 2018).

Konan, D. E., and K. E. Maskus. 2006. Quantifying the Impact of Services Liberalization in a Developing Country. *Journal of Development Economics* 81(1): 142–162. https://doi.org/10.1016/j.jdeveco.2005.05.009 (accessed 31 October 2018).

Kravis, I. B., A. W. Heston, and R. Summers. 1983. The Share of Services in Economic Growth. In *Global Econometrics: Essays in Honor of Lawrence R. Klein*, edited by F. G. Adams and B. G. Hickman. Cambridge, MA: Massachusetts Institute of Technology Press.

Levine, R., and D. Renelt. 1992. A Sensitivity Analysis of Cross-Country Growth Regressions. *The American Economic Review* 82(4): 942–963. https://doi.org/10.2307/2117352 (accessed 31 October 2018).

Mattoo, A., and L. Payton. 2007. *Services Trade and Development: The Experience of Zambia.* Washington, DC: World Bank and Palgrave Macmillan.

Mattoo, A., R. Rathindran, and A. Subramanian. 2006. Measuring Services Trade Liberalization and Its Impact on Economic Growth: An Illustration. *Journal of Economic Integration* 21(1): 64–98.

Miroudot, S., and B. Shepherd. 2016. Trade Costs and Global Value Chains in Services. In *Research Handbook on Trade in Services*, edited by P. Sauvé and M. Roy. Cheltenham: Edward Elgar.

Ngai, L. R., and B. Petrongolo. 2017. Gender Gaps and the Rise of the Service Economy. *American Economic Journal: Macroeconomics* 9(4): 1–44. https://doi.org/10.1257/mac.20150253 (accessed 31 October 2018).

OECD and World Trade Organization (WTO). 2017. *Aid for Trade at a Glance 2017: Promoting Trade, Inclusiveness and Connectivity for Sustainable Development.* Geneva/Paris: OECD/WTO.

Rendall, M. 2010. Brain Versus Brawn: The Realization of Women's Comparative Advantage. Working Paper No. 491 (Revised). Zurich: University of Zurich, Institute for Empirical Research in Economics.

Rodriguez, F., and D. Rodrik. 2014. Trade Policy and Economic Growth: A Skeptic's Guide to the Cross-National Evidence. In *NBER Macroeconomics Annual*, edited by B. S. Bernanke and K. Rogoff. Cambridge, MA: Massachusetts Institute of Technology Press.

Saez, J. S., C. H. Hollweg, D. Taglioni, E. van der Marel, E. Leendert, and V. Zavacka. 2015. *Valuing Services in Trade: A Toolkit for Competitiveness Diagnostics* 93714: 1–171. Washington, DC: World Bank. http://documents.worldbank.org/curated/en/2015/01/23811491/valuing-services-trade-toolkit-competitiveness-diagnostics (accessed 31 October 2018).

Schettkat, R., and L. Yocarini. 2006. The Shift to Services Employment: A Review of the Literature. *Structural Change and Economic Dynamics* 17(2): 127–147. http://dx.doi.org/10.1016/j.strueco.2005.04.002 (accessed 31 October 2018).

Ssozi, J., and S. Amlani. 2015. The Effectiveness of Health Expenditure on the Proximate and Ultimate Goals of Healthcare in Sub-Saharan

Africa. *World Development* 76: 165–179. http://dx.doi.org/10.1016 /j.worlddev.2015.07.010 (accessed 31 October 2018).

United Nations. 2014. *Open Working Group Proposal for Sustainable Development Goals.* New York: United Nations.

United Nations. 2015. *Transforming Our World: The 2030 Agenda for Sustainable Development.* New York: United Nations.

Van der Marel, E. 2012. Trade in Services and TFP: The Role of Regulation. *The World Economy* 35(11): 1387–1429.

Wagner, J. 2012. International Trade and Firm Performance: A Survey of Empirical Studies Since 2006. *Review of World Economics* 148(2): 235–267. https://doi.org/10.1007/s10290-011-0116-8 (accessed 31 October 2018).

World Bank. 2010. *International Trade in Services, Trade and Development.* Washington, DC: World Bank.

WTO. 2016. *World Trade Statistical Review* (Technical Report WTO). Geneva: WTO.

Young, A. 2014. Structural Transformation, the Mismeasurement of Productivity Growth, and the Cost Disease of Services. *American Economic Review* 104(11): 3635–3667. https://doi.org/10.1257 /aer.104.11.3635 (accessed 31 October 2018).

Appendix A

Goal 1: End poverty in all its forms everywhere.

Goal 2: End hunger, achieve food security and improved nutrition and promote sustainable agriculture.

Goal 3: Ensure healthy lives and promote well-being for all at all ages.

Goal 4: Ensure inclusive and equitable quality education and promote lifelong learning opportunities for all.

Goal 5: Achieve gender equality and empower all women and girls.

Goal 6: Ensure availability and sustainable management of water and sanitation for all.

Goal 7: Ensure access to affordable, reliable, sustainable and modern energy for all.

Goal 8: Promote sustained, inclusive and sustainable economic growth, full and productive employment and decent work for all.

Goal 9: Build resilient infrastructure, promote inclusive and sustainable industrialization and foster innovation.

Goal 10: Reduce inequality within and among countries.

Goal 11: Make cities and human settlements inclusive, safe, resilient and sustainable.

Goal 12: Ensure sustainable consumption and production patterns.

Goal 13: Take urgent action to combat climate change and its impacts.

Goal 14: Conserve and sustainably use the oceans, seas and marine resources for sustainable development.

Goal 15: Protect, restore and promote sustainable use of terrestrial ecosystems, sustainably manage forests, combat desertification, and halt and reverse land degradation and halt biodiversity loss.

Goal 16: Promote peaceful and inclusive societies for sustainable development, provide access to justice for all and build effective, accountable and inclusive institutions at all levels.

Goal 17: Strengthen the means of implementation and revitalize the global partnership for sustainable development.

Appendix B

Table B1 Services Trade Restrictiveness Index Countries and Estimation Sample Coverages

HIC OECD		HIC Non-OECD		Upper MIC		Lower MIC		LIC	
CODE	Samples	CODE	Samples	CODE	Samples	CODE	Samples	CODE	Samples
AUS	G, F, C, T	BHR	G, F, C, T	ALB	G, F, C, T	ARM	G, F, C, T		G, F, C, T
AUT	G, F, C, T	KWT	G, F, C, T	ARG	F, C, T	BOL	G, F, C, T		G, F, C, T
BEL	G, F, C, T	LTU	G, F, C, T	BGR	G, F, C, T	CIV	G, C, T		G, F, C, T
CAN	G, F, C, T	OMN	F, C, T	BLR	F, C, T	CMR	G, F, C, T		F, C, T
CHL	G, F, C, T	QAT	G, F, C, T	BRA	G, F, C, T	EGY	G, F, C, T		G, F, C, T
CZE	G, F, C, T	RUS	G, F, C, T	BWA	G, F, C, T	GEO	F, C, T	KHM	G, F, C, T
DEU	G, F, C, T	SAU	G, F, C, T	CHN	G, F, C, T	GHA	G, F, C, T	MDG	F, C, T
DNK	G, F, C, T	TTO	G, F, C	COL	G, F, C, T	GTM	G, F, C, T	MLI	G, F, C, T
ESP	G, F, C, T	URY	G, F, C, T	CRI	G, F, C, T	HND	G, F, C, T	MOZ	G, F, C, T
FIN	G, F, C, T			DOM	G, F, C, T	IDN	G, F, C, T	MWI	G, F, C, T
FRA	G, F, C, T			DZA	G, F, C, T	IND	G, F, C, T	NPL	G, F, C, T
GBR	G, F, C, T			ECU	G, F, C, T	KGZ	G, C, T	RWA	G, F, C, T
GRC	G, F, C, T			HUN	G, F, C, T	LKA	G, F, C, T	TZA	G, F, C, T
IRL	G, F, C, T			IRN	F, C, T	LSO	G, F, C, T	UGA	G, F, C, T
ITA	G, F, C, T			JOR	G, F, C, T	MAR	G, F, C, T	ZWE	G, F, C, T
JPN	G, F, C, T			KAZ	G, F, C, T	MNG	G, F, C, T		
KOR	G, F, C, T			LBN	F, C, T	NGA	F, C, T		
NLD	G, F, C, T			MEX	G, F, C, T	NIC	G, F, C, T		
NZL	G, F, C, T			MUS	G, F, C, T	PAK	G, F, C, T		
POL	G, F, C, T			MYS	G, F, C, T	PHL	G, F, C, T		
PRT	G, F, C, T			NAM	G, C, T	PRY	G, F, C, T		
SWE	G, F, C, T			PAN	G, F, C, T	SEN	G, F, C, T		
USA	G, F, C, T			PER	G, F, C, T	UKR	G, F, C, T		
				ROU	G, F, C, T	UZB	F, C, T		
				THA	G, F, C, T	VNM	G, F, C, T		
				TUN	G, F, C, T	YEM	F, C, T		
				TUR	G, F, C, T	ZMB	G, F, C, T		
				VEN	G, F, C, T				
				ZAF	G, F, C, T				

HIC = high-income country, LIC = low-income country, MIC = middle-income country, OECD = Organisation for Economic Co-operation and Development.

Notes: CODE refers to the 3-digit International Organization for Standardization country codes. Samples are G for growth regression (Table 3.3); F for Sustainable Development Goal (SDG) finance regression (Columns 1–3 in Table 3.5); C for SDG information and communications technology regression (Columns 4–6 in Table 3.5); and T for SDG transport regression (Columns 7–9 in Table 3.5).

Source: Author.

Table B2 Summary Statistics—Growth Regressions

Variable	Source	#	Mean	Median	SD	Min.	Max.
Dependent variable							
Growth of GDP per capita (PPP), average 2008–2013	World Development Indicators, World Bank	92	1,946	1,931	2.3	–4,656	8,452
STRI variables (All modes available)							
All sectors	Services Trade Restrictiveness Database, World Bank	92	27,316	23.4	13,562	6.2	65.7
Finance	Services Trade Restrictiveness Database, World Bank	92	20,609	19.5	16,927	0.0	71.3
Telecommunications	Services Trade Restrictiveness Database, World Bank	92	25,136	25.0	24,197	0.0	100.0
Transport	Services Trade Restrictiveness Database, World Bank	92	30,398	28.9	17,374	3.1	79.8
Professional	Services Trade Restrictiveness Database, World Bank	92	47,842	45.0	17,047	11.0	90.0
STRI variables (Mode 3)							
All sectors	Services Trade Restrictiveness Database, World Bank	92	25,652	21.29	15,386	0	69.34
Finance	Services Trade Restrictiveness Database, World Bank	92	19,574	18,965	18,271	0	75.00
Transport	Services Trade Restrictiveness Database, World Bank	92	31,433	30.56	19,959	0	81.25
Professional	Services Trade Restrictiveness Database, World Bank	92	39,348	37.5	26,984	0	100.00
Other growth controls							
Log initial GDP per capita (PPP), 2008	World Development Indicators, World Bank	92	8,315	8,336	1,622	5,012	10,958
Education, secondary school enrollment, 2005	Barro and Lee Educational Attainment Data	92	43,617	41,890	19,351	3,943	87,966
Investment, gross capital formation (% of GDP), average 2005–2013	World Development Indicators, World Bank	92	24,346	23,171	6,088	11,476	46,524
Crisis, = 1 if systemic crisis during 2007–2011	Laeven-Valencia, Systemic Banking Crises Database	92	0.207	0	0.407	0	1

continued on next page

Table B2 *continued*

Variable	Source	#	Mean	Median	SD	Min.	Max.
Political stability, average 2008–2013	World Governance Indicators, World Bank	92	-0.116	-0.068	0.870	-2,661	1,396
GVT consumption, general government final consumption (% of GDP), average 2008–2013	World Development Indicators, World Bank	92	15,850	15,089	5,724	2,804	37,389
Share of tropical land, year 2000	Köppen-Geiger climate classification	92	37,297	6,151	43,355	0	100
Sub-Saharan Africa dummy	World Bank region classification	92	0.217	0	0.415	0	1
Latin American Countries dummy	World Bank region classification	92	0.185	0	0.39	0	1

GDP = gross domestic product, Max. = maximum, Min. = minimum, PPP = power purchasing parity, SD = standard deviation, STRI = services trade restrictiveness index.
Source: Author.

Table B3 Summary Statistics— Sustainable Development Goals Regressions

Variable	Source	#	Mean	Median	SD	Min.	Max.
Financial services							
Account at a formal financial institution (% age 15+), average 2010–2011	Global Financial Database, World Bank	100	48,683	40,584	30,301	3,660	99,737
STRI finance (all modes)	Services Trade Restrictiveness Database, World Bank	100	21,878	20.8	18,049	0	87.4
STRI finance (Mode 3)	Services Trade Restrictiveness Database, World Bank	100	20,993	25	19,791	0	100
Log of GDP per capita (constant 2005 US dollars), average 2010–2012	World Development Indicators Database, World Bank	100	8,308	8,389	1,563	4,998	10,999
Regulatory quality, average 2010–2012	World Governance Indicators, World Bank	100	0.155	0.088	0.893	-1,935	1,872
ICT services							
Internet users (per 100 people), average 2010–2012	Millennium Development Indicators, World Bank	103	38,936	36,867	26,748	1,110	91,983

continued on next page

Table B3 *continued*

Variable	Source	#	Mean	Median	SD	Min.	Max.
STRI telecommunications (all modes/Mode 3)	Services Trade Restrictiveness Database, World Bank	103	26,942	25	25,411	0	100
Log of GDP per capita (constant 2005 US dollars), average 2010–2012	World Development Indicators, World Bank	103	8,268	8,335	1,570	4,998	10,999
Regulatory quality, average 2010–2012	World Governance Indicators, World Bank	103	0.133	0.071	0.892	–1,935	1,872
Transport services							
Logistic Performance Index, average 2010 and 2012	World Development Indicators, World Bank	102	2,957	2,825	0.527	1,610	4.07
STRI transport (all modes)	Services Trade Restrictiveness Database, World Bank	102	31,034	29.15	17,857	3.1	79.8
STRI transport (Mode 3)	Services Trade Restrictiveness Database, World Bank	102	31,759	29.17	20,945	0	87.5
Log of GDP per capita (constant 2005 US dollars), average 2010–2012	World Development Indicators Database, World Bank	102	8,255	8,296	1,573	4,998	10,999
Regulatory quality, average 2010–2012	World Governance Indicators, World Bank	102	0.131	0.021	0.896	–1,935	1,872

GDP = gross domestic product, ICT = information and communications technology, Max. = maximum, Min. = minimum, SD = standard deviation, STRI = services trade restrictiveness indices, US = United States, WDI = World Development Indicators.
Source: Author.

Appendix C

Table C1 Services Trade Policy and Economic Growth in Developing Countries

	Dependent Variable: Per Capita GDP Growth					
	(1)	(2)	(3)	(4)	(5)	(6)
STRI overall	0.016					
	(0.016)					
STRI finance		0.006				0.004
		(0.016)				(0.019)
STRI telecommunications			0.013			0.016
			(0.010)			(0.011)
STRI transport				-0.018		-0.026**
				(0.012)		(0.012)
STRI professional					0.012	0.015
					(0.014)	(0.016)
Log initial pc GDP	-0.658**	-0.599**	-0.564*	-0.512*	-0.744**	-0.622**
	(0.278)	(0.291)	(0.285)	(0.269)	(0.297)	(0.282)
Education	0.023*	0.023*	0.024*	0.024**	0.026**	0.028**
	(0.013)	(0.012)	(0.012)	(0.011)	(0.012)	(0.011)
Investment	0.122***	0.123***	0.120***	0.130***	0.125***	0.133***
	(0.037)	(0.037)	(0.036)	(0.034)	(0.036)	(0.031)
Crisis	-0.251	-0.366	-0.276	-0.457	-0.145	-0.038
	(0.807)	(0.786)	(0.803)	(0.799)	(0.831)	(0.908)
Political stability	0.541	0.487	0.414	0.300	0.514	0.355
	(0.353)	(0.336)	(0.310)	(0.342)	(0.333)	(0.314)
GVT consumption	-0.052	-0.050	-0.047	-0.045	-0.050	-0.044
	(0.043)	(0.045)	(0.042)	(0.045)	(0.044)	(0.048)
Share of tropical land	0.011*	0.013*	0.011**	0.015**	0.012**	0.012*
	(0.006)	(0.006)	(0.006)	(0.006)	(0.006)	(0.006)
SSA dummy	-0.288	-0.304	-0.361	-0.419	-0.245	-0.461
	(0.522)	(0.509)	(0.538)	(0.504)	(0.524)	(0.587)
LAC dummy	0.218	-0.025	0.055	-0.507	0.301	-0.014
	(0.791)	(0.694)	(0.683)	(0.694)	(0.846)	(0.856)
Constant	3.632	3.417	2.920	3.146	3.778	2.774
	(2.748)	(2.764)	(2.672)	(2.599)	(2.701)	(2.434)
Observations	61	61	61	61	61	61
Adjusted Rsq	0.377	0.368	0.388	0.395	0.376	0.412

GDP = gross domestic product, GVT = government, LAC = Latin America and Caribbean, pc = per capita, Rsq = R-squared, SSA = sub-Saharan Africa, STRI = services trade restrictiveness index.

Notes: Robust standard errors in parentheses. * 0.1, ** 0.05, *** 0.01.

Source: The sources of all variables used in the regressions are provided in Table B2.

Table C2 Mode 3 Services Trade Policy and Economic Growth in Developing Countries

	Dependent Variable: Per Capita GDP Growth				
	(1)	(2)	(3)	(4)	(5)
STRI overall	0.013				
	(0.014)				
STRI finance		0.007			0.004
		(0.015)			(0.019)
STRI telecommunications					0.016
					(0.011)
STRI transport			−0.015		−0.020*
			(0.010)		(0.011)
STRI professional				0.005	0.006
				(0.008)	(0.009)
Log initial pc GDP	−0.671**	−0.603**	−0.485*	−0.696**	−0.523*
	(0.277)	(0.294)	(0.267)	(0.287)	(0.264)
Education	0.023*	0.023*	0.025**	0.025**	0.027**
	(0.012)	(0.012)	(0.012)	(0.012)	(0.011)
Investment	0.122***	0.125***	0.126***	0.123***	0.126***
	(0.036)	(0.037)	(0.034)	(0.036)	(0.033)
Crisis	−0.255	−0.391	−0.566	−0.244	−0.335
	(0.818)	(0.780)	(0.811)	(0.834)	(0.919)
Political stability	0.544	0.501	0.314	0.512	0.384
	(0.352)	(0.346)	(0.339)	(0.326)	(0.309)
GVT consumption	−0.052	−0.051	−0.043	−0.048	−0.040
	(0.043)	(0.046)	(0.044)	(0.044)	(0.046)
Share of tropical land	0.011*	0.012*	0.015**	0.013**	0.013**
	(0.006)	(0.006)	(0.006)	(0.006)	(0.006)
SSA dummy	−0.316	−0.318	−0.475	−0.341	−0.651
	(0.514)	(0.501)	(0.519)	(0.496)	(0.568)
LAC dummy	0.197	0.009	−0.477	0.137	−0.141
	(0.800)	(0.727)	(0.699)	(0.788)	(0.820)
Constant	3.828	3.453	2.847	3.929	2.536
	(2.718)	(2.762)	(2.608)	(2.655)	(2.451)
Observations	61	61	61	61	61
Adjusted Rsq	0.375	0.369	0.393	0.372	0.401

GDP = gross domestic product, GVT = government, LAC = Latin America and Caribbean, pc = per capita, Rsq = R-squared, SSA = sub-Saharan Africa, STRI = services trade restrictiveness indices.

Notes: Robust standard errors in parentheses. * 0.1, ** 0.05, *** 0.01.

Source: The sources of all variables used in the regressions are provided in Table B2.

PART II
Services and Manufacturing Intertwined

4

Services and Manufacturing in Global Value Chains— Is the Distinction Obsolete?

Sébastien Miroudot

4.1 Introduction

There is an ongoing debate on the "deindustrialization" of economies in both developed countries (Rowthorn and Wells 1987; Palma 2005; Neuss 2018) and developing countries (Palma 2014; Rodrik 2016). At the same time, other authors are discussing the "servicification" of economies (National Board of Trade 2012; Lodefalk 2013). At first glance, the two could be seen as symmetric trends describing the same shift from manufacturing activities to service activities. This shift was first observed in developed countries and is now being seen in developing countries. "Deindustrialization" puts the emphasis on the decline in manufacturing employment (the "glass half-empty"), while servicification points to the creation of new jobs in the service sector (the "glass half-full").

However, the two strands of literature do not describe the same phenomenon. The deindustrialization debate is focused on employment effects in relation to trade (offshoring), technological progress (productivity gains), and the evolution of demand (consumers' preferences). Although it is unclear whether there is less manufacturing today in terms of value added or output, the share of employment in manufacturing has clearly decreased, at least in developed countries. Concerns about the negative impact of deindustrialization first arise with regard to low-skilled jobs in developed countries, in relation to the "China shock"[1] (Autor, Dorn, and Hanson 2016) and a literature

---

[1]   The term "China shock" refers to the surge in exports from the People's Republic of China after the country joined the World Trade Organization in 2001.

that points the finger at globalization for causing the rise in inequality and poverty. In developing countries, the concern is that a *premature* deindustrialization would slow development by preventing countries from benefiting from the accumulation of capital, skills, and know-how traditionally gained by specializing in core manufacturing industries before moving to service activities. Authors concerned about deindustrialization are also often in favor of state capitalism and industrial policy as a mechanism to enable developing countries to catch up and create the foundations of their future growth.

In contrast, the literature on servicification focuses on transformations at the firm level. This literature is less about the shift to services at the aggregate level (i.e., employment moving from agriculture to manufacturing and then from manufacturing to services) and more about the transformation of manufacturing itself. Servicification takes stock of the increased use of services inputs by manufacturing firms (the outsourcing and offshoring of services), the increase in service activities within manufacturing firms (in-house provision of services), and the fact that services are increasingly sold together with goods as part of "solutions" or "bundles" (referred to as the "servitization" of manufacturing) (Vandermerwe and Rada 1988). The impact of this practice on jobs is largely related to high-skilled employment as this servicification aims to increase the value of products by adding services that are generally knowledge-intensive. When emerging economies bring new competition for these services, developed countries may perceive this as a negative development and cause for concern. In terms of policies, the literature on servicification leans toward the idea of "leapfrogging," that is, services-led development by focusing on the opportunities for developing countries to join global manufacturing through the provision of services inputs.

Although authors discussing deindustrialization and servicification often hold different views, they build their analyses on the idea that economists and statisticians can distinguish manufacturing from service activities. The purpose of this chapter is to question first whether this distinction makes any sense in the context of global value chains (GVCs) and new production arrangements between firms, and second, whether some analytical tools are more useful than others in dealing with the blurring lines between manufacturing and services. It will be argued that value-added analyses and approaches that take GVCs into account are better, although they do not fully address the fundamental data issues identified. Since data on manufacturing and services are used to answer key policy questions on globalization and development, it is important to be aware of the weaknesses of these data and of the analytical tools that can mitigate some of these.

4.2 Manufacturing and Services in the Age of Global Value Chains

4.2.1 How Are Manufacturing and Service Activities Defined?

When talking about "manufacturing" and "services," an important distinction must first be made between "products" and "firms" (or activities). Following the System of National Accounts (SNA) 2008, on which national accounts and gross domestic product (GDP) statistics are based, there are two types of "products": goods and services.[2] Firms are classified into different industries and generic categories such as "manufacturing" or "services" based on their "principal activity" (although they can produce both of these). A manufacturing firm is simply one that produces mostly goods or that derives most of its income from sales of goods, while service firms sell mainly services.

The distinction between manufacturing and services is therefore based on the difference between goods and services. The SNA defines goods as "physical, produced objects for which a demand exists, over which ownership rights can be established and whose ownership can be transferred from one institutional unit to another by engaging in transactions on markets"; and services as "the result of a production activity that changes the conditions of the consuming units, or facilitates the exchange of products or financial assets."[3]

Although there is some debate about whether these definitions are consistent and operational, this issue is beyond the scope of this chapter. However, it should be noted that from 1993 to 2008 the SNA definition of services evolved to take into account criticisms about the identification of services as "intangibles" and the fact that—particularly with the digital economy—there are also such things as "intangible goods" (Hill 1999). The definition of services is now based on a change in the condition of the consumer or the facilitation of an exchange, a definition broad enough to encompass all sorts of services.

Manufacturing itself is not defined in the SNA, and it is necessary to look at industry classifications, especially the International Standard

---

[2] To make things more complicated, the latest version of the Central Product Classification, the international classification for products, indicates that some products fail to meet the strict definitions of goods or services and should be regarded as bundles; two examples of this are photographs and meals.

[3] There are thus two types of services: "change effecting services" and "margin services."

Industrial Classification (ISIC), to identify manufacturing industries. Such classifications also include a primary sector (agriculture and mining activities) understood as separate from manufacturing. In the ISIC Revision 4, manufacturing corresponds to Section C (Section A being "agriculture, forestry and fishing" and Section B "mining and quarrying"), which includes activities that are services, such as "repair and installation of machinery and equipment" (Division 33). Other categories, such as Section D ("electricity, gas, steam and air conditioning supply") comprise a mix of activities involving the production of goods and services. It is also questioned whether "construction" (Section F) should be considered part of services. Since services are not defined, there is a tendency to include all of the sections beyond A, B, and C (with a gray area for D and F) in services.

The measurement of manufacturing and services output or employment based on national accounts is therefore based on (i) the determination of the principal activity of the firm for which data are collected, and (ii) the way this activity is classified in the list of industries used to aggregate the data. Yet, a manufacturing firm can produce services (as a secondary activity) and a services firm can produce goods.

This criterion of principal activity is easy to implement when the goods and services are produced and sold separately, but becomes more difficult when they are bundled together. Many services are provided embedded in goods (i.e., knowledge-capturing products). For example, the information in a newspaper or a book—whether in paper or electronic form—is regarded as a service despite the use of a physical object over which ownership rights can be established. Moreover, through servitization and digital technologies, goods such as electric machines, home appliances, and cars are increasingly incorporating software and complementary services that are no longer "secondary" but part of the core product. This tends to increase the approximation (that is, the fact that data cannot strictly separate goods from services) in any measurement of manufacturing and services.

4.2.2 Global Value Chain Framework: Taking the Role of Services in Global Production into Account

The purpose of a GVC analysis is precisely to address some of the shortcomings of traditional economic analysis at the industry level by looking at all firms from various industries involved in the production of a specific product, from its conception to the consumer's hands (Gereffi and Fernandez-Stark 2016). National statistics that list the output of different industries provide a rather artificial decomposition of production, since any good or service is the result of a combination of inputs from these different industries. By starting from a final product, a GVC framework introduces some consistency into the analysis by linking together all of the industries involved in producing an actual good or service.

In such a framework, there is no reason to distinguish manufacturing from services since any good or service is produced through both. In a stylized GVC such as that depicted in Figure 4.1, activities at both the beginning (research and development [R&D] and design) and the end of the value chain (distribution, marketing, and services) are typically services, while the core manufacturing (raw materials, processed inputs, final assembly) takes place in the middle of the value chain. However, since logistics services are needed for the core production activity (as well as other services such as maintenance and repair of the production infrastructure or financial services), there is no clear distinction between the manufacturing and service production stages. Manufacturing itself (the assembly of the final product, the production of all inputs, or both) can be outsourced and become a service for some manufacturing firms. Moreover, each material input is also the result of its own value chain, as it also must be designed, marketed, and distributed, for example. Therefore, manufacturing and services are combined in all stages.

Thus, it may be advisable to move from a distinction between manufacturing and services industries to one between manufacturing and services value chains, which would be defined based on the final product (either a good or a service). Stabell and Fjeldstad (1998) suggest that

Figure 4.1 A Generic "Manufacturing" Global Value Chain

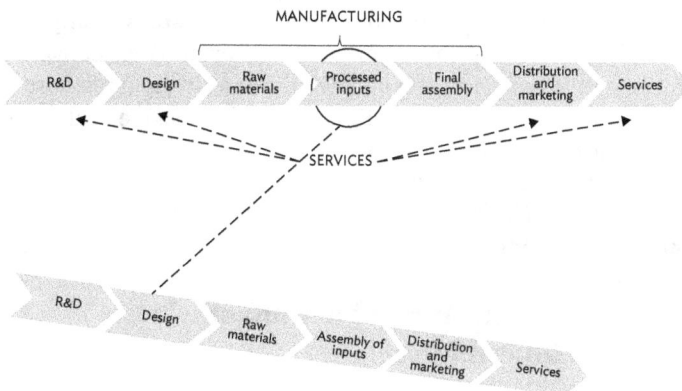

R&D = research and development.
Source: Author.

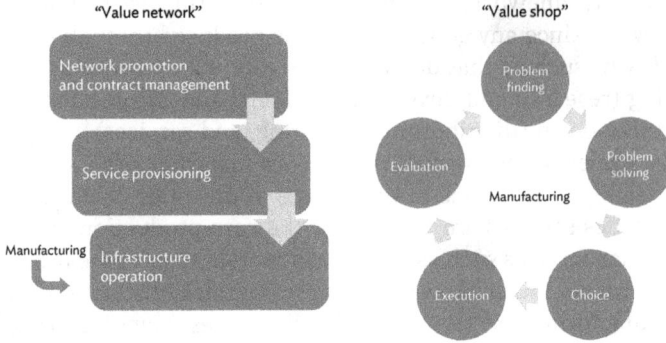

Figure 4.2 Examples of Service Value Chains—
Value Networks and Value Shops

"Value network"

Network promotion and contract management

Service provisioning

Manufacturing

Infrastructure operation

"Value shop"

Problem finding

Evaluation

Problem solving

Manufacturing

Execution

Choice

Source: Based on Stabell, C., and Ø. Fjeldstad. 1998. Configuring Value for Competitive Advantage: On Chains, Shops, and Networks. *Strategic Management Journal* 19: 413–437.

services value chains look a bit different from manufacturing value chains (Figure 4.2) and propose two additional models: (i) the "value network," which is the business model in both physical network (e.g., transport, telecoms, and electricity) and virtual network industries (e.g., banking, insurance, and social media); and (ii) the "value shop," which is the model for all consulting, business supporting, and personal services. In the value network, value is created by linking customers, while in the value shop, value creation originates in the solution brought to the consumer.

However, these value chains also include some manufacturing (e.g., the physical network in value networks) or are typically dedicated to providing solutions for manufacturing firms (e.g., consulting and engineering). Some services, such as food catering and restaurants, also follow the traditional model of Figure 4.1 with a sequential value chain in which the end product is a service. Finally, servitization suggests that many final products are bundles of goods and services, or "solutions" for customers. Therefore, it would also be artificial to try to distinguish manufacturing from services value chains, as they are intertwined.

4.2.3 The Servicification of Manufacturing: What Does It Mean?

We can also refer to GVC analysis to describe the different dimensions of the shift toward services or the "servicification" of manufacturing. Table 4.1 provides an overview of what is generally discussed in the

Table 4.1 Servicification of Manufacturing:
Taxonomy of Service Activities in Manufacturing Global Value Chains

Role of services	Related concepts	Additional distinctions	Relevant data
Services as inputs in the manufacturing value chain	Embodied services	Sourced from other firms (i.e., outsourced)	Input-output tables, trade in value-added statistics
		Produced in-house (i.e., insourced)	Occupations and tasks data
Manufacturing or final assembly as a service	Factory-less goods producers	Ownership of inputs by the company asking for the manufacturing service	When offshored: balance of payments (manufacturing services on inputs owned by others)
		Ownership of inputs by the company providing for the manufacturing service	When offshored: balance of payments (merchanting, trade in goods)
Services sold together with a good	Embedded services: product-service systems (PSS); servitization	Product-oriented PSS	Production or trade statistics for goods only or goods plus services
		Use-oriented PSS	Production or trade statistics for renting and leasing services
		Result-oriented PSS	Production or trade statistics for services corresponding to the result

Source: Author's elaboration based on the servicification literature.

related literature and introduces some of the concepts used in the rest of the chapter. It also indicates the relevant sources of data to analyze these dimensions in an international context (this part of the table is explained further in the next section).

The starting point of the taxonomy is the role played by services along the value chain. Services can be first used as inputs in the GVC as part of the production stages shown in Figure 4.1. Services used as inputs are consumed during the production process. They are also described as embodied services when referring to the good they were used to produce. These services include, inter alia, R&D, design, transport, logistics, finance, marketing, and advertising. They can be either produced in-house by a department within the firm or bought from external suppliers (i.e., outsourced).

Service inputs are used in the value chain, but the core manufacturing or final assembly stage can also be outsourced and become a service. Some "manufacturing" companies are not doing any manufacturing and only focus on the service stages shown in Figure 4.1. Such companies are described as "factory-less goods producers." Whether they buy the inputs used by their manufacturer themselves or also ask the manufacturer to source material inputs impacts how this type of production is measured in trade statistics.

Finally, some services are produced by manufacturing firms and sold to the consumer as a bundle with the good. Services not used as inputs but sold to the consumer as part of a good are described as embedded services. In the management literature, these bundles are regarded as "solutions" for the customer or "product-service systems" (Baines et al. 2009). The expression "servitization" is also specific to these bundled services as opposed to "servicification," which would cover all of the elements in Table 4.1. A more detailed analysis of these different categories is provided in section 4.3.

4.3 Relative Share of Manufacturing and Service Activities—Statistical Challenges

The World Input–Output Database (WIOD) is a set of world input–output tables covering 43 countries and 56 industries from 2000 to 2014 (Timmer et al. 2016). These data will be used in the rest of the chapter to illustrate the main statistical challenges in measuring manufacturing and service activities, and how they can to some extent be addressed by relying on GVC approaches. Although the country coverage is limited (covering only developed countries and the BRICS countries [Brazil, the Russian Federation, India, and the People's Republic of China]), these tables account for 85% of world output. The remaining 15% of output falls into the "rest of the world" category, so that any trend observed reflects the entire world economy.[4] Yet, these data cannot capture heterogeneity among countries in the rest of the world, particularly small developing countries.

Figure 4.3 provides a decomposition of employment for all WIOD economies across three types of activities: the primary, manufacturing, and services sectors. Since the WIOD follows national accounts and the ISIC classification, the decomposition is based on the principal activity of firms.

---

[4]   All variables are available for the "rest of the world" except data on employment.

Figure 4.3 Share of Manufacturing and Services Employment, World Input–Output Database Countries, 2000–2014

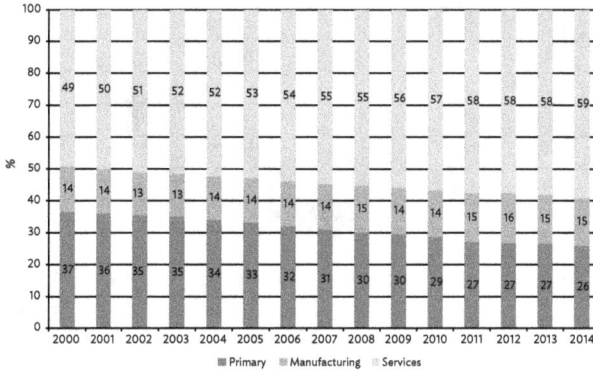

Source: World Input–Output Database. http://www.wiod.org/database/wiots16 (accessed 4 January 2017).

Interestingly, no deindustrialization is observed at the aggregate level. Employment remained stable in the manufacturing sector during 2000–2014, and even increased slightly from 14% to 15%. Any deindustrialization must have occurred before 2000; yet, the share of employment in the primary sector decreased, causing an increase in employment in services industries. Since data for all countries are aggregated, this may reflect two parallel trends of developing countries moving from the primary sector to manufacturing industries, and developed countries moving from the manufacturing sector to services. However, individual country data also suggest some "leapfrogging," that is, when jobs from the primary sector are directly replaced by jobs from the services sector, as pointed out in the literature on premature deindustrialization.

When looking at the same decomposition in terms of value added instead of employment (Figure 4.4), the primary sector appears much smaller and services account for three-quarters of the world GDP.[5] The share of manufacturing is slightly higher because of higher productivity

---

[5] The data in Figure 4.4 include all WIOD countries (excluding "rest of the world") for comparison with Figure 4.3; however, the shares observed are almost the same when including the rest of the world.

Figure 4.4 Share of Manufacturing and Services Value Added, World Input–Output Database Countries, 2000–2014

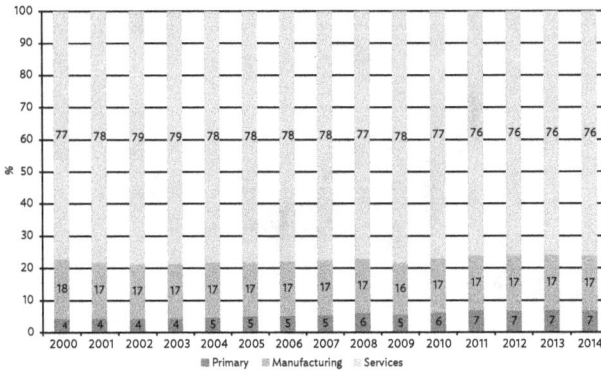

Source: World Input–Output Database. http://www.wiod.org/database/wiots16 (accessed 4 January 2017).

(17% in 2014), but the difference between employment in services (59%) and value added in services (76%) suggests that labor productivity is much higher in the services sector, contrary to what is often believed.

Figure 4.4 reveals no deindustrialization or servicification. Thus, these trends either must have occurred before 2000 or are observed only at the country level. This suggests that the primary issue at hand is the specialization of countries in manufacturing and service activities. Nevertheless, these data cannot answer our initial question satisfactorily because, for various reasons (explored below), the manufacturing and services industries do not clearly indicate the type of activity (and hence jobs) involved in the production process.

4.3.1 Services Used as Inputs in Manufacturing Global Value Chains: Inside or Outside the Firm?

When services are intermediate inputs in the production of goods, they are captured in input–output and supply-use tables in national accounts. The output of the manufacturing sector includes the intermediate consumption of service inputs. This is not an issue for the measurement of GDP since the value added by service suppliers is correctly allocated to the service industries. There is an issue for trade statistics that are in gross terms (and thus include the services inputs in exports of goods) but trade in value-added (TiVA) statistics can reveal the contribution of services inputs and provide trade data consistent with GDP.

However, only the services inputs sourced from other firms (i.e., outsourced) are included in input–output tables. When services are produced in-house by manufacturing firms, they contribute to output and value added in the manufacturing sector to which the firm belongs, but there is no intermediate consumption. Therefore, whether services are produced in-house or outsourced affects the boundaries of manufacturing firms and the size of the manufacturing sector. When a service is outsourced and is provided by a service firm, some value added is shifted from the manufacturing sector to the services sector (and to another country in the case of offshoring).

Miroudot and Cadestin (2017a) provide estimates of the in-house provision of services in manufacturing industries for selected countries, based on labor force surveys and the identification of occupations that correspond to service tasks. Combining these data with input–output information from the Organisation for Economic Co-operation and Economic Development (OECD) TiVA database, they calculate the share of services that are insourced, outsourced, and offshored in manufacturing output (Figure 4.5). Insourced services are those provided in-house, outsourced services are those no longer provided in-house and carried out by independent domestic firms, and offshored services (or foreign outsourced) are those imported from other countries.

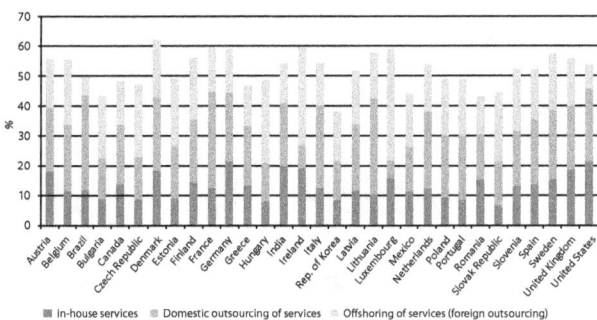

Figure 4.5 In-House, Outsourced, and Offshored Services Value Added in Manufacturing Output (%), 2011

Source: Miroudot, S., and C. Cadestin. 2017a. Services in Global Value Chains: From Inputs to Value-Creating Activities. Organisation for Economic Co-operation and Development Trade Policy Paper 197. Paris: Organisation for Economic Co-operation and Development Publishing. http://dx .doi.org/10.1787/465f0d8b-en (accessed 19 April 2019).

Figure 4.5 highlights that a large share of manufacturing output is composed of services: when adding the insourced and outsourced services (domestic and foreign), an average of more than 50% of manufacturing output is services. While this confirms the kind of model described by GVC analysis, there are differences across countries, and the same level of service value added can be obtained by a different mix of in-house, outsourced, and offshored services. This implies that the respective sizes of the manufacturing and services sectors are influenced by outsourcing strategies with differences across countries based on factors such as transaction costs, regulatory barriers, and firm heterogeneity. For example, Figure 4.5 suggests that in-house provision of services is higher in countries where manufacturing firms are headquartered (e.g., the US or Luxembourg) than in countries where manufacturing firms are more focused on core manufacturing and assembly tasks (e.g., Bulgaria or the Slovak Republic).

Generally, only a value-added analysis can shed light on the actual contribution of the manufacturing and services sectors to output. Industry analysis primarily relies on value added and a decomposition of GDP (as in Figure 4.4). However, caution should be used when working with concepts such as gross exports for trade or the sales or output of foreign affiliates (a variable broadly used in the analysis of the role of multinational enterprises in global production), as these gross measures include the value of all intermediate inputs from all sectors.

Figure 4.6 Manufacturing and Services Value Added in World Gross Exports and Output of Foreign Affiliates, 2014 ($ trillion)

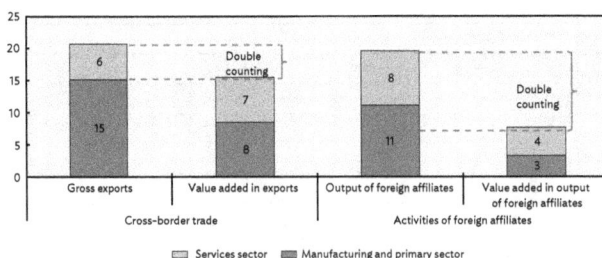

Source: Cadestin, C., K. De Backer, I. Desnoyers-James, S. Miroudot, D. Rigo, and M. Ye. 2018. Multinational Enterprises and Global Value Chains: New Insights on the Trade-Investment Nexus. Organisation for Economic Co-operation and Development Science, Technology and Industry Working Papers 2018/05. Paris: Organisation for Economic Co-operation and Development Publishing. https://doi.org/10.1787/194ddb63-en (accessed 19 April 2019).

Figure 4.6 illustrates that, for both trade and the output of foreign affiliates, the respective shares of manufacturing and services are quite different in gross and value-added terms. Because many services inputs are used in manufacturing industries (and more so with the rise in outsourcing), gross figures overestimate the contribution of manufacturing. The gross figures also include some double counting that can be misleading; this is avoided in national accounts by measuring income or production through GDP.

4.3.2 Manufacturing or Final Assembly as a Service: Uncertainties about Factory-Less Goods Producers and the Debate on Goods for Processing

It is possible to outsource, not only services inputs, but also the core manufacturing or assembly activities of firms producing goods. An extreme case of this is when "manufacturing" companies decide to not produce anything at all and to outsource fully the manufacturing of their products. This was illustrated in Apple's production of the iPod, iPhone, and iPad (Dedrick, Kraemer, and Linden 2009). However, it is not limited to the computer and electronics industry, and can also be found in the household appliance industry (e.g., Dyson), the toy industry (e.g., Hasbro), and the apparel industry (e.g., Abercrombie & Fitch).

According to Bernard and Fort (2015), factory-less goods producers (FGPs) are disproportionately found in the pharmaceutical (24% of firms) and apparel industries in the US (24% of firms). They estimate that, on average, only 12% of US firms are FGPs, but these firms are larger and employ twice as many workers as other firms.

Yet, it is unclear exactly where FGPs are in the statistics of Figures 4.3 and 4.4. Firms that design and sell products but do not manufacture them are not considered manufacturing firms in these figures, but are part of the distribution sector. In the case of the US, where company information is collected at the establishment level, FGPs are identified through a survey on contract manufacturing. An FGP is a wholesale firm that is engaged in contract manufacturing and has no manufacturing establishment. The US decided as of 2017 to include FGPs in its statistics for the manufacturing sector. This will certainly increase the share of manufacturing in the US GDP. Yet, most countries have no information to identify FGPs (only five countries so far could produce statistics as recommended by the international statistics community in order to improve the measurement of global production).

If one is concerned with employment and the types of jobs provided by companies, FGPs may be better placed in the services sector. They combine the high-skilled jobs required for the R&D, design, and engineering of products with the high- and medium-skilled jobs found in marketing and distribution. But companies without factories do not provide jobs for low-skilled workers and also may not bring the capital and skill accumulation associated with the development of manufacturing.

While FGPs have no factory, they still involve manufacturing activity taking place in another company, which is likely to be in the manufacturing sector. Although this company can be in another country (offshoring), the manufacturing activities themselves have not disappeared. Some developing countries now specialize in contract manufacturing and processing trade; however, the new SNA 2008 is again making it more complicated to identify such activities.

As an implementation of the "ownership principle," the SNA 2008 has introduced a new distinction in the measurement of contract manufacturing and processing trade. If the principal (the company that requests the manufacture of a product it has designed) owns the inputs used in the production process and the processor is only assembling the inputs received from the principal (and not buying them), the processor provides "manufacturing services on inputs owned by others." This company will still be considered a manufacturing company since, under the ISIC classification, these manufacturing services are part of the manufacturing industry; but it will produce a service and, in terms of trade flows, the goods sent for processing and the resulting processed good that is returned to the principal economy are no longer "traded." Instead, imports of inputs and exports of processed products by the processor country are recorded in the balance of payments of the principal economy (even if none of the shipments transit through the principal economy), as set out in the Balance of Payments Manual, Revision 6 (BPM6). In addition, there is a manufacturing service export from the processor to the principal corresponding to the processing fee.

From a conceptual point of view, outsourcing the production of a good by sending inputs that the company owns to be assembled in another country is like sending a vessel abroad for repair and maintenance: it is a service transaction. Nonetheless, the implementation of the SNA 2008 and BPM6 is quite problematic for countries, and only a minority of them have switched to the new system. Trade statistics, in particular, are not yet fully recorded according to the new rules, and this creates discrepancies with national accounts.

Although the manufacturing value added should not be affected (beyond the issue of the offshoring of manufacturing activities previously discussed with FGPs), trade statistics definitely record a different share of manufacturing and services in the BPM5 versus BPM6. This matters for indicators of competitiveness based on trade data, such as revealed comparative advantage (RCA) indices.

4.3.3 Services Sold Together with a Good: No Possible Identification of Product–Service Systems in Statistics Based on a Distinction Between Goods and Services

The biggest challenge, and the least discussed, may be bundles of goods and services and the servitization of manufacturing. Using French firm-level data, Crozet and Milet (2017) find that 76% of manufacturing firms sell services and 22% report more sales of services than sales of goods.[6] With regard to Germany, Kelle (2013) indicates that 25% of exports of services are by manufacturing firms.

The management literature has explored in more detail what can be described as "product service systems" (Baines et al. 2009), in which goods and services are really combined and not sold as separate products by the same firm. There are three types of product service systems (PSSs). In the case of "product-oriented" PSSs, the ownership of a good is transferred to the customer with additional services. For example, a car sold with a maintenance contract and a financing scheme is considered a PSS because the customer purchases a full solution that takes care of the financing and maintenance, meaning that the customer need not deal with other companies and spend time making the required arrangements to own the car. Fulfilling customer needs is the objective of PSSs.

In the case of "use-oriented" PSSs, the ownership of the product remains with the provider but the usage rights are sold to the customer. Instead of buying a car, the customer can, for example, rent or lease a car. The difference from the previous example is that the contracting company keeps the ownership of the car, while the customer receives a very similar solution in terms of having a car without dealing with its maintenance and financing. However, the company that rents or leases the car provides a service and will be classified as a service company if this is its principal activity.

Lastly, in the case of "result-oriented" PSSs, the product's functional results that directly fulfill the customer needs are sold. For example, when taxis or private drivers sell the customer transportation in a car from one location to another, what is provided is a transport service, and the company will again be classified in the services sector, if that is its main activity.

---

[6] Although this may seem paradoxical (since, in this case, they should not be labeled as manufacturing firms), as indicated before, some services (such as manufacturing services or repair and maintenance services) are classified within manufacturing industries under the ISIC classification. A firm mostly producing such services will still be a manufacturing firm while still selling mostly services in terms of products.

These three types of PSSs can address the same customer's needs, and the above examples all involve a car to be produced. The way in which this car is combined with services leads to three different economic trends. In addition to an extra car sold, there is a rise in manufacturing value added in the car industry (with the value of services regarded as manufacturing output) in the first example, an increase in rental services in the second example, and an increase in transport services in the third example. PSSs thus clearly affect the distribution of value added across industries. While they create value, this value can end up in the manufacturing sector or in different services industries depending on the type of PSS, making it impossible to distinguish clearly what is or is not coming from a PSS in each of these sectors.

A GVC approach can tackle this issue to some extent by starting from a PSS at the end of the value chain or from the consumer's needs and then identifying all the different PSSs that can fulfill them. However, it becomes very difficult to link this to any production or trade statistics, and the approach can only work in the context of very specific case studies. Only firm-level data with some detailed information on the products sold by companies can allow some analysis.

PSSs blur the lines between manufacturing and services. Although no study provides systematic evidence as to their prevalence, many examples in different industries indicate that they are not anecdotal. Studies on services sold by manufacturing firms cannot always identify whether or not there is a PSS; yet, the high share of firms selling both goods and services suggests that product-oriented PSSs are quite common, particularly with regard to maintenance and repair, as well as the installation services that come with a machine or equipment.

For use-oriented PSSs, in addition to the growth of the renting and leasing industry, there are also many examples of companies that switch to business models in which they rent their product (Kowalkowski et al. 2017). For example, in the airplane industry, Rolls-Royce rents its aircraft engines by the hour ("power by the hour"). With regard to aircraft tires, air companies buy a number of landings and not the tires themselves. Due to the costs involved and extensive security and safety standards, air companies prefer "solutions" instead of buying and maintaining the airplanes themselves. Many contractors are involved, and the income of the airplane industry is re-shuffled across a mix of manufacturing and services industries.

Another example of results-oriented PSSs found in the literature is Xerox, the company that invented and produced photocopy machines and is now selling "office document solutions," with most photocopy machines now provided as part of a subscription covering all office document-related needs with a fixed price per copy. As with

International Business Machines in the computer industry (Spohrer 2017), Xerox moved from the manufacturing sector to the services sector in national accounts when its principal activity became services, which impacted the boundary between manufacturing and services. Firms that switch industries can explain a significant part of the deindustrialization observed in some economies (Bernard, Smeets, and Warzynski 2017).

4.3.4 Other Challenges: Price Issues

Lastly, to address the statistical challenges that impact the relative size of the manufacturing and services sectors comprehensively, we should also mention some price issues. Although Figure 4.4 uses current prices, authors often rely on constant prices to compare value added over time, as this method better accounts for changes in relative prices between the two sectors. However, finding the right deflators is problematic. Houseman et al. (2011) in particular have pointed out a bias related to offshoring. Manufacturing firms often switch to importing foreign inputs because these are generally much cheaper than domestic inputs. According to the authors, price indices used to deflate inputs do not accurately track the decrease in their price due to offshoring, thus underestimating the volume growth of intermediate consumption. Consequently, real value added (and then productivity) in manufacturing industries is overestimated, since value added is the difference between output and intermediate consumption. If so, there is more deindustrialization than suggested by the data.[7]

Moreover, in a different paper, Houseman and other co-authors suggest that the measure of value added in the manufacturing sector is affected by the industry composition and by industries in which prices are rapidly falling and productivity quickly increasing due to rapid technological progress (Houseman, Bartik, and Sturgeon 2015). For example, the authors estimate that most of the increase in US manufacturing is driven by computer-related industries. When these are removed, the deindustrialization observed in the employment data is also visible in terms of value added.

Price issues should not be underestimated and may in some cases be linked to the servitization of manufacturing. Price indices are also created for industries that are becoming increasingly heterogeneous in terms of the products that they sell. When manufacturing firms try to

---

[7] It is also assumed that services are not affected or are less affected by the bias because of lower shares of offshoring. Hence, this has an impact on the relative share of manufacturing and services in GDP.

provide tailored solutions to customers by adding services, the difficulty of creating price indices for tailored services in the services sector is extended to the manufacturing sector. One reason why it is difficult to measure productivity in services industries is precisely that there are no identified homogeneous products, and that the price changes for almost every customer. The servitization of manufacturing tends to generalize this situation to all products.

All of the different data issues reviewed so far lead to the same conclusion: the statistics on the respective share of manufacturing and services in employment, GDP, output, or trade cannot be trusted. Thus, the next question is whether some approaches are better than others and can mitigate some of the statistical issues described.

4.4 Relying on Global Value Chain Approaches to Address Some of the Statistical Challenges

In this section, we review three types of measures that can, to some extent, provide a better understanding of a country's income, competitiveness, and productivity in the context of GVCs. However, it should be understood that, while they improve the conclusions one can draw from the data, these measures are still imperfect. In particular, they cannot fully address the challenge of PSSs. We also do not discuss the important challenge of how to improve price indices and conduct an analysis in constant prices; but the measures described below at least take into account the value chain and its combination of manufacturing and service activities.

4.4.1 Global Value Chain Income

By using a world input–output table and input–output analysis techniques, it is possible to look at the entire value chain and track the origin of value added in a final product, that is, to measure the value added by all the firms in all countries and industries that have participated in the value chain (Timmer et al. 2013). The "GVC income" is simply a value-added decomposition of final demand, following the seminal model introduced by Leontief (1936), which is the foundation of input–output analysis. This highlights the origin of value added, namely the initial country and industry that used labor and capital to produce value.

GVC income can first be calculated at the global level for the products of a given industry. To illustrate this, Figure 4.7 decomposes the GVC income in the automotive industry by country of origin. The share

Figure 4.7 Distribution of Global Value Chain Income in the World Automotive Industry, 2000 and 2014

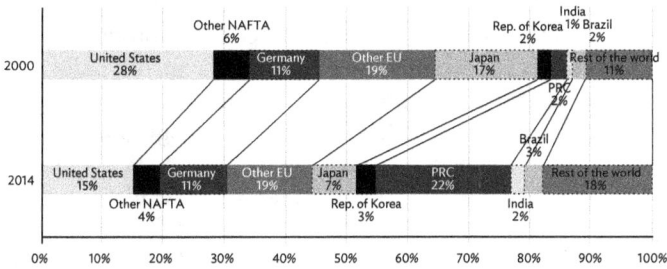

PRC = People's Republic of China, EU = European Union, NAFTA = North American Free Trade Agreement, Rep. of Korea = Republic of Korea.

Source: Author's calculations based on the World Input–Output Database. http://www.wiod.org/database/wiots16 (accessed 4 January 2017).

of each country indicates the share of value added that it contributes to sales of cars and other products from the global automotive industry. For example, 7% of the value added in world sales came from Japan in 2014.

This approach takes the value chain into account in the sense that Japan's contribution includes (i) the direct value added in sales of Japanese cars (and other products from the automotive industry), (ii) the indirect value added from Japanese suppliers in sales of Japanese cars, and (iii) the indirect value added from Japanese suppliers in sales of any foreign manufacturer. The indirect value added can come from any industry, including services industries, thus providing some GVC consistency to this type of decomposition.

The category "sales of cars and other products from the automotive industry" includes bundles of goods and services, as well as any service sold by car manufacturers. For example, if maintenance and financing services are provided along with cars sold by these manufacturers, this bundling is also included in this decomposition. The GVC income approach does not indicate any PSSs, but only because the underlying national accounts do not contain the relevant information. This limitation is related not to the methodology but to the construction of national accounts.

Between 2000 and 2014, the distribution of income in the automotive GVC changed significantly. The share of the US was almost halved from 28% to 15%, while that of the People's Republic of China (PRC) increased from 2% to 22%. This kind of change is precisely what authors discussing deindustrialization are interested in. In a traditional analysis of value added or output in the automotive sector, the GVC income figures are not affected by outsourcing. The decline in the US figure cannot be explained by US car manufacturers having outsourced the production of their inputs or even having moved from the manufacturing industry to the services sector. Although offshoring affects these figures when the value added is shifted to other countries, the methodology could also further identify how offshoring is responsible for the decline in US value added.

One interesting finding is that Germany, unlike all other developed countries, maintained its share of value added in the automotive GVC between 2000 and 2014, despite the rise of the PRC. Yet, statistics on exports of German cars or the output of the automotive industry in Germany do not capture Germany's role in the world automotive value chain. It should also be noted that the GVC income includes the domestic market (domestic final demand), thus explaining why the share of the US, for example, is higher than that of Germany although Germany exports more cars than the US. However, the final demand can easily be decomposed into a domestic component and foreign component for a different analysis focusing on the role of trade.

As Figure 4.7 is in percentages, it may appear misleading in terms of the "decline" observed for some countries, such as the US. Figure 4.8 introduces values in constant billion US dollars and points out that, for all countries with a lower share, the observed decline is relative in terms of the value added derived from the automotive GVC, and is not an absolute decline. In summary, although the US and Japan have a smaller share of a larger "pie," there is no decline in their value added. What happened was that the PRC's contribution to the world GVC income in this industry more than quadrupled, mostly as a consequence of the expansion of its domestic market. This has arguably benefited other countries more than it has introduced new competition.

The point is not to debate the outcome in the automotive industry, but to illustrate how the GVC income offers a better means of assessing each country's contribution to global production for a given product. As illustrated in Figure 4.8, this analysis can be done in constant prices by using the value-added deflators provided in the WIOD socioeconomic accounts (although these deflators are subject to the type of criticism noted above). While the WIOD database includes tables in previous-year prices that allow for a full analysis in constant prices, the deflators for intermediate consumption (particularly imported inputs) remain problematic as they are estimated by statistical methods and made consistent with value added and output through rebalancing. This implies that one should use any analysis with absolute values cautiously.

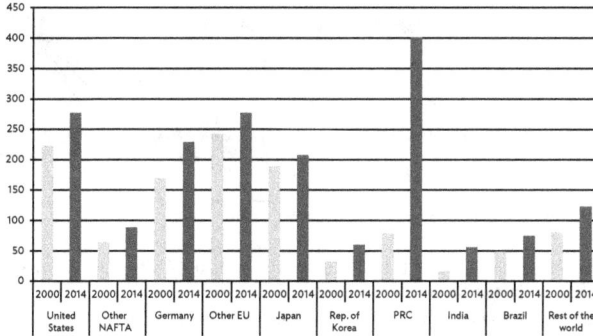

Figure 4.8 World Global Value Chain Income in the Automotive Industry, 2000 and 2014 ($ billion in constant prices)

PRC = People's Republic of China, EU = European Union, NAFTA = North American Free Trade Agreement, Rep. of Korea = Republic of Korea.

Source: Author's calculations based on the World Input–Output Database. http://www.wiod.org/database/wiots16 (accessed 4 January 2017).

Relative values (i.e., percentages, as in Figure 4.7) are also affected but to a lesser extent.

In Figure 4.8, GVC income was calculated for the world final demand of products from the automotive industry, merging the final demand from all countries. It can also be calculated for the final demand addressed to the products of a specific country. In Figure 4.9, which depicts the distribution of GVC income for all products sold by the Japanese automotive industry, most of the value added comes from Japan, as Japanese cars are produced mostly with Japanese value added. The case would be similar for any country, with domestic value added being dominant in domestic production (except for very small open economies).

In Figure 4.9, the Japanese value added has been divided between manufacturing and services, illustrating how the source industry can also be identified in the GVC income framework. This is not especially recommended in light of the previous discussion and the fact that the manufacturing–services dichotomy is quite artificial and affected by production arrangements and firm outsourcing strategies. A better decomposition could be direct and indirect value added, with indirect coming both from manufacturing and services industries.

Figure 4.9 Distribution of Global Value Chain Income in the Japanese Automotive Industry, 2000 and 2014

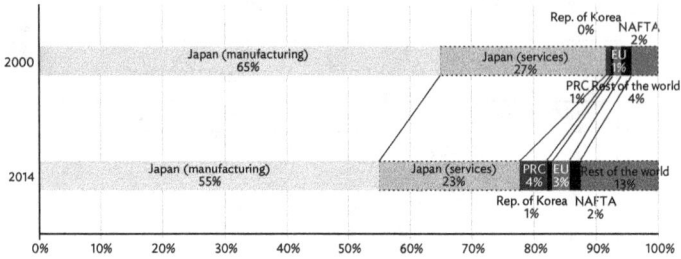

PRC = People's Republic of China, EU = European Union, NAFTA = North American Free Trade Agreement, Rep. of Korea = Republic of Korea.

Source: Author's calculations based on the World Input–Output Database. http://www.wiod.org/database/wiots16 (accessed on 4 January 2017).

4.4.2 Global Value Chain Income Revealed Comparative Advantage

In trade theory, economists rely on the concept of comparative advantage and its empirical assessment through an RCA index (Balassa 1965). The RCA is generally calculated as the share of a country's exports of a given product in total exports, divided by the share of world exports of this product in total world exports. An index above 1 indicates that the country has a comparative advantage for this product, that is, it exports this product relatively more often than do other countries.

Following Timmer et al. (2013), this concept can be applied to GVCs by calculating an RCA based on the GVC income. The formula is simply the share of a country in the GVC income of a specific industry divided by the share of this country in all GVCs (i.e., all industries, equivalent to world GDP). In Figure 4.10, such an RCA is calculated for the "computer, electronics, and optical products" industry for selected countries, and compared with the traditional RCA based on gross exports. Results are reported for countries where the GVC income RCA and gross exports RCA tell a different story.

Figure 4.10 shows that in the GVC the comparative advantage goes beyond what is reflected by exports of products. For example, although the Czech Republic, Finland, Ireland, Sweden, and Switzerland have no particular RCA when gross exports are considered (values below 1 indicate no RCA), RCAs are observable when looking at the GVC income

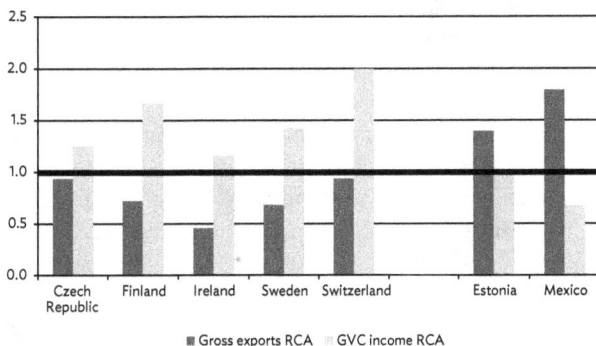

Figure 4.10 Gross Exports and Global Value Chains Income Revealed Comparative Advantage for Selected Countries, "Computer, Electronics, and Optical Products," 2014

GVC = global value chain, RCA = revealed comparative advantage.

Source: Author's calculations based on the World Input–Output Database. http://www.wiod.org/database/wiots16 (accessed 4 January 2017).

(these are particularly strong for Switzerland and Finland). While these countries are not strong exporters of computers and related products, their value-added contribution to the value chain of these products is high, as they supply inputs (including services inputs) that are embodied in both domestic and foreign products from the "computer, electronics, and optical products" GVC.

In contrast, Estonia and Mexico, which are exporters of similar products and have an RCA above 1 based on gross exports, have a smaller contribution in terms of GVC income. These countries may specialize more in the area of assembly tasks or in parts of the value chain that have a lower level of value added, and consequently reveal no particular comparative advantage in terms of GVC income.

Since the GVC income RCA takes into account the services inputs and income all along the value chain, it would appear to be a better metric to assess whether countries have a comparative advantage in manufacturing (acknowledging that manufacturing includes the provision of services). The fact that the output of the "computer, electronics, and optical products" industry might be bundles of goods and services is also not particularly an issue in terms of assessing the comparative advantage since it includes such bundles. Nevertheless, it still presents a problem in terms of other PSSs related to this industry that are later classified under other industries (e.g., computer services). A workaround in this case would be to compare or merge GVC income RCAs for the relevant industries (e.g., computer products, and computer services).

As specialization in GVCs occurs in tasks rather than industries (Grossman and Rossi-Hansberg 2008), it is also useful to go below the industry level and decompose the GVC income in different types of tasks or "business functions" (Sturgeon et al. 2013). For example, Miroudot and Cadestin (2017b) use labor force survey data to identify business functions within each industry based on occupations, and calculate a GVC income RCA by business function (Figure 4.11).

For the textile and apparel industry, most of the countries in Figure 4.11 have an RCA in "R&D and engineering" and other support service business functions (only RCAs above 1 are shown). Few countries have an RCA in "operations" corresponding to the manufacturing of textile and apparel products (Estonia, Hungary, India, Indonesia, Portugal, and the Slovak Republic). This is because the countries that actually manufacture most of the textile products in the world (such as the PRC, Bangladesh, Pakistan, and Viet Nam) are not included in the figure. The results are in line with the prevalence of FGPs and the fact that leading firms in developed countries specialize in design and distribution rather than operations.

An analysis of functional specialization in trade (Timmer et al. 2019) might be more useful for policy purposes to identify what countries actually do in the value chain. Such an analysis could also yield more concrete insights as to the meaning of functional upgrading in GVCs, since developing and emerging countries do not intend to remain in stages of production associated with lower levels of value added.

4.4.3 Global Value Chain Productivity

Lastly, GVC income can also be used as a component of an assessment to capture "GVC productivity." With GVC income, there is a decomposition of value added along the value chain for a given final demand in an industry. Using employment data, labor productivity can be calculated along the value chain by dividing this value added by the labor needed in each country and industry to create it. The GVC productivity is the number of jobs in the global production system needed to produce one unit of final demand. Dietzenbacher and Los (2012) explain this methodology using labor productivity; however, given the capital stocks in each country and industry, it is also be possible to calculate GVC productivity based on multifactor productivity.

An interesting characteristic of GVC productivity is that it is calculated from the point of view of the final product, like GVC

Figure 4.11 Global Value Chain Income Revealed Comparative Advantage in "Manufacture of Textiles, Wearing Apparel, and Leather Products," by Business Function, 2014

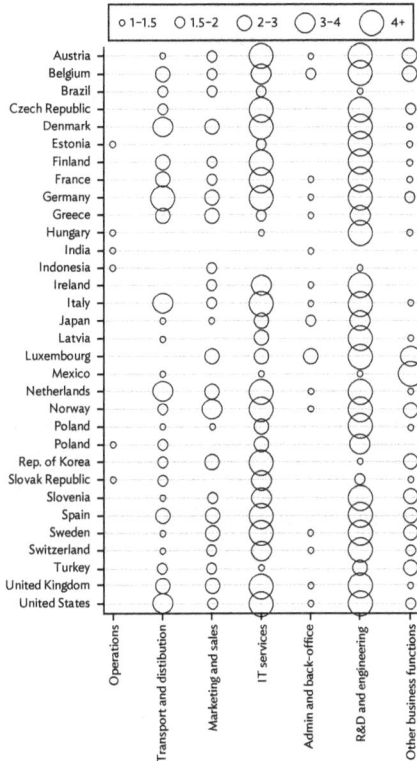

Legend: ○ 1–1.5 ○ 1.5–2 ○ 2–3 ○ 3–4 ○ 4+

Countries (rows): Austria, Belgium, Brazil, Czech Republic, Denmark, Estonia, Finland, France, Germany, Greece, Hungary, India, Indonesia, Ireland, Italy, Japan, Latvia, Luxembourg, Mexico, Netherlands, Norway, Poland, Poland, Rep. of Korea, Slovak Republic, Slovenia, Spain, Sweden, Switzerland, Turkey, United Kingdom, United States

Business functions (columns): Operations, Transport and distibution, Marketing and sales, IT services, Admin and back-office, R&D and engineering, Other business functions

Admin = administration, IT = information technology, Rep. of Korea = Republic of Korea, R&D = research and development.

Source: Miroudot, S., and C. Cadestin. 2017a. Services in Global Value Chains: From Inputs to Value-Creating Activities. Organisation for Economic Co-operation and Development Trade Policy Paper 197. Paris: OECD Publishing. http://dx.doi.org/10.1787/465f0d8b-en.

income. Traditional productivity calculated at the industry level is a mix of activities contributing to different products and different value chains, and is difficult to interpret and to link to other data (such as trade) at the product level. Studies at the firm level always report some heterogeneity in the same industry precisely because the "industry" is not well connected to the production of specific products. In addition, productivity in a given industry ignores the contribution of other industries (and other countries) to the value added achieved per unit of labor. Productivity can be high because other countries and industries supply efficient inputs. Without these inputs, domestic productivity would be lower, and an analysis of domestic productivity in isolation from other industries and countries could give the impression that a domestic industry is strong, when it is merely "lucky" to benefit from efforts in other countries and industries.

GVC productivity takes into account the use of primary inputs all along the value chain and allows for a better productivity analysis (see Table 4.2). For each country (and for both the manufacturing and commercial services industries),[8] Table 4.2 reports the GVC productivity growth (the ratio of levels) for 2014 and 2000, the growth of the "domestic segment" of GVC productivity (i.e., the productivity contributed by all domestic industries in the GVC), and traditional labor productivity growth. When we first compare the growth in GVC productivity and labor productivity, we see differences and possibly a different interpretation of countries' performance. For example, Brazil and Mexico appear to have small growth in terms of labor productivity in the manufacturing sector, but their productivity appears higher when the GVC approach is used. Checking whether the domestic GVC productivity is equal to or higher than the overall GVC productivity (which includes the contribution of other countries) confirms that these countries have benefited from this higher productivity. In contrast, in Indonesia the labor productivity growth in the manufacturing sector appears smaller (but still high) when using the GVC productivity. Since this measure takes into account the productivity induced by industries contributing inputs (including services industries), it is a better metric of the performance of a country in the production of a specific product.

Table 4.2 is also useful in that it shows that productivity growth in the services sector is not lower than in the manufacturing sector. This is clear from looking at traditional labor productivity growth, and even more so from GVC productivity. For example, in the US productivity growth appears higher in the manufacturing sector based on traditional labor productivity, but appears higher in services when the GVC approach is used. Although this is not systematically true in all countries, GVC productivity tends to rebalance productivity across supplying industries, eliminating a systematic bias against services based on the final product.

---

[8] Commercial services exclude public administration, education, health, and social services that are partly or fully provided by the public sector depending on the country.

Table 4.2 Global Value Chain Productivity Growth Rates, Manufacturing, and Commercial Services, Selected Countries, Ratios of Levels for 2014 and 2000

Country	Manufacturing			Commercial services		
	Growth in GVC producivity	Growth in domestic GVC producivity	Growth in labour GVC producivity	Growth in GVC producivity	Growth in domestic GVC producivity	Growth in labour GVC producivity
Australia	1.22	1.21	1.06	1.20	1.17	1.18
Brazil	1.23	1.25	1.04	1.11	1.11	1.06
Canada	1.22	1.20	1.23	1.16	1.15	1.05
China, People's Rep. of	1.51	1.52	1.82	1.65	1.64	1.28
France	1.65	2.06	1.87	1.54	1.74	1.47
Germany	1.59	1.83	1.83	1.53	1.62	1.48
India	2.12	2.17	1.72	2.18	2.19	1.85
Indonesia	2.30	2.35	3.26	5.55	5.64	2.25
Japan	1.48	1.91	1.44	1.27	1.35	1.32
Rep. of Korea	1.69	1.95	2.39	1.33	1.38	1.28
Mexico	1.09	1.09	1.01	1.40	1.43	0.94
Russian Federation	0.97	0.87	0.95	0.94	0.92	0.83
United Kingdom	1.50	1.71	1.46	1.54	1.59	1.45
United States	1.57	1.86	1.75	1.77	1.89	1.31

GVC = global value chain.

Source: Miroudot, S., and C. Cadestin. 2017a. Services in Global Value Chains: From Inputs to Value-Creating Activities. Organisation for Economic Co-operation and Development Trade Policy Paper 197. Paris: OECD Publishing. http://dx.doi.org/10.1787/465f0d8b-en; based on the World Input–Output Database. http://www.wiod.org/database/wiots16 (accessed 4 January 2017).

4.5 Concluding Remarks

To conclude, manufacturing and services are intertwined in GVCs, not because the different production stages can be decomposed between manufacturing and service activities, but because all stages comprise a mix of manufacturing and services, and the final products themselves are no longer clearly goods or services. Statistical classifications and rules of national accounts play an important and often arbitrary role in deciding whether a firm is part of the manufacturing or services sector, and firms themselves engage in strategies that cause them to shift from one category to another.

Therefore, it becomes almost impossible to draw a clear line between manufacturing and service activities, and any analysis based on the evolution of the share of manufacturing and services in employment, output, or trade should be received with caution. The statistical issues described in this chapter affect all types of indicators that try to compare the performance of the manufacturing and services sectors, such as productivity measures or RCA indices. One way to deal with this is to no longer try to compare manufacturing and service activities, particularly when focusing on "commercial" activities as opposed to public services, health, education, or other activities that are "services" of a different nature and not "mixed" with manufacturing in the same way as are commercial services.

However, to answer key policy questions in terms of development, specialization, or industrial policy, it is still necessary to compare activities, such as knowing where to provide support or improve regulations. In this case, following a GVC approach seems more appropriate than looking at industries. Starting from final products makes it possible to take into account all firms in all industries and countries that are actually needed to produce a good or a service. Better measures of performance, productivity, or RCAs can be derived through such an approach, as illustrated in this chapter. Still, the GVC approach is being challenged by the blurring lines between manufacturing and services in the sense that final products themselves are less and less clearly identified, and there is no panacea for this problem.

At the international level, it should be noted that there is an effort to improve the collection of data that are relevant for global production. For example, the OECD has an Expert Group on Extended Supply-Use Tables whose goal is to add new dimensions to national accounts and to disaggregate output data according to ownership, the size of firms, or a firm's export status. Initiatives such as the WIOD or the OECD-World Trade Organization TiVA database have also provided new tools for analysing GVCs through the creation of a global input–output matrix. However, disaggregated input–output statistics are not available for all countries in the world. Collecting such data is costly, and developing countries are generally unable to gather this information although they stand to benefit the most from its collection, which would help them design development policies.

It will take time to adjust the statistical and national account systems to the challenges of globalization in the digital age. Nonetheless, policy makers must change their traditional way of looking at these issues and understand that manufacturing and services can no longer be distinguished.

References

Autor, D., D. Dorn, and G. Hanson. 2016. The China Shock: Learning from Labor-Market Adjustment to Large Changes in Trade. *Annual Review of Economics* 8: 205–240. http://dx.doi.org/10.1146/annurev -economics-080315-015041 (accessed 18 February 2017).

Baines, T. S., H. W. Lightfoot, O. Benedettini, and J. M. Kay. 2009. The Servitization of Manufacturing: A Review of Literature and Reflection on Future Challenges. *Journal of Manufacturing Technology Management* 20(5): 547–567. http://dx.doi.org /10.1108/17410380910960984 (accessed 13 February 2017).

Balassa, B. 1965. Trade Liberalisation and Revealed Comparative Advantage. *The Manchester School* 33(2): 99–123.

Bernard, A., and T. Fort. 2015. Factoryless Goods Producing Firms. *American Economic Review* 105(5): 518–523. http://dx.doi.org /10.1257/aer.p20151044 (accessed 11 June 2018).

Bernard, A., V. Smeets, and F. Warzynski. 2017. Rethinking Deindustrialization. *Economic Policy* 32(89): 5–38. http://dx.doi.org /10.1093/epolic/eiw016 (accessed 11 June 2018).

Cadestin, C., K. De Backer, I. Desnoyers-James, S. Miroudot, D. Rigo, and M. Ye. 2018. Multinational Enterprises and Global Value Chains: New Insights on the Trade-Investment Nexus. Organisation for Economic Co-operation and Development (OECD) Science, Technology and Industry Working Papers 2018/05. Paris: OECD Publishing. https://doi .org/10.1787/194ddb63-en (accessed 19 April 2019).

Crozet, M., and E. Milet. 2017. Should Everybody Be in Services? The Effect of Servitization on Manufacturing Firm Performance. *Journal of Economics & Management Strategy* 26(4): 820–841. http://dx.doi.org /10.1111/jems.12211 (accessed 11 June 2018).

Dedrick, J., K. Kraemer, and G. Linden. 2009. Who Profits from Innovation in Global Value Chains? A Study of the iPod and Notebook PCs. *Industrial and Corporate Change* 19(1): 81–116 http://dx .doi.org/10.1093/icc/dtp032 (accessed 11 June 2018).

Dietzenbacher, E., and B. Los. 2012. Quantification of the Contributions of Productivity Growth and Globalization to World Consumption Growth Rates (1995–2008). Paper prepared for the 32nd General Conference of the International Association for Research in Income and Wealth, 7 August 2012.

Gereffi, G., and K. Fernandez-Stark. 2016. Global Value Chain Analysis: A Primer. 2nd ed. Duke Center on Globalization, Governance and Competitiveness, July. https://globalvaluechains.org/publication /global-value-chain-analysis-primer-2nd-edition (accessed 19 April 2019).

Grossman, G., and E. Rossi-Hansberg. 2008. Trading Tasks: A Simple Theory of Offshoring. *American Economic Review* 98(5): 1978–1997. http://dx.doi.org/10.1257/aer.98.5.1978 (accessed 12 June 2018).

Hill, P. 1999. Tangibles, Intangibles and Services. *Canadian Journal of Economics* 32(2): 426–446.

Houseman, S., T. Bartik, and T. Sturgeon. 2015. Measuring Manufacturing: How the Computer and Semiconductor Industries Affect the Numbers and Perceptions. In S. Houseman and B. Mandel (eds), *Measuring Globalization: Better Trade Statistics for Better Policy*, Vol. 1, pp.151–194. Kalamazoo, MI: W. E. Upjohn Institute for Employment Research.

Houseman, S., C. Kurz, P. Lengermann, and B. Mandel. 2011. Offshoring Bias in U.S. Manufacturing. *Journal of Economic Perspectives* (25)2: 111–132. http://dx.doi.org/10.1257/jep.25.2.111 (accessed 12 June 2018).

Kelle, M. 2013. Crossing Industry Borders: German Manufacturers as Services Exporters. *World Economy* 36(12): 1494–1515. http://dx.doi.org/10.1111/twec.12111 (accessed 17 August 2018).

Kowalkowski, C., H. Gebauer, B. Kamp, and G. Parry. 2017. Servitization and Deservitization: Overview, Concepts, and Definitions. *Industrial Marketing Management* 60: 4–10.

Leontief, W. 1936. Quantitative Input and Output Relations in the Economic System of the United States. *Review of Economic and Statistics* 18(3): 105–125.

Lodefalk, M. 2013. Servicification of Manufacturing—Evidence from Sweden. *International Journal of Economics and Business Research* 6(1): 87–113. http://dx.doi.org/10.1504/IJEBR.2013.054855 (accessed 17 August 2018).

Miroudot, S., and C. Cadestin. 2017a. Services in Global Value Chains: From Inputs to Value-Creating Activities. OECD Trade Policy Paper 197. Paris: OECD Publishing. http://dx.doi.org/10.1787/465f0d8b-en (accessed 17 August 2018).

Miroudot, S., and C. Cadestin. 2017b. Services in Global Value Chains: Trade Patterns and Gains from Specialisation. OECD Trade Policy Paper 208. Paris: OECD Publishing http://dx.doi.org/10.1787/06420077-en (accessed 20 December 2017).

National Board of Trade. 2012. *Everybody Is in Services—The Impact of Servicification in Manufacturing on Trade and Trade Policy*. Stockholm: National Board of Trade.

Neuss, L. 2018. Globalization and Deindustrialization in Advanced Countries. *Structural Change and Economic Dynamics* 45: 49–63. http://dx.doi.org/10.1016/j.strueco.2018.02.002 (accessed 13 June 2018).

Palma, J. G. 2005. Four Sources of De-Industrialisation and a New Concept of the Dutch-Disease. In J. A. Ocampo (ed), *Beyond Reforms: Structural Dynamic and Macroeconomic Vulnerability*, pp.71–116. Stanford, CA; Washington, DC: Stanford University Press; World Bank.

Palma, J. G. 2014. Industrialization, 'Premature' Deindustrialization and the Dutch Disease. *Revista Núcleo de Estudos de Economia Catarinense* 3(5): 7–23.

Rodrik, D. 2016. Premature Deindustrialization. *Journal of Economic Growth* 21(1): 1–33. http://dx.doi.org/10.1007/s10887-015-9122-3 (accessed 12 June 2018).

Rowthorn, R., and J. Wells. 1987. *De-Industrialization and Foreign Trade.* Cambridge: Cambridge University Press.

Spohrer J. 2017. IBM's Service Journey: A Summary Sketch. *Industrial Marketing Management* 60: 167–172.

Stabell, C., and Ø. Fjeldstad. 1998. Configuring Value for Competitive Advantage: On Chains, Shops, and Networks. *Strategic Management Journal* 19: 413–437.

Sturgeon, T., P. B. Nielsen, G. Linden, G. Gereffi, and C. Brown. 2013. Direct Measurement of Global Value Chains: Collecting Product- and Firm-Level Statistics on Value Added and Business Function Outsourcing and Offshoring. In A. Mattoo, Z. Wang, and S.-J. Wei (eds), *Trade in Value Added: Developing New Measures of Cross-Border Trade*, pp.291–321. Washington, DC: Center for Economic and Policy Research and World Bank.

Timmer, M. P., B. Los, R. Stehrer, and G. J. de Vries. 2013. Fragmentation, Incomes and Jobs: An Analysis of European Competitiveness. *Economic Policy* 28(76): 613–661 http://dx.doi.org/10.1111/1468 -0327.12018 (accessed 1 August 2018).

Timmer, M. P., B. Los, R. Stehrer, and G. J. de Vries. 2016. An Anatomy of the Global Trade Slowdown Based on the World Input–Output Database 2016 Release. Groningen Growth and Development Centre Research Memorandum 162, October.

Timmer, M. P., S. Miroudot, and G. J. de Vries. 2019. Functional Specialization in Trade. *Journal of Economic Geography*, 19(1): 1–30. https://doi.org/10.1093/jeg/lby056 (accessed 26 November 2018).

Vandermerwe, S., and J. Rada. 1988. Servitization of Business: Adding Value by Adding Services. *European Management Journal* 6(4): 314–324.

5

The Servicification of Manufacturing in Asia— A Conceptual Framework

Valerie Mercer-Blackman and Christine Ablaza

5.1 Introduction

Services are becoming increasingly prominent in terms of both output and employment. In 2016, services accounted for 66% of world gross domestic product (GDP). The shift from manufacturing to services, otherwise known as the "deindustrialization-tertiarization phenomenon," is not just limited to advanced economies. A number of studies have pointed out that many developing countries are also transitioning to a services-led economy (Felipe and Mehta 2016). The fact that this shift is occurring even though manufacturing has yet to develop fully has prompted some to call the deindustrialization "premature" (Rodrik 2016).

Given the widespread premise that manufacturing is the driver of growth, the deindustrialization of economies around the world has incorrectly raised concerns about the role of services. Since services were considered less productive than manufacturing, and largely nontradable, Baumol (1967) predicted that growth would eventually slow down. However, in line with other recent studies, we argue against this for several reasons. First, the sectoral approach to measuring output ignores the increasing fragmentation of production wherein tasks may be outsourced to other sectors either domestically or internationally. This practice may create a notional increase in the output of services without creating new value added in services (Hallward-Driemeier and Nayyar 2018; Nayyar 2010). Thus, the contribution of these services to the manufacturing process is not properly captured.

We show that current productivity measures suffer from biases in definition and measurement. Such measures also do not account for the indirect effect of services on other industries. For example, although the additional value generated by services for manufactured goods can be substantial, it is difficult to measure their contribution given their indivisible, intangible nature. At the same time, the contribution of services is multifaceted and becoming even more important in a knowledge-based economy: as the digital economy has grown, measuring the value of output in many spheres has become even more challenging. This chapter discusses the concept of "servicification" in manufacturing in Asia. We explain how certain services are intrinsically performed as part of the manufacturing process, have a symbiotic relationship with the physical manufacturing of goods, and are subordinate to the final output. We also explain why national accounts do not capture this, and propose a new methodology using the principle of time use.

5.2 The Role of Services in the Economy: Some Basics

5.2.1 Definitions and Key Concepts

Services encompass a wide range of activities that fall outside the agriculture and manufacturing industries, among others (Andersen and Corley 2003; OECD 2000). These activities result in the transformation of a good or a person's state (Hill 1977), often through the creation of value added by individuals (OECD 2000). Services differ from other sectors of the economy in several ways. Unlike manufacturing, which produces physical goods, many services are intangible and difficult to store. Moreover, the production of services (such as cutting hair and teaching) requires direct interaction with consumers. In contrast to goods, which are relatively homogeneous, most services are highly customized or personalized. For instance, the treatments administered by doctors are tailored to the needs of each individual.

Nevertheless, the distinction between services and manufacturing is becoming increasingly blurred. Advances in technology have allowed some services to acquire characteristics that were previously unique to manufacturing (OECD 2000). In particular, technological progress has allowed some types of services to be stored. For example, movies, music, and other performing arts can now be streamed, recorded, or digitally stored for consumers to watch at their convenience. This development has enabled services to be traded and distributed to a broader market. Likewise, technology is gradually eliminating the need for personal interaction. For instance, customers can now execute financial transactions through internet banking. Electronic commerce has also enabled goods and other services to be bought and sold virtually.

Given their heterogeneous nature, the literature has classified services in several different ways. One of the most commonly used classification systems is based on the primary product of a firm or enterprise (Andersen and Corley 2003). For example, the latest revision of the International Standard Industrial Classification (ISIC) system divides services into 12 broad groups (excluding publicly provided), which can be disaggregated further into more specific activities (see the Table in the Appendix for the ISIC revision 3.1 classification). Moreover, the classification allows for the possibility that some firms or enterprises produce more than one type of service.

As a second alternative, services can be classified into two broad groups: *traditional* or *"stagnant"* services; and *modern, hi-tech,* or *"progressive"* services (Baumol 1985). Traditional services include wholesale and retail trade, personal services (e.g., barbershops), and publicly provided services such as defense. Most of these services are characterized by a high degree of face-to-face interaction as well as limited use of information and communications technology (ICT) (World Bank 2009). On the other hand, modern services, such as finance, insurance, and business-related services, are heavily dependent on technology. This has contributed to their increasing transportability (e.g., through satellite and telecommunications networks) and tradability (World Bank 2009). Traditional services typically dominate the early stages of economic development, while modern services emerge as countries reach higher levels of income (Eichengreen and Gupta 2011).

A third classification is based on how services are used or consumed (Petit 1986; Montresor and Vittucci Marzetti 2011). Services that mainly satisfy final demand (such as hotels and restaurants, recreation, and personal care) are known as consumer services. In contrast, services that primarily cater to intermediate demand are known as producer services. These include finance, insurance, real estate, and research and development (R&D). Producer services act as inputs to all sectors of the economy, from agriculture to mining to manufacturing. Services can also function as inputs to other service sectors.

In terms of their role in manufacturing, services can be considered either horizontal or vertical. For example, R&D and product design typically occur prior to the fabrication of a good, while sales and marketing activities are usually conducted in the latter stages of production. These services, which are common to all manufacturing firms, are also known as "horizontal services." In addition, some firms may require vertical services specific to their industry or subsector, such as clinical tests in the pharmaceutical sector (Gereffi and Fernandez-Stark 2010). Additionally, services such as transportation act as the "glue" that holds global value chains (GVCs) together (Low 2013).

However they are classified, services can be supplied for either domestic or foreign use. With regard to foreign use, the General Agreement on Trade in Services identifies four modes through which services can be distributed internationally (Lanz and Maurer 2015). Mode 1 is through traditional cross-border supply, which is similar to how goods are traded across borders. Alternatively, services can be supplied through the movement of labor and capital, that is, when people move abroad either to consume services (Mode 2) or to supply services (Mode 4). Likewise, firms may establish a commercial presence in another country through the movement of capital (Mode 3). Modes 1, 2, and 4 are captured through the balance of payments system. Services provided through commercial presence are covered by the Foreign Affiliates Statistics framework (Lanz and Maurer 2015).

5.2.2 Trends and Issues

Globally, services account for a large and increasing share of output and employment. Between 1995 and 2016, services' contribution to world GDP rose from 58% to 66%, while employment grew from 36% to 51% (World Bank 2010). Among advanced economies, the growth of services has occurred as a natural progression from the industrial stage of development. In contrast, many developing countries' employed populations are shifting to services even before their manufacturing sectors have "peaked" in earlier stages of development. This has been called "premature deindustrialization" (Rodrik 2016).

This "premature deindustrialization" has raised concerns about the future of growth given the lower productivity of services compared to manufacturing, but there are differing reasons for this. For one, the growth of services and concomitant decline of manufacturing may be more notional than real. As Hallward-Driemeier and Nayyar (2018) point out, the outsourcing or splintering of services creates an artificial increase in services output followed by a commensurate decline in manufacturing output. In this case, the change is caused by a reorganization of production and not by a real change in the value of output produced by the two sectors. Using data on 40 countries from the World Input–Output Database, Cruz and Nayyar (2017) found that the outsourcing of services by manufacturing firms accounted for only 10% of the growth in services' value added between 2000 and 2014. Yet, in looking at the reasons for firms switching activities from manufacturing to services in Denmark, Bernard, Smeets, and Warzynski (2017) find that those that splinter into services and specialize tend to become much more productive than those that do not, suggesting that the results are different at the firm level.

Aggregate statistics also mask considerable differences in the composition of services within an economy and the fact that there are comparatively fewer high-tech services in developing Asia. As Noland, Park, and Estrada (2013) point out, most of developing Asia is still characterized by traditional services, such as wholesale and retail trade, hotels and restaurants, transport, and personal services. Only a handful of economies in the region—Hong Kong, China; the Republic of Korea; and Singapore, in particular—have services sectors that are comparable with those in OECD economies in terms of sophistication. Distinguishing among different types of services is important because productivity rates vary significantly within the sector. In general, consumer services exhibit lower productivity than do producer services. Some services, such as transport and communications and financial intermediation and business activities, have productivity rates on par with, or even greater than, those of manufacturing (International Monetary Fund 2018a). The key message is that some types of services could be just as effective as manufacturing in driving growth.

Current productivity estimates may be biased due to measurement issues. Simply defined, productivity is the amount of real output produced by a given set of real inputs.[1] This implies that the quantity of output and inputs, as well as the prices used to deflate both components, must be captured accurately. This is difficult to do in practice given the inherent characteristics of services discussed below. As a result, the output of manufacturing would appear larger and its productivity higher relative to services. Given the increasingly important role played by services in the manufacturing process, this bias could be significant.

More importantly, intersectoral comparisons overlook the indirect contribution of services to the productivity of other sectors. For example, telecommunications enable knowledge diffusion by acting as a "transport mechanism" for information and other digitized products. Similarly, technological innovation would not be possible without R&D. Even "unproductive" services, such as retail and wholesale trade, and health and education, can indirectly contribute to the productivity of other sectors. The former plays a key role in linking producers with

---

[1]   There are many different types of productivity measures. Broadly speaking, these can be classified according to the number of inputs used (i.e., single-factor productivity measures versus multifactor productivity measures), or how output is defined (i.e., gross output versus value-added output). For a detailed explanation of these measures, see OECD (2001).

consumers, while the latter helps improve the quality of the workforce, which is a key factor of production (Hoekman and Mattoo 2008).

More generally, the splintering of services from manufacturing has paved the way for specialization to occur (Francois 1990). The resulting economies of scale not only translate to greater output for manufacturing firms, but also to lower prices for the services used as inputs to production. One way to gauge the contribution of services to the productivity of manufacturing is to examine the link between the two sectors more closely. By quantifying the contribution of services to the manufacturing sector, we can capture one of the ways in which services indirectly contribute to productivity. [2] In the next section, we explore the concept of "servicification" in more detail and provide some evidence for Asia.

5.3 The Servicification of Manufacturing

5.3.1 Definitions, Concepts, and Drivers

The servicification of manufacturing, otherwise known as "manuservice," pertains to the increasing reliance of manufacturing firms on services, which manifests in several ways. First, production in services is becoming more intensive, as reflected by the number of services used as intermediate inputs by manufacturers (Low 2013). Second, manufacturing jobs are becoming more service-oriented: the number of workers performing service-related activities within the manufacturing sector has grown, while the number of those engaged in core production has declined (Miroudot and Cadestin 2017; Miroudot 2016). In addition, services are increasingly being embedded in or bundled with goods to create more value. Servicification is therefore a multidimensional phenomenon (Figure 5.1).

Services may also be embedded in, or bundled with, a manufactured good, a phenomenon known as "servitization."[3] This idea goes back to Vandermerwe and Rada (1988) who described the practice as "the increased offering of fuller market packages or 'bundles' of customer-focused combinations of goods, services, support, self-service, and

---

[2]   The IMF (2018a: Box 3.1) measured the services content of manufacturing for a set of advanced and developing countries between 1995 and 2011, and found that the change during that period was quite small at about 6%, most of which was due to growth in consumer services. However, due to the level of aggregation of the sectors, as well as the time period studied (before high-tech services became more prominent), they are unlikely to capture the contribution of services embodied in the manufactured good.

[3]   We thank Sebastien Miroudot for clarifying this terminology.

Figure 5.1 The Various Dimensions of Servicification

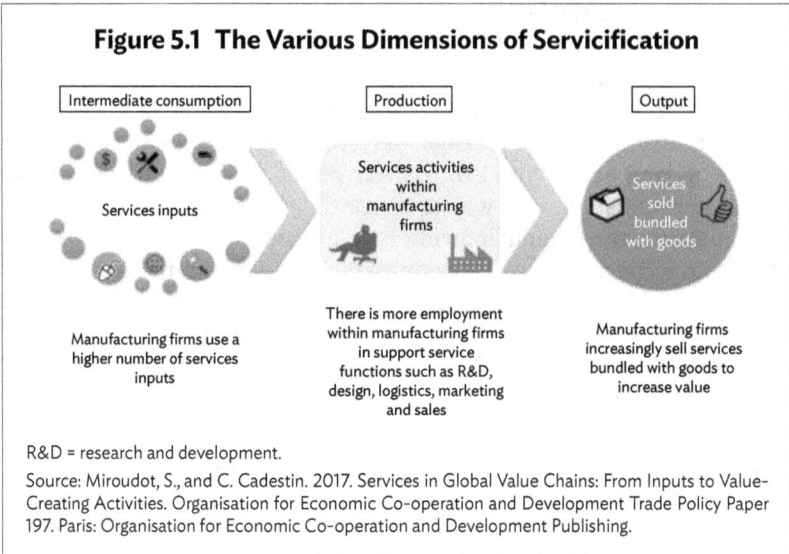

| Intermediate consumption | Production | Output |

Services inputs

Services activities within manufacturing firms

Services sold bundled with goods

Manufacturing firms use a higher number of services inputs

There is more employment within manufacturing firms in support service functions such as R&D, design, logistics, marketing and sales

Manufacturing firms increasingly sell services bundled with goods to increase value

R&D = research and development.
Source: Miroudot, S., and C. Cadestin. 2017. Services in Global Value Chains: From Inputs to Value-Creating Activities. Organisation for Economic Co-operation and Development Trade Policy Paper 197. Paris: Organisation for Economic Co-operation and Development Publishing.

knowledge in order to add value to core product offerings." Some examples of these include warranties and aftersales services, as well as financing schemes designed to facilitate the purchase of a product. Moreover, the types of services that can be embedded in or bundled with a good have expanded with advances in technology. One example of this is the smartphone: while the phone itself is a good, users can download applications that use different types of services ranging from audiovisual (e.g., the streaming of music or movies) to publishing services (e.g., e-books) (Hallward-Driemeier and Nayyar 2018). Consequently, manufacturing firms are employing more workers in service-related activities (such as R&D, design, and marketing) than in activities directly related to production (Miroudot 2016).

To understand the types of services offered by manufacturing firms, services are classified in two broad groups (Table 5.1). In line with Cusumano, Kahl, and Suarez (2015), the first group includes all services that act as complements to the manufactured good. These can be divided further into two types, namely *smoothing* services and *adapting* services. Smoothing services are designed to facilitate the purchase and use of the good without changing the product's features significantly. Financing schemes, warranties, and maintenance and technical support are all examples of smoothing services. On the other hand, adapting services enhance the overall value of a product by augmenting it with new features or making it more personalized. For instance, Xerox now offers

Table 5.1 Types of Services Offered by Manufacturing Firms

	Complementary with Products		Replacement
	Smoothing	Adapting	Substituting
Definition	Services that "smooth" the product sale or usage without significantly altering the product functionality	Services that expand the functionality of a product or help the customer develop new uses	Services that replace the purchase of a product
Examples	• Financing • Warranty/insurance • Maintenance/repair • Technical support • Training in basic uses	• Customizations that create new features specific to a user • Training or consulting that introduces new uses • Integration with other products or "solutions"	• Data-processing services in lieu of mainframes • Software as a service instead of a software product • Zapmail service (Fedex) offered instead of fax machines • Rolls-Royce "Power by the Hour" instead of engine sales

Source: Cusumano, M. A., S. J. Kahl, and F. F. Suarez. 2015. Services, Industry Evolution, and the Competitive Strategies of Product Firms. Strategic Management Journal 36(4): 559–575. doi:10.1002/smj.2235

"document solutions," which are essentially printer or photocopying machine bundles that include services such as document management (Benedettini et al. 2009). In some cases services replace rather than complement goods. IBM, for instance, has evolved from a computer manufacturer to an information technology and business services provider (Ahamed, Inohara, and Kamoshida 2013).

A second important form of servicification of manufacturing happens through splintering. The splintering of production could manifest itself if manufacturing firms are closing their services departments and outsourcing. Essentially, this allows businesses to subcontract part of their operations to independent suppliers located in the same country (e.g., domestic outsourcing) or abroad (e.g., offshore outsourcing). This is usually done for noncore activities, such as back office processing, accounting, or customer support. The new services are provided through "arm's length" contracts, where firms have separate ownership and management (although they can customize the service for their clients). Such a process can facilitate true specialization at every stage of production.

Figure 5.2 The Servicification of Manufacturing

Traditional transformation process	Servitization process	Splintering process
Stage 1: Manufacturing process automated but transformation mostly managed by factory workforce.	Stage 2: Manufacturing process fully automated, with specific departments (inside or outside the factory) providing back - office, information technology, and logistics support.	Stage 3: Outsourcing of all services except those specifically related to the manufacturing process (e.g., quality control, flow management). Manufacturing process itself completely automated.

Source: Authors.

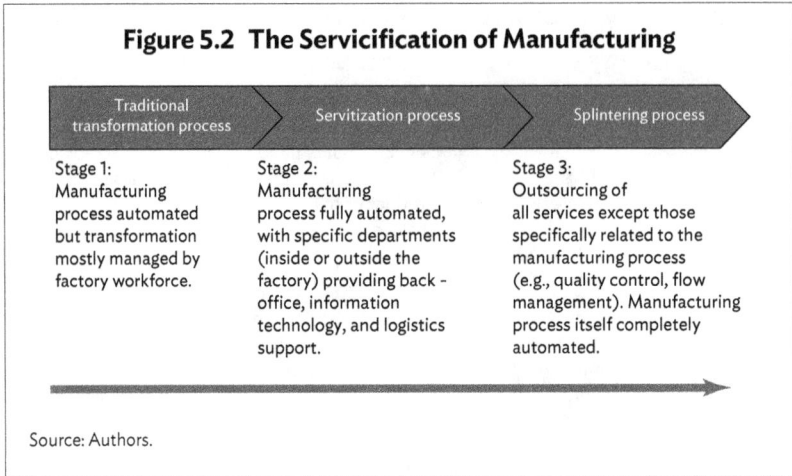

The gradual transformation of the manufacturing process to a service-oriented one is what creates the symbiotic relationship between goods and services (Figure 5.2). Servicification, which is perhaps a more general term (see the definition in the Swedish National Board of Trade 2016), can come in the form of servitization (in-house provision) or servification (splintering and outsourcing). One variant of this relationship is the movement from producing songs on compact disks to making them available digitally, where the music industry is still alive but is reclassified from producing a "good" to producing a "service." Another example is when an automobile company separates its auto maintenance and leasing business: each unit can act separately, but the efficiency and survival of the service and leasing units depend on the extent of sales of that type of car (subordination of the service to the manufacturing process).

In the next section, we survey the extent of servicification based on the literature as well as our own analysis for Asia.

5.3.2 Trends and Patterns of Servificification

5.3.2.1 Evidence from Recent Studies and New Data

The main empirical contribution of this chapter is the use of an updated global dataset to provide a broad but fuller examination of servicification in the manufacturing sector in Asia. Most recent studies have focused on the impact on trade and GVCs. In this section, we examine trends and patterns of servicification using the Multiregional Input–Output (MRIO) tables of the Asian Development Bank (ADB). The ADB MRIO builds on the World Input–Output Database, and extends it to cover more Asian economies. [4] It divides economies into 35 broad sectors, including 14 manufacturing sectors and 17 services sectors (see Appendix Table A1). For our analysis, we utilize the latest release of the MRIO, which covers a total of 62 individual economies (with the remainder denoted the "rest of world") for 9 years (i.e., 2000, 2010–2017).

The literature estimating the importance of services in manufacturing is fairly new and focuses on manufacturing exports. ADB (2015) and the OECD (OECD and the World Trade Organization 2012) have begun reporting comprehensive indicators in trade in value added (most recently updated in OECD [2018]). Heuser and Mattoo (2017) showed that the share of services exports in gross exports globally has remained at roughly 20% since the 1980s, whereas the contribution of services to value-added exports has grown very quickly globally, from below 30% in 1980 to more than 40% in 2009. Using the updated MRIO 2017, our data show similar trends for Asia. Services exports as a share of total exports for Asia between 2000 and 2017 has remained steady at 16.6%–16.8% on average (Figure 5.3). Excluding Japan, it has declined

Figure 5.3 Services Exports Versus Export Servicification in Asia (% of total gross exports)

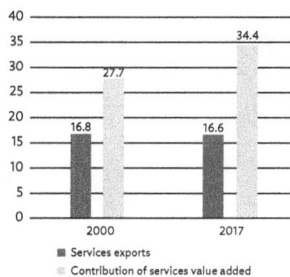

Source: Authors' calculations based on trade in value added statistics, in the Asian Development Bank's Multi-Regional Input-Output Tables (accessed 30 September 2018).

---

[4] The ADB MRIO includes 24 economies in Asia equivalent to 97% of developing Asia's GDP: Bangladesh; Bhutan; Brunei Darussalam; Cambodia; Fiji; Hong Kong, China; India; Indonesia; Japan; Kazakhstan; the Kyrgyz Republic; the Republic of Korea; Lao People's Democratic Republic; Malaysia; Maldives; Nepal; Pakistan; People's Republic of China; Philippines; Singapore; Sri Lanka; Taipei,China; Thailand; and Viet Nam. The other 42 economies are mostly OECD economies, but an included region called the "rest of the world" ensures that the system is closed, as any economy not included individually is part of the rest of the world.

from 18% to 16%. However, in terms of value added, the contribution of services to total exports of goods and services has increased from 27.7% in 2000 to 34.4% in 2017.

The share of services value added in exports was about the same in 2017 in Asia and non-Asia, although this share varies significantly across economies (Figure 5.4).[5] In part, these differences reflect various areas of specialization. For instance, economies that primarily export commodities (e.g., Mongolia and Brunei Darussalam) and manufactured

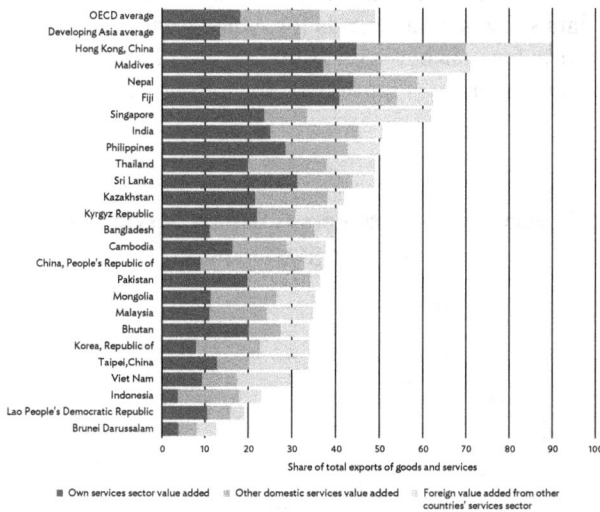

Figure 5.4 Own Services, Other Domestic Services, and Foreign Services Value-Added Contribution to Value Added of Exports by Economy, 2017

OECD = Organisation for Economic Co-operation and Development.

Note: Own services sector value added refers to value added originating from within the services sector to produce its own exports. Other domestic services value added refers to value added contributed by other domestic services sectors used to produce exports. Foreign value added from other economies' services sectors refers to value added contributed by foreign services sectors to produce exports. The Republic of Korea is in both the OECD and developing Asia.

Source: Authors, based on the Asian Development Bank's Multiregional Input–Output Table 2017 (accessed 15 November 2018).

---

5   The value added of services to gross exports can be broken down into its foreign and domestic component. The latter can be disaggregated further into three parts: (i) direct domestic services value added; (ii) indirect domestic services value added; and (iii) reimported domestic services value added (Heuser and Mattoo 2017).

goods (e.g., Viet Nam, the Republic of Korea) use fewer services as inputs than economies that actually export services, such as Hong Kong, China (where services contribute over 70%) and Maldives. However, the relationship is not straightforward. This result is consistent with Heuser and Mattoo (2017), who find that, during 1980–2011, services accounted for 33% of value-added exports on average among advanced economies, with the majority being domestically provided. Lanz and Maurer (2015) also look at services contribution and find that this ratio is a full 13 percentage points higher in advanced economies than in developing economies, with the gap largely explained by indirect exports of services. Indeed, the availability of services within an economy appears to be crucial for the development of export sectors.

Our data also show that more advanced economies have a higher contribution of services to GDP. More specifically, the higher the GDP per capita, the higher this ratio is (Figure 5.5). This is not surprising given the specific sectors that play a key role in the manufacturing process and the "nontradable" nature of many services sectors, such as retail trade, telecommunications, and infrastructure services, which are more developed in advanced economies. This result was found in Chen et al. (2018).

Figure 5.5 Direct and Indirect Inputs of Services as a Share of Gross Domestic Product Against Gross Domestic Product per Capita, 2000–2017 (Multiregional Input–Output)

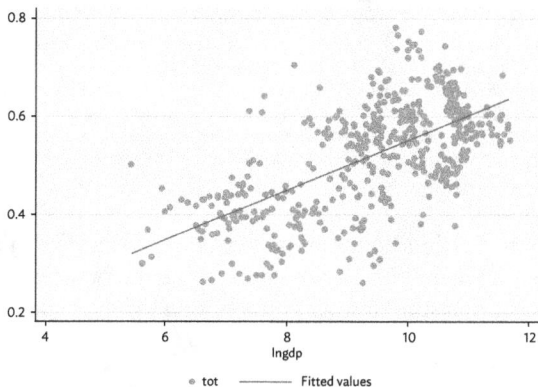

lngdp = in gross domestic product, tot = terms of trade.
Source: Authors, based on the Asian Development Bank's Multiregional Input–Output Table 2017.

Services provided in-house within manufacturing firms (servitization) could be substantial but are difficult to observe. Miroudot (2016) matched job functions to occupation data from labor force surveys using data for 37 countries, mostly from the OECD, to describe how the composition of employment in manufacturing firms has changed since 1995.[6] Overall, he found that the servitization of manufacturing jobs has increased in all countries for which data are available. Moreover, the analysis reveals large variations across sectors. Jobs related to core operating activities range from almost 30% for coke and petroleum to more than 90% in the case of agriculture (Figure 5.6). On average, only about 50% of jobs in the manufacturing sector are in production, with the rest in support services.

Figure 5.6 Decomposition of Jobs Embodied in Gross Manufacturing Exports by Function and Industry, 2011

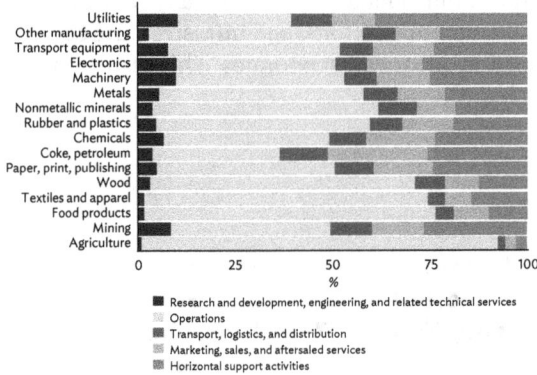

Source: Heuser, C., and A. Mattoo. 2017. Services Trade and Global Value Chains. In *Measuring and Analyzing the Impact of GVCs on Economic Development*, edited by World Bank, Institute of Developing Economies Japan External Trade Organization, Organisation for Economic Co-operation and Development (OECD), University of International Business and Economics, and World Trade Organization. Washington, DC: World Bank; based on Miroudot, S. 2016. Services in Global Value Chains: From Inputs to Value-Creating Activities. OECD Trade Policy Paper. Paris: OECD.

Services provided in-house are not only used as inputs in production but are also bundled with goods sold by manufacturing firms, thus complicating the measure of their contribution to value added. In theory,

---

[6] The analysis was expanded further in Miroudot and Cadestin (2017) to include 41 countries. These are the 28 European Union countries, Australia, Brazil, Canada, India, Iceland, Japan, the Republic of Korea, Mexico, New Zealand, Norway, Switzerland, Turkey, and the United States.

national accounts should reflect the division between in-house goods and services of servicification. For example, the total output of a manufacturing firm that offers financing should be recorded as two separate transactions: first as a good, and second as a service. In practice, there are likely to be differences across countries and industries regarding how output is measured and recorded by national statistical offices. It is especially difficult to disaggregate output when the sale is conducted as a single transaction or when the service is not "consumed" simultaneously with the good (e.g., maintenance or repair). As a result, the servitization of manufacturing output is likely to be understated in national accounts. Crozet and Milet (2017) thus refer to this phenomenon as "hidden deindustrialization." Box 5.1 discusses the main challenges for national accounts.

Box 5.1 Can National Accounts Adequately Measure Today's Productivity?

National accounts were first conceived of in the 1930s by Colin Clark, Simon Kuznets, and Richard Stone of the United Kingdom. At this time, which was very different from the situation today, manufacturing and construction were the engines of growth. The production of goods was a clearly tangible process of man "working" with machines or tools to transform mostly physical goods into consumable outputs. While services were sometimes supportive (e.g., transportation utilities), they were mostly consumable or publicly provided, and were considered marginal to production or a leisure activity. To determine what should be considered value added in a given year, Kuznets included only "productive" activities in the new economic statistics. These were defined as activities that produced goods or services that could be bought or sold in the market economy. Thus, their unit value was the price. It was also important to be able to measure the activities, and the industrial classification developed thus "treat[ed] services as 'immaterial' (i.e., everything that is not manufacturing or agriculture), while ignoring that the activity of services in the economy, as well as the corporate structure of firms, transcend such classification schemes at any level of aggregation" (Andersen and Corley 2003). However, as the definitions of a "productive activity" or a "unit" of service became increasingly blurred in the age of high-tech manufacturing, artificial intelligence, and mobile phone applications, the compilation of national accounts as originally conceived is experiencing serious challenges measuring intangibles.

The example of the national accounting of the Korean automobile company Hyundai illustrates how difficult it is to measure every process. Its factory in Montgomery, Alabama in the United States, with 3,000 employees, can produce almost 400,000 cars and trucks each year for distribution across North America; the company also leases the vehicles and finances their purchase, while its 800 dealerships provide servicing.

continued on next page

Box 5.1 *continued*

Almost all of the parts, including sophisticated electronic components and sensors, are produced elsewhere around the world. Thus, the question arises, how should national accountants determine Hyundai's economic contribution? First, they will request revenues and costs for all of Hyundai's operations, and will divide the main activities into primary, secondary, and tertiary activities, for example. At some reasonable cutoff for the number of "principal" activities of Hyundai United States, they will assign the value added (revenues minus costs) to the different subsector categories under the North American Industry Classification System. Services contracted out to third parties (such as leasing, repair, engineering services, logistics, and accounting) will be considered a cost for Hyundai and a revenue for the service providers. Thus, the input–output links will clearly show that these activities are linked (although presentation of national accounts on the production side will not show the links). Labor compensation will be classified depending on the worker's place of affiliation. Overall, the value added will be fully accounted for in aggregate in one sector or another.

Four important problems in this measurement undermine the contribution of services to productivity.

(i) First, the labor productivity of the plant (e.g., number of cars per worker/hour, 400,000 autos per year/300 plant workers in man-hours) will be solely attributed to the auto manufacturing sector in the national accounts, and not to the myriad of services that contributed. Due to the bundling of services, batching of computer programming, and robotics installed in earlier years, for example, most of the unit average costs in that period will be components, parts and utilities, and consumption of fixed capital defined under statutory depreciation rules, among others. Although the contribution of services in that period will be small, the output would be impossible without the provision of "indivisible" services with huge economies of scale. Their contribution cannot be accounted for as a share of the final output if it is included elsewhere as a stand-alone "service."

(ii) Second, workers involved in services within the Hyundai plant are unlikely to appear as even separate services employees in the accounting, and thus cannot contribute to an increase in services value added in the national accounts, particularly if they comprise a small or ancillary cost of production. The extent of servitization mismeasurement is greater when the service is provided in-house (Crozet and Milet 2017).

(iii) Third, services are typically priced through bundling, cognizant of their indivisibility property. It is common for insurance, accounting services, and television and phone services to be priced as "monthly services," meaning that two users of the same plan may use vastly different amounts of the "bundled" service. In practice, the difference in productivity derived from the service by each user may be huge. For example, national accounts will show the "phone services" of the customer service desk as being equal to the "phone services" of the staff lounge room and attach to it the bundle

continued on next page

Box 5.1 *continued*

price, erroneously attributing the same value added to these two users. When deflated, services with different usage rates are assumed to be equally productive. This is compounded by the lack of homogeneity of the service unit once used up. Goods, on the other hand, are tangible and clearly divisible, and their unit value can be more easily measured.

(iv) Finally, many services are becoming almost free because they rely on a repetitive, previously designed code, as we rely on the accumulation of knowledge by others. For example, an algorithm designed to optimize the shipping routes for Hyundai cars ready for delivery has a fixed cost (charged by the programmers), but no marginal cost. Again, national accounts may attribute the efficiency of the distribution process to the manufacturing process itself, when in fact it was the infinite economies of scale of the network specialist's algorithm that enabled this shipping efficiency.

Other issues discussed in the literature exacerbate these problems. However, various studies (e.g., International Monetary Fund 2018b) argue that the size of the estimated effects is insufficient to explain the fall in labor productivity over the last 2 decades. Going forward, these issues will lead to large measurement biases. There are perhaps five main issues that arise:

(i) Deflators of new goods or high-tech goods do not reflect goods' "unit value" when calculating real gross domestic products, and not all statistical offices adjust appropriately.

(ii) "Free" goods, such as Facebook, Wikipedia, and pictures from a mobile phone, are not included in national accounts (because their price is zero), which underestimates the value they contribute to gross domestic product. If these platforms are used for e-commerce, for example (which is very common in developing Asia), their contribution to efficient distribution is not properly accounted for.

(iii) Goods or services produced but not remunerated (e.g., unpaid household work, family help) are also not included because they are free.

(iv) When corporations splinter production offshore, the valuation of each of the stages of production sometimes relies on inaccurate pricing by multinational companies, who declare their ownership of each stage of production in the locality that minimizes their tax liability (transfer pricing). Even if all production stages could be valued accurately, this would require all countries to provide full, accurate reporting and to share their data on companies with other national accounts statistics offices (this is beyond the capacity of most countries' institutions) (Moulton and van de Ven 2018).

(v) The spillover effects from agglomeration economies of a talented team working together to produce new knowledge is crucial to productivity and is generally not accounted for. The human capital of a university scientist in the team, for example, is classified as an "education" service. Such a service is valued at cost (sometimes subsidized if provided by the public sector) because there is no tangible output.

Given the limitations of national accounts and trade statistics, studies on servitization have relied on firm-level data, which allow output to be disaggregated into a goods component and a services component, and most focus on Europe (Walter and Dell'mour 2010; Kelle 2013). Federico and Tosti (2017) utilized a dataset with 3,000 exporters in Italy and found that 30% of services exports are produced by manufacturing firms. Crozet and Milet (2017) used French time-series data (as did Lodefalk [2010] for Sweden), and found that the servitization of manufacturing output has indeed grown. Miroudot and Cadestin (2017) utilized the Orbis dataset, which contains firm-level data for 50 developed and developing countries (nine of which are from Asia). Although the estimates are subject to a number of caveats, they also reveal that a significant number of firms produce both goods and services. The most common type of service bundled with goods is "distribution," followed by transport services. However, some services are tied to the production of specific goods. For example, engineering and R&D services usually accompany exports of chemicals and minerals, while construction is linked with exports of wood products.

A good example of servitization is in the very capital-intensive oil and gas sector. Originally dominated by large oil and gas conglomerates, the complexity of the oil and gas production chain has led to both servitization and splintering of oil and gas services. Major oil companies have become resource owners and project managers of many smaller outfits that do the technical work, both inside and outside the consortiums. As the sector becomes more complex, this process is expected to increase (Box 5.2).

Box 5.2 Servitization in Oil and Gas Services

Examples from the United States and Kazakhstan
The oil and gas services sector provides a pointed example of the servitization of production of nonrenewable resources. Oil production and exploration are performed by multinational companies organized around joint ventures that contract the services of all sorts of experts, such as geologists and geophysicists, lessors of oil rigs, drilling services, welders, lawyers, pipeline companies, shippers, and distributors. These services are tightly linked to production and extraction but are typically provided at arm's length by oil field and exploration services companies (OFS).

Oil field services (OFS) companies have driven innovation in oil and gas, increasing in scale and scope and enabling extraction from fields at levels impossible to conceive before 2000. By 2011, the global revenue of

continued on next page

Box 5.2 *continued*

OFS was estimated at $750 billion (The Economist 2012). In mid-2018, the market capitalization of the largest supplier, Schlumberger, stood at $95 billion and exceeded that of major international oil companies, such as ENI and Statoil. It carries out most of the tasks involved in finding and extracting oil. Most recent innovations in oil and gas production and distribution are the result of OFS work, and the rate of innovations in the sector is astounding. The 2006 oil price increases unleashed innovation, and horizontal drilling and shale oil and gas (three-dimensional seismology and directional drilling), as well as enhanced oil recovery techniques, flourished. This allowed accessible oil and gas reserves to flow much more easily, and also gave producers the ability to draw on capacity in shorter periods of time. More importantly, it gave the sector the ability to splinter the production process even further and refine the value chains. Another discovery has been the ability to transport natural gas more economically in liquefaction boats, such as small liquefied natural gas carriers and bunker vessels.

Figure B2.1 Stock Market Value of Oil Production and Oil Field Services, 2000–2018

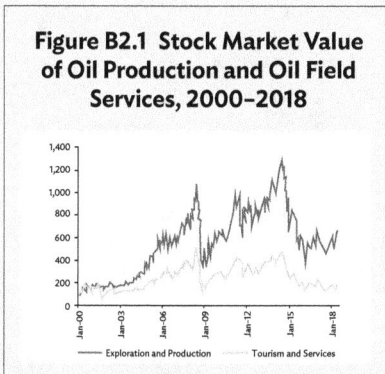

In the United States (US) the technological advances have, in turn, increased the value of the oil and gas companies as well, with positive spillovers. In the US, at least, these spillovers have translated into a large valuation growth for producing companies, although not for service companies. According to national accounts, value added in oil and gas extraction soared during 2000–2016, while employment as a share of nonfarm employment in the US stayed roughly the same, implying significant growth in labor productivity (Table B2.1). Although measured value added of oil and gas services barely rose (from 1.2% in 2000 to 1.3% in 2015), employment as a share of total US employment rose by almost 20 percentage points to 0.42%. When employment grows faster than value added, this implies flat productivity for oil and gas service companies based on the national accounts; however, other evidence suggests otherwise. Moreover, while oil production has increased with oil prices, oil services have been much less volatile, and their value is not attributed appropriately in the stock prices (Figure B2.1). In other words, the production sector is getting all the "credit" despite the large amount of talent employed in many different areas in oil and gas services.

continued on next page

Box 5.2 *continued*

**Table B2.1 United States Economy: Share of Employment
and Value Added to Total Employment and Value Added (Selected Sectors)**

Concept	Employment (full- and part-time)		Value added (GDP)	
Year	2000	2016	2000	2016
Oil and gas extraction	0.28%	0.3%	1.3%	1.7%
Downstream	0.4%	0.3%	1.1%	1.3%
Oil and gas services 1/	0.35%	0.42%	1.2%	1.3%
Memo item: Services over extraction	1.25	1.4	0.92	0.76

1/ = excludes waste management and remediation services, GDP = gross domestic product.

Source: United States Bureau of Economic Analysis, Bureau of Labor Statistics. www.bea.gov (accessed 25 May 2018); and authors' estimates.

Similarly, in Kazakhstan the importance of OFS is not obvious in national accounts. Kazakhstan is a typical highly resource-dependent country in central Asia, and like many it has struggled to diversify. One way it has done this is through a concerted effort to establish local-content regulations, providing a chance for local engineers and oil services firms to get involved. On average, between 1994 and 2014 oil and gas production accounted for only 0.5% of total employment in Kazakhstan. However, the indirect impact on total employment through forward linkages was considerable, as the spending of oil rents supported the growth of labor-intensive services. The share of service jobs in total employment grew from 38% in 2001 to 48% in 2014.

The direct and indirect inputs by services in Kazakhstan suggest considerable servicification. Between 2005 and 2015, the oil and gas sector purchased over 50% of all its intermediate inputs from the services sector, growing from 55% in 2005 to 74% in 2015 (Table B2.2). This likely underestimates the importance of know-how and skills that went with it: R&D services were crucial in developing the Kashagan field in the northern Caspian Sea, one of the largest in the world with an estimated 13 billion recoverable barrels of oil. It was discovered in 2000, but the geological and technological challenges led to $50 billion being spent on R&D over 17 years; of this amount, almost one-quarter went to local services firms, as joint ventures and consortiums between local and foreign OFS companies were promoted as vehicles for transferring technologies and skills. Despite the huge inputs of services, the national accounts show large increases in oil and gas production, but only slight services output increases by domestic services firms.

continued on next page

Box 5.2 *continued*

Table B2.2 Share of Services in Intermediate Inputs Purchased by the Oil and Gas Sector

Services	2005	2010	2015
Repairs	1.08	0.48	3.28
Auxiliary mining services	17.17	13.99	20.67
Construction	1.61	0.48	1.68
Professional services	7.8	3.5	11.16
Oil field services	27.7	18.5	36.8
Total services (%)	55.36	36.95	73.59

Source: Asian Development Bank (2018a) using the Kazakhstan National Committee on Statistics.

5.3.2.2 Some Evidence Specific to Asia

Perhaps the earliest evidence of servicification in Asia was provided by Baldwin, Forslid, and Ito (2015) and Baldwin, Ito, and Sato (2014). Using the concept of the smile curve, the authors find that in all nine Asian economies in their sample[7] between 1985 and 2005, the primary source of value added has recently shifted away from the manufacturing sector and moved to the services sector. This is particularly true for the semiconductors and electronics production process, with the major producers being based in Asia (Figure 5.7). Until 1995, the manufacturing sector still accounted for the majority of value added.

The MRIO tables allow us to measure sector-level components of servicification using some refinements on the well-known direct and Leontief coefficients. Using the technical coefficient matrix, we can quantify the number of services used directly as inputs in manufacturing sectors for arm's-length transactions. By subtracting this matrix from the Leontief matrix, we also obtain an estimate of services used indirectly by a particular sector (see ADB [2018b] for a detailed description of the decomposition). The Leontief coefficients themselves give us the total number of services used in manufacturing, that is, they represent the sum of what we denote as direct and indirect components. To illustrate these concepts, consider the case of an automobile manufacturer that uses equipment leased by another company to produce one vehicle. The

---

7   These are Indonesia; Japan; Malaysia; the PRC; Philippines; Republic of Korea; Singapore; Taipei,China; and Thailand.

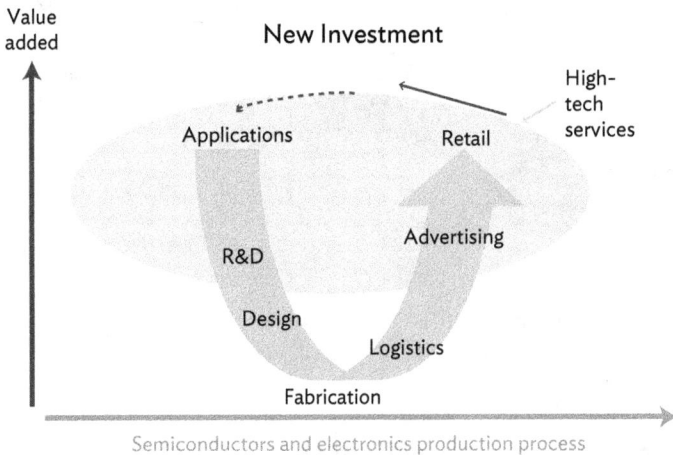

Figure 5.7 The Role of High-Tech Services in the Manufacturing Value Chain

R&D = research and development.
Source: Authors, based on Asian Development Bank. 2018. *Asian Development Outlook: Technology and Jobs in Asia*, April. Manila: Asian Development Bank.

rent paid for the equipment is an example of a direct service used as an input by the automobile manufacturer; however, this does not account for all of the equipment rentals that are paid for in the process of producing one vehicle. For instance, the automobile manufacturer may require basic metals as part of its raw materials. Assuming these metals are also produced using leased equipment, then the rent serves as an indirect input to the manufacture of a vehicle. Figure 5.8 shows that the direct contribution of services to manufacturing's value added between 2000 and 2017 stayed broadly constant: on average, $1.00 of demand for manufacturing production generates nearly $0.20 of services globally. The indirect component is not only about twice as large but it has grown by more than 15 percentage points: the total (direct and indirect) contribution of services to a $1.00 value added in manufacturing increased from $0.55 in 2000 to $0.62 in 2017.

The degree of servification varies widely across economies but is generally lower in Asia than in OECD economies (Figure 5.9). In terms of direct inputs, Viet Nam's manufacturing sector is the least servified. On average, only 8% of a good's value is derived from services. The

---

Figure 5.8 Global Direct and Indirect Contribution of Services to Manufacturing Value Added (% of manufacturing value added)

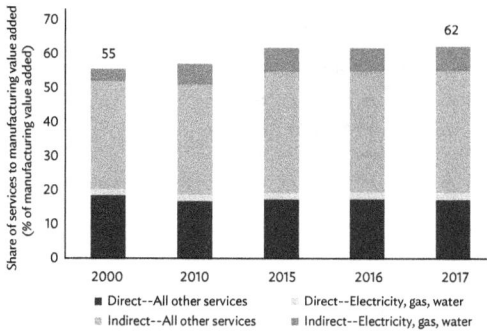

mfg = manufacturing.

Notes: Figures represent the average of all manufacturing sectors, weighted by the country's gross domestic product. Services sectors include publicly provided and community sectors, but exclude construction.

Source: Authors' calculations based on the trade in value added statistics, in the Asian Development Bank's Multiregional Input–Output tables (accessed 10 September 2018).

---

opposite is true for Hong Kong, China, the most servified economy in the group, where services directly account for two-thirds of manufacturing output.[8] In contrast, Singapore and Thailand are more servified than the average OECD economy (both just over 60%), with two-thirds of this attributed to the indirect contribution of services to manufacturing value added. India, Malaysia, and the People's Republic of China exhibit values similar to the US. The indirect contribution is generally slightly larger than the direct contribution for Asian economies, except for Pakistan and Bangladesh. Services in developing Asia in total contribute 43% to manufacturing value added (unweighted average); however, many of the larger and more advanced economies in developing Asia are close to OECD average levels.

---

[8] This result partly reflects the very small manufacturing base in Hong Kong, China, which in some sense magnifies the share of services and makes it an outlier. However, it also reflects its trade openness. It is worth remembering that the direct and indirect contributions of an economy's services sectors can originate either domestically or from a foreign economy.

Figure 5.9 Direct and Indirect Contribution of Services to Manufacturing Value Added, 2017

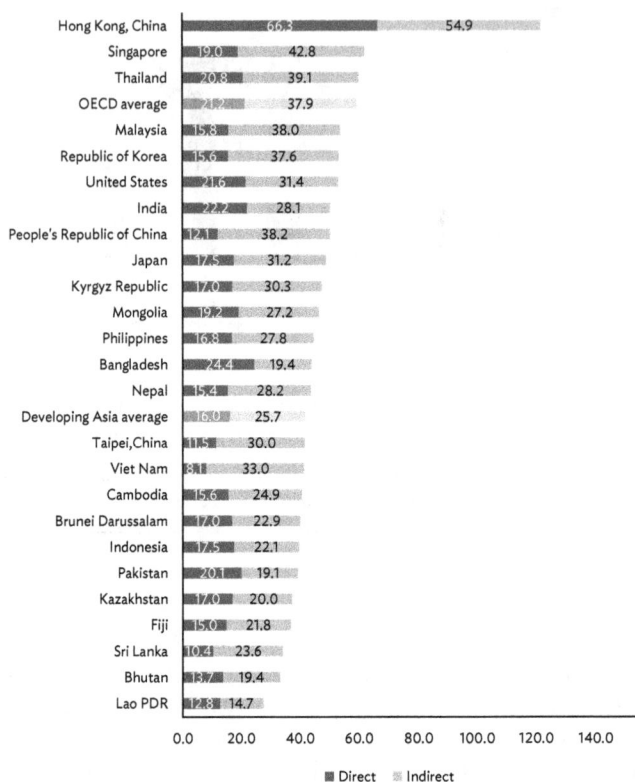

Economy	Direct	Indirect
Hong Kong, China	66.3	54.9
Singapore	19.0	42.8
Thailand	20.8	39.1
OECD average	21.2	37.9
Malaysia	15.8	38.0
Republic of Korea	15.6	37.6
United States	21.6	31.4
India	22.2	28.1
People's Republic of China	12.1	38.2
Japan	17.5	31.2
Kyrgyz Republic	17.0	30.3
Mongolia	19.2	27.2
Philippines	16.8	27.8
Bangladesh	24.8	19.4
Nepal	15.4	28.2
Developing Asia average	18.0	25.7
Taipei,China	11.4	30.0
Viet Nam	8.1	33.0
Cambodia	15.6	24.9
Brunei Darussalam	17.0	22.9
Indonesia	17.5	22.1
Pakistan	20.1	19.1
Kazakhstan	17.0	20.0
Fiji	15.0	21.8
Sri Lanka	10.4	23.6
Bhutan	13.7	19.4
Lao PDR	12.8	14.7

Lao PDR = Lao People's Democratic Republic, OECD = Organisation for Economic Co-operation and Development.

Notes: Figures represent the average of all manufacturing sectors for each economy. The original data are expressed in terms of one dollar of manufacturing output, so these were multiplied by 100 in order to convert them to percentages.

Source: Authors' calculations, based on the trade in value added statistics, in the Asian Development Bank's Multiregional Input–Output tables (accessed 28 September 2018).

Globally, all manufacturing sectors show that services account for 50%–60% of their value added, and this phenomenon is not only limited to high-tech manufacturing sectors. Some services contribute more than others, with the category "renting of machinery and equipment and other business services" (abbreviated henceforth as business services) having the strongest arm's-length links with manufacturing,

Figure 5.10 Total (Direct and Indirect) Contribution of Services to Manufacturing Value Added by Sector (2000 and 2017)

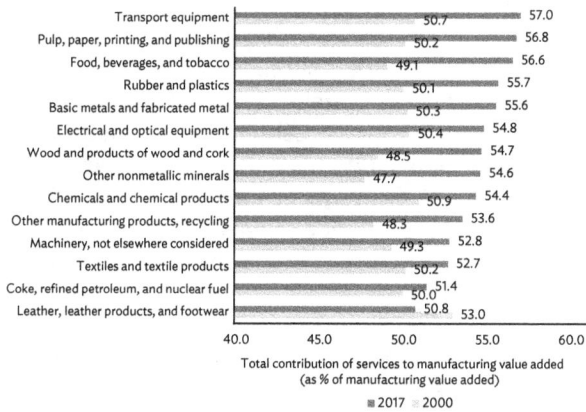

Sector	2017	2000
Transport equipment	50.7	57.0
Pulp, paper, printing, and publishing	50.2	56.8
Food, beverages, and tobacco	49.1	56.6
Rubber and plastics	50.1	55.7
Basic metals and fabricated metal	50.3	55.6
Electrical and optical equipment	50.4	54.8
Wood and products of wood and cork	48.5	54.7
Other nonmetallic minerals	47.7	54.6
Chemicals and chemical products	50.9	54.4
Other manufacturing products, recycling	48.3	53.6
Machinery, not elsewhere considered	49.3	52.8
Textiles and textile products	50.2	52.7
Coke, refined petroleum, and nuclear fuel	50.0	51.4
Leather, leather products, and footwear	50.8	53.0

Total contribution of services to manufacturing value added
(as % of manufacturing value added)

■ 2017 ▨ 2000

mfg = manufacturing.

Note: Figures represent the average input coefficient of services for all 62 economies. The original data are expressed in terms of one dollar of manufacturing output.

Source: Authors' calculations based on the Asian Development Bank's Multiregional Input–Output Table 2017 (accessed 30 September 2018).

especially in the United States.[9] Figure 5.10 shows the direct and indirect contribution of services to the value added of each manufacturing sector globally. Transportation equipment, which is deeply embedded in GVCs, is not only the most servified manufacturing sector (at 57% in 2017), but also saw its contribution grow the most of all manufacturing sectors between 2000 and 2017. This is not surprising: transport equipment, particularly automobiles, is also one of the most automated sectors (using robots), in line with the complementarity of high-tech services with capital intensity (ADB 2018b). Other sectors, such as paper printing and publishing, and food, beverages, and tobacco, tend to be mostly nontraded, and are directly linked to services such as publishing and restaurants, respectively. Only one sector, leather and footwear, became less servified between 2000 and 2017, although services still

---

[9]   The key services used by manufacturers are distribution and business services, with each sector contributing about one-third to the value added of services in manufactured exports. The remainder is divided among transport, finance, and other services (Miroudot and Cadestin 2017).

contribute to 50% of their value added. The textile and garments sector is not excessively servified, which perhaps explains why Pakistan and Bangladesh (two large garments exporters) have lower than average values of servicification.

In terms of the source of the contribution of services to manufacturing, there are stark differences across economies, although no discernible patterns are evident (Table 5.2). Most manufacturing sectors are embedded in long GVCs, with both domestic and foreign arm's-length links. The magnitude of the increase varied significantly between 2000 and 2017. The indirect contribution, which is perhaps the most interesting, registered a wide range of changes, from an increase of almost 100 percentage points in Brunei Darussalam, an oil-producing economy, to a decline of 48 percentage points in Fiji. While most of the direct contribution comes from domestic services inputs, the opposite is true for indirect contribution, in which the foreign component is somewhat larger. For developing Asia, the direct contribution of services grew by 8 percentage points, although the indirect contribution remains more important. The direct foreign services contribution is low ($0.04 for every dollar of manufacturing value added) but growing, with indirect foreign services contributing to 17% of manufacturing value added, on

Table 5.2 Change in the Direct and Indirect Contribution of Services to Manufacturing Value Added by Source, 2000–2017 (%)

Economy	% Change in Direct Contribution			% Change in Indirect Contribution		
	Total	Domestic	Foreign	Total	Domestic	Foreign
Growth, 2000–2017						
OECD average	9%	–1%	62%	14%	–8%	33%
Developing Asia average	8%	6%	18%	6%	8%	5%
Share of servicification, 2017 (% services input to manufacturing value added)						
OECD average	21%	17%	4%	38%	15%	23%
Developing Asia average	18%	15%	4%	28%	10%	17%

OECD = Organisation for Economic Co-operation and Development.

Notes: Figures represent averages for all manufacturing sectors. Developing Asia excludes Japan.

Source: Authors' calculation based on the Asian Development Bank's Multiregional Input–Output Table 2017 (accessed 30 September 2018).

average. It is worth noting that, for OECD advanced economies, the contribution of domestic services has fallen precipitously since 2000, while the contribution of foreign services has soared.

We also examined "servification of services" and found that it is not as large as for manufacturing, although the variation across services sectors is huge. The most servified sectors are business services and financial services. A $1.00 increase in the demand for business services elicits a $1.70 increase in the value added of services in 2017 (this number is particularly high for OECD countries). This figure is $1.61 in the "wholesale trade and commission trade" sector. Financial services are also highly servified, although this phenomenon is limited to just a few countries (especially those with large offshore centers, and Bangladesh). Except for the PRC, servification of high-tech services is very low in developing Asia.

Business services tend to be a key player in the development of high-income economies, despite being barely traded internationally. Since the majority of services are not directly exported, but only contribute to the value of other exported goods, it is easy to undervalue their importance in the growth of manufacturing and an export-led development strategy. When high-tech manufacturing products are exported, this tends to stimulate business services, including legal and professional services. Indeed, the greater the direct and indirect linkages (servification) of business services in manufacturing value added, the more developed the economy is (Figure 5.11). This number is generally low for most of Asia except for Singapore and Hong Kong, China. Interestingly, both direct and indirect linkages increase quickly in the early stages of development. Indirect linkages are highly correlated with development, particularly for advanced economies (Figure 5.11, right panel).[10]

---

[10] There are some pointed examples of servification in developing countries as well. Mercer-Blackman, Foronda, and Mariasingham (2017) found that the subsector in Bangladesh with the highest linkages to the manufacturing of machinery is a services subsector: "sale, maintenance, and repair of motor vehicles." According to the statistics, these services are purely nontraded and make up less than 0.25% of gross value added. This reflects the informal but thriving vehicle repair shops in Bangladesh that allow vehicles that would have otherwise surpassed their useful life in 10 years in most countries to continue for 20 or more years through continued servicing.

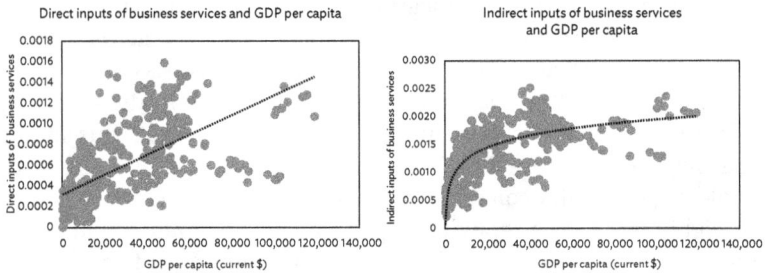

Figure 5.11 Impact of Services Sectors on Manufacturing and Business Services and Economic Development

GDP = gross domestic product, USD = United States dollar.

Source: Authors' calculations using the Asian Development Bank's Multiregional Input–Output Table 2017 (accessed 30 September 2018).

Taken together with the earlier evidence, the data seem to suggest that what is being couched as "premature deindustrialization" may simply be the process of splintering services from manufacturing, or servification. Contrary to interpretations by Rodrik (2016), this implies that the barometer for the speed of economic development may no longer be the increased share of employment in manufacturing, but instead the degree of links (servicification) between high-tech services such as business services and manufacturing value added.

Patterns of employment can shed some light on the underlying drivers of servitization. So far, we have looked at what could be considered arm's-length servicification that may happen as a result of splintering, but not in-house servitization. Splintering allows firms to specialize, which in turn raises their productivity. In manufacturing, this should manifest itself through a reallocation of labor from noncore activities to core production activities. We examine whether this has occurred in Asia by looking at changes in manufacturing occupations for five major emerging economies: India, Indonesia, the Philippines, Thailand, and Viet Nam. To do this, we use one-digit occupation codes from labor force surveys mapped to each of the manufacturing sectors in the MRIO.[11] To maximize

---

[11]   The one-digit International Standard Classification of Occupations breaks down occupations into the following broad groups: (1) armed forces occupations; (2) managers; (3) professionals; (4) technicians and associate professionals; (5) clerical support workers; (6) services and sales workers; (7) skilled agricultural, forestry, and fishery workers; (8) craft and related trades workers; (9) plant and machine operators and assemblers; and (10) elementary occupations.

the period covered, we use the earliest and latest available data for each of the five developing member countries.

Our analysis shows that the composition of occupations within manufacturing has changed significantly. Most of these changes have occurred in two occupation groups: craft and related trades workers, and plant and machine operators and assemblers (Figure 5.12). These two groups arguably account for the highest share of production workers when compared to other occupations. In Indonesia, employment in these two occupations increased by nearly 30 percentage points while the number of workers in elementary occupations decreased by a similar magnitude. In Thailand and Viet Nam, there was a notable decrease in craft and related trades workers, which was offset by a growth in the number of plant and machine operators and assemblers. However, the pattern is quite different for India and the Philippines, where the share of workers in managerial positions and elementary occupations grew (this increase was much less pronounced in India).

We find partial evidence of the role of splintering in these occupational changes, although further analysis is warranted

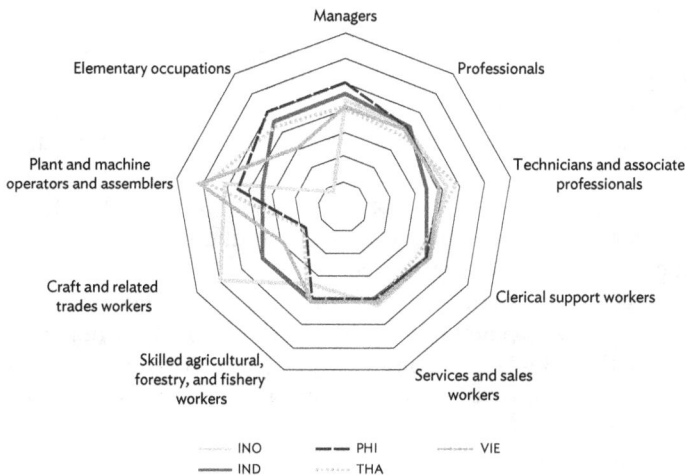

Figure 5.12 Change in Occupations within Manufacturing (in percentage points, earliest to latest year)

IND = India, INO = Indonesia, PHI = the Philippines, THA = Thailand, VIE = Viet Nam.
Note: IDN: 2000–2014; IND: 2000–2012; PHI: 2001–2013; THA: 2000–2010; VNM: 2007–2013.
Source: Authors' calculations based on country labor force surveys.

(Figure 5.13). Specifically, the higher the share of production workers in a country's sector, the more servicified the sector, meaning that manufacturing sectors with a higher share of production workers use more services as inputs.

5.4 Implications of Servicification for Productivity Measurements and Blueprints for a Proposal

5.4.1 Implications for Measurement

If there is servicification, how does that improve productivity? If it is the result of splintering where services previously produced in-house within firms are outsourced to become an arm's-length transaction, then servicification merely reflects the reclassification of an activity from the manufacturing to the services sector. Assuming there is no improvement in efficiency, measured productivity—if properly accounted for—will stay the same. What is not appropriately accounted for is the role of the underlying service in the transformation of the raw material into the manufactured good, because the service itself does not become "measurably" embodied in the physical manufactured good.

Alternatively, the growth of the product's value could arise from relative price changes. Where manufacturing activities are offshored to low-wage countries, their share of total value added decreases relative to services. We observe this in the data for advanced economies. At the same time, servicification can result from a real increase in the output of the sector, propelled by the rise of GVCs: as production becomes fragmented into geographically separate units, connecting services (such as telecommunications, transportation, or infrastructure services) become even more important. The changing nature of goods is another factor. The growing services content of manufactured goods implies that an increase in the demand for such products would also raise the demand for complementary services.

A new conceptualization of the future production model is required. A recent paper notes that "fully 28 of 29 other countries for which the OECD has compiled productivity growth data saw a deceleration in labor productivity growth over the last few decades. The unweighted average annual labor productivity growth rate across these countries was 2.3% from 1995 to 2004 but only 1.1% from 2005 to 2015" (Brynjolfsson, Rock, and Syverson 2017: 6). Although this is a robust result, the results come from the sole use of traditional measures of TFP using national accounts.

5.4.2 Measurement Issues: The Old and the New

The traditional Solow-based models characterize the aggregate production function as a function of in-house factors of production. Real value added at time t (denoted Y_t) is modelled as a function (g) of essentially two factors of production: labor hours worked (L) and the contribution of capital (K). Technology and innovation from year t to $t+1$ can be described by a scalar A with an exponent. This characterizes well the output of a manufacturing firm in the last century.

$$Y_t = A^t g\, (K_t, L_t) \tag{1}$$

This characterization is not accurate when the output is a modern service or automated manufacturing firm with outsourced services. The contribution of services and innovation to manufacturing productivity will be underestimated (Brynjolfsson, Rock, and Syverson 2017). In the Solow model, assuming capital and labor are measured appropriately, the unexplained growth portion is labeled *total factor productivity*, which captures the efficiency created through better use of existing factors, better management, institutions, and technology, for example. This made sense when conceived in the 1950s; "productive" activities typically showed people working with machines to transform inputs. However, it is an inadequate characterization of the production of a typical firm or production unit in 2018, as it leaves room neither for production fragmentation, offshoring, or process specialization, nor for the contribution of services to boosting manufacturing production. A better characterization of modern manufacturing is a node or web showing the contribution of different goods and services spread out geographically (in other words, a GVC). Consider instead the characterization of the production of, for example, the automobiles GVC:

$$Y^{AU} = V^{AU}\, \{f_1, f_2, f^*_3 ... f_n, L^{AU}, S_1, S_2, S_3 ... S_m\}, \tag{2}$$

where Y^{AU} is the production of automobiles, with inputs being a function of a series of production units that produce intermediate goods such as auto parts, each with its own production function: $f_1 .. f_i$ with $i = 1 .. n$ production units,[12] L^{AU} is in-house labor used in the production and/or assembly of automobiles, and S_j, $j = 1 ... m$ denotes the services inputs provided directly to the plant (such as energy, shipping, and

---

[12]   The * superscript denotes that the production unit is foreign.

quality control). In turn, $S_j = V^j(f_{j1}, f_{j2}..f_{jr}, L^j, s_{j1}, s_{j2}...s_{ju})$ would be a service produced by unit j, which uses as inputs other goods, L^j, and other services components. V^{AU} is the value added, which can be computed by combining—using factor costs as weights—the cost of f_i's, wages for labor L^{AU}, and some artificial aggregator unit (a regulated or "bundle" price) for services S_j. The combination or transformation function for autos V^{AU} could be a standard Cobb-Douglas form; for our purposes this is immaterial. In turn, each production unit will take form $f_i = V^i\{f_{i1}, f_{i2}, f_{i3}...f_{ip}, L^i s^*{}_{i1}, s^*{}_{i2}, s_{i3}...s_{iq}\}$. We can also denote f_{i1} in the traditional way:

$$f_i = V^i \equiv Ag(K^i, L^i) \tag{3}$$

Equation (3) characterizing production unit i looks very much like Equation (1). K^i, capital services, only denotes the services provided in-house. This means that the TFP incorporated in A also incorporates the productivity that should be attributed to outsourced services, but its value is biased upwards because Solow models erroneously attribute to it only improved efficiency. The traditional notation implies that the greater productivity emanates from inside the firm or production unit.

In contrast, each input in Equation (2) could come either from a separate unit of the same company (in-house provision), from a different entity, or from a foreign entity. The combination chosen minimizes costs over time for a given state of technology. In most cases, it minimizes costs through economies of scale, which are infinitely larger for services inputs. Another challenge is that, while it is possible to add up similar goods, it is not possible to add up services for the purposes of measuring productivity because they are infinitely divisible and have different values over time, which is why they must be bundled for easier pricing (see Box 5.1).

Using this new characterization, the distinction between a manufactured good and a service becomes more blurred. This gradual transformation of manufacturing production characterized as an evolution from a single production function of a firm in the 1950s (Stage 1), to the specialization of labor (Stage 2), to the splintering of production units (Stage 3) is illustrated in Figure 5.13. Y_M is the output of manufacturing, whereas Y_s is the output of services. In the past, manufacturing was more capital-intensive, and a simple measure of labor productivity would always yield a greater number in the manufacturing sector than in the service sector ($Y_M/L_M > Y_S/L_S$). Once the output of manufacturing is characterized as the result of a value chain of production units (Stage 3), it becomes less clear that output per worker is higher for manufacturing than for services, because the distinction is blurred.

The suggested setup divides inputs into *production units*, not a *good* or a *service*, as the distinction is increasingly irrelevant. The argument of whether we are talking about a good or a service becomes semantic for the purposes of measuring productivity, and the "products" will often be bundles of goods and services. For example, 20 years ago a disk jockey providing music services for a wedding would have brought a CD collection; now he or she may use an online music service to provide entertainment. Although the main input used has changed from a physical good (CD) to a service (e.g., Spotify), the output is the same: musical entertainment.

This leads to the understanding of activities as labor efforts within the production unit in time and space. Time use, through activity and technical competence, is still important. This entails classifying activities by degree of effort and valuing them according to difficulty or technical competence as already done for time use surveys (TUSs). Manufacturing or activities that transform physical goods (e.g., cooking, weaving, welding, building a car, and painting) can still be conceptually separated from service activities (e.g., waitressing, teaching, strategizing, planning, and designing); however, comparing their productivity will depend on context and time.

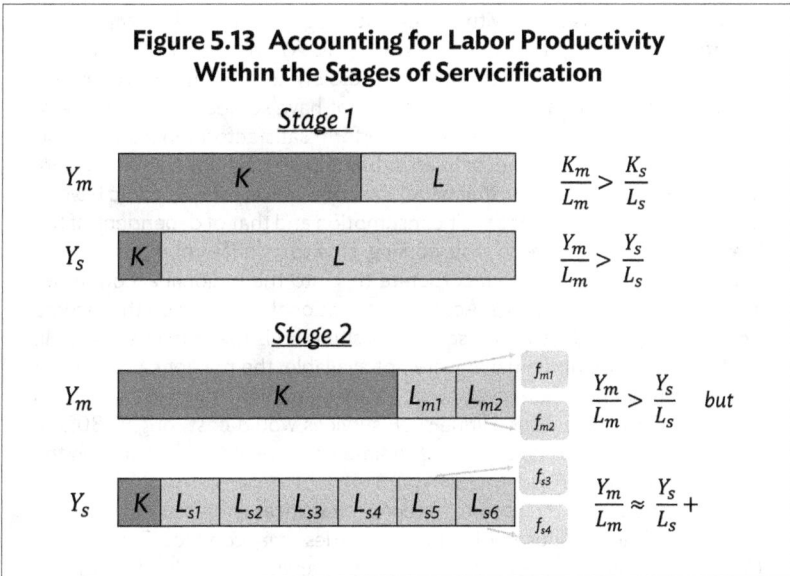

Figure 5.13 Accounting for Labor Productivity Within the Stages of Servicification

Stage 1

Y_m : K | L $\qquad \dfrac{K_m}{L_m} > \dfrac{K_s}{L_s}$

Y_s : K | L $\qquad \dfrac{Y_m}{L_m} > \dfrac{Y_s}{L_s}$

Stage 2

Y_m : K | L_{m1} | L_{m2} $\quad \begin{matrix} f_{m1} \\ f_{m2} \end{matrix} \quad \dfrac{Y_m}{L_m} > \dfrac{Y_s}{L_s}$ but

Y_s : K | L_{s1} | L_{s2} | L_{s3} | L_{s4} | L_{s5} | L_{s6} $\quad \begin{matrix} f_{s3} \\ f_{s4} \end{matrix} \quad \dfrac{Y_m}{L_m} \approx \dfrac{Y_s}{L_s} +$

continued on next page

Figure 5.13 *continued*

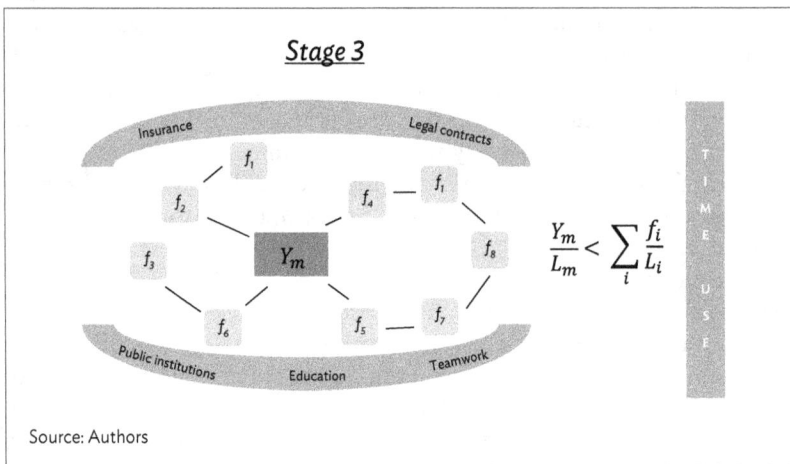

Source: Authors

Box 5.3 Measuring Time Use as a New Measurement Approach

Unpaid care could be characterized as a servitization relationship within the family and, like other services, it has been difficult to measure. Consider two adults in a household, with one earning wages in the market (Mr. Z) and the other performing unpaid home work (Ms. A). Mr. Z and Ms. A have a "servitization" relationship (in addition possibly to a marital relationship). Their work is codependent. If Mr. Z does not have someone to take care of and cook for dependents, he may not perform satisfactorily in his work and may have to work half-time, or in an extreme case may not be able to work outside the home. On the other hand, the homemaker, Ms. A, would have to find employment to finance their consumption and that of dependents if the breadwinner, Mr. Z, were to stop working. Due to its different measurement unit (time), it is difficult to incorporate this into the national accounts, let alone productivity measures. According to national accounts on the income side, the only "productive" person in this situation is the market earner, Mr. Z. However, if the homemaker were not available, the market earner would have to hire a child-care giver, cook, cleaner, and activity driver, as well as possibly a family manager. Hiring such services would cost roughly 30% of the total average income according to time use survey (TUS) results in the United States and United Kingdom.

Mainstreaming TUSs into national statistical systems has been a challenge. Only a subset of Asian countries has conducted full TUSs (Table B3.1). Since the purpose is generally to analyze household bargaining and gender roles, there is little appreciation of why countries should conduct

continued on next page

Box 5.3 *continued*

TUS on a regular basis. As an alternative, many countries have undertaken a modular approach by adding on TUS questions to other surveys such as a labor force survey. Typically, the use of these surveys for policy makers rarely goes beyond measures of gender inequality of nonmarket work. Based on high-quality surveys, the value of unpaid care work as a share of GDP varies from about 25% to 35% of gross domestic product, with the majority of the work being performed by women. The United States and United Kingdom have initiatives to include TUS in the national accounts on a more permanent basis, as the valuation of time use can be adjusted for different purposes. In Asia, Bhutan and the Republic of Korea have advanced the most on this front.

Table B3.1 Status of Time Use Surveys in Developing Asia and Some Advanced Economies

Status	Countries or Territories
Developed countries where a time use survey (TUS) is mainstreamed	Australia, Japan, New Zealand, Republic of Korea, United States (satellite account), United Kingdom
No TUS conducted	Afghanistan, Brunei Darussalam, Maldives, Marshall Islands, Myanmar, Palau, Singapore
Small TUS only	Indonesia, Fiji, Kiribati, Papua New Guinea, Samoa, Solomon Islands, Sri Lanka, Tuvalu, Vanuatu
Official pilot TUS only	Philippines
Only rural or urban TUS	Iran (Islamic Republic of)—only urban TUS
National modular TUS	Cambodia, Lao People's Democratic Republic, Nepal, Timor-Leste, Malaysia, Viet Nam, Cook Islands
National or large TUS using a time diary	Bangladesh, Bhutan, People's Republic of China, India, Mongolia, Pakistan, Thailand

Source: Hirway, I. 2016. Unpaid Work: An Obstacle to Gender Equality and Economic Empowerment including Women's Labour Force Participation. Chennai: Centre For Development Alternatives. http://www.unescap.org/sites/default/files/Session_2Ab_Unpaid_Work_and_Domestic_Care_Indira_Hirway.pdf (accessed 10 June 2018); and authors.

Measuring time use in the future will be the only way to gauge the level of productivity of individuals. As services become more prominent, time increases in value, many professionals' work weeks constantly exceed 40 hours, the distinction between "work" and "nonwork" becomes increasingly blurred, and the current measurement of labor productivity makes less sense. Fortunately, as survey tools have advanced, monitoring time use has become less intrusive (see University of Oxford, Centre for Time Use Research).

5.4.3 National Accounts Versus Time Use Surveys: An Example

In this section, we use an example to show how the mismeasurement of productivity of services has as much to do with servicification as it does with the concept of what constitutes "work." Most modern workers will perform a myriad of tasks in a given period, including community work and personal management tasks. One typical task could be the repair of a roof leak. How can the value of this service be accounted? How should that person's time spent repairing the roof be measured? Circumstances matter in traditional national accounting (although they should not). For example, to define a task performed (quantity), such as "fixing a roof leak measuring 20 centimeters x 20 centimeters," it is important to ask, how can this service be valued? For many activities, the best way to value it is to use the local market price (how much the community is willing to pay to get a task completed).

The appropriate valuation of the same function should be equal irrespective of context, although the context should be reported, as illustrated in the following example. Suppose person A spends 3 hours on Sunday afternoon fixing a leaky roof in his or her house at the behest of his or her spouse. Person B spends 3 hours fixing a neighbor's leak in the neighborhood, because he or she is good at it and is part of a church volunteer group helping elderly people with home repair. Person C works at a roofing company called "Roofs and More" (RM) and spends 3 hours fixing a leak. Each of these activities should have the same value or labor productivity (assuming they use the same technology and work with similar tools). The difference is purpose: Person A, based at home, performs unpaid work and thus loses 3 hours of leisure time; Person B may have received a small compensation from the church (say, a free pizza and a thank-you note from the neighborhood board of directors); while Person C will have received wage compensation from his or her company (denoted w_{RM}) for the job of fixing the roof.[13]

Using national accounts valuation, the marginal product of labor of Mr. C equals:

$$\frac{\Delta Y_C^{RM}}{\Delta L_C} \equiv w_{RM} > \frac{\Delta Y_B^{CH}}{\Delta L_B} > \frac{\Delta Y_A^{HH}}{\Delta L_A} = 0, \qquad (4)$$

---

[13] Here we are also abstracting from the recording of improvements to the housing capital stock, which is depreciation.

where Y^J_i measures the real output or activity in a unit of time performed by individual $i \in \{A,B,C\}$ in sector $j \in \{RM, CH, HH\}$. In the example, RM is the roofing manufacturing and installation sector, CH is the charity and community sector, and HH is the household sector. L_i is the labor of person i. Since the market wages of persons A and B are 0, Equation (1) erroneously ascribes their marginal productivity as zero too.

How will these tasks be classified in national accounts? If the roofing company also manufactures products (sector RM), the value of person C's labor will appear as part of the manufacturing sector. In the case of person B, their labor would be recorded as a community service (a "service"), which may incorrectly appear as a very small share of charitable income deflated by the consumer price index, and the cost of materials and pizza may be subtracted. Person B's work does not appear at all in national accounts if calculated on the income or expenditure side. In the case of person A's labor, it does not appear in the national accounts at all and the effort is considered "unproductive," even though Mr. A also became more "time poor" because he had to spend part of his day of rest and leisure—assuming he had a full-time job in the market on weekdays—performing an activity he did not enjoy.

According to Equation (4) above, manufacturing production is more productive than services if we use the national accounts methodology. Under the TUS methodology proposed, all activities have the same value because they required the same amount of effort and the same technology. If the sectors $j = \{CH, HH\}$ are in the services sectors, then twice the amount of value per worker was produced than in the manufacturing sector ($Y_{HH} + Y_{CH} > Y_{RM}$). Since $Y^{HH} = Y^{CH} = Y^{RM}$ and $L_A = L_B = L_C$ (assuming all persons use the same technology and the same amount of time), then the services sector should be more productive, as in Equation 5. There is no need to be concerned about premature deindustrialization-type arguments.

$$\frac{\Delta(Y_A^{HH} + Y_B^{CH})}{\Delta(L_A + L_B)} > \frac{\Delta Y_C^{RM}}{\Delta L_C} \cong w_{RM}, \qquad (5)$$

There are many reasons why the labor productivity of an activity is better measured by TUSs than by national accounts. This does not mean we should do away with national accounts, as these are still the most useful gross accounting framework. What does need to be considered in the digital age and an era of increasing servicification is the use of TUSs to measure real labor productivity. This would have the additional challenge or requirement to measure, say, artificial intelligence capital and other factors (see Brynjolfsson, Rock, and Syverson [2017] for some ideas). TUSs enable different valuations of activities, depending on the values given by society.[14] This valuation can be decided by citizens and governments using the same methods used to value public goods, such as the value of a walk in the neighborhood park, of breathing fresh air, or of leading a healthy life.

5.5 Conclusions

The premature deindustrialization hypothesis is based on the assumption that there is something inherently "special" about the organization of manufacturing production activities that neither agriculture nor services possess, making labor there more productive. The arguments presented and preliminary evidence using recent data suggest otherwise. Part of the problem is that services are being measured and valued using the same tools we use to measure tangible manufactured goods.

This chapter argues that services are fundamentally very different from goods in character, but are traditionally measured in the same way. Due to their indivisibility and heterogeneity, among other characteristics, services are priced in a very different way (usually bundled as packages or as an extension to the manufacturing output's value). Consequently, labor productivity in each sector is also mismeasured. Moreover, many services are integrated and intertwined with the production of goods, which is why they have a symbiotic relationship in production (a term we define as "subordinate servicification"). However, only goods are visible and tangible. As a result, the contribution of services to economic growth may be underestimated. We show evidence of the extent of servicification in Asia and globally, defined as increasing in-house production of services by firms classified as manufacturing firms, as well as outsourcing to services firms both domestically and abroad. While servicification is large and growing in Asia, it is still much more prevalent outside of Asia, particularly in advanced economies. Finally, we explain why national accounting is not able to capture properly the productivity derived from services. Although these measurement issues have been known for some time, they were considered small in size and thus not problematic. However, with the introduction of disruptive technologies in all spheres of life this measurement bias is likely to grow.

---

[14] As with national accounts, measuring time use does not necessarily say anything about the utility derived from the activity. In the above example, person A derives disutility from fixing the roof despite his appreciating the urgency of the work.

Policy makers and statistical offices need to adopt alternative measures of labor productivity sooner rather than later. The only method that could be expanded and institutionalized by countries to capture some of these changes—particularly in services—is the use of TUSs over distinct activities or production units. TUSs also have the advantage of measuring disparities in workloads of different factions of the population (given the value of time), while providing an opportunity to value activities in more useful ways—something that market prices cannot do properly in the age of servicification.

References

Ahamed, Z., T. Inohara, and A. Kamoshida. 2013. The Servitization of Manufacturing: An Empirical Case Study of IBM Corporation. *International Journal of Business Administration* 4(2): 18–26.

Andersen, B., and M. Corley. 2003. The Theoretical, Conceptual and Empirical Impact of the Service Economy (Vol. UNU-WIDER Discussion Paper No. 2003/22). Helsinki: United Nations University World Institute for Development Economics Research.

Arnold, J. M., B. Javorcik, M. Lipscomb, and A. Mattoo. 2016. Services Reform and Manufacturing Performance: Evidence from India. *Economic Journal* 126(590): 1–39. doi:10.1111/ecoj.12206

Asian Development Bank (ADB). 2015. Global Value Chains Indicators for International Production Sharing. In *Key Indicators for Asia and the Pacific, 2015, September*. Manila: ADB.

ADB. 2018a. *Asian Development Outlook: Technology and Jobs in Asia, April*. Manila: ADB.

ADB. 2018b. *Key Indicators of Asia and the Pacific,* 49th edition. Manila: ADB.

Baldwin, R., R. Forslid, and T. Ito. 2015. Unveiling the Evolving Sources of Value Added in Exports. Institute of Developing Economies, Japan External Trade Organization Joint Research Program Series 161. Chiba: Institute of Developing Economies, Japan External Trade Organization.

Baldwin, R., T. Ito, and H. Sato. 2014. *Portrait of Factory Asia: Production Network in Asia and its Implication for Growth—The "Smile Curve."* Institute of Developing Economies, Japan External Trade Organization Joint Research Program Series 159. Chiba: Institute of Developing Economies, Japan External Trade Organization.

Baumol, W. J. 1967. Macroeconomics of Unbalanced Growth: The Anatomy of Urban Crisis. *American Economic Review* 57(3): 415–426.

Baumol, W. J. 1985. Managing the Service Economy: Prospects and Problems. In R. P. Inman (ed), *Managing the Service Economy: Prospects and Problems*, New York: Cambridge University Press.

Bernard, A., V. Smeets, and F. Warzynski. 2017. Rethinking Deindustrialization. *Economic Policy* 32(89): 5–38. https://doi.org/10.1093/epolic/eiw016

Benedettini, O., B. Clegg, M. Kafouros, and A. Neely. 2009. Guest Editorial: The Myths of Manufacturing. *Operations Management Research* 2: 28–32. doi:10.1007/s12063-009-0023-5

Brynjolfsson, E., D. Rock, and C. Syverson. 2017. Artificial Intelligence and the Modern Productivity Paradox: A Clash of Expectations and

Statistics. National Bureau of Economic Research (NBER) Working Paper 24001, November. Cambridge, MA: NBER.

Chen, L., J. Felipe, A. Kam, and A. Mehta. 2018. Is Employment Globalizing? ADB Economics Working Paper 556. Manila: ADB.

Crozet, M., and E. Milet. 2017. Should Everybody Be in Services? The Effect of Servitization on Manufacturing Firm Performance. *Journal of Economics and Management Strategy* 26(4): 820–841. doi:10.1111/jems.12211

Cruz, M., and G. Nayyar. 2017. Manufacturing and Development: What Has Changed? Unpublished manuscript. Washington, DC: World Bank.

Cusumano, M. A., S. J. Kahl, and F. F. Suarez. 2015. Services, Industry Evolution, and the Competitive Strategies of Product Firms. *Strategic Management Journal* 36(4): 559–575. doi:10.1002/smj.2235

Eichengreen, B., and P. Gupta. 2011. The Two Waves of Service-Sector Growth. *Oxford Economic Papers* 65(1): 96–123. doi:10.1093/oep/gpr059

The Economist. 2012. The Unsung Masters of the Oil Industry. July 21. http://www.economist.com/node/21559358 (accessed 28 March 2019).

Federico, S., and E. Tosti. 2017. Exporters and Importers of Services: Firm-Level Evidence on Italy. *World Economy* 40(10): 2078–2096. doi:10.1111/twec.12462

Felipe, J., and A. Mehta. 2016. Deindustrialization? A Global Perspective. *Economics Letters* 149(C): 148–151. doi:10.1016/j.econlet.2016.10.038

Francois, J. 1990. Producer Services, Scale, and the Division of Labor. *Oxford Economic Papers* 42(4): 715. doi:10.1093/oxfordjournals.oep.a041973

Gereffi, G., and K. Fernandez-Stark. 2010. The Offshore Services Value Chain: Developing Countries and the Crisis. Policy Research Working Paper 5262. Washington, DC: World Bank.

Hallward-Driemeier, M., and G. Nayyar. 2018. *Trouble in the Making? The Future of Manufacturing-Led Development*. Washington, DC: World Bank.

Heuser, C., and A. Mattoo. 2017. Services Trade and Global Value Chains. In *Measuring and Analyzing the Impact of GVCs on Economic Development*, edited by World Bank, Institute of Developing Economies Japan External Trade Organization, Organisation for Economic Co-operation and Development (OECD), University of International Business and Economics, and World Trade Organization. Washington, DC: World Bank.

Hill, T. P. 1977. On Goods and Services. *Review of Income and Wealth* 23(4): 315–338. doi:10.1111/j.1475-4991.1977.tb00021.x

Hirway, I. 2016. Unpaid Work: An Obstacle to Gender Equality and Economic Empowerment including Women's Labour Force Participation. Chennai: Centre For Development Alternatives. http://www.unescap.org/sites/default/ files/Session_2Ab_Unpaid _Work_and_Domestic_Care_Indira_Hirway.pdf (accessed 19 April 2019).

Hoekman, B., and A. Mattoo. 2008. Services Trade and Growth. Policy Research Working Paper 4461. Washington, DC: World Bank.

International Monetary Fund (IMF). 2018a. Manufacturing Jobs: Implications for Productivity and Inequality. *World Economic Outlook*. pp.129–171. Washington, DC: IMF.

IMF. 2018b. Measuring the Digital Economy, a Report by the Staff of the IMF. February 28. Washington, DC: IMF.

Kelle, M. 2013. Crossing Industry Borders: German Manufacturers as Services Exporters. *World Economy* 36(12): 1494–1515. doi:10.1111 /twec.12111

Lanz, R., and A. Maurer. 2015. Services and Global Value Chains: Servicification of Manufacturing and Services Networks. *Journal of International Commerce, Economics, and Policy* 6(03). doi:10.1142 /S1793993315500143

Lodefalk, M. 2010. Servicification of Manufacturing—Evidence from Swedish Firm and Enterprise Group Level Data. Swedish Business School Working Paper 3/2010. Orebro: Orebro University.

Low, P. 2013. Changing Features of Global Value Chains: The Role of Services. In *Global Value Chains in a Changing World*, edited D. K. Elms and P. Low. Geneva: World Trade Organization.

Mercer-Blackman, V., A. Foronda, and J. Mariasingham. 2017. Using Input–Output Analysis Framework to Explain Economic Diversification and Structural Transformation in Bangladesh. ADB Economics Working Paper 513. Manila: ADB.

Miroudot, S. 2016. Services in Global Value Chains: From Inputs to Value-Creating Activities. OECD Trade Policy Paper. Paris: OECD.

Miroudot, S., and C. Cadestin. 2017. Services in Global Value Chains: From Inputs to Value-Creating Activities. OECD Trade Policy Paper 197. Paris: OECD Publishing.

Montresor, S., and G. Vittucci Marzetti. 2011. The Deindustrialisation/ Tertiarisation Hypothesis Reconsidered: A Subsystem Application to the OECD7. *Cambridge Journal of Economics* 35(2): 401–421. doi:10.1093/cje/beq009

Moulton, B., and P. van de Ven. 2018. Addressing the Challenges of Globalization in National Accounts. NBER Conference. http://papers.nber.org/conf_papers/f100570/f100570.pdf (accessed 5 June 2018).

Nayyar, G. 2010. Growth of the Services Sector in India: Notional or Real? *Economics Bulletin* 30(4): 3282–3287.

Noland, M., D. Park, and G. E. B. Estrada. 2013. Developing the Service Sector as Engine of Growth for Asia: An Overview. In *Developing the Service Sector as Engine of Growth for Asia*, edited by M. Noland and D. Park. Manila: ADB.

OECD. 2000. *The Service Economy*: Paris: OECD Publishing.

OECD. 2001. *Measuring Productivity: OECD Manual*. Paris: OECD Publishing.

OECD. 2018. *Trade in Value Added*. Paris: OECD Publishing. http://www.oecd.org/sti/ind/measuringtradeinvalue-addedanoecd-wtojointinitiative.htm (accessed 15 June 2018).

OECD and World Trade Organization. 2012. *Trade in Value-Added: Concepts, Methodologies and Challenges*. Paris: OECD.

Petit, P. 1986. Services: Problem or Solution. In *Slow Growth and the Service Economy*, edited by P. Petit. London: Pinter.

Rajan, R., and L. Zingales. 1998. Financial Dependence and Growth. *American Economic Review* 88(3): 559–586. doi:10.2307/116849

Rodrik, D. 2016. Premature Deindustrialization. *Journal of Economic Growth* 21(1): 1–33. doi:10.1007/s10887-015-9122-3

Swedish National Board of Trade. 2016. *The Servicification of EU Manufacturing, Building Competitiveness in the Internal Market, National Board of Trade Sweden, October.* https://www.kommers.se/Documents/dokumentarkiv/publikationer/2016/Publ-the-servicification-of-eu-manufacturing_webb.pdf (accessed 10 November 2018).

University of Oxford, Centre for Time Use Research. https://www.timeuse.org/ (accessed 19 April 2019).

Vandermerwe, S., and J. Rada. 1988. Servitization of Business: Adding Value by Adding Services. *European Management Journal* 6(4): 314–324. doi:10.1016/0263-2373(88)90033-3

Walter, P., and R. Dell'mour. 2010. Firm Level Analysis of International Trade in Services. International Finance Corporation Working Paper 4. Basel: Bank for International Settlements.

World Bank. 2009. *The Service Revolution in South Asia*. Washington, DC: World Bank.

World Bank. 2010. World Development Indicators. http://datatopics.worldbank.org/world-development-indicators/ (accessed 15 May 2018).

World Bank. 2016. *World Development Report 2016: Digital Dividends*. Washington, DC: World Bank.

Appendix

Table: Breakdown of Multiregional Input–Output Sectors

Code	Sector	Classification
1	Agriculture, forestry, fishery	Agriculture and natural resources
2	Mining and quarrying	Agriculture and natural resources
3	Food, beverages, and tobacco	Manufacturing
4	Textiles and textile products	Manufacturing
5	Leather, leather products, and footwear	Manufacturing
6	Wood and products of wood and cork	Manufacturing
7	Pulp, paper, printing, and publishing	Manufacturing
8	Coke, refined petroleum, and nuclear fuel	Manufacturing
9	Chemicals and chemical products	Manufacturing
10	Rubber and plastics	Manufacturing
11	Other nonmetallic mineral	Manufacturing
12	Basic metals and fabricated metal	Manufacturing
13	Machinery, not classified elsewhere	Manufacturing
14	Electrical and optical equipment	Manufacturing
15	Transport equipment	Manufacturing
16	Manufacturing not classified elsewhere; recycling	Manufacturing
17	Electricity, gas, and water supply	Industry
18	Construction	Industry
19	Sale, maintenance and repair of motor vehicles and motorcycles; retail sale of fuel	Services
20	Wholesale trade and commission trade except for motor vehicles and motorcycles	Services
21	Retail trade except for motor vehicles and motorcycles; repair of household goods	Services
22	Hotels and restaurants	Services
23	Inland transport	Services
24	Water transport	Services
25	Air transport	Services
26	Other supporting and auxiliary transport activities; activities of travel agencies	Services
27	Post and telecommunications	Services

continued on next page

Table *continued*

Code	Sector	Classification
28	Financial intermediation	Services
29	Real estate activities	Services
30	Renting of machinery and equipment and other business activities	Services
31	Public administration and defense; compulsory social security	Services
32	Education	Services
33	Health and social work	Services
34	Other community, social, and personal services	Services
35	Private households with employed persons	Services

Source: United Nations, Department of Economic and Social Affairs (2002), International Standard Industrial Classification of all Economic Activities, Revision 3.1. New York, United Nations. https://unstats.un.org/unsd/publication/seriesm/seriesm_4rev3_1e.pdf (accessed 19 April 2019).

6

Services Policies and Manufacturing Exports

Ben Shepherd

6.1 Introduction

Services and manufacturing are closely intertwined, as manufacturers use services as inputs into their production process. It is difficult to imagine a modern global value chain working without efficient transport services, financial services, logistics, and business services. The Organisation for Economic Co-operation and Development (OECD)-World Trade Organization (WTO) Trade in Value Added (TiVA) dataset gives us a first indication of just how important services are for exporters of manufactured goods. Focusing on Asia, we see that, since the 1990s, the proportion of services value added in gross exports of manufactured goods has averaged just under 33% in the Asia-Pacific Economic Cooperation, Association of Southeast Asian Nations, and the East Asian economies. Interestingly, though, the split between domestic- and foreign-origin services value added has changed significantly. Figure 6.1 shows that domestic-origin services value added declines in all three subregions from 1995 to 2011. However, as the constant total share of services implies, Figure 6.2 shows that the foreign-origin share increased. The 1990s and 2000s saw substantial liberalization of services markets all around the world, including in Asia. Indeed, the People's Republic of China's 2001 WTO Accession Agreement was associated with real and meaningful changes in policy that significantly opened key services markets to international competition (Mattoo 2003).

What does this dynamic mean for policy? Clearly, manufacturers need access to high-quality, competitively priced services. In the context of developing countries in particular, this necessarily involves some recourse to world markets. Indeed, we can see that reliance on world services markets by manufacturers has generally been increasing over time. This dynamic suggests intuitively that services policies can have direct and indirect effects on the performance of manufacturers, including in terms of export market gains. First, and best known, there is an indirect effect: opening up services markets to foreign competition by lowering trade costs increases competitive pressure and favors the reallocation of resources from less productive firms to more productive ones, and sectoral productivity in services sectors increases as a result (Miroudot, Sauvage, and Shepherd 2012). Hoekman and Shepherd (2017) have shown that this dynamic operates at the level of individual firms: since many services are supplied locally, there is evidence of a productivity linkage between manufactured goods exporters and services suppliers in the same locality, which in turn fosters greater trade integration through the standard productivity self-selection channel as in Melitz (2003).

Less well-known is the prospect that services policies could have a direct impact on exporters of manufactured goods. The mechanism is simple: as shown in Figure 6.1, manufacturers source a substantial proportion of their total services inputs from world markets. As a result, the liberalization of trade policies that increase trade costs allows manufacturers to acquire those services at a lower price, which acts like a productivity shock, and promotes export market success in the same way as the indirect effect referred to in the previous paragraph.

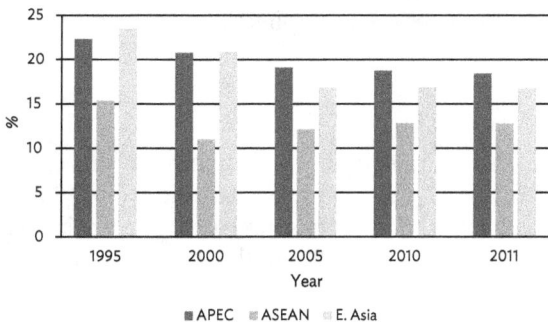

Figure 6.1 Domestic Services Value Added Embodied in Manufacturing Exports, by Region, 1995–2011, Percent of Gross Exports

APEC = Asia-Pacific Economic Cooperation, ASEAN = Association of Southeast Asian Nations, E. Asia = East Asia.

Source: Organisation for Economic Co-operation and Development-World Trade Organization Trade in Value Added database. https://stats.oecd.org/index.aspx?queryid=75537 (accessed 1 April 2019).

Hoekman and Shepherd (2017) again provide evidence suggesting such an effect using a gravity model, but this is little explored in the literature.

Against this background, this chapter adds to the literature in two main ways. First, we take account of recent developments in the gravity model literature to improve on the estimation framework used by Hoekman and Shepherd (2017). Like them, we introduce a measure of services policies directly into a gravity model of manufactured goods trade. We also examine the relationship of this measure to tariffs and take account of domestic (intra-national) trade flows. Second, we take advantage of recently uncovered properties of the Poisson Pseudo-Maximum Likelihood (PPML) estimator to conduct policy-relevant counterfactual simulations that are fully consistent with the constraints imposed by theory. We separately consider 10% reductions in applied tariffs and the restrictiveness of services policies. In summary, we find that the trade and real output effects of the latter are significantly larger than the former. This is a striking result. The liberalization of services policies typically produces larger welfare effects than tariff liberalization in computable general equilibrium models, but not for the reason we examine here, namely the way in which it changes the ability of manufacturers to acquire services at world market prices. From a policy standpoint, this finding is particularly important in regions like developing Asia, where there is skepticism of the growth potential of services. An additional reason for moving forward on reforming services sectors is that such action can promote growth in manufacturing, which is an objective of all economies in the region.

The chapter proceeds as follows. The next section discusses data and sources. Section 6.3 presents our econometric model and discusses the simulation methodology. Section 6.4 presents results. Section 6.5 concludes and discusses policy implications.

6.2 Data

Table 6.1 presents a summary of the data used in this chapter. Sources are standard for gravity control variables, and we use Larch's regional trade agreement (RTA) dataset to source a dummy variable equal to one when both countries are members of the same trade agreement (Egger and Larch 2008).

Table 6.1 Data and Sources

Variable	Definition	Years	Source
Colony	Dummy variable equal to one for country pairs that were ever in a colonial relationship	N/A	CEPII
Common border	Dummy variable equal to one for countries that share a common land border	N/A	CEPII
Common colonizer	Dummy variable equal to one for country pairs that were colonized by the same power	N/A	CEPII
Common language	Dummy variable equal to one for countries that have a common official language	N/A	CEPII
Exports	Total manufacturing exports from country i to country j in time period t	2010	OECD-WTO TiVA
International	Dummy variable equal to one if country i and country j are not the same		
Log(distance)	Distance between country i and country j	N/A	CEPII
Log(STRI)	Overall and sectoral Services Trade Restrictiveness Index	2010	World Bank
Log(1+tariff)	Simple average effectively applied tariff on manufactured goods imports	2010	TRAINS

CEPII = Centre d'Études Prospectives et d'Informations Internationales, N/A = not applicable, OECD = Organisation for Economic Co-operation and Development, TiVA = Trade in Value Added, TRAINS = Trade Analysis Information System, WTO = World Trade Organization.
Source: Author.

Table 6.2 Summary Statistics

Variable	Observations	Mean	Std. Dev.	Min.	Max.
Colony	2,898	0.03	0.17	0.00	1.00
Common border	2,898	0.04	0.19	0.00	1.00
Common colonizer	2,898	0.01	0.10	0.00	1.00
Common language	2,898	0.07	0.26	0.00	1.00
Exports	2,898	11.74	189.23	0.00	8,537.31
International	2,898	0.98	0.13	0.00	1.00
Log(distance)	2,898	1.60	1.07	-2.82	2.99
Log(STRI)	2,898	3.14	0.44	2.40	4.19
Log(tariff)	2,805	0.05	0.05	0.00	0.30

Max. = maximum, Min. = minimum, Std. Dev. = standard deviation, STRI = Services Trade Restrictiveness Index.
Source: .Author.

Table 6.3 Correlation Matrix

	Colony	Common border	Common colonizer	Common language	Exports
Colony	1.00				
Common border	0.18	1.00			
Common colonizer	-0.02	0.08	1.00		
Common language	0.29	0.16	0.10	1.00	
Exports	-0.01	0.00	-0.01	-0.01	1.00
International	0.02	0.03	0.01	0.04	-0.38
Log(distance)	-0.08	-0.36	-0.04	-0.04	-0.11
Log(STRI)	-0.05	-0.03	0.12	0.01	0.02
Log(tariff)	-0.02	-0.11	0.09	-0.01	-0.05

	International	Log(Dist)	Log(STRI)	Log(Tariff)
Colony				
Common border				
Common colonizer				
Common language				
Exports				
International	1.00			
Log(distance)	0.35	1.00		
Log(STRI)	0.00	0.15	1.00	
Log(tariff)	0.13	0.37	0.39	1.00

STRI = Services Trade Restrictiveness Index.
Source: Author.

The standard source for trade data is United Nations Comtrade. However, it does not include data on self-trade, that is, goods and services that are produced and consumed within the same country. Yotov et al. (2017) show that such data should ideally be included in gravity models, which rely for their theoretical basis on summing exports across all destinations—including the home country—to produce aggregates like total output and expenditure. We therefore use the OECD-WTO TiVA dataset, which has balanced gross trade data by International Standard Industrial Classification sector, along with gross production data at the same level of disaggregation. By subtracting world exports from total production, we can obtain a measure of self-trade (for intermediate and final goods, we work directly with the input–output tables to obtain the required figures). It should be emphasized that we work with trade and production data in gross, not value added, terms. Although using trade data in value added terms would be an interesting extension for our work, the theoretical foundation does not lend itself as easily to modeling in a gravity framework, and in particular to the same combined approach to estimation and simulation that we use here (see Noguera 2012, for an attempt to embed value-added trade in gravity logic).

The TiVA data are available for 63 exporting and importing economies, which account for over 90% of world gross domestic product. Although the data focus on OECD countries, they also include developing economies from all regions, and as such can be informative about bilateral trade patterns beyond the developed world, and between developed and developing regions. As far as coverage of Asian economies is concerned, the OECD dataset covers 20 of the 21 APEC economies (all except Papua New Guinea), and 8 of the 10 ASEAN countries (missing only Myanmar and the Lao People's Democratic Republic. It also includes partner countries, such as all European Union members, the United States, and Canada.

For our empirical analysis, we use data on exports of manufactured goods (International Standard Industrial Classification sectors 15–37). We start with a balanced panel of 63 exporters and importers in each sector aggregate for the year 2010. The number of observations falls as we introduce policy data. We draw data on effectively applied tariffs from the Trade Analysis Information System. Our source for services policies is the World Bank's Services Trade Restrictiveness Index (STRI). The STRI aims to capture policy measures that discriminate against foreign service providers, and is constant across all exporters. We therefore interact it with a dummy variable equal to one for international (as opposed to intra-national) trade in the way that Yotov et al. (2017) recommend for policy measures that are constant at the importer level.

6.3 Econometric Model

Theory-consistent gravity models are well known in the trade literature. Anderson, Larch, and Yotov (2018) developed a simple method for conducting theory-consistent policy simulations using the familiar structural gravity model derived from constant elasticity of substitution preferences across countries for national varieties differentiated by origin (the Armington assumption). The model takes the following form:

$$X_{ij} = \left(\frac{t_{ij}}{\Pi_i P_j}\right)^{1-\sigma} Y_i E_j \qquad (1)$$

$$P_j^{1-\sigma} = \sum_i \left(\frac{t_{ij}}{\Pi_i}\right)^{1-\sigma} Y_i \qquad (2)$$

$$\Pi_i^{1-\sigma} = \sum_j \left(\frac{t_{ij}}{P_j}\right)^{1-\sigma} E_j \qquad (3)$$

$$p_j = \frac{Y_j^{\frac{1}{1-\sigma}}}{\gamma_j \Pi_j} \qquad (4)$$

where X is exports in value terms from country i to country j; E is expenditure in country j; Y is production in country i; t captures bilateral trade costs; σ is the elasticity of substitution across varieties; P is inward multilateral resistance, which captures the dependence of bilateral shipments into j on trade costs across all inward routes; Π is outward multilateral resistance, which captures the dependence of bilateral shipments out of i on trade costs across all outward routes; p is the exporter's supply price of country i; and γ is a positive distribution parameter of the constant elasticity of substitution function.

Most commonly, the model represented by (1) through (4) is estimated by fixed effects, which collapses it into the following empirical setup:

$$X_{ij} = exp\left(T_{ij}\beta + \pi_i + \chi_j\right)e_{ij} \qquad (5)$$

where T is a vector of observables capturing different elements of trade costs; π is a set of exporter fixed effects; χ is a set of importer fixed effects; and e is a standard error term.

The model has a number of salient features, which are well known but deserve restating. First, its structure makes clear that the elasticity of trade with respect to particular bilateral trade costs—such as membership in an RTA—specified within t is not an accurate summary of the impact of a change of trade costs on trade. The reason is that the multilateral resistance indices depend on trade costs across all partners, meaning that the model takes account of general equilibrium effects. This point is typically recognized at the estimation stage, when fixed effects by exporter and by importer are included to account for multilateral resistance. However, when a counterfactual simulation is conducted, the effects need to be passed through the two price indices, not simply extracted from the relevant regression coefficient. This point is much less commonly appreciated in the literature.

Second, if the model is estimated by PPML with fixed effects as recommended by Santos Silva, and Tenreyro (2006), then Fally (2015) shows that the estimated fixed effects correspond exactly to the terms required by the structural model. In other words, if (5) is estimated correctly, then it follows that:

$$\widehat{\Pi_i^{1-\sigma}} = E_0 Y_i \exp(-\pi_i) \tag{6}$$

$$\widehat{P_j^{1-\sigma}} = \frac{E_j}{E_0} \exp(-\pi_i) \tag{7}$$

where E_0 corresponds to the expenditure of the country corresponding to the omitted fixed effect (typically an importer fixed effect) in the empirical model, and the normalization of the corresponding price terms in the structural model.

Let $\hat{\beta}$ be the PPML estimates of the trade cost parameters in (5). To see the impact of a counterfactual change in trade costs, such as the elimination of an RTA between two trading partners, we can re-estimate (5) imposing $\hat{\beta}$ as a constraint and with counterfactual trade costs T_{ij}^c:

$$X_{ij} = exp\left(T_{ij}^c \hat{\beta} + \pi_i + \chi_j\right) e_{ij} \tag{8}$$

Estimating (8) with PPML and the original trade data means that output and expenditure remain constant, so the PPML fixed effects adjust to take account of changes in multilateral resistance brought about by the change in bilateral trade costs. Once estimates have been obtained, counterfactual values of relevant indices can be calculated; however, these are conditional on fixed output and expenditure although they take account of general equilibrium reallocations. In particular, $\widehat{X_{ij}}$ from (8) provides counterfactual values of bilateral trade that are consistent with the general equilibrium restrictions of theory, but which still sum to give observed output and expenditure, consistent with a remarkable property of the PPML estimator (Arvis and Shepherd 2013; Fally 2015).

It is possible to push the model further, by allowing counterfactual changes in factory-gate prices to drive changes in output and expenditure, which in turn lead to additional changes in trade flows, until the system converges. Specifically, endogenous responses in output and expenditure are as follows in an endowment economy where trade imbalance ratios $\phi_i = E_i/Y_i$ remain constant:

$$Y_i^c = \left(\frac{p_i^c}{p_i}\right) Y_i \qquad (9)$$

$$E_i^c = \left(\frac{p_i^c}{p_i}\right) E_i \qquad (10)$$

Anderson, Larch, and Yotov (2018) propose an iterative approach to solving the system. First, use structural gravity to translate changes in output and expenditure into changes in trade flows:

$$X_{ij}^c = \frac{\left(t_{ij}^{1-\sigma}\right)^c}{t_{ij}^{1-\sigma}} \frac{Y_i^c E_j^c}{Y_i E_j} \frac{\Pi_i^{1-\sigma} P_j^{1-\sigma}}{\left(\Pi_i^{1-\sigma}\right)^c \left(P_j^{1-\sigma}\right)^c} \qquad (11)$$

where superscript c indicates counterfactual values obtained from constrained estimation of (8) and calculation of relevant indices. Counterfactual values of output and expenditures come from applying market-clearing conditions $p_i = \left(\frac{Y_i}{Y}\right)^{1/1-\sigma} \frac{1}{\gamma_i \Pi_i}$, making it possible to translate changes in the fixed effects between (8) and (5) into first-order changes in factor-gate prices:

$$\frac{p_i^c}{p_i} = \frac{exp(\widehat{\pi_i^c})}{exp(\widehat{\pi_i})} \qquad (12)$$

Further changes occur in a second-order sense, as changes in prices lead to further changes in output and expenditure, which in turn drive changes in trade. By iterating the PPML estimation and calculation of changes until convergence, it is possible to obtain full-endowment general equilibrium estimates of trade flows and relevant indices.

To summarize, Anderson, Larch, and Yotov (2018) show that starting with the standard structural gravity model, it is possible to design a simple approach for first estimating the model's parameters, and then using the estimated parameters to perform counterfactual simulations in a way that is fully consistent with the general equilibrium implications of gravity theory. The methodology can be broken down as follows:

(i) Estimate the model using PPML and fixed effects to obtain estimates of trade costs and trade elasticities for the baseline.

(ii) Solve the gravity system using the output from step (i) to provide baseline values of all indices.

(iii) Define a counterfactual scenario in terms of an observable trade cost variable.

(iv) Solve the counterfactual model in conditional general equilibrium, that is, direct and indirect changes in trade flows at constant output and expenditure.

(v) Solve the counterfactual model in full general equilibrium, that is, direct and indirect changes in trade flows with endogenous output and expenditure driven by trade-induced changes in factory-gate prices.

Yotov et al. (2017) provide a detailed explanation of the above steps, as well as Stata code for implementing them in a general setting. We adopt their approach and freely adapt their code here. Concretely, we use PPML to estimate (8) for 2010. This setup allows us to introduce importer and exporter fixed effects to account for multilateral resistance, expenditure, and output. We specify the trade costs function as follows:

$$T_{ij}\beta = \beta_0 Policy_{ij} + \beta_1 \ln dist_{ij} + \beta_2 contig_{ij}$$
$$+ \beta_3 colony_{ij} + \beta_4 comcol_{ij}$$
$$+ \beta_5 comlang_{ij} + \beta_6 intl_{ij}$$

The policy variable is either effectively applied tariffs or the STRI. The coefficient of primary interest is , which gives the elasticity of bilateral trade flows with respect to changes in policy. Ideally, we would estimate the model over multiple years to attenuate simultaneity bias and control for country-pair unobservables, but the STRI is currently only available for a single year, 2010.

Once we have isolated from the regression, we again use data for 2010 to conduct the counterfactual simulations. We impose the estimated coefficients from the first stage as constraints, then proceed as in Anderson, Larch, and Yotov (2018) to obtain counterfactual estimates of trade and real output effects.

6.4 Results

This section presents the results of our analysis. We first discuss our econometric results and then move to a consideration of the trade and real output effects of the liberalization of goods and services policies through our counterfactual simulations.

6.4.1 Estimation Results

Table 6.4 presents the estimation results. Each column uses a different STRI, moving from the overall measure in Column 1 to the sectoral STRIs in the other columns. We enter the sectoral STRIs in separate regressions, rather than all at once, because they are strongly correlated, as would be expected; thus, regression performance is poor due to inflated standard errors.

Table 6.4 Estimation Results

	Overall	Banking	Insurance	Professional	Retail	Telecom	Transport
Log(STRI)	-0.017 ***	-0.017 ***	-0.014 ***	0.003	-0.010 **	-0.006 **	-0.007
	(0.005)	(0.004)	(0.005)	(0.005)	(0.004)	(0.003)	(0.005)
Log(tariff)	-1.972	-0.482	-1.515	-3.594 **	-2.707 **	-2.243 *	-3.401 ***
	(1.207)	(1.221)	(1.235)	(1.428)	(1.236)	(1.261)	(1.275)
Log(distance)	-0.725 ***	-0.743 ***	-0.747 ***	-0.731 ***	-0.718 ***	-0.747 ***	-0.714 ***
	(0.050)	(0.041)	(0.045)	(0.048)	(0.052)	(0.051)	(0.048)
Common border	0.241	0.254	0.225	0.208	0.231	0.203	0.239
	(0.254)	(0.249)	(0.255)	(0.262)	(0.252)	(0.255)	(0.255)
Colony	0.234 *	0.151	0.200	0.330 **	0.273 *	0.272 *	0.308 **
	(0.137)	(0.128)	(0.131)	(0.143)	(0.142)	(0.140)	(0.141)
Common colonizer	0.062	0.011	-0.023	-0.140	-0.001	-0.069	-0.007
	(0.120)	(0.110)	(0.116)	(0.160)	(0.118)	(0.151)	(0.153)
Common language	0.158	0.232	0.187	0.163	0.152	0.164	0.146
	(0.157)	(0.155)	(0.158)	(0.151)	(0.156)	(0.149)	(0.155)
International	-2.269 ***	-2.454 ***	-2.411 ***	-2.782 ***	-2.550 ***	-2.512 ***	-2.491 ***
	(0.166)	(0.117)	(0.133)	(0.264)	(0.141)	(0.142)	(0.206)
Observations	2,805.000	2,805.000	2,805.000	2,805.000	2,805.000	2,805.000	2,805.000
R^2	0.414	0.414	0.414	0.414	0.414	0.414	0.414
Exporter fixed effects	Yes	Yes	Yes	Yes	Yes	Yes	Yes
Importer fixed effects	Yes	Yes	Yes	Yes	Yes	Yes	Yes

STRI = Services Trade Restrictiveness Index, Telecom = telecommunications.

Note: Estimation is by Poisson Pseudo-Maximum Likelihood in all cases. The STRI sector is indicated at the top of each column. Robust standard errors corrected for clustering by country pair appear in parentheses below the coefficient estimates. Statistical significance is indicated as follows: * (10%), ** (5%), and *** (1%).

Source: Author.

Standard gravity variables typically have the expected signs in all models, although only distance and the colony dummy are statistically significant at the 10% level or better. In terms of the policy variables, the STRI has a negative and statistically significant coefficient in five out of seven regressions, namely the overall STRI and the sectoral STRIs for banking, insurance, retail, and telecommunications. Applied tariffs have a negative and statistically significant coefficient in four of the seven models; moreover, their coefficient is marginally significant when paired with the overall STRI (prob. = 0.102). We therefore conclude that the policies in goods and services markets both have a direct impact on trade costs affecting manufactured goods, and a less liberal stance in either area is associated with lower trade values. However, the regression results on their own do not allow a simple comparison between magnitudes of the two types of policies, given that they are measured on different scales (percent ad valorem and an index) and that the tariff coefficient is an elasticity while the STRI coefficient is a semi-elasticity. A counterfactual simulation that considers comparable shocks to the two variables can give a clearer idea of their relative influences on bilateral trade in manufactured goods. The next subsection turns to that issue.

6.4.2 Counterfactual Simulations

With the estimating platform in place, we can proceed to conduct counterfactual simulations as per the Anderson, Larch, and Yotov (2018) methodology. We consider two scenarios, both based on the estimation results from Column 1 of Table 6.4. The first scenario considers the trade effects of a 10% reduction in the restrictiveness of services policies, which we capture by a 10% reduction in the importing country's STRI. The second scenario considers a 10% reduction in effectively applied tariffs.

Table 6.5 reports changes in trade flows and real manufacturing output under the two scenarios. We limit consideration to non-OECD Asian economies only. We only report full general equilibrium estimates, using the terminology of Anderson, Larch, and Yotov (2018). First, the table shows that the impacts on trade flows of decreasing services policy restrictiveness are much larger than those for reducing tariffs, although the impacts are strictly positive in both cases, as would be expected. Changes in exports and imports are typically two to three times higher under the first scenario than under the second. Second, impacts on real manufacturing output are smaller than trade impacts in both cases, but this is in line with the fact that the Anderson, Larch, and Yotov (2018) model falls into the class of models analyzed by Arkolakis, Costinot, and Rodriguez-Clare (2012). These authors show that the welfare gains to the United States from the totality of its international trade account for

**Table 6.5 Counterfactual Simulation Results
for Total Trade, Percentage Change Over Baseline**

	STRI			Tariffs		
	Delta Xi %	Delta Mi %	Delta Y %	Delta Xi %	Delta Mi %	Delta Y %
CAM	1.51	1.47	0.87	0.43	0.44	0.34
PRC	3.71	5.35	0.05	0.93	1.71	0.00
INO	5.82	4.70	0.23	0.72	0.92	0.00
IND	7.49	5.81	0.16	1.68	1.74	-0.01
MAL	4.34	5.76	0.22	0.70	1.06	-0.02
PHI	4.87	5.15	0.42	0.59	0.97	0.05
THA	4.73	6.38	0.15	1.46	1.83	-0.03
VIE	4.87	3.53	0.44	1.07	1.00	0.08

CAM = Cambodia, PRC = People's Republic of China, INO = Indonesia, IND = India, MAL = Malaysia, PHI = Philippines, STRI = Services Trade Restrictiveness Index, THA = Thailand, VIE = Viet Nam.
Source: Author's calculations.

0.7%–1.4% of the country's GDP. Against that background, our figures for the impact of the two liberalization scenarios are in fact quite large. However, whereas the real output impacts of services liberalization are strictly positive, there are some small negative impacts in the case of tariffs, due to general equilibrium effects. Third, as would be expected from larger import impacts, the effects on real output of liberalizing services policies are considerably larger than those from liberalizing tariffs. The difference is qualitatively large for all of the countries in Table 6.5. This result sits well with existing computable general equilibrium evidence that the welfare implications of services liberalization are typically much larger than they are for goods, but it is striking that the result flows from a consideration of the impact of services policies on manufacturing only, not on the services sector itself.

6.5 Conclusion and Policy Implications

This chapter used the latest developments in the gravity model literature, specifically the general equilibrium PPML approach of Anderson, Larch, and Yotov (2018), to analyze the trade and real output implications of liberalizing services policies versus liberalizing tariffs. Our key finding is that the former scenario has much larger trade and real output effects than the latter scenario. This is a striking result, given that the policy change is essentially a cross-sectoral effect. However, it is quite consistent with the evidence presented above to the effect that exporters of manufactured goods typically source a substantial amount of their inputs from world services markets; thus, facilitating that access by liberalizing policies acts as a positive productivity shock and induces greater exports. Although we estimate using a reduced form based on this relationship, the evidence we have provided is consistent with the firm-level model in Hoekman and Shepherd (2017), which focuses on input linkages and indirect, as opposed to direct, effects of services liberalization on manufacturers.

From a policy perspective, our results are of particular importance in a region like developing Asia, where policy makers are strongly focused on manufacturing. In reality, the development of manufacturing cannot be divorced from the development of services. The two are closely intertwined, as the results in this chapter make clear. Nonetheless, it is typically challenging to give services the policy priority they deserve in developing Asia due to the strong belief that manufacturing is the key to medium-term productivity and income growth. That challenge is only made more daunting by the growth of "services pessimism" driven in part by the premature deindustrialization thesis.

Our results suggest that a weightier argument for policy makers in the region may be that services liberalization can boost manufacturing output and exports. In other words, policies that can bring about more competitive and integrated services markets are in fact perfectly aligned with the goal of promoting manufacturing. There is an opportunity to realize a win–win scenario that should appeal both to those convinced that the future of the region is in services and to those who argue that the manufacturing sector needs to continue to develop in much of the region.

On an intuitive level, our findings reinforce the argument that there is no simple dichotomy between manufacturing and services. Instead, the two sectors are intimately linked, and the evidence suggests that this linkage is only growing tighter over time. While we do not discuss the merits of the premature deindustrialization thesis from the standpoint of productivity levels and dynamics, our results nonetheless suggest that a simplistic implementation of policies to promote manufacturing over services would perhaps be self-defeating. In a world economy and a regional economy that are becoming increasingly "servicified," developing a competitive services sector, which is helped by pro-market services policies, is in fact a key component of promoting manufacturing. Policy makers would do well to act cautiously when considering altering the balance of incentives between manufacturing and services, as apparently sensible policies could have undesirable outcomes in a setting in which the two sectors are as closely interlinked as they now are.

References

Anderson, J., M. Larch, and Y. Yotov. 2018. GEPPML: General Equilibrium Analysis with PPML. *The World Economy* 41(10): 2750–2782.

Arkolakis, C., A. Costinot, and A. Rodriguez-Clare. 2012. New Trade Models, Same Old Gains? *American Economic Review* 102(1): 94–130.

Arvis, J. F., and B. Shepherd. 2013. The Poisson Quasi-Maximum Likelihood Estimator: A Solution to the Adding Up Problem in Gravity Models. *Applied Economics Letters* 20(6): 515–519.

Egger, P., and M. Larch. 2008. Interdependent Preferential Trade Agreement Memberships: An Empirical Analysis. *Journal of International Economics* 76(2): 384–399.

Fally, T. 2015. Structural Gravity and Fixed Effects. *Journal of International Economics* 97(1): 76–85.

Hoekman, B., and B. Shepherd. 2017. Services Productivity, Trade Policy, and Manufacturing Exports. *World Economy* 40(3): 499–516.

Mattoo, A. 2003. China's Accession to the WTO: The Services Dimension. *Journal of International Economic Law* 6(2): 299–339.

Melitz, M. 2003. The Impact of Trade on Intra-Industry Reallocations and Aggregate Industry Productivity. *Econometrica* 71(6): 1695–1725.

Miroudot, S., J. Sauvage, and B. Shepherd. 2012. Trade Costs and Productivity in Services Sectors. *Economics Letters* 114(1): 36–38.

Noguera, G. 2012. Trade Costs and Gravity for Gross and Value Added Trade. Working Paper.

Santos Silva, J. M. C., and S. Tenreyro. 2006. The Log of Gravity. *Review of Economics and Statistics* 88(4): 641–658.

Yotov, Y., R. Piermartini, J. A. Monteiro, and M. Larch. 2017. *An Advanced Guide to Trade Policy Analysis: The Structural Gravity Model (Online Revised Version)*. Geneva: United Nations and World Trade Organization.

PART III
Productivity Growth in Services: What Prospects for Developing Countries?

7

Productivity Spillovers from Services Firms in Low- and Middle-Income Countries: What Is the Role of Firm Characteristics and Services Liberalization?

Deborah Winkler

7.1 Introduction

In recent years, several studies have suggested that services usage within sectors and firms has a performance-enhancing effect. However, there is still a shortage of studies on productivity spillovers from services to other sectors and firms, especially for low- and middle-income countries. Spillovers generally refer to productivity improvements resulting from knowledge diffusion (in the form of either unintentional transmission or intentional transfer) encompassing both technology and all forms of codified and "tacit knowledge" related to production, including management and organizational practices (Hoekman and Javorcik 2006).

The lacuna of empirical literature on productivity spillovers from services firms is surprising, given the relevance of services inputs to downstream industries, manufacturing sectors in particular. A recent World Bank study suggests that countries with a higher content of services in the downstream economy are also those producing more complex goods (Saez et al. 2015), while another study by the Organisation for Economic Co-operation and Development (OECD) finds that services represent at least 30% of the value added in manufacturing exports (OECD 2014). These developments are also strongly linked to the emergence of global value chains (GVCs), which depend on the quality of embedded services, including quality control, logistics, storage facilities, packaging, insurance, and distribution (Taglioni and Winkler 2016).

The heavy dependence of firms on services inputs implies that improvements in services sectors, including the services firms' performance and services reforms, are likely to affect all downstream sectors. Second, the performance of downstream sectors depends, to a large extent, on the quality and availability of domestic services firms due to the limited cross-border tradability of services compared to material inputs. This makes services sectors a relevant source of vertical productivity spillovers (Javorcik 2008).

This study is based on the premise that spillovers from services firms are not equally distributed among manufacturing firms, but are mediated by the services firms' characteristics. These determine the spillover potential. The absorptive capacity of manufacturing firms to internalize spillovers also matters for actual spillovers (as depicted in the conceptual framework shown in Figure 7.1). The spillover potential also depends on the extent of services liberalization in a given country, leading to market restructuring by increasing the availability of services inputs and providers, and thus magnifying the potential for productivity spillovers.

Possible transmission channels from services to manufacturing firms include learning externalities that could arise when purchased services improve the productivity of the workers (e.g., due to new software being

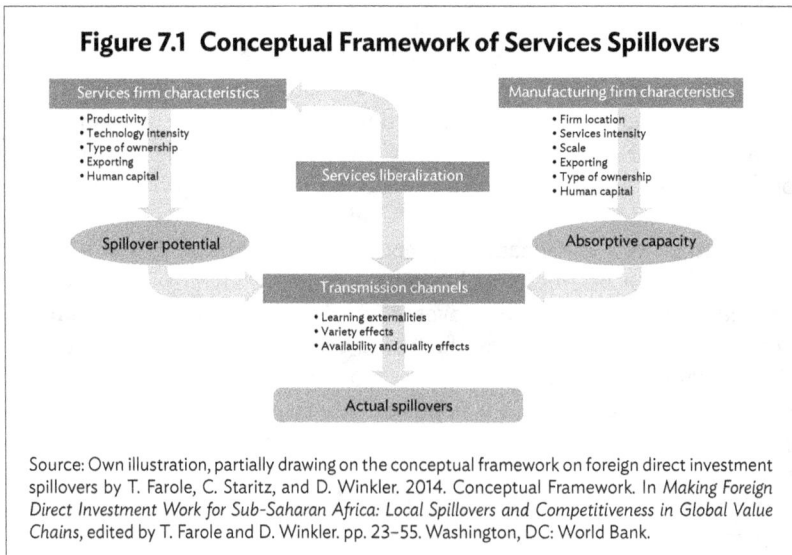

Figure 7.1 Conceptual Framework of Services Spillovers

Source: Own illustration, partially drawing on the conceptual framework on foreign direct investment spillovers by T. Farole, C. Staritz, and D. Winkler. 2014. Conceptual Framework. In *Making Foreign Direct Investment Work for Sub-Saharan Africa: Local Spillovers and Competitiveness in Global Value Chains*, edited by T. Farole and D. Winkler. pp. 23–55. Washington, DC: World Bank.

used). Variety effects could raise productivity when new services inputs are used (Amiti and Wei 2009, Ethier 1982). In addition, spillovers can increase via supply chain linkages as new or better services inputs become available (availability and quality effect) (Javorcik 2008).

The ability of manufacturing firms to access new services and invest more in services infrastructure depends on their absorptive capacity. This chapter hypothesizes that manufacturing firms with a higher absorptive capacity (i.e., that are located closer to services firms, such as within the same region) have a higher services intensity, are larger, export, have foreign ownership status, and show a higher share of human capital, enjoy higher spillovers from services firms. Similarly, this study predicts that the spillover potential of services firms increases for firms that are more productive, have a higher technology intensity, are foreign-owned, export, and are more skill-intensive, as such services firms tend to have a higher knowledge intensity that can diffuse to manufacturing firms in downstream sectors.

Besides firm-level characteristics, this study examines the role of a country's services liberalization in influencing spillovers from services firms. Services liberalization involves eliminating barriers to entry, privatizing state-owned enterprises, and abolishing monopolies, among other things. More services liberalization, including in services trade, opens markets to new services providers, both domestic and foreign, and forces existing services firms either to increase their productivity or to exit (Arnold, Javorcik, and Mattoo 2011). Services liberalization thus increases the spillover potential of services firms, and also influences the functioning of the transmission channels.

Using a cross-section of more than 38,000 manufacturing and 24,000 services firms in 105 low- and middle-income countries from 2010 to 2017 (World Bank, Enterprise Surveys), this chapter focuses on productivity spillovers from services to manufacturing firms, as well as the role of firm characteristics and a country's services liberalization in mediating spillovers.

This chapter attempts to answer the following four questions:

(i) Are there productivity and technology spillovers from services to manufacturing firms?

To shed light on this question, we relate a manufacturing firm's labor productivity to several measures of services spillovers using a linear regression analysis. Labor productivity is measured as value added per worker. We include capital intensity as additional control variable. The findings confirm positive spillovers resulting from a higher average regional productivity and technology intensity of services firms, but rejects the existence of spillovers from services firm presence alone.

Differentiating between income levels, the results suggest a U-shaped effect, meaning that productivity spillovers are larger in upper middle- and low-income countries than in lower middle-income countries. The results are different for technology spillovers from services firms. Here, upper middle-income countries benefit the least from spillovers, while manufacturing firm productivity in lower middle- and low-income countries is more strongly correlated with the regional technology intensity of services firms.

(ii) Which manufacturing firms benefit most from spillovers?

Next, the analysis focuses on the role of manufacturing firms' absorptive capacity in mediating productivity and technology spillovers. Analytically, we assess this by including interaction terms between the spillover variable and selected manufacturing firm characteristics. The findings suggest that several manufacturing firm characteristics increase productivity and technology spillovers from services firms, including large firm size, foreign ownership status, and exporting. In contrast, manufacturing firms with a larger services intensity show lower spillovers, while skill intensity does not matter.

(iii) Which services firm characteristics increase the spillover potential?

Given the positive relationship between services and manufacturing firm productivity, this chapter then assesses the characteristics of services firms with higher productivity and technology intensity levels, as these determine the services spillover potential. We find that foreign ownership status and the extent of the top manager's experience in a given sector are positively associated with services firms' output per worker and technology intensity. Exporting status only shows a positive correlation with technology intensity, not labor productivity for services firms.

(iv) Can services trade liberalization increase spillovers?

The chapter also examines if policy mediates productivity spillovers from services to manufacturing firms in a region. Reforms in the upstream services sectors may translate into a higher spillover potential and thus higher actual productivity spillovers. For this analysis, we rely on the World Bank's Services Trade Restrictions database, which is based on surveys that were mostly collected in 2008. Analytically, we include interaction terms between the spillover variable and the measures of services trade restrictiveness at the country level. The results suggest that lower regulations increase productivity spillovers, but only for Mode 1 services trade. We also test for the direct link between services liberalization and services firm productivity, and find a positive connection across all modes of supply available in the dataset (Modes 1, 3, and 4).

Our study is closest in nature to the study by Hoekman and Shepherd (2017), who find evidence for regional productivity spillovers from services to manufacturing firms using a set of 58,000 firms from the World Bank Enterprise Surveys across 119 countries from 2006 to 2011. Despite similarities with regard to the research question and database, there are also substantial differences in terms of model specification, measures, and the time period used. Importantly, our study not only includes a measure of spillovers based on the average services firm productivity in a region, but also tests for the existence of regional spillovers from a higher technology intensity and presence of services firms.

Second, borrowing from the rich literature on spillovers from foreign direct investment (FDI) (e.g., Paus and Gallagher 2008; Farole, Staritz, and Winkler 2014), our study also examines the role of absorptive capacity in mediating spillovers and identifies characteristics of services firms that correlate with higher spillover potential. Finally, this study also assesses the role of services liberalization in shaping productivity spillovers, while Hoekman and Shepherd (2017) examine the relationship between services liberalization and manufacturing exports at the sector level using a gravity model. Reassuringly, our study confirms the general findings of Hoekman and Shepherd (2017) that a higher regional productivity of services firms is positively correlated with manufacturing firm labor productivity, while a higher services trade restrictiveness has negative implications for the manufacturing sector.

7.2 Literature Review

This study is related to three streams of empirical literature: (i) studies on the relationship between services usage and performance, (ii) studies on the role of services and services liberalization for the competitiveness of downstream sectors, and (iii) studies on productivity spillovers from FDI and the role of mediating factors. For an extensive literature overview on the connection between services (in particular trade, FDI, and liberalization) and economic performance, see Francois and Hoekman (2010).

Several studies explore the relationship between the intensity of importing services (or services offshoring) and productivity. Several studies at the sectoral level find evidence that a higher services offshoring intensity significantly increases productivity, while the effect of materials offshoring intensity is smaller or insignificant; these include Amiti and Wei (2009) for United States (US) manufacturing between

1992 and 2000, Crinò (2008) for nine European Union countries between 1990 and 2004, Winkler (2010) for German manufacturing industries between 1995 and 2006, and Michel and Rycx (2014) for Belgian manufacturing industries between 1995 and 2004. This final study also examines the impact of inter-industry spillover effects from services offshoring, but finds only a little evidence of this.

A few studies analyze the relationship between services offshoring and productivity using firm-level data. Görg and Hanley (2003) analyze the impact of services offshoring intensity on labor productivity for Ireland using plant-level data (the effect was positive in the electronics industry between 1990 and 1995). In a more recent plant-level study, Görg, Hanley, and Strobl (2008) evaluate the productivity effects of materials and services offshoring intensity for Irish manufacturing for the period 1990–1998, differentiating between exporting and non-exporting firms. They only find a significantly positive impact of services offshoring on total factor productivity (TFP) for exporting firms.

Other studies focus on the role of services for other performance indicators. Using a sample of Swedish manufacturing firm-level data, Lodefalk (2014) studies the relationship between a firm's services intensity and its export intensity, and finds that a higher share of services in in-house production raises a firm's exports share in total sales. The effect is stronger for services that are produced in-house compared to external services purchases. Debaere, Görg, and Raff (2013) examine the role of services for manufacturing firms' sourcing intensities using Irish plant-level survey data. A higher services availability, defined as the number of local and foreign services firms in a region in a specific year, significantly increases a firm's share of imported materials in total sales. Interestingly, access to local service providers in this sample matters only for domestic firms, while access to foreign service providers matters only for foreign firms.

The second stream of literature focuses on the role of services for the competitiveness of downstream sectors. Rajan and Zingales (1998) relate financial sector development to growth in downstream sectors and conclude that sectors that are more reliant on finance show higher growth in countries with well-developed financial markets. Similarly, Guiso, Sapienza, and Zingales (2004) find that local financial development in Italy enhances firm entry and the likelihood of individuals to start a business, and increases competition and growth. Focusing on spillovers at the regional level using a set of 58,000 firms across 119 countries for the period 2006–2011, Hoekman and Shepherd (2017) find evidence for productivity spillovers from services to manufacturing firms.

Focusing specifically on services liberalization, Nicoletti and Scarpetta (2003) postulate a positive link between services liberalization and productivity growth in manufacturing sectors in OECD countries. Similarly, Conway and others (2006) find that a country's manufacturing productivity catches up to the leading OECD country more quickly if its services market is relatively more open. Hoekman and Shepherd (2017) find that more services restrictions negatively affect manufacturing exports. Using firm-level data, Arnold, Javorcik, and Mattoo (2011) and Arnold and others (2015) examine the relationship of services liberalization with the productivity of firms in downstream manufacturing sectors. While the first study focuses on firms in the Czech Republic over the period 1998–2003, the second study covers Indian firms for the period 1993–2005. In both cases, the authors conclude that services reforms are linked to higher performance on the part of manufacturing firms.

A vast set of empirical studies has been undertaken on the existence and direction of FDI-generated horizontal and vertical spillovers (for a review of the literature, see, e.g., Görg and Greenaway 2004; Lipsey and Sjöholm 2005; Smeets 2008; and Havranek and Irsova 2011). In a comprehensive meta-analysis, Havranek and Irsova (2011) take into account 3,626 estimates from 55 studies on vertical spillovers, and find evidence for positive and economically important backward spillovers from multinational corporations on domestic suppliers in upstream sectors and smaller positive effects on domestic customers in downstream sectors. However, the study rejects the existence of horizontal spillovers. Overall, the results are mixed, and suggest that the postulated spillover effects often do not materialize automatically (Farole and Winkler 2015).

As a result, more and more research has been devoted to understanding the various conditions that may explain these mixed results. Three major types of mediating factors have been identified: (i) characteristics of foreign firms that shape spillover potential; (ii) characteristics of domestic firms that determine absorptive capacity to internalize spillovers; and (iii) differences in host country factors (Castellani and Zanfei 2003; Lipsey and Sjöholm 2005) that shape both domestic and foreign firm characteristics, as well as the transmission channels for spillovers (Paus and Gallagher 2008, Farole, Staritz, and Winkler 2014).

In summary, these studies suggest a performance-enhancing effect of services within sectors and firms, as well as for downstream sectors and firms. However, most of these studies focus on industrialized countries and neglect the role of firm heterogeneity in mediating these links.

7.3 Model and Data

7.3.1 Empirical Model

We postulate the following value added function:

$$(Y\text{-}inp) = VA = F(K, L, T) \tag{1}$$

where capital K and labor L are the input factors, and $VA = (Y\text{-}inp)$ designates the value added and is the difference between output Y and intermediate inputs inp. The technology shifter $T = T(spill)$ is a function services spillovers, $spill$.

We are interested in labor productivity, lp, defined as value added per worker, as the dependent variable and estimate the following equation in log-linear form:

$$\ln lp_{isrt} = \alpha + \beta X_{isrt} + \gamma spill_{rt} + D_{cs} + D_t + \varepsilon_{isrt} \tag{2}$$

where subscript i stands for firm, r for (subnational) region, s for sector, c for country, and t for year. α designates the constant, D_{cs} the sector fixed effects, D_t the year fixed effects, and ε_{isrt} the idiosyncratic error term.

X is a proxy for the firm-level determinants of labor productivity, namely a firm's capital intensity, $capint$. $spill$ designates the services spillover variable, measured at the regional level. Our main spillover measure is the median output per worker (which equals productivity) of services firms in a region. We also use an alternative measure, namely the median technology intensity of services firms in a region.[1] A detailed description of the measures used can be found in section 7.3.3.

Since firm characteristics can mediate the capacity of manufacturing firms to internalize regional services spillovers, we also assess different types of absorptive capacities. They enter Equation (2) in the form of interaction terms with the spillover variable:

$$\ln lp_{isrt} = \alpha + \beta X_{isrt} + \gamma spill_{rt} + \delta_1 spill_{rt} \\ * AC_{isrt} + D_{cs} + D_t + \varepsilon_{isrt} \tag{3}$$

The joint effect of $spill$ is the sum of γ plus $\delta_1 * AC$. Since AC (absorptive capacity) is positive, the mediating effect of the interaction term is positive for $\delta_1 > 0$.

---

[1] We also test for spillovers from the presence of services firms in the region.

AC includes a firm's services intensity, as well as firm size, foreign ownership status, exporting behavior, skill intensity, and the top manager's experience. Firm size, type of ownership, exporting, and human capital have been shown to mediate the productivity impacts of FDI, and it will be interesting to find out if they also matter for the absorption of services spillovers.

Lastly, we assess whether policies at the country level mediate regional services spillovers. As in Equation (3), policy variables enter the equation in the form of interaction terms with the spillover variable:

$$\ln lp_{isrt} = \alpha + \beta X_{isrt} + \gamma spill_{rt} + \delta_1 spill_{rt} \\ * policy_c + D_{cs} + D_t + \varepsilon_{isrt} \qquad (4)$$

Our policy variables are based on the World Bank's Services Trade Restrictions Index. They are available for certain sectors (telecommunications, finance, transportation, retail, and professional services), and also in aggregate form. While the measures focus on the trade openess of services, we postulate that they correlate highly with a country's overall services liberalization.

7.3.2 Data

Our dataset draws on two underlying datasets published by the World Bank Enterprise Analysis Unit: the Enterprise Surveys Global Database and the Firm-Level TFP Estimates and Factor Ratios. The Enterprise Surveys Global Database covers 242 surveys in 140 countries from 2006 to 2017.

Enterprise surveys represent a comprehensive source of firm-level data in emerging markets and developing economies. One major advantage of the enterprise surveys is that the survey questions are the same across all countries. Moreover, the surveys represent a stratified random sample of firms using three levels of stratification: sector, firm size, and region. Sectors are based on the International Standard Industrial Classification (ISIC) Revision 3.1 classification.

The Enterprise Surveys Global Database covers a wide range of indicators on firm characteristics, business environment, innovation and technology, and workforce and skills, among others. We merged this dataset with data on firm-level output, value added, and capital stock obtained from the Firm-Level TFP Estimates and Factor Ratios dataset. All local currencies have been converted into US dollars and deflated using a gross domestic product deflator in US dollars (base year 2009). Exchange rates and deflators have been obtained from the World Development Indicators.

We apply the following rules to the dataset: (i) include only the most recent Enterprise Surveys for each country; (ii) drop high-income countries to cover only emerging or developing countries;[2] (iii) only cover the years 2010 to 2017, to account for the shock of the global economic crisis of 2008; (iv) drop construction firms (ISIC 45), restaurants and hotels (ISIC 55), and some outliers from the sample,[3] as these are not considered business services firms; and (v) drop countries with fewer than 100 firms after applying the previous steps.

This procedure yielded more than 63,031 firms in 105 countries, of which 38,344 are manufacturing and 24,687 are services firms. The list of countries, year of the most recent survey, and number of manufacturing and services firms by country can be found in Appendix 7.1. After computing the regional spillover measures, we focus only on the productivity spillovers for domestic manufacturing firms, since TFP and labor productivity measures are unavailable for services firms. The distribution of firms across ISIC sectors is shown in Appendix 7.2.

While the use of Enterprise Survey data allows us to capture dynamics at the firm-level, one downside of computing the spillover variables at the regional level is the heterogeneity of regional size. In countries where regions are defined as larger geographical entities covering more firms, spillovers may be more difficult to materialize for certain manufacturing firms due to larger geographical distances. However, the strong correlation between a region's median services and manufacturing firm productivity across the full sample of regions (see Figure 7.2 in section 7.4.1) reassures us that heterogeneity in regional size across countries does not seem to be a major concern.

Finally, we merge the firm-level data with country-level scores on services trade restrictions from the World Bank (Borchert, Gootiiz, and Mattoo 2012; World Bank, Development Economics Research Group). The database focuses on policies and regulations that discriminate against foreign services or foreign service providers, as well as other aspects of the country's regulatory environment that substantially affect trade in services. The data are based on surveys and offer comparable information on services trade policy for over 100 countries, covering five sectors (telecommunications, finance, transportation, retail, and professional services). As almost all surveys were collected in 2008, endogeneity between the dependent variable and policy is a minor issue. Scores range from 0 ("open") to 100 ("closed"). The database covers

---

[2] These are dropped because the database only included 15 high-income countries that were not representative of high-income countries (i.e., eight Eastern European countries, five Caribbean islands, Israel, and Sweden).

[3] Some firms were classified as non-commercial services (ISIC 75–95).

the most relevant "modes of supply" within each sector: commercial presence or FDI (Mode 3); cross-border supply (Mode 1) of financial, transportation, and professional services; and the presence of individuals supplying the service (Mode 4) in professional services.

7.3.3 Measures

We use labor productivity at the firm-level as the dependent variable, which is measured as value added per employee and available only for manufacturing firms.[4] The measure is provided by the Enterprise Survey Analysis Unit and reported in 2009 US dollars.[5]

We include the firm-level determinant of labor productivity, as suggested by theory: *capital intensity*, ln*capint* = capital stock per employee in natural logarithms. We analyze two spillover variables from services firms: ln*prod_med* = median productivity level of services firms in a region, defined as output per employee (in natural logarithms); and *tech_med* = median technology intensity of services firms in a region (*tech = iso + tech_for* $\in$ {0, 1, 2}, where *iso* = 1 if firm owns internationally-recognized quality certification and 0 otherwise, and *tech_for* = 1 if firm uses technology licensed from foreign firms and 0 otherwise). This technology indicator is a narrower spillover measure and mainly captures technology spillovers.

Characteristics of manufacturing firms that can mediate productivity spillovers from services firms include:

(i) *services intensity*, *serv_int* = services inputs as % of value added;

(ii) *large* = 1 if number of employees >= 100, and 0 if otherwise;

(iii) *fdi* = 1 if foreign private ownership >= 10%, and 0 if otherwise;

(iv) *exp* = 1 if direct export share in sales >= 10%, and 0 if otherwise;

(v) *shs* = number of skilled production workers as % of total production workers as a measure of skill intensity; and

(vi) *manager* = years of top manager's experience in the sector (in natural logarithms) as alternative measure of skill intensity.

Finally, we include services trade restrictions policy measures from the World Bank that all range from 0 to 100, where 0 means "open" and 100 "closed":

(i) *overall*: overall services trade restriction

(ii) *telecom*: services trade restriction in telecommunications

---

[4] Hoekman and Shepherd (2017) use output per worker as the dependent variable.

[5] Labor productivity is part of the "Firm-Level TFP Estimates and Factor Ratios" dataset.

(iii) *finance:* services trade restriction in finance (banking and insurance)
(iv) *transp:* services trade restriction in transportation
(v) *retail:* services trade restriction in retail distribution
(vi) *prof:* services trade restriction in professional services (accounting and legal)

The analysis also differentiates by mode of services supply (Modes 1, 3, and 4).

7.4 Analysis of Spillovers from Services Firms

7.4.1 Are There Productivity and Technology Spillovers from Services to Manufacturing Firms?

This section assesses whether manufacturing firms experience productivity spillovers from services firms. To fix ideas, we assess the relationship between the median services and manufacturing firm labor productivity visually at the subnational regional level. Figure 7.2 suggests

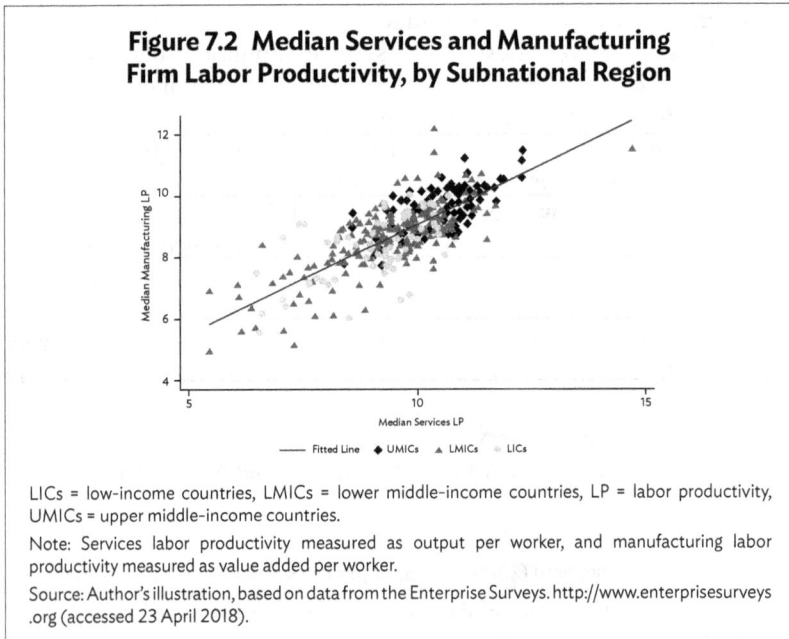

Figure 7.2 Median Services and Manufacturing Firm Labor Productivity, by Subnational Region

LICs = low-income countries, LMICs = lower middle-income countries, LP = labor productivity, UMICs = upper middle-income countries.
Note: Services labor productivity measured as output per worker, and manufacturing labor productivity measured as value added per worker.
Source: Author's illustration, based on data from the Enterprise Surveys. http://www.enterprisesurveys.org (accessed 23 April 2018).

that there is a clear positive relationship between the two, as shown by the bivariate regression line. In addition, it appears that both services and manufacturing labor productivity increase as income levels increase, although, on the lower end of the spectrum for each, we find regions from both low- (gray circle) and lower middle-income countries (triangle). Lower middle-income countries in particular appear to have a larger variation across regions with regard to their median productivity levels.

As a first step, we assess whether the presence of services firms alone is correlated with productivity gains. The summary statistics can be found in Appendix 7.3. All estimations produce standard errors robust to both heteroscedasticity and any form of intra-cluster correlation at the subnational level. We apply two measures of service presence: (i) the number of services firms as a percent of total number of firms by region, *serv_no*; and (ii) the output of services firms as a percent of total output of firms by region, *serv_out*. The latter measure follows the approach of the FDI spillovers literature where foreign presence in a sector is measured by the share of output by foreign firms in a sector's total output. The results in Appendix 7.4 suggest that a higher number and output of services firms as a percent of the total number and output of firms in a region is not correlated with manufacturing firm productivity.

While the quantity or output of services firms does not matter, the productivity and technology intensity of services firms matter for spillovers. Table 7.1 shows that the median productivity of services firms in a region is positively associated with manufacturing labor productivity and the results are significant at the 1% level (Column 1). Additionally controlling for capital intensity slightly reduces the coefficient size, but not the statistical significance (Column 2). The results imply that a 1 percentage point increase in median services productivity in a region is related to a 0.23 percentage point increase in manufacturing labor productivity, confirming the general findings by Hoekman and Shepherd (2017). Using a region's median technology intensity of services firms as an alternative spillover measure confirms the findings (Columns 3–4).[6] All estimates are significant at the 1% level.

In a next step, we test whether the correlations differ across countries' income levels. The full regression results are reported in Appendix 7.5. Figure 7.3 suggests a U-shaped effect using a region's median services productivity as spillover measure (dark gray bars). Upper middle-income

---

[6] In a previous analysis, we also included whether a firm uses a website or email to communicate with clients into the technology spillover measure. While the correlation with services productivity was also positive, the coefficient was smaller, indicating that the productivity-enhancing spillover potential is higher from having an internationally recognized quality certification and/or technology licensed from a foreign firm.

Table 7.1 Services Productivity and Technology Intensity in a Region and Manufacturing Firm Productivity, Ordinary Least Squares

Dependent Variable: lnlp_{isrt}	ln$prod\_med$		tech$\_med$	
	(1)	(2)	(3)	(4)
spill$_{rt}$	0.2606***	0.2371***	0.3012***	0.4411***
	(0.000)	(0.000)	(0.000)	(0.000)
lncapint$_{isrt}$		0.2969***		0.3029***
		(0.000)		(0.000)
constant	6.8576	4.2482***	9.3558	7.0139***
	(0.998)	(0.000)	(0.000)	(0.000)
Observations	25,155	17,819	25,176	17,836
R-squared	0.36	0.50	0.35	0.50

lncapint$_{isrt}$ = capital stock per employee in natural logarithms, lnlp_{isrt} = value added per employee in natural logarithms, ln$prod\_med$ = median output per employee of services firms in a region in natural logarithms, spill$_{rt}$ = spillover variable, tech$\_med_{rt}$ = median technology intensity of services firms in a region.

Note: p*<0.1, p**<0.05, p***<0.01 (p-values in parentheses). All regressions include country-sector, and year fixed effects and are clustered at the subnational level.

Source: Enterprise Surveys. http://www.enterprisesurveys.org (accessed 23 April 2018).

Figure 7.3 Services Productivity and Technology Intensity in a Region and Manufacturing Firm Productivity, by Income, Ordinary Least Squares

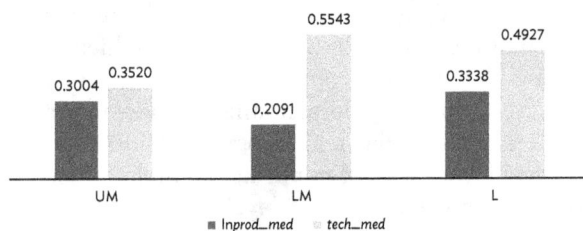

ln$prod\_med$ = median productivity level of services firms in a region, defined as output per employee (in natural logarithms); tech$\_med$ = median technology intensity of services firms in a region; L = low-income countries; LM = lower middle-income countries; UM = upper middle-income countries.

Note: All estimates significant at the 1% level. Based on regressions in Appendix 7.5.

Source: Enterprise Surveys. http://www.enterprisesurveys.org (accessed 23 April 2018).

countries show the highest correlation, which is somewhat higher than for low-income countries, while lower middle-income countries enjoy the lowest positive productivity spillovers. This finding may imply that upper middle-income countries rely more strongly on high-quality services inputs than countries with lower income levels (see Figure 7.2). In contrast, the strong assocation for low-income countries could point to some large untapped spillover potential that services can generate.

Using a region's median technology intensity of services firms as an alternative spillover measure yields different results (see the light gray bars in Figure 7.3). Here, upper middle-income countries benefit the least from spillovers, while manufacturing firm productivity in lower middle- and low-income countries is more strongly correlated with the regional technology intensity of services firms. One explanation could be that manufacturing firms in upper middle-income countries are much closer to the technology frontier, and technology improvements in services firms have lower productivity effects as a result.

7.4.2 Which Manufacturing Firms Benefit Most from Spillovers?

Since not all manufacturing firms benefit equally from services spillovers, this section studies the role of absorptive capacity to internalize such productivity spillovers. Table 7.2 focuses on our first spillover measure (median productivity of services firms in a region). The first absorptive capacity measure is a manufacturing firm's services intensity, which interacts negatively with spillovers (Column 1). That is, regional productivity spillover from services firms more strongly benefits those manufacturing firms that rely less on external services as a percent of their value added. In other words, the potential to absorb productivity spillovers from services firms in the same region declines for manufacturing firms that already make use of more external services relative to their value added.[7]

---

[7]   The literature on services outsourcing mostly relates purchases of services inputs to either value added or total intermediate inputs (see, e.g., the literature review in Crinò 2009 or Winkler 2013). Using total intermediate inputs, defined as the difference between sales and value added, as an alternative denominator confirms the negative mediating effect. Our results differ from Hoekman and Shepherd (2017) who find a positive mediating effect of services intensity, which could be related to the different measures of services intensity being used. While they relate services purchases to total costs, we use value added as a denominator. Second, their services purchases include electricity, communications, transport, and water, while our study additionally includes rental.

Table 7.2 Services Productivity in a Region and Manufacturing Firm Productivity, Absorptive Capacity, Ordinary Least Squares

Dependent Variable: lnlp_{isrt}	Absorptive Capacity (AC)					
	(1) serv_int	(2) large	(3) fdi	(4) exp	(5) shs	(6) manager
ln prod_med$_{rt}$	0.2314***	0.2174***	0.2329***	0.2317***	0.2247***	0.2330***
	(0.000)	(0.000)	(0.000)	(0.000)	(0.000)	(0.000)
ln prod_med$_{rt}$*AC$_{isrt}$	−0.0374***	0.0329***	0.0301***	0.0301***	−0.0000	0.0022
	(0.000)	(0.000)	(0.000)	(0.000)	(0.640)	(0.312)
ln capint$_{isrt}$	0.3025***	0.2944***	0.2933***	0.2925***	0.3052***	0.2947***
	(0.000)	(0.000)	(0.000)	(0.000)	(0.000)	(0.000)
constant	5.2047***	4.8638***	4.4042	3.3864	4.7716***	5.2119***
	(0.000)	(0.000)	(0.999)	(0.998)	(0.000)	(0.000)
Observation	17,355	17,819	17,810	17,775	15,182	17,635
R−squared	0.61	0.51	0.51	0.51	0.50	0.50
F−test[a]	0.0000	0.0000	0.0000	0.0000	0.0000	0.0000

AC$_{isrt}$ = absorptive capacity, exp = exporter dummy, fdi = foreign ownership dummy, ln capint$_{isrt}$ = capital stock per employee in natural logarithms, lnlp_{isrt} = value added per employee in natural logarithms, ln prod_med$_{rt}$ = median output per employee of services firms in a region in natural logarithms, large = large firm dummy, manager = years of top manager's experience in the sector in natural logarithms, serv_int = services inputs as % of value added in natural logarithms, shs = number of skilled production workers as % of total production workers.

Note: p*<0.1, p**<0.05, p***<0.01 (p-values in parentheses). All regressions include country-sector and year fixed effects and are clustered at the subnational level.

[a] F-test of joint significance between spill$_{rt}$ and spill$_{rt}$*AC$_{isrt}$ (Prob > F).

Source: Enterprise Surveys. http://www.enterprisesurveys.org (accessed 23 April 2018).

For other absorptive capacity measures, we borrow from the rich FDI spillovers literature and include firm characteristics that have been shown to mediate spillovers, including firm size, foreign ownership status, exporting behavior, and skill intensity. The interaction term with large firm size (*large*) is positive and significant (Column 2). In other words, large firms show higher spillovers (joint coefficient = 0.25) than do small or medium-sized firms (coefficient = 0.22). Foreign and exporting firms also enjoy spillovers from a region's median services productivity (Columns 3 and 4), which are higher (joint coefficient = 0.26) than those of domestic or non-exporting firms (coefficient = 0.23). In contrast, a higher skill intensity of manufacturing firms, measured as both the share of skilled production workers and the manager's years of experience in the sector, does not influence the extent of spillovers individually. However, the mediating effect is jointly significant with the spillover measure, as shown by the F-test.

**Table 7.3 Services Technology Intensity in a Region
and Manufacturing Firm Productivity, Absorptive
Capacity, Ordinary Least Squares**

Dependent Variable: $lnlp_{isrt}$	Absorptive Capacity (AC)					
	(1) serv_int	(2) large	(3) fdi	(4) exp	(5) shs	(6) manager
$tech\_med_{rt}$	0.3109***	0.3730***	0.4346***	0.4183***	0.3777**	0.4362**
	(0.006)	(0.000)	(0.000)	(0.000)	(0.018)	(0.034)
$tech\_med_{rt}*AC_{isrt}$	−0.1528***	0.1736**	0.1693	0.1637**	0.0013	0.0008
	(0.000)	(0.024)	(0.412)	(0.035)	(0.496)	(0.991)
$lncapint_{isrt}$	0.3030***	0.3034***	0.3029***	0.3030***	0.3120***	0.3013***
	(0.000)	(0.000)	(0.000)	(0.000)	(0.000)	(0.000)
constant	9.1836***	7.0117***	9.1858***	7.0132***	5.1599	9.2061***
	(0.000)	(0.000)	(0.000)	(0.000)	(0.000)	(0.000)
Observation	1,7372	17,836	17,827	17,791	15,199	17,652
R–squared	0.50	0.50	0.50	0.50	0.49	0.50
F–test[a]	0.0000	0.0000	0.0000	0.0000	0.0000	0.0000

AC_{isrt} = absorptive capacity, *exp* = exporter dummy, *fdi* = foreign ownership dummy, $lncapint_{isrt}$ = capital stock per employee in natural logarithms, $lnlp_{isrt}$ = value added per employee in natural logarithms, *tech_med* = median technology intensity of services firms in a region, *large* = large firm dummy, *manager* = years of top manager's experience in the sector in natural logarithms, *serv_int* = services inputs as % of value added in natural logarithms, *shs* = number of skilled production workers as % of total production workers.

Note: p*<0.1, p**<0.05, p***<0.01 (p-values in parentheses). All regressions include country-sector and year fixed effects, and are clustered at the subnational level.

[a] F-test of joint significance between $spill_{rt}$ and $spill_{rt}*AC_{isrt}$ (Prob > F).

Source: Enterprise Surveys. http://www.enterprisesurveys.org (accessed 23 April 2018).

Focusing on our alternative spillover measure in Table 7.3 instead (median technology intensity of services firms in region) confirms the previous findings. A larger services intensity lowers spillovers, while technology spillovers are increased for large and exporting firms, but not foreign firms.. Again, skill intensity does not matter for regional services spillovers.

7.4.3 Which Services Firm Characteristics Increase the Spillover Potential?

To understand which services firm characteristics have the potential to increase the spillover potential, we rerun the labor productivity model specified in Equation (2) on the sample of services firms only.

Due to data constraints on services firms in the Enterprise Surveys, we have to make several amendments to the model.

First, our dependent variable becomes output per worker, rather than value added per worker, since value added data are unavailable for services firms. Using output as the left-hand side numerator requires us to control for intermediates. We therefore add services expenses as a percent of a firm's output, *serv_int*, as an additional control variable. Services intensity in the previous section was measured relative to value added. Second, we cannot directly control for capital intensity as a determinant of labor productivity, as such data are only available for manufacturing firms. Thus, we add a firm's technology intensity as a proxy for a firm's technology and skill intensity.

Despite these amendments, the model can give us some insights into which firm characteristics are correlated with services firm productivity. Besides the share of intermediate services in output, we also add several firm-level characteristics as independent variables that have been shown to be correlated with firm-level productivity, including exporting status,[8] foreign ownership status, and skill intensity as proxied by the years of top manager's experience in the sector (in natural logarithms). The summary statistics for services firms can be found in Appendix 7.6.

The results are shown in Table 7.4 (Column 1). A higher share of intermediate services in output is negatively correlated with output per worker. Focusing on the predictors of labor productivity, the results show that foreign ownership status is positively and strongly associated with labor productivity, while exporting status does not matter. This is surprising given the strong connection between exporting and productivity for manufacturing firms. Finally, a higher skill intensity as proxied by the years of experience of the top manager, is positively correlated with labor productivity.

Columns 2–4 replicate the model by income status and find differences across groupings. It seems that the labor productivity of services firms in low-income countries is more sensitive to changes in other firm-level factors. A higher services intensity is more negatively correlated with labor productivity in low-income countries compared to middle-income countries. By contrast, FDI status and a longer experience of the top manager in the sector are more positively associated with labor productivity in low-income countries. Interestingly, exporting only shows a positive correlation with labor productivity for low-income

---

8   Rather than using direct exports to compute the export dummy, we use total exports, as indirect exports (via an intermediary agent) may be a more common export channel for services firms.

Table 7.4 Determinants of Services Firm Productivity, Ordinary Least Squares

Dependent Variable: $lnprod_{isrt}$	(1) All	(2) UM	(3) LM	(4) L
$lnserv\_int_{isrt}$	−0.4889***	−0.4776***	−0.4602***	−0.5833***
	(0.000)	(0.000)	(0.000)	(0.000)
fdi_{isrt}	0.3084***	0.2148***	0.2873***	0.3713***
	(0.000)	(0.001)	(0.000)	(0.000)
exp_{isrt}	0.0422	0.0556	−0.0620	0.2476***
	(0.286)	(0.318)	(0.341)	(0.008)
$manager_{isrt}$	0.0691***	0.0638***	0.0452*	0.1062***
	(0.000)	(0.008)	(0.051)	(0.003)
constant	7.2392***	9.3961***	7.2174***	4.7523***
	(0.000)	(0.000)	(0.000)	(0.000)
Observations	13,902	4,531	6,681	2,220
R-squared	0.57	0.53	0.52	0.53

exp_{isrt} = exporter dummy, fdi_{isrt} = foreign ownership dummy, $lnprod_{isrt}$ = output per employee in natural logarithms, $lnserv\_int_{isrt}$ = services inputs as % of output in natural logarithms, $manager_{isrt}$ = years of top manager's experience in the sector in natural logarithms, L = low-income countries, LM = lower middle-income countries, UM = upper middle-income countries.

Note: p*<0.1, p**<0.05, p***<0.01 (p-values in parentheses). All regressions include country-sector and year fixed effects.

Source: Enterprise Surveys. http://www.enterprisesurveys.org (accessed 23 April 2018); and World Bank income classification.

countries, which also explains the lack of statistical significance in the overall sample (Column 1). There are also slight differences between upper middle- and lower middle-income countries. FDI status matters more strongly for productivity gains in lower middle-income countries. On the other hand, services productivity in upper middle-income countries benefits more strongly from a longer experience of the top manager.

Table 7.5 replicates the analysis using a services firm's technology intensity as the dependent variable. The overall findings from the labor productivity regressions are supported, suggesting that a higher services intensity is negatively correlated with technology intensity, whereas foreign ownership status, managerial experience, and now also exporting status show a positive relationship with technology intensity (Column 1). Focusing on the determinants by income category in Columns 2–4 suggests that the negative correlation with services intensity is solely

Table 7.5 Determinants of Services Technology Intensity, Ordinary Least Squares

Dependent Variable: $tech_{isrt}$	(1) All	(2) UM	(3) LM	(4) L
lnserv_int_{isrt}	−0.0051***	−0.0045	−0.0032	−0.0136***
	(0.008)	(0.260)	(0.198)	(0.007)
fdi_{isrt}	0.1258***	0.1641***	0.1300***	0.0713***
	(0.000)	(0.000)	(0.000)	(0.003)
exp_{isrt}	0.1459***	0.1826***	0.1087***	0.1372***
	(0.000)	(0.000)	(0.000)	(0.000)
$manager_{isrt}$	0.0118**	0.0155	0.0056	0.0226**
	(0.011)	(0.109)	(0.377)	(0.018)
constant	−0.1180***	−0.0541*	0.9758***	−0.1624***
	(0.000)	(0.061)	(0.000)	(0.000)
Observations	14,582	5,049	6,789	2,266
R-squared	0.21	0.18	0.21	0.19

exp_{isrt} = exporter dummy, fdi_{isrt} = foreign ownership dummy, $tech_{isrt}$ = technology intensity, lnserv_int_{isrt} = services inputs as % of output in natural logarithms, $manager_{isrt}$ = years of top manager's experience in the sector in natural logarithms, L = low-income countries, LM = lower middle-income countries, UM = upper middle-income countries.

Note: p*<0.1, p**<0.05, p***<0.01 (p-values in parentheses). All regressions include country-sector and year fixed effects.

Source: Enterprise Surveys. http://www.enterprisesurveys.org (accessed 23 April 2018); and World Bank income classification.

driven by low-income countries. Similarly, managerial experience only matters positively for technology intensity in low-income countries, but not in middle-income countries. In addition, the richer a country the stronger the role of FDI as a predictor for services firm technology intensity. Finally, there seems to be a U-shaped effect of exporting, which matters more strongly for upper middle- and low-income countries compared to lower middle-income countries. In summary, this section suggests that improving the business environment with regard to skills building, trade, and investment can boost the labor productivity and technology intensity of services firms, and thus magnify the spillover potential of services firms for manufacturing productivity.

7.4.4 Can Services Trade Liberalization Increase Spillovers?

In summary, we find that a higher median productivity and technology intensity of services firms in a region are positively associated with manufacturing firm productivity levels. We also showed that several manufacturing firm characteristics increase spillovers, including large firm size, foreign ownership status, and exporting status. Due to the positive relationship between services and manufacturing firm productivity, we assessed which firm characteristics determine services firm productivity and technology intensity. We found that foreign ownership status and the top manager's experience are positively associated with services firms' output per worker and technology intensity. Exporting status only shows a positive correlation with technology intensity, but not labor productivity for services firms.

This raises the question of whether policy can influence the spillover potential and ultimately increase manufacturing firm productivity. In particular, we are interested in the role of services trade liberalization in mediating services spillovers.

Figure 7.4 Overall Services Trade Restrictions Index and Median Services Labor Productivity

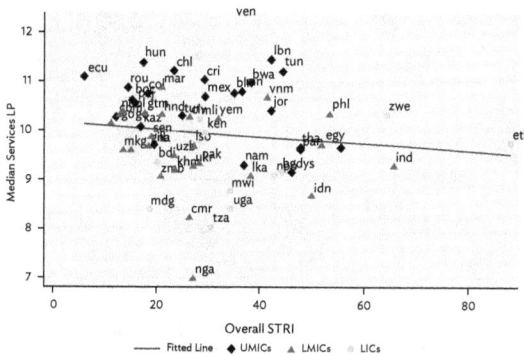

LICs = low-income countries, LMICs = lower middle-income countries, LP = labor productivity, STRI = Services Trade Restrictions Index, UMICs = upper middle-income countries.

Note: Services labor productivity measured as output per worker. A lower STRI indicates more services liberalization. Country abbreviations taken from the World Bank income classification dataset.

Source: Author's illustration, based on data from the Enterprise Surveys http://www.enterprisesurveys .org (accessed 23 April 2018) and Services Trade Restrictions Database. http://iresearch.worldbank .org/servicetrade/ (accessed 7 June 2018).

As a first step, we plot the overall services trade restrictions index on the x-axis against a country's median services output per worker on the y-axis (Figure 7.4). The graph confirms the hypothesis that a more liberal services trade environment is associated with a higher median labor productivity of services firms in a country. The scatterplot also shows that countries with higher income levels tend to have a higher median services productivity. The highest median services productivity levels are found in upper middle-income countries. In addition, high services trade restrictiveness is less common for upper middle-income countries.

Table 7.6 sheds further light on the question of whether services trade liberalization is beneficial for productivity spillovers from services to manufacturing firms. The findings suggest that higher services trade restrictions in a country, both overall and at the sector level, interact

Table 7.6 Productivity Spillovers from Services to Manufacturing Firms and the Role of the Services Trade Restrictions Index, Ordinary Least Squares

Dependent Variable: $lnlp_{isrt}$	STRI, All Modes					
	(1) overall	(2) telecom	(3) finance	(4) transp	(5) retail	(6) prof
$lnprod\_med_{rt}$	0.3942***	0.4024***	0.4119***	0.2650***	0.3465***	0.3520***
	(0.000)	(0.000)	(0.000)	(0.001)	(0.000)	(0.002)
$lnprod\_med_{rt}*AC_c$	−0.0033	−0.0041	−0.0046	−0.0008	−0.0024	−0.0018
	(0.173)	(0.106)	(0.111)	(0.721)	(0.103)	(0.361)
$lncapint_{isrt}$	0.2980***	0.2984***	0.2983***	0.2992***	0.2977***	0.2986***
	(0.000)	(0.000)	(0.000)	(0.000)	(0.000)	(0.000)
constant	3.8346***	3.1561***	2.3312***	6.2419***	3.5126***	4.1532***
	(0.000)	(0.000)	(0.000)	(0.000)	(0.000)	(0.000)
Observation	15,325	15,325	15,325	15,325	15,325	15,325
R-squared	0.48	0.48	0.48	0.48	0.48	0.48
F-test[a]	0.0000	0.0000	0.0000	0.0000	0.0000	0.0000

AC_c = absorptive capacity, $lncapint_{isrt}$ = capital stock per employee in natural logarithms, $lnlp_{isrt}$ = value added per employee in natural logarithms, $lnprod\_med_{rt}$ = median output per employee of services firms in a region in natural logarithms, prof = professional, telecom = telecommunications, transp = transportation, STRI = Services Trade Restrictions Index.

Note: p*<0.1, p**<0.05, p***<0.01 (p-values in parentheses). All regressions include country-sector and year fixed effects, and are clustered at the subnational level.

[a] F-test of joint significance between $lnprod\_med_{rt}$ and $lnprod\_med_{rt}*stri_c$ (Prob > F). A lower STRI indicates more services liberalization.

Source: Enterprise Surveys. http://www.enterprisesurveys.org (accessed 23 April 2018); and Services Trade Restrictions Index.

Table 7.7 Productivity Spillovers from Services to Manufacturing Firms and the Role of the Services Trade Restrictions Index, Modes 1 and 4, Ordinary Least Squares

Dependent Variable: lnlp_{isrt}	STRI, Mode 1				STRI, Mode 4	
	(1) overall	(2) finance	(3) transp	(4) prof	(5) overall	(6) prof
ln$prod\_med_{rt}$	0.4274***	0.3592***	0.4609***	0.3587***	-0.1288	-0.1288
	(0.000)	(0.000)	(0.000)	(0.000)	(0.456)	(0.456)
ln$prod\_med_{rt}$*AC$_c$	-0.0040**	-0.0029*	-0.0059*	-0.0023**	0.0050**	0.0050**
	(0.023)	(0.092)	(0.057)	(0.021)	(0.034)	(0.034)
ln$capint_{isrt}$	0.2975***	0.2991***	0.2978***	0.2971***	0.2996***	0.2996***
	(0.000)	(0.000)	(0.000)	(0.000)	(0.000)	(0.000)
constant	5.0125***	6.0387***	1.7671	2.9029***	4.8576***	4.8576***
	(0.000)	(0.000)	(0.150)	(0.000)	(0.000)	(0.000)
Observation	15,325	15,325	15,325	15,325	15,325	15,325
R-squared	0.48	0.48	0.48	0.48	0.48	0.48
F–test[a]	0.0000	0.0000	0.0000	0.0000	0.0000	0.0000

AC$_c$ = absorptive capacity, ln$capint_{isrt}$ = capital stock per employee in natural logarithms, lnlp_{isrt} = value added per employee in natural logarithms, ln$prod\_med_{rt}$ = median output per employee of services firms in a region in natural logarithms, prof = professional, transp = transportation, STRI = Services Trade Restrictions Index.

Note: p*<0.1, p**<0.05, p***<0.01 (p-values in parentheses). All regressions include country-sector and year fixed effects, and are clustered at the subnational level.

[a] F-test of joint significance between ln$prod\_med_{rt}$ and ln$prod\_med_{rt}$*stric (Prob > F). A lower STRI indicates more services liberalization.

Source: Enterprise Surveys. http://www.enterprisesurveys.org (accessed 23 April 2018); and Services Trade Restrictions Index.

negatively with productivity spillovers, although none of the interaction terms is individually significant. These surprising results could be related to the measure of the Services Trade Restrictions Index (STRI), which does not differentiate between the modes of services supply.[9]

Rerunning the analysis for STRI for Mode 1 services only (cross-border trade) shows negative interaction terms, which are statistically significant for STRI in all sectors, but also in finance, transporation,

---

[9] Under the General Agreement on Trade in Services, one can differentiate between four modes of services trade: cross-border trade (Mode 1), consumption abroad (Mode 2), commercial presence abroad (Mode 3), and presence of natural persons (Mode 4). The STRI differentiates between Mode 1, Mode 3, and Mode 4.

and professional services (Table 7.7, Columns 1–4). That is, a higher restrictiveness in Mode 1 services trade translates into lower productivity spillovers for manufacturing firms. In contrast, less restrictiveness in Mode 4 services trade (presence of natural persons) overall and in professional services increases the productivity spillovers overall (Columns 5 and 6). In these regressions, however, the spillover variable is no longer significant. Finally, running the analysis with the STRI measures for Mode 3 services (commercial presence abroad) shows negative interaction terms that are individually insignificant, but jointly significant with the spillover variable (Appendix 7.7).

Replicating the analysis for our alternative measure of technology spillovers shows no significant results on the individual interaction terms, but the F-tests suggest joint significance between the spillover variable and the interaction term across all specifications. This also holds for the different modes of services supply (results not shown). We conclude that higher services trade restrictiveness reduces productivity spillovers from services firms, except for restrictiveness in Mode 4 services. This seems to be beneficial to labor productivity, while its impact on technology spillovers is ambiguous.

The previous analysis examined the effects of services trade liberalization on services firm productivity. The way the estimation equation was specified allowed for direct effects (on services firms in the same sector) and indirect effects (on services firms in other sectors) due to services liberalization. In this section, we test for the direct effects of sectoral services liberalization on the productivity of firms in the same sector. We first narrow down the data sample to the five sectors for which we have country-sector measures of services trade restrictions: telecommunications (ISIC 64), finance (ISIC 66), transportation (ISIC 60-63), retail (ISIC 52), and professional services (ISIC 71-74). In the next step, we add the sectoral measure of services trade restriction, *stri*, as an independent variable to the labor productivity regressions.

The results in Table 7.8 confirm our earlier findings that more services trade liberalization (a lower *stri*) increases the productivity of services firms (Column 1). This holds for the overall STRI measure as well as Modes 1 and 3 services supply (cross-border trade and commercial presence abroad). In contrast, more restrictions in Mode 4 services trade (presence of natural persons) seems to be beneficial to the labor productivity of services firms. Replicating the results using technology intensity as the dependent variable in Table 7.9 mostly confirms those findings. While more services trade liberalization overall, and specifically in Mode 3 services, are associated with productivity gains, more liberalization in Mode 4 services seems to be correlated with the productivity losses of services firms.

Table 7.8 Services Trade Restrictions Index and Services Firm Productivity, Ordinary Least Squares

Dependent Variable: lnprod_{isrt}	(1) Overall	(2) Mode 1	(3) Mode 3	(4) Mode 4
stri_{cs}	−0.0262***	−0.0263***	−0.0171***	0.0077***
	(0.000)	(0.000)	(0.000)	(0.007)
lnserv_int_{isrt}	−0.4256***	−0.3743***	−0.4256***	−0.4143***
	(0.000)	(0.000)	(0.000)	(0.000)
fdi_{isrt}	0.3105***	0.0465	0.3105***	−0.1477
	(0.000)	(0.681)	(0.000)	(0.283)
exp_{isrt}	0.0497	0.3273**	0.0497	0.4183*
	(0.650)	(0.016)	(0.650)	(0.060)
manager_{isrt}	0.1064***	0.0943	0.1064***	0.2011*
	(0.000)	(0.175)	(0.000)	(0.064)
constant	9.7979***	9.0388***	8.7574***	8.0632***
	(0.000)	(0.000)	(0.000)	(0.000)
Observations	6,906	1,778	6,906	625
R-squared	0.54	0.56	0.54	0.56

exp_{isrt} = exporter dummy, fdi_{isrt} = foreign ownership dummy, $lnprod_{isrt}$ = output per employee in natural logarithms, $lnserv\_int_{isrt}$ = services inputs as % of output in natural logarithms, $manager_{isrt}$ = years of top manager's experience in the sector in natural logarithms, $stri_{cs}$ = Services Trade Restrictions Index.

Note: p*<0.1, p**<0.05, p***<0.01 (p-values in parentheses). All regressions include country-sector and year fixed effects and are clustered at the country-sector level. A lower $stri$ indicates more services liberalization.

Source: Enterprise Surveys http://www.enterprisesurveys.org (accessed 23 April 2018); and Services Trade Restrictions Index.

Table 7.9 Services Trade Restrictions Index and Services Technology Intensity, Ordinary Least Squares

Dependent Variable: tech_{isrt}	(1) Overall	(2) Mode 1	(3) Mode 3	(4) Mode 4
stri_{cs}	−0.0052***	−0.0007	−0.0048***	0.0015*
	(0.000)	(0.384)	(0.000)	(0.068)
lnserv_int_{isrt}	−0.0066*	−0.0122	−0.0066*	0.0026
	(0.053)	(0.149)	(0.053)	(0.883)
fdi_{isrt}	0.1279***	0.1822***	0.1279***	0.1092
	(0.000)	(0.000)	(0.000)	(0.181)

continued on next page

Table 7.9 *continued*

Dependent Variable: tech$_{isrt}$	(1) Overall	(2) Mode 1	(3) Mode 3	(4) Mode 4
exp$_{isrt}$	0.1010***	0.0750**	0.1010***	0.1213***
	(0.000)	(0.038)	(0.000)	(0.000)
manager$_{isrt}$	0.0118	0.0563	0.0118	0.1582**
	(0.298)	(0.170)	(0.298)	(0.028)
constant	0.0725**	-0.1647	-0.0674**	-0.5595***
	(0.025)	(0.315)	(0.049)	(0.004)
Observations	7,258	1,892	7,258	663
R-squared	0.21	0.27	0.21	0.27

exp$_{isrt}$ = exporter dummy, fdi$_{isrt}$ = foreign ownership dummy, tech$_{isrt}$ = technology intensity, Inserv_int$_{isrt}$ = services inputs as % of output in natural logarithms, manager$_{isrt}$ = years of top manager's experience in the sector in natural logarithms, stri$_{cs}$ = Services Trade Restrictions Index.

Note: p*<0.1, p**<0.05, p***<0.01 (p-values in parentheses). All regressions include country-sector and year fixed effects, and are clustered at the country-sector level. A lower stri indicates more services liberalization.

Source: Enterprise Surveys. http://www.enterprisesurveys.org (accessed 23 April 2018); and Services Trade Restrictions Index.

7.5 Summary and Conclusions

In recent years, several studies have suggested a performance-enhancing effect of services usage within sectors and firms. However, there is still a shortage of studies on the productivity spillovers from services firms to downstream sectors and firms, in particular for low- and middle-income countries. Using a cross-section of more than 38,000 manufacturing and 24,000 services firms in 105 low- and middle-income countries over the period 2010–2017 from the World Bank's Enterprise Surveys, this chapter focuses on productivity spillovers from services to manufacturing firms, as well as the role of firm characteristics and a country's services liberalization in mediating spillovers.

The chapter confirms positive spillovers to manufacturing firms resulting from a higher average regional productivity and technology intensity of services firms, but rejects the existence of spillovers from services firm presence alone. This finding is of high policy relevance, as it suggests that the number of services firms in a region and their share in a region's total output are not sufficient to generate spillovers—what matters is the quality of services firms. This chapter assesses two characteristics of services firms that are associated with a higher manufacturing firm productivity, namely, their output per worker and technology intensity.

The analysis also shows that the extent of spillovers varies and depends on the characteristics of manufacturing firms (which determine their absorptive capacity), the characteristics of services firms (which determine their spillover potential), and country characteristics, including income status and services trade liberalization efforts. The findings suggest that certain types of manufacturing firms benefit more strongly from productivity and technology spillovers of services firms, in particular large, foreign-owned, and exporting manufacturing firms. Manufacturing firms with a larger services intensity, by contrast, have lower spillovers, and skill intensity does not matter.

Regarding the spillover potential of services firms, the results show that foreign ownership status and the top manager's experience in a sector are positively associated with services firms' output per worker and technology intensity. Exporting status only shows a positive correlation with technology intensity, but not labor productivity for services firms. This implies that policies aiming at upgrading skills and technology can not only increase the spillover potential of services firms, but also help manufacturing firms absorb spillovers. In addition, policies facilitating the growth of manufacturing firms can generate higher productivity and technology spillovers.

Country characteristics, including a country's income status, also matter. The results suggest a U-shaped effect for productivity spillovers from services firms, meaning that spillovers are larger in upper middle- and low-income countries than in lower middle-income countries. The results are different for technology spillovers where lower middle- and low-income countries benefit more strongly. Similarly, the results show that labor productivity of services firms in low-income countries is more sensitive to FDI status and the experience of the top manager in the sector. In addition, exporting and labor productivity are positively associated in low-income countries only. This implies that policy interventions to improve the productivity of services firms or the absorptive capacity of manufacturing firms have a larger impact in low-income countries.

As a last step, the chapter examines whether policy mediates productivity spillovers from services to manufacturing firms in a region. It is possible that reforms in the upstream services sectors translate into higher spillover potential and thus higher actual productivity spillovers. The results suggest that lower regulations in Mode 1 services trade (cross-border trade) increase productivity spillovers, whereas a lower restrictiveness in Mode 4 services trade (presence of natural persons) seems to reduce them. We also test for the direct link between services liberalization and services firm productivity, and find a positive connection overall and for Mode 1 and Mode 3 (commercial presence abroad) services trade, but not for Mode 4 services trade. Linking services restrictiveness to the technology intensity of services firms confirms the positive correlation overall and for Mode 1 services, as well as the negative association for Mode 4 services. In summary, the findings suggest that more liberalization in Mode 1 and Mode 3 services trade increases spillovers from services firms to manufacturing firms via a productivity-enhancing effect in the services sectors.

While there has been substantial empirical work in the area of services spillovers, much promising ground for research remains. Our findings suggest two areas in particular. First, this chapter highlights the importance of firm heterogeneity in mediating spillovers, from the perspective of both manufacturing and services firms. Improving our understanding of the underlying transmission channels of services spillovers can help guide policies to strengthen services firms and promote spillovers to manufacturing firms.

Finally, research should focus more on understanding the services spillover potential, especially in the context of GVC dynamics. Recent research suggests that services play an important role in economic upgrading within GVCs, as they add value to a given unit of output. In the apparel GVC, for instance, countries can increase their value added by moving from the lower value-added cut, make, and trim segment into original design manufacturing or original brand manufacturing. This is particularly important for small and low-income countries that increasingly rely on GVC participation.

References

Amiti, M., and S.-J. Wei. 2009. Service Offshoring and Productivity: Evidence from the US. *The World Economy* 32(2): 203–220.

Arnold, J., B. Javorcik, and A. Mattoo. 2011. Does Services Liberalization Benefit Manufacturing Firms?: Evidence from the Czech Republic. *Journal of International Economics* 85(1): 136–146.

Arnold, J., B. Javorcik, M. Lipscomb, and A. Mattoo. 2015. Services Reform and Manufacturing Performance: Evidence from India. *The Economic Journal* 126(590): 1–39.

Borchert, I., B. Gootiiz, and A. Mattoo. 2012. Policy Barriers to International Trade in Services: Evidence from a New Database. Policy Research Working Paper 6109. Washington, DC: World Bank.

Castellani, D., and A. Zanfei. 2003. Technology Gaps, Absorptive Capacity and the Impact of Inward Investments on Productivity of European Firms. *Economics of Innovation and New Technology* 12.

Conway, P., D. de Rosa, G. Nicoletti, and F. Steiner. 2006. Regulation, Competition and Productivity Convergences. *Organisation for Economic Co-operation and Development (OECD) Economics Department Working Paper* 509.

Crinò, R. 2008. Service Offshoring and Productivity in Western Europe. *Economics Bulletin* 6: 1–8.

Crinò, R. 2009. Offshoring, Multinationals and Labor Market: A Review of the Empirical Literature. *Journal of Economic Surveys* 23(2): 197–249.

Debaere, P., H. Görg, and H. Raff. 2013. Greasing the Wheels of International Commerce: How Services Facilitate Firms' International Sourcing. *Canadian Journal of Economics* 46(1): 78–102.

Ethier, W. 1982. National and International Returns to Scale in the Modern Theory of International Trade. *The American Economic Review* 72(3): 389–405.

Farole, T., and D. Winkler. 2015. The Role of Foreign Firm Characteristics, Absorptive Capacity and the Institutional Framework for FDI Spillovers.*The Journal of Banking and Financial Economics* 1(3): 77–112.

Farole, T., C. Staritz, and D. Winkler. 2014. Conceptual Framework. In T. Farole and D. Winkler (eds), *Making Foreign Direct Investment Work for Sub-Saharan Africa: Local Spillovers and Competitiveness in Global Value Chains*, pp. 23–55. Washington, DC: World Bank.

Francois, J., and B. Hoekman. 2010. Services Trade and Policy. *Journal of Economic Literature* 48(3): 642–92.

Görg, H., and A. Hanley. 2003. International Outsourcing and Productivity: Evidence from Plant Level Data. Research Paper Series: Globalisation, Productivity and Technology. Research Paper 20/2003. Nottingham: University of Nottingham.

Görg, H., and D. Greenaway. 2004. Much Ado About Nothing? Do Domestic Firms Really Benefit from Foreign Direct Investment? *The World Bank Research Observer* 19(2): 171–197.

Görg, H., A. Hanley, and E. Strobl. 2008. Productivity Effects of International Outsourcing: Evidence from Plant-Level Data. *Canadian Journal of Economics* 41(2): 670–688.

Guiso, L., P. Sapienza, and L. Zingales. 2004. Does Local Financial Development Matter? *Quarterly Journal of Economics* 119: 929–969.

Havranek, T., and Z. Irsova. 2011. Estimating Vertical Spillovers from FDI: Why Results Vary and What the True Effect Is. *Journal of International Economics* 85: 234–244.

Hoekman, B., and B. Javorcik. 2006. Lessons from Empirical Research on Technology Diffusion through Trade and Foreign Direct Investment. In *Global Integration and Technology Transfer*, edited by B. Hoekman and B. Javorcik. Washington, DC: Palgrave and World Bank.

Hoekman, B., and B. Shepherd. 2017. Services Productivity, Trade Policy and Manufacturing Exports. Special Issue: Services and Manufacturing Activity. *World Economy* 40(3): 499–516.

Javorcik, B. 2008. Can Survey Evidence Shed Light on Spillovers from Foreign Direct Investment? *World Bank Research Observer* 23(2): 139–159.

Lipsey, R. E., and F. Sjöholm. 2005. The Impact of Inward FDI on Host Countries: Why Such Different Answers? In T. H. Moran, E. Graham, and M. Blomström (eds), *Does Foreign Direct Investment Promote Development?*, pp. 23–43. Washington, DC: Peterson Institute for International Economics and Center for Global Development.

Lodefalk, M. 2014. The Role of Services for Manufacturing Firm Exports. *Review of World Economics* 150(1): 59–82.

Michel, B., and F. Rycx. 2014. Productivity Gains and Spillovers from Offshoring," *Review of International Economics* 22(1): 73–85.

Nicoletti, G., and S. Scarpetta. 2003. Regulation, Productivity and Growth: OECD Evidence. *Economic Policy* 18(36): 9–72.

OECD. 2014. Global Value Chains and Africa's Industrialisation. *African Economic Outlook 2014*. Paris: OECD.

Paus, E., and K. Gallagher. 2008. Missing Links: Foreign Investment and Industrial Development in Costa Rica and Mexico. *Studies of Comparative International Development* 43(1): 53–80.

Rajan, R. G., and L. Zingales. 1998. Financial Dependence and Growth. *American Economic Review* 88(3): 559–586.

Saez, S., D. Taglioni, E. van der Marel, C. H. Hollweg, and V. Zavacka. 2015. *Valuing Services in Trade: A Toolkit for Competitiveness Diagnostics*. Washington, DC: World Bank.

Smeets, R. 2008. Collecting the Pieces of the FDI Knowledge Spillovers Puzzle. *World Bank Research Observer* 23(2): 107–138.

Taglioni, D., and D. Winkler. 2016. *Making Global Value Chains Work for Development*. Washington, DC: World Bank.

Winkler, D. 2010. Services Offshoring and Its Impact on Productivity and Employment: Evidence from Germany, 1995–2006. *The World Economy* 33(12): 1672–1701.

Winkler, D. 2013. Services Offshoring and the Relative Demand for White-Collar Workers in German Manufacturing. In A. Bardhan, D. Jaffee, and C. Kroll (eds), *The Oxford Handbook of Offshoring and Global Employment*, pp. 72–99. New York: Oxford University Press.

World Bank, Development Economics Research Group. Services Trade Restrictions Database. http://iresearch.worldbank.org/servicetrade (accessed 7 June 2018).

World Bank, Enterprise Surveys. http://www.enterprisesurveys.org (accessed 23 April 2018).

Appendix 7.1 Number of Firms by Country and Sector

Country	Year	Total	Mfg	%	Services	%
Afghanistan	2014	337	139	41.2%	198	58.8%
Albania	2013	292	111	38.0%	181	62.0%
Angola	2010	195	78	40.0%	117	60.0%
Argentina	2017	931	650	69.8%	281	30.2%
Armenia	2013	297	111	37.4%	186	62.6%
Azerbaijan	2013	320	121	37.8%	199	62.2%
Bangladesh	2013	1,360	1,179	86.7%	181	13.3%
Belarus	2013	337	117	34.7%	220	65.3%
Belize	2010	111	72	64.9%	39	35.1%
Benin	2016	134	70	52.2%	64	47.8%
Bhutan	2015	144	83	57.6%	61	42.4%
Bolivia	2017	327	118	36.1%	209	63.9%
Bosnia and Herzegovina	2013	324	117	36.1%	207	63.9%
Botswana	2010	226	85	37.6%	141	62.4%
Bulgaria	2013	251	111	44.2%	140	55.8%
Burundi	2014	127	60	47.2%	67	52.8%
Cambodia	2016	294	135	45.9%	159	54.1%
Cameroon	2016	309	102	33.0%	207	67.0%
Central African Republic	2011	131	37	28.2%	94	71.8%
Chile	2010	1,012	780	77.1%	232	22.9%
China, People's Republic of	2012	2,406	1,686	70.1%	720	29.9%
Colombia	2010	917	708	77.2%	209	22.8%
Costa Rica	2010	473	322	68.1%	151	31.9%
Côte d'Ivoire	2016	325	106	32.6%	219	67.4%
Democratic Republic of the Congo	2013	466	241	51.7%	225	48.3%
Djibouti	2013	216	62	28.7%	154	71.3%
Dominican Republic	2016	326	111	34.0%	215	66.0%
Ecuador	2017	323	103	31.9%	220	68.1%
Egypt	2016	1,613	1,173	72.7%	440	27.3%
El Salvador	2016	678	405	59.7%	273	40.3%

continued on next page

Appendix 7.1 *continued*

Country	Year	Total	Mfg	%	Services	%
Ethiopia	2015	723	383	53.0%	340	47.0%
Georgia	2013	302	111	36.8%	191	63.2%
Ghana	2013	631	377	59.7%	254	40.3%
Guatemala	2013	559	356	63.7%	203	36.3%
Guinea	2010	125	27	21.6%	98	78.4%
Guyana	2016	141	71	50.4%	70	49.6%
Honduras	2010	303	92	30.4%	211	69.6%
India	2016	8,686	7,163	82.5%	1,523	17.5%
Indonesia	2014	1,251	1,069	85.5%	182	14.5%
Iraq	2015	618	475	76.9%	143	23.1%
Jamaica	2011	336	121	36.0%	215	64.0%
Jordan	2010	531	335	63.1%	196	36.9%
Kazakhstan	2013	523	202	38.6%	321	61.4%
Kenya	2013	717	414	57.7%	303	42.3%
Kosovo	2013	170	71	41.8%	99	58.2%
Kyrgyz Republic	2013	207	104	50.2%	103	49.8%
Lao People's Democratic Republic	2013	286	110	38.5%	176	61.5%
Latvia	2016	293	117	39.9%	176	60.1%
Lebanon	2013	489	239	48.9%	250	51.1%
Lesotho	2013	134	76	56.7%	58	43.3%
Liberia	2016	131	75	57.3%	56	42.7%
Lithuania	2017	233	107	45.9%	126	54.1%
Macedonia	2013	288	125	43.4%	163	56.6%
Madagascar	2013	358	264	73.7%	94	26.3%
Malawi	2014	455	171	37.6%	284	62.4%
Malaysia	2015	928	585	63.0%	343	37.0%
Mali	2016	166	99	59.6%	67	40.4%
Mauritania	2014	129	52	40.3%	77	59.7%
Mexico	2010	1,440	1,171	81.3%	269	18.7%
Moldova	2013	310	110	35.5%	200	64.5%
Mongolia	2013	279	115	41.2%	164	58.8%
Montenegro	2013	129	50	38.8%	79	61.2%

continued on next page

Appendix 7.1 *continued*

Country	Year	Total	Mfg	%	Services	%
Morocco	2013	339	187	55.2%	152	44.8%
Myanmar	2016	536	367	68.5%	169	31.5%
Namibia	2014	456	181	39.7%	275	60.3%
Nepal	2013	413	242	58.6%	171	41.4%
Nicaragua	2016	281	110	39.1%	171	60.9%
Niger	2017	134	41	30.6%	93	69.4%
Nigeria	2014	2,377	1,427	60.0%	950	40.0%
Pakistan	2013	1,188	1,086	91.4%	102	8.6%
Panama	2010	331	119	36.0%	212	64.0%
Paraguay	2017	334	117	35.0%	217	65.0%
Peru	2017	932	551	59.1%	381	40.9%
Philippines	2015	1,271	1,037	81.6%	234	18.4%
Romania	2013	468	175	37.4%	293	62.6%
Russian Federation	2012	3,624	1,380	38.1%	2,244	61.9%
Rwanda	2011	178	81	45.5%	97	54.5%
Senegal	2014	450	249	55.3%	201	44.7%
Serbia	2013	325	118	36.3%	207	63.7%
Sierra Leone	2017	131	77	58.8%	54	41.2%
Solomon Islands	2015	133	42	31.6%	91	68.4%
South Sudan	2014	588	89	15.1%	499	84.9%
Sri Lanka	2011	562	362	64.4%	200	35.6%
St. Lucia	2010	112	63	56.3%	49	43.8%
St. Vincent and the Grenadines	2010	128	49	38.3%	79	61.7%
Sudan	2014	606	84	13.9%	522	86.1%
Suriname	2010	126	75	59.5%	51	40.5%
Swaziland	2016	131	75	57.3%	56	42.7%
Tajikistan	2013	284	122	43.0%	162	57.0%
Tanzania	2013	648	440	67.9%	208	32.1%
Thailand	2016	956	726	75.9%	230	24.1%
Timor-Leste	2015	100	60	60.0%	40	40.0%
Togo	2016	117	45	38.5%	72	61.5%
Tunisia	2013	536	329	61.4%	207	38.6%
Turkey	2015	1,911	1,139	59.6%	772	40.4%

continued on next page

Appendix 7.1 *continued*

Country	Year	Total	Mfg	%	Services	%
Uganda	2013	650	378	58.2%	272	41.8%
Ukraine	2013	951	737	77.5%	214	22.5%
Uruguay	2017	333	114	34.2%	219	65.8%
Uzbekistan	2013	332	133	40.1%	199	59.9%
Venezuela	2010	287	85	29.6%	202	70.4%
Viet Nam	2015	906	694	76.6%	212	23.4%
Yemen	2013	302	117	38.7%	185	61.3%
Zambia	2013	578	364	63.0%	214	37.0%
Zimbabwe	2016	529	289	54.6%	240	45.4%
Total		63,031	38,344	60.8%	24,687	39.2%

Mfg = manufacturing.
Source: Enterprise Surveys. http://www.enterprisesurveys.org (accessed 23 April 2018).

Appendix 7.2 Number of Manufacturing Firms by Sector

ISIC Rev. 3	Sector Name	No. of Firms	%
15	Manufacture of food products and beverages	7,147	18.6%
16	Manufacture of tobacco products	193	0.5%
17	Manufacture of textiles	2,428	6.3%
18	Manufacture of wearing apparel; dressing and dyeing of fur	3,791	9.9%
19	Tanning and dressing of leather; manufacture of luggage, handbags, saddlery, harness and footwear	816	2.1%
20	Manufacture of wood and of products of wood and cork, except furniture	1,138	3.0%
21	Manufacture of paper and paper products	589	1.5%
22	Publishing, printing and reproduction of recorded media	1,615	4.2%
23	Manufacture of coke, refined petroleum products and nuclear fuel	132	0.3%
24	Manufacture of chemicals and chemical products	2,725	7.1%
25	Manufacture of rubber and plastics products	2,795	7.3%
26	Manufacture of other non-metallic mineral products	2,955	7.7%
27	Manufacture of basic metals	1,380	3.6%
28	Manufacture of fabricated metal products, except machinery and equipment	3,271	8.5%
29	Manufacture of machinery and equipment N.E.C.	2,151	5.6%
30	Manufacture of office, accounting and computing machinery	20	0.1%
31	Manufacture of electrical machinery and apparatus N.E.C.	1,399	3.6%
32	Manufacture of radio, television and communication equipment and apparatus	200	0.5%
33	Manufacture of medical, precision and optical instruments,watches and clocks	296	0.8%
34	Manufacture of motor vehicles, trailers and semi-trailers	940	2.5%

continued on next page

Appendix 7.2 *continued*

ISIC Rev. 3	Sector Name	No. of Firms	%
35	Manufacture of other transport equipment	143	0.4%
36	Manufacture of furniture; manufacturing N.E.C.	1996	5.2%
	Undefined*	224	0.6%
	Total	38,344	100.0%

ISIC = International Standard Industrial Classification, N.E.C. = not elsewhere classified, No. = number, Rev. = revision.

Note: ISIC classification based on the most important product of a firm. *Some firms were classified as Manufacturing in the Enterprise Surveys, but their largest product was a service.

Source: Enterprise Surveys. http://www.enterprisesurveys.org (accessed 23 April 2018).

Appendix 7.3 Summary Statistics, Manufacturing Firms

Variable	Obs	Mean	Std. Dev.	Min	Max
$lnlp_{isrt}$	26,033	9.108	1.418	0.131	16.684
$lncapint_{isrt}$	20,719	8.182	1.960	−8.814	18.745
$serv\_no_{rt}$	36,758	31.063	17.727	0.000	97.468
$serv\_out_{rt}$	36,755	26.118	23.553	0.000	99.980
$lnprod\_med_{rt}$	35,342	9.760	1.109	5.472	14.706
$tech\_med_{rt}$	36,755	0.061	0.237	0.000	2.000
$lnserv\_int_{isrt}$	24,244	0.810	2.731	−11.220	11.273
$large_{isrt}$	35,619	0.252	0.434	0.000	1.000
fdi_{isrt}	35,601	0.096	0.295	0.000	1.000
exp_{isrt}	35,080	0.187	0.390	0.000	1.000
shs_{isrt}	28,432	70.651	29.963	0.000	100.000

exp_{isrt} = exporter dummy, fdi_{isrt} = foreign ownership dummy, $lncapint_{isrt}$ = capital stock per employee in natural logarithms, $lnlp_{isrt}$ = value added per employee in natural logarithms, $lnprod\_med_{rt}$ = median output per employee of services firms in a region in natural logarithms, $lnserv\_int_{isrt}$ = services inputs as % of value added in logarithms, $large_{isrt}$ = large firm dummy, $manager_{isrt}$ = years of top manager's experience in the sector in natural logarithms, Max = maximum, Min = minimum, Obs = observations, $prof$ = professional, shs_{isrt} = number of skilled production workers as % of total production workers, $serv\_no_{rt}$ = number of services firms as a percent of total number of firms by region, $serv\_out_{rt}$ = output of services firms as a percent of total output of firms by region, Std. Dev. = standard deviation, $tech\_med_{rt}$ = median technology intensity of services firms in a region.

Source: Enterprise Surveys. http://www.enterprisesurveys.org (accessed 23 April 2018).

Appendix 7.4 Services Presence in a Region and Manufacturing Firm Productivity, Ordinary Least Squares

Dependent Variable: $lnlp_{isrt}$	serv_no		serv_out	
	(1)	(2)	(3)	(4)
$spill_{rt}$	−0.0010	0.0041	−0.0022	0.0000
	(0.777)	(0.219)	(0.102)	(0.996)
$lncapint_{isrt}$		0.3014***		0.3015***
		(0.000)		(0.000)
constant	9.3451	7.5690***	10.2647***	7.6401***
	(.)	(0.000)	(0.000)	(0.000)
Observations	25,179	17,839	25,176	17,836
R-squared	0.35	0.50	0.35	0.50

$lncapint_{isrt}$ = capital stock per employee in natural logarithms, $lnlp_{isrt}$ = value added per employee in natural logarithms, $spill_{rt}$ = spillover variable, serv_no = number of services firms as a percent of total number of firms by region, serv_out = output of services firms as a percent of total output of firms by region.

Note: p*<0.1, p**<0.05, p***<0.01 (p-values in parentheses). All regressions include country-sector and year fixed effects, and are clustered at the subnational level.

Source: Enterprise Surveys. http://www.enterprisesurveys.org (accessed 23 April 2018).

Appendix 7.5 Services Productivity and Technology Intensity in a Region and Manufacturing Firm Productivity, by Income, Ordinary Least Squares

Dependent Variable: $\ln lp_{isrt}$	lnprod_med			tech_med		
	(1) UM	(2) LM	(3) L	(4) UM	(5) LM	(6) L
spill_rt	0.3004***	0.2091***	0.3338***	0.3520***	0.5543***	0.4927**
	(0.000)	(0.000)	(0.001)	(0.006)	(0.000)	(0.031)
lncapint_isrt	0.2749***	0.2989***	0.3157***	0.2842***	0.3049***	0.3191***
	(0.000)	(0.000)	(0.000)	(0.000)	(0.000)	(0.000)
constant	3.5587***	4.5128***	2.3450***	7.1043***	6.6121***	6.2758***
	(0.000)	(0.000)	(0.004)	(0.000)	(0.000)	(0.000)
Observations	6,041	8,772	2,687	6,041	8,789	2,687
R-squared	0.38	0.41	0.52	0.37	0.41	0.51

lncapint_isrt = capital stock per employee in natural logarithms, lnprod_med = median output per employee of services firms in a region in natural logarithms, lnlp_isrt = value added per employee in natural logarithms, spill_rt = spillover variable, tech_med = median technology intensity of services firms in a region, L = low-income countries, LM = lower middle-income countries, UM = upper middle-income countries.

Note: p*<0.1, p**<0.05, p***<0.01 (p-values in parentheses). All regressions include country-sector and year fixed effects, and are clustered at the subnational level.

Source: Enterprise Surveys. http://www.enterprisesurveys.org (accessed 23 April 2018); and World Bank income classification.

Appendix 7.6 Summary Statistics, Services Firms

Variable	Obs	Mean	Std. Dev.	Min	Max
lnprod_{isrt}	17,536	9.893	1.774	0.866	20.261
lnserv_int_{isrt}	14,960	-4.736	1.960	-19.773	5.886
tech_{isrt}	22,169	1.293	1.035	0.000	4.000
fdi_{isrt}	21,396	0.100	0.300	0.000	1.000
exp_{isrt}	22,169	0.105	0.307	0.000	1.000
manager_{isrt}	20,761	2.548	0.764	0.000	4.970

exp_{isrt} = exporter dummy, fdi_{isrt} = foreign ownership dummy, lnprodis_{rt} = output per employee in natural logarithms, lnserv_int_{isrt} = services inputs as % of output in natural logarithms, manager_{isrt} = years of top manager's experience in the sector in natural logarithms, Max = maximum, Min = minimum, Obs = observations, Std. Dev. = standard deviation, tech_{isrt} = technology intensity.

Source: Enterprise Surveys. http://www.enterprisesurveys.org (accessed 23 April 2018).

Appendix 7.7 Productivity Spillovers from Services to Manufacturing Firms and the Role of Services Trade Restrictions Index, Mode 3, Ordinary Least Squares

Dependent Variable: $\ln lp_{isrt}$	STRI, Mode 3					
	(1) overall	(2) telecom	(3) finance	(4) transp	(5) retail	(6) prof
$\ln prod\_med_{rt}$	0.3660***	0.4024***	0.3883***	0.2476***	0.3465***	0.3081***
	(0.000)	(0.000)	(0.000)	(0.001)	(0.000)	(0.000)
$\ln prod\_med_{rt}{}^*stri_c$	−0.0027	−0.0041	−0.0039	−0.0004	−0.0024	−0.0011
	(0.205)	(0.106)	(0.128)	(0.823)	(0.103)	(0.374)
$\ln capint_{isrt}$	0.2981***	0.2984***	0.2985***	0.2993***	0.2977***	0.2985***
	(0.000)	(0.000)	(0.000)	(0.000)	(0.000)	(0.000)
constant	2.6121***	3.1561***	3.9556***	6.4076***	3.5126***	4.4366***
	(0.000)	(0.000)	(0.000)	(0.000)	(0.000)	(0.000)
Observations	15,325	15,325	15,325	15,325	15,325	15,325
R-squared	0.48	0.48	0.48	0.48	0.48	0.48
F-test[a]	0.0000	0.0000	0.0000	0.0000	0.0000	0.0000

$\ln capint_{isrt}$ = capital stock per employee in natural logarithms, $\ln lp_{isrt}$ = value added per employee in natural logarithms, $\ln prod\_med_{rt}$ = median output per employee of services firms in a region in natural logarithms, prof = professional, stri = Services Trade Restrictions Index, telecom = telecommunications, transp = transportation.

Note: p*<0.1, p**<0.05, p***<0.01 (p-values in parentheses). All regressions include country-sector, and year fixed effects, and are clustered at the subnational level.

[a] F-test of joint significance between $\ln prod\_med_{rt}$ and $\ln prod\_med_{rt}{}^*stri_c$ (Prob > F). A lower stri indicates more services liberalization.

Source: Enterprise Surveys. http://www.enterprisesurveys.org (accessed 23 April 2018); and Services Trade Restrictions Database.

8

Productivity and Trade Growth in Services: How Services Helped Power "Factory Asia"

Ben Shepherd

8.1 Introduction

One key aspect of the "premature deindustrialization" argument is the hypothesis that services are low in productivity relative to manufacturing, and that the prospects for rapid and sustained productivity growth, which are the primary source of gains in per capita income, are greater in manufacturing than in services. For instance, Rodrik (2016) argued that manufacturing plays a special role in development and growth, as it is technologically dynamic and tradeable (i.e., not constrained by small domestic markets). Measuring productivity in services sectors is fraught with difficulties. This chapter takes a different approach by focusing on trade data. According to Ricardian logic, productivity differences are a key driver of trade flows between economies. If the relative productivity hypothesis behind the premature deindustrialization argument is true, we would expect the trade data to reflect it. Specifically, we would expect economies to experience different patterns of revealed productivity growth between manufacturing and services.

Until recently, analysts commonly used the Balassa measure of revealed comparative advantage (RCA) to draw inferences about the patterns of comparative advantage across sectors and economies. Although the measure is intuitively appealing, it lacks a theoretical foundation and imposes an arbitrary threshold for a "comparative advantage" and "comparative disadvantage" based on a comparison of an economy's sectoral trade patterns and those of the world as a whole. Such an approach would not be informative in the present case, as considerably more nuance is necessary.

We therefore use Costinot, Donaldson, and Komunjer's (2012) recently developed Ricardian model of trade. Under Ricardian logic, the productivity driver for trade is not absolute differences but relative differences in productivity. In other words, we are interested in whether the People's Republic of China (PRC) or Singapore is better at producing financial services relative to electronics, for example. A by-product of this model is a simple and intuitive methodology for estimating a theory-consistent measure of RCA using a standard gravity model. The authors applied their insight to the data using trade in goods only, and Lemain and Orefice (2013) extended their work to a more disaggregated level. To our knowledge, our work here is the first to apply the same methodology to services and, in particular, to allow for patterns of comparative advantage across goods and services sectors.

Traditionally, economists often subsumed services under the heading of the "non-tradeable" economy. That approach no longer applies given the regulatory and technological changes over recent decades (van der Marel and Shepherd 2013). First, under the World Trade Organization (WTO) General Agreement on Trade in Services (GATS), any service is potentially tradeable, accounting for the four modes of supply. While it is true that some services remain rarely traded, this is due to high trade costs, not physical or legal impossibility. For instance, the textbook example of a "non-tradeable" service is a haircut. However, every year, for Fashion Week in New York or Paris, hairstylists move from country to country to supply such services under GATS Mode 4 (movement of service providers). Capturing statistics for such trade is challenging, and it only represents a small segment of the market; nonetheless, it exists. Similarly, in other sectors, pure cross-border trade (GATS Mode 1) has become possible thanks to innovations in information and communications technology (ICT). From a technological point of view, a lawyer in Shanghai can advise a client in Bangkok by phone, Voice over Internet Protocol, or email; the resulting payment of his or her fee is an export of services from the PRC to Thailand. This kind of trade in services is quantitatively important in many sectors and continues to grow as internet penetration rates increase and the digital economy extends its reach.

As a result of these two dynamics—changes in regulation and changes in technology—we can no longer consider services to be "non-tradeable." As such, it makes sense to include them in models of comparative advantage, just like goods. Since economic actors choose to allocate resources across goods and services sectors based on similar considerations, there is no a priori barrier to including them in the same model, provided that we take appropriate account of the possibility of cross-sectoral heterogeneity, as is already the case for disaggregated models of goods trade.

The key constraint in implementing this approach is the availability of bilateral services trade data disaggregated by subsector. We elaborate on this issue in section 8.2. In essence, we use a database of gross exports of goods and services by International Standard Industrial Classification (ISIC) sector developed by the Organisation for Economic Co-operation and Development (OECD)-WTO Trade in Value Added (TiVA) project. To be clear, we do not use estimates of value-added trade as these would not fit with our chosen theory. Instead, we use carefully cleaned, harmonized, and estimated values for trade in goods and services in gross shipment terms as an input into the value-added exercise.

This chapter is organized as follows. Section 8.2 discusses the data issues in more detail and presents some descriptive statistics based on the observed patterns of export growth in developing Asia. The key insight of the descriptive analysis is that it is utterly artificial to separate trade growth in goods and services markets: they belong together in a profound sense, even in "Factory Asia," where manufacturing has been paramount over recent decades. Section 8.3 discusses our model and estimation and presents the results. Our focus in the discussion of the results is on showing that productivity differences and growth potential vary at least as much within manufacturing and services aggregates as they do between them. In other words, sectoral specialization at the micro-level matters for growth and development potential, not the aggregate level of goods or services production in an economy. Section 8.4 concludes and presents policy implications.

8.2 Data and Descriptive Statistics

Data on trade in services are notoriously incomplete. Recent efforts to compile global databases have focused on trade with the world as an aggregate partner (e.g., Loungani et al. 2017). While informative for descriptive purposes, these databases are largely unhelpful for empirical work, because they do not disaggregate by partner economy. As a result, we cannot use them with standard trade models like gravity.

The difficulty of constructing a database of bilateral trade in services is that many economies simply do not record the relevant data within their balance of payments statistics. Although it is possible to construct estimates by modeling, this subsequently creates problems when using synthetic observations in regressions that take a similar form to the model used to fill in the missing cells in the trade matrix. A recent effort in this direction was the WTO's experimental Balanced Trade in Services dataset; however, as it is still undergoing testing and development, we do not use it here. Experience with it suggests that it models rather than directly observing most bilateral data for developing Asian economies, particularly when applying sectoral disaggregation.

The OECD–WTO TiVA database strikes an appropriate balance among these competing concerns. It contains not only information on TiVA, but also the components necessary to produce those estimates that include gross trade flows in goods and services. The database harmonizes all of the reported data using the ISIC classification, balances the reported exports and imports, and fills in missing cells in the trade matrix using an econometric model when necessary. The database includes 12 non-OECD members from East, Southeast, and South Asia. The advantage of this dataset for the present chapter is that it presents harmonized data on trade in goods and services, making it possible to analyze comparative advantages across sectors. We therefore use gross export data from the TiVA database as our primary data source for all the analyses.

Before moving to a fully developed model in the next section, we can present some simple descriptive statistics. Intuitively, as policy distortions fall, as they largely have over recent decades, comparative advantage sectors should experience faster trade growth than should comparative disadvantage sectors. It is therefore useful to compare aggregate trade growth (with the rest of the world) across major sectors. We take the full period for which annual TiVA data are available (1995–2011) and decompose the total trade into the following macro-sectors: agriculture, mining, manufacturing, and services. For services, we only consider business sector services, not government

Figure 8.1 Breakdown of Exports by Macro-Sector, Developing Asia, 1995–2011

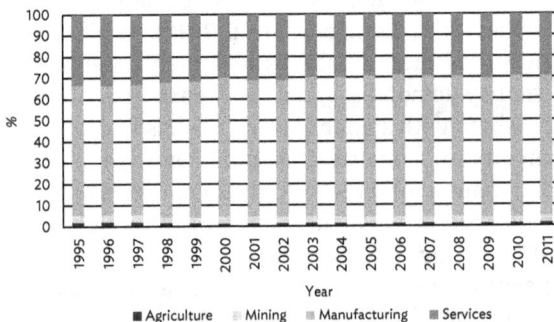

Source: Author's calculations; and Organisation for Economic Co-operation and Development, World Trade Organization Trade in Value Added Database. https://stats.oecd.org/index.aspx ?queryid=75537 (accessed 1 April 2019).

services. In the case of services, we only consider the portion of the total that economies record in the balance of payments, namely Mode 1 and some Mode 2 trade. No internationally comparable data on Mode 3 trade are available outside the OECD, and no comparable data on Mode 4 trade are available at all. The WTO is undertaking an experimental effort to produce a modal breakdown of services trade data, but it is basing it on significant simplifications of existing data rather than direct collection; in any event, this is not yet available to researchers.

Figure 8.1 shows a breakdown of total exports, that is, a summing across macro-sectors, for the full sample period. In this and the following figures, we limit our consideration to what we call "developing Asia," namely East, Southeast, and South Asian economies, in the TiVA dataset, with the exception of OECD member economies. It is important to keep in mind that this period largely represented a period of rapid growth in manufacturing exports from developing Asia. It is therefore remarkable that the share of manufacturing grew by only 5 percentage points over the nearly 2 decades that the figure represents. Mining remained essentially constant in proportional terms over time, but agriculture lost ground, as did services, which accounted for 33% of the total exports in 1995 but only 29% in 2011. Yet, this relative loss of ground belies what was in fact a very strong growth performance over time, only slightly less rapid than the explosive growth in manufactured goods exports.

To show this more clearly, Figure 8.2 presents growth in nominal gross exports over time, rebasing all of the sectors to equal 100 at the

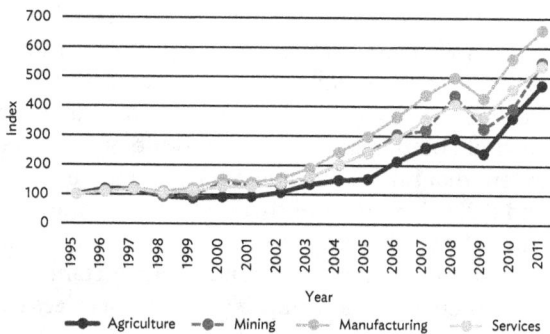

Figure 8.2 Exports by Macro-Sector, Developing Asia, 1995 = 100

Source: Author's calculations; and Organisation for Economic Co-operation and Development-World Trade Organization Trade in Value Added Database. https://stats.oecd.org/index.aspx?queryid=75537 (accessed 1 April 2019).

beginning of the sample and making it possible to interpret the changes in percentage terms. Although growth in manufactured goods exports outstripped that in other sectors in the golden age of development of "Factory Asia," services in fact also enjoyed explosive export growth over time. The significant difference between manufacturing and services by 2011 is due to compounding over time. In fact, the average annualized growth rates were very close: 12.5% per year for manufacturing and 11.1% per year per services. In any other environment, researchers would consider such a growth rate for services exports to be evidence of the rapid and successful development of the services sector. Comparing rates of growth across macro-sectors suggests that, although developing Asia enjoys a comparative advantage in manufacturing relative to all other sectors, there is nonetheless evidence of a comparative advantage in services relative to agriculture and, arguably, mining. In other words, the secondary and tertiary sectors are both sources of a comparative advantage relative to the primary sector. From a development standpoint, this finding is important, as it suggests that movement out of low-productivity agriculture benefits both the manufacturing and services sectors. Secondly, these data do not support the assertion either that manufactured goods are tradeable in a way that services are not or that they have prospects for dynamic growth that services do not.

Of course, even the relatively small sample of economies used by this analysis displays significant heterogeneity. To make this clear, Figure 8.3 shows the average annualized growth rates of exports in each macro-sector for the individual economies that constitute developing Asia in our sample. In several economies (Brunei Darussalam; Cambodia; Hong Kong, China; India; the Philippines; Singapore; and Taipei,China), the growth rate of services exports is either higher than the growth rate of manufacturing exports or very close to it. Even in a manufacturing powerhouse like the PRC, the two rates are surprisingly close, as they are again in Malaysia, a country that relies heavily on manufacturing in its effort to move from middle- to high-income status. The overall conclusion from Figure 8.3 is that there is a broad basis for arguing that services are a vital component of the total trade growth in developing Asia; to the extent that this conclusion does not emerge as strongly from Figures 8.1 and 8.2, this is apparently due largely to the PRC, which is responsible for a large share of the total manufacturing exports and which has a small but—when compounded—important differential in growth rates between manufacturing exports and services exports.

Thus far, we have only examined trade performance by macro-sector. However, comparative advantage is a force that operates at a much more disaggregated level. It is therefore important to look within the services sector, by economy, to examine the subsectors in which trade

Figure 8.3 Average Annualized Growth Rates of Exports by Macro-Sector, 1995–2011, Developing Asia

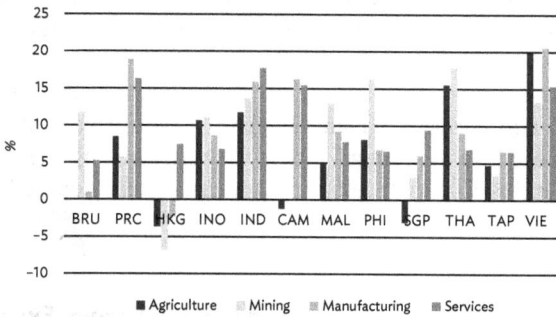

BRU = Brunei Darussalam; CAM = Cambodia; PRC = People's Republic of China; HKG = Hong Kong, China; INO = Indonesia; IND = India, MAL = Malaysia; PHI = the Philippines; SIN = Singapore; TAP = Taipei,China; THA = Thailand; VIE = Viet Nam.

Source: Author's calculations; and Organisation for Economic Co-operation and Development-World Trade Organization Trade in Value Added Database. https://stats.oecd.org/index.aspx?queryid=75537 (accessed 1 April 2019).

growth has been particularly sustained and rapid. It is also important to take account of the special role of transport services, which are to some extent subject to demand from manufacturing, since goods exports need transport services to move from the factory gate to the final consumer or the next user.

Table 8.1 presents the results, again for the full sample period. The entries in bold represent the average annualized growth rates of exports of 10% or more over this period of nearly 2 decades. Three facts stand out. First, known high performers in trade, like the PRC, have experienced rapid export growth in all of the services subsectors, not just transport. The same is true of known services specialists, like India. The second major finding is that, even in other economies, there is typically evidence of rapid trade growth in some services subsectors, suggesting that, at a disaggregated level, some services subsectors may exhibit a comparative advantage relative to other subsectors in the economy, in either the primary or secondary sector. Finally, the pattern of sectoral specialization in exports, as evidenced by growth patterns, is quite different across economies. Business services stand out in some economies, as do computer services in India and finance in some cases, as well as construction. The sectoral pattern of specialization is important, because different levels of productivity and patterns of productivity growth are associated with different services subsectors. Intuitively, we would expect to see strong productivity growth associated with specialization in business or computer services, but significantly less associated with hotels and restaurants or construction. In thinking about the development trajectories of the economies in the table, the relative pattern of export growth is important.

Of course, it is not possible to draw strong conclusions about patterns of comparative advantage from descriptive statistics alone. Section 3 presents a modeling framework with a strong theoretical basis that makes it possible to develop more nuanced and detailed insights.

Table 8.1 Average Annualized Growth Rate of Exports by Services Subsector, 1995–2011, Developing Asia

Economy	Construction	Wholesale and Retail	Hotels and Restaurants	Transport	Telecom
BRU	4.18%	8.91%	6.83%	4.76%	4.34%
CAM	24.25%	14.72%	24.76%	14.99%	17.50%
PRC	15.77%	16.25%	11.55%	14.35%	17.44%
HKG	8.66%	5.46%	8.81%	7.39%	8.65%
INO	6.59%	8.80%	2.51%	5.20%	4.03%
IND	20.67%	13.37%	13.23%	20.11%	22.98%
MAL	9.26%	8.87%	7.57%	5.77%	11.54%
PHI	−4.06%	5.84%	6.77%	7.31%	4.68%
SIN	19.20%	6.30%	5.94%	9.79%	10.02%
TAP	10.33%	5.50%	8.14%	8.04%	3.45%
THA	33.10%	6.86%	7.50%	6.02%	5v.70%
VIE	9.26%	16.23%	15.52%	19.84%	5.33%

Economy	Finance	Real Estate	Renting	Computer	Business Services
BRU	4.38%	9.98%	4.29%	2.40%	3.91%
CAM	21.02%	14.11%	25.18%	8.14%	36.23%
PRC	11.37%	12.57%	19.41%	19.25%	28.97%
HKG	8.65%	7.03%	9.44%	8.66%	8.65%
INO	4.03%	2.69%	7.48%	4.03%	4.03%
IND	22.99%	11.59%	14.65%	22.99%	22.99%
MAL	7.83%	7.05%	6.86%	22.77%	5.74%

continued on next page

Table 8.1 *continued*

Economy	Finance	Real Estate	Renting	Computer	Business Services
PHI	9.45%	6.25%	7.02%	8.67%	6.67%
SIN	12.46%	10.87%	7.52%	9.66%	11.82%
TAP	9.21%	7.77%	9.63%	7.59%	8.89%
THA	9.14%	5.86%	9.68%	-1.41%	12.61%
VIE	-1.88%	21.02%	15.78%	12.96%	13.21%

BRU = Brunei Darussalam; CAM = Cambodia; PRC = People's Republic of China; HKG = Hong Kong, China; INO = Indonesia; IND = India, MAL = Malaysia; PHI = the Philippines; SIN = Singapore; TAP = Taipei,China; Telecom = telecommunications; THA = Thailand; VIE = Viet Nam.

Source: Author's calculations; and Organisation for Economic Co-operation and Development, World Trade Organization Trade in Value Added Database. https://stats.oecd.org/index.aspx?queryid=75537 (accessed 1 April 2019).

8.3 Model and Results

Costinot, Donaldson, and Komunjer (2012) developed a Ricardian model of trade, extending the work of Eaton and Kortum (2002). Their objective was to quantify the importance of productivity differences as a driver of trade. However, as a by-product of their investigation, they developed a simple method for analyzing patterns of comparative advantage that is fully consistent with their theoretical setup. Like many models of trade, it is possible to reduce theirs to a gravity-like relation. Specifically, their theory predicts that bilateral trade flows by sector should satisfy the following relation:

$$\ln x_{ij}^k = d_{ij} + d_j^k + \theta \ln z_i^k + e_{ij}^k \qquad (1)$$

where: x_{ij}^k is exports from country i to country j in sector k; d_{ij} is a country pair fixed effect capturing the structural features of the model, such as trade costs; θ is a parameter from the theory capturing intra-industry heterogeneity in productivity; z_i^k is the fundamental productivity of country i in sector k, taking into account factors like climate, infrastructure, and institutions that affect all of the producers within a country; and e_{ij}^k is an error term satisfying the standard assumptions. As the use of a parameter like this suggests, the objective of the exercise is to quantify a comparative advantage rather than to uncover its sources, as in models like that of Chor (2010), which van der Marel (2011) applied to services.

Costinot, Donaldson, and Komunjer (2012) initially estimated Equation (1) directly, using productivity estimates that they drew from the available data. However, such an approach is not practical for application to a wide range of countries, particularly developing ones, as such estimates are not readily available on a comparable basis. As the authors noted, they also suffer from significant concerns regarding measurement error.

An alternative approach is therefore to replace the productivity variable with an exporter sector fixed effect:

$$\ln x_{ij}^k = d_{ij} + d_j^k + d_i^k + e_{ij}^k \qquad (2)$$

The standard ordinary least squares estimate will produce consistent estimates of the exporter sector fixed effects. Once the estimates have been obtained, we can use a value of from the literature to construct revealed productivity measures by exponentiation, that is, $z_i^k = \exp(d/\theta)$. There are important advantages to proceeding in this way. First, the only limit to the method's application is the availability of trade data. There is no a priori reason why it cannot be applied to trade in services as well as goods, even though there are greater concerns about productivity data in services sectors than is the case for goods. Second, it is possible to interpret the revealed productivity measure, as the authors did, in terms of a theoretical RCA measure. Following the original paper, we express all of the estimates relative to the revealed productivity level in agriculture in each economy.

To implement the model empirically, we use data on trade flows in goods and services covering the 27 ISIC sectors that the TiVA database contains. We use trade data in gross shipments, not value added, terms. The estimation sample includes 62 exporting and importing economies. We discard observations for which trade is equal to 0, as the estimation procedure is in logarithms. We then estimate separately for each year, pooling across sectors. To convert the estimated fixed effects into theory-consistent RCA measures, we use the same estimate of as did Costinot, Donaldson, and Komunjer (2012), namely 6.53.

We present the results for the manufacturing sector in Table 8.2 and for the services sector in Table 8.3. Although the estimates are available for all of the years in the sample, we initially limit our consideration to the last year in the sample, 2011. Unsurprisingly, Table 8.2 shows that developing Asian economies typically have a comparative advantage in manufacturing sectors relative to agriculture. However, the most important point is that the degree of advantage varies considerably across economies within sectors and across sectors within economies. Economies like the PRC; Singapore; and Taipei,China have a strong comparative advantage in the electronics

Table 8.2 Revealed Productivity in Selected Manufacturing Sectors, Developing Asia, 2011

Economy	Food Products	Textiles and Clothing	Chemicals	Plastics
CAM	1.09	1.51	0.77	0.85
PRC	1.28	1.71	1.64	1.47
HKG	1.39	1.83	1.63	1.42
INO	1.11	1.08	1.11	0.97
IND	1.19	1.32	1.53	1.17
MAL	1.31	1.02	1.34	1.29
PHI	1.33	1.14	1.28	1.12
SIN	1.85	1.53	2.61	1.71
TAP	1.26	1.61	2.03	1.79
THA	1.35	1.10	1.29	1.25
VIE	1.19	1.13	0.92	1.00

Economy	Metal Products	Machinery	Electronics	Vehicles
CAM	0.88	0.77	0.73	0.71
PRC	1.48	1.87	2.11	1.40
HKG	1.40	1.84	1.27	1.17
INO	0.73	1.02	1.10	0.86
IND	1.06	1.28	1.22	1.25
MAL	1.01	1.29	1.59	0.93
PHI	1.00	1.15	1.65	1.17
SIN	1.86	2.47	3.05	1.42
TAP	1.88	2.15	2.43	1.68
THA	1.05	1.47	1.39	1.36
VIE	0.91	0.97	1.18	0.75

CAM = Cambodia; PRC = People's Republic of China; HKG = Hong Kong, China; INO = Indonesia; IND = India, MAL = Malaysia; PHI = the Philippines; SIN = Singapore; TAP = Taipei,China; THA = Thailand; VIE = Viet Nam.

Note: All the estimates are relative to agriculture (1.00). We drop Brunei Darussalam from the sample, as estimates are typically not available in the baseline sector.

Source: Author's calculations.

sector, for example. By contrast, Indonesia's comparative advantage in manufacturing is much more modest and focuses on the chemicals sector. Interpreting these results in terms of relative productivity levels confirms that most developing Asian economies have manufacturing sectors that are more productive than their own agricultural sectors, although the

**Table 8.3 Revealed Productivity in Selected
Services Sectors, Developing Asia, 2011**

Economy	Construction	Wholesale and Retail	Hotels and Restaurants	Transport
CAM	0.73	1.39	0.99	1.31
PRC	0.85	1.79	1.31	1.59
HKG	1.56	2.05	2.24	3.06
INO	0.51	1.24	0.85	1.01
IND	0.74	1.47	1.04	1.41
MAL	0.87	1.43	1.14	1.29
PHI	0.78	1.44	1.15	1.53
SIN	1.76	2.46	2.43	2.95
TAP	0.84	2.02	1.30	1.76
THA	0.64	1.41	1.23	1.32
VIE	0.53	1.18	0.82	1.14

Economy	Telecom	Finance	Computer Services	Other Business Services
CAM	0.93	0.73	0.59	0.65
PRC	0.90	0.46	0.73	1.02
HKG	1.78	1.70	0.78	1.39
INO	0.63	0.36	0.38	0.41
IND	0.86	0.52	0.98	0.96
MAL	0.91	0.64	0.67	0.74
PHI	1.18	0.63	0.76	0.98
SIN	1.48	2.03	1.66	1.77
TAP	1.07	0.77	0.66	0.93
THA	0.76	0.51	0.35	0.63
VIE	0.48	0.37	0.37	0.39

CAM = Cambodia; PRC = People's Republic of China; HKG = Hong Kong, China; INO = Indonesia; IND = India, MAL = Malaysia; PHI = the Philippines; SIN = Singapore; TAP = Taipei,China; Telecom = telecommunications; THA = Thailand; VIE = Viet Nam.

Note: All the estimates are relative to agriculture (1.00). We drop Brunei Darussalam from the sample, as estimates are typically not available in the baseline sector.

Source: Author's calculations.

degree of the productivity differential is highly variable. Interestingly, a country like Viet Nam, which has emphasized the development of its manufacturing sector in recent years, only exhibits a relatively limited degree of comparative advantage in manufacturing subsectors relative to a more established manufacturer like the PRC. Of course, these data are for 2011, and substantial changes are likely to have taken place in the intervening 7 years.

A comparison of the results in Table 8.2 with those in Table 8.3 suggests that we cannot draw a simple conclusion about the relative patterns of comparative advantage in goods and services in developing Asia. While the results are highly variable across economies and sectors, there are many instances in which developing Asian economies have a comparative advantage in services subsectors relative to agriculture and (comparing the two tables) in certain services subsectors relative to some manufacturing subsectors. In the PRC, for example, the extent of comparative advantage in wholesale and retail trade relative to agriculture is comparable to the figure for textiles and clothing or machinery in manufacturing. Similarly, the degree of comparative advantage in transport services in the Philippines relative to agriculture is stronger than we can observe in all of the manufacturing sectors except for electronics. While it is true that typically higher income economies have a stronger comparative advantage in services subsectors—Singapore and Hong Kong, China stand out—there are important instances of middle-income economies with significant revealed productivity advantages in services subsectors. In addition to those already listed, Viet Nam's comparative advantage in wholesale and retail trade relative to agriculture is identical to that in electronics and only slightly lower than that in food products, while that in transport is nearly as strong. There are numerous instances of this type. The objective here is not to catalogue them all but simply to highlight that, even in "Factory Asia," we cannot reduce patterns of revealed productivity to a simple dichotomy between relatively high-productivity manufacturing and relatively low-productivity services. The reality is much more complicated and nuanced, suggesting that simple narratives based on the observed prevalence of services relative to manufacturing are likely to miss important truths. This finding sits well with the descriptive statistics presented above, in which we showed that, even in a region like developing Asia, where most analyses have focused on rapid growth in manufacturing exports over recent years, the observed patterns of services trade have actually been strikingly similar.

As the model covers a lengthy period of time, it is informative to look at the changes in revealed productivity in manufacturing and services. This point is important in light of the argument in the premature deindustrialization literature that manufacturing has unique prospects for technological change over time and thus for sustained productivity growth.

Tables 8.4 and 8.5 consider the absolute change in our theory-consistent RCA measures between 1995 and 2011. We use the full period because it represents the spread of manufacturing activity from the tiger

Table 8.4 Change in Revealed Productivity in Selected Manufacturing Sectors, Developing Asia, 1995–2011

Economy	Food Products	Textiles and Clothing	Chemicals	Plastics
CAM	0.38	0.60	0.08	0.13
PRC	0.15	0.32	0.25	0.38
HKG	0.07	0.23	0.25	0.06
INO	0.12	-0.05	0.13	0.08
IND	0.16	0.13	0.31	0.20
MAL	0.25	0.15	0.31	0.29
PHI	0.10	0.00	0.16	0.19
SIN	0.47	0.37	1.06	0.40
TAP	-0.02	-0.22	0.13	0.00
THA	-0.11	-0.27	0.05	-0.17
VIE	0.16	0.04	0.06	0.18

Economy	Metal Products	Machinery	Electronics	Vehicles
CAM	0.21	0.13	0.06	0.20
PRC	0.34	0.56	0.74	0.47
HKG	0.12	0.20	-0.39	0.17
INO	-0.10	0.15	0.19	0.23
IND	0.15	0.31	0.35	0.39
MAL	0.21	0.23	0.30	0.20
PHI	0.04	0.07	0.14	0.22
SIN	0.61	0.82	0.88	0.45
TAP	0.11	0.09	0.03	0.14
THA	-0.02	0.11	-0.04	0.29
VIE	0.19	0.13	0.23	0.09

CAM = Cambodia; PRC = People's Republic of China; HKG = Hong Kong, China; INO = Indonesia; IND = India, MAL = Malaysia; PHI = the Philippines; SIN = Singapore; TAP = Taipei,China; THA = Thailand; VIE = Viet Nam.

Note: All the estimates are relative to agriculture (1.00). We drop Brunei Darussalam from the sample, as estimates are typically not available in the baseline sector.

Source: Author's calculations.

economies to other parts of Asia, and has witnessed explosive export growth in economies like the PRC and Viet Nam, among others. Thus, we would expect to see evidence of a deepening comparative advantage in manufacturing sectors over that time.

Table 8.5 Change in Revealed Productivity in Selected Services Sectors, Developing Asia, 1995–2011

Economy	Construction	Wholesale and Retail	Hotels and Restaurants	Transport
CAM	0.23	0.45	0.33	0.55
PRC	0.22	0.39	0.53	0.46
HKG	0.66	0.32	0.59	1.17
INO	0.08	0.10	-0.08	0.08
IND	0.07	0.22	0.23	0.36
MAL	0.24	0.27	0.22	0.22
PHI	-0.14	0.13	0.07	0.14
SIN	1.02	0.76	0.91	1.24
TAP	0.22	-0.01	0.13	0.15
THA	0.07	-0.09	-0.13	-0.14
VIE	-0.10	0.02	-0.04	0.21

Economy	Telecom	Finance	Computer Services	Other Business Services
CAM	0.23	0.01	0.04	0.24
PRC	0.22	-0.33	0.21	0.45
HKG	0.67	-0.21	0.17	0.46
INO	-0.06	-0.37	0.00	-0.01
IND	0.19	-0.32	0.33	0.29
MAL	0.12	-0.42	0.29	0.08
PHI	0.03	-0.47	0.08	-0.03
SIN	0.61	0.11	0.73	0.79
TAP	-0.02	-0.55	0.08	0.08
THA	-0.17	-0.42	-0.15	0.06
VIE	-0.30	-0.83	-0.02	-0.06

CAM = Cambodia; PRC = People's Republic of China; HKG = Hong Kong, China; INO = Indonesia; IND = India, MAL = Malaysia; PHI = the Philippines; SIN = Singapore; TAP = Taipei,China; Telecom = telecommunications; THA = Thailand; VIE = Viet Nam.

Note: All the estimates are relative to agriculture (1.00). We drop Brunei Darussalam from the sample, as estimates are typically not available in the baseline sector.

Source: Author's calculations.

This what we observe in Table 8.4. The entries in the table are typically positive, meaning that the revealed productivity relative to agriculture has increased over time in most cases. Unsurprisingly, the

PRC stands out as having made significant revealed productivity gains in all of the manufacturing subsectors. However, this phenomenon is by no means limited to the PRC: the data are consistent with a general increase in revealed productivity of manufacturing activities relative to agriculture all across Asia, from lower income economies like Cambodia to higher income ones like Singapore.

However, a comparison of Table 8.4 (manufacturing) with Table 8.5 (services) shows that productivity gains were also strong in services. In the PRC, for example, the absolute increase in the revealed productivity of the other business services sector relative to agriculture was comparable to that for motor vehicles and larger than was the case for manufacturing sectors like textiles and clothing. The contrast is even stronger for transport services. Other than the PRC, the higher income economies in the region again stand out as having particularly strong gains in revealed productivity in services; yet, it is important to stress that this phenomenon is by no means limited to them. Cambodia's second-largest absolute gain in revealed productivity was in transport services, which outstripped the absolute gains in all of the manufacturing sectors except textiles and clothing, and is a well-known success story in terms of industrial development. Similarly, Malaysia's absolute gain in revealed productivity in computer services was equal to that in plastics and only slightly below the gains in the electronics and chemicals sectors. Again, there is no easy way to classify the patterns in Tables 8.4 and 8.5 according to a supposed dichotomy between manufactured goods and services. The data do not support the proposition that the productivity gains in manufacturing are systematically stronger in a dynamic sense than those in services. Rather, what we see is a complex set of results that varies across economies and sectors. Again, therefore, precise patterns of specialization, not gross patterns (manufacturing versus services), are relevant to an economy's growth path. As above, however, we stress that, even in manufacturing success stories like the PRC and Viet Nam, there is evidence of revealed productivity gains in services that are quantitatively significant and in some cases of comparable magnitude.

8.4 Conclusion and Policy Implications

We have reviewed the recent evidence on trade growth in goods and services, focusing on developing (non-OECD) Asia. Researchers widely consider the 1990s and 2000s to have been the golden age of manufacturing in developing Asia, with the movement of industrial activity from the tiger economies of the 1970s and 1980s to the PRC and subsequently to other parts of the region. Consistent with this view, we find that developing Asia as a whole indeed experienced very rapid growth in manufacturing exports over that period. Moreover, our modeling suggests that increases in revealed productivity or theoretical RCA drove this export growth. Thus far, our findings are consistent with the intuition that the development of the manufacturing sector, through outward orientation in particular, is the surest way to promote productivity upgrading and economic transformation.

However, this widely accepted story is only half of what actually happened in developing Asia. We show that the export growth in commercial services was nearly as spectacular as that in manufacturing. This is not a well-known fact. Even less appreciated is the fact that the significant increase in revealed productivity in services subsectors similarly drove this increase in trade. In other words, in developing Asia, manufacturing and services have tended to grow together in terms of trade integration. There is no simple pattern of changes in revealed productivity over time as there is between goods and services. We certainly do not observe in the data that only manufacturing sectors enjoy high levels of revealed productivity, are tradeable, or enjoy rapid and sustained productivity growth. Rather, we see a complex pattern of results at the level of individual subsectors and economies, as we would expect if the relationship between specialization and productivity growth depended in a complex way on resources, institutions, and firm-level behavior. In other words, what we observe is the full complexity of trade growth in a context in which comparative advantages matter in both a quantitative and a qualitative sense.

Bearing this insight in mind, the key conclusion is that policy makers should be wary of oversimplifying the relationship between manufacturing and services. On the one hand, the servicification of economies all around the world (e.g., Bamber et al. 2017), including in Asia, means that it is now impossible to talk about trade or productivity growth in manufacturing without considering services inputs. However, we have also shown that the experience of developing Asia has not been that economies choose "manufacturing" or "services" in an aggregate sense, potentially at the expense of the other, but that the two interact in complex ways. Similarly, our results suggest that we cannot justify "services pessimism" in developing Asia—the idea that only manufacturing can produce rapid and sustained productivity growth— as a general proposition. Rather, we see that, in individual economies, particular services subsectors have exhibited rates of revealed productivity growth that are absolutely comparable to those apparent during the golden age of Factory Asia. In other words, it is important to consider the realities of performance at a disaggregated level before drawing strong conclusions about the development potential of particular sectors.

The premature deindustrialization story has a certain intuitive appeal, especially in classroom settings in which highly stylized and simplified models can nonetheless be of great expositional value. However, as a guide to policy, it is far too simple to be useful. In a servicified economy, the distinction between "manufactured goods" and "services" is increasingly blurred; many firms produce and use both, and a substantial proportion of gross exports of manufacturing (32% in the Association of Southeast Asian Nations and East Asia) is in fact embodied services value added (OECD-WTO TiVA database). In addition, as we have shown in this chapter, it is not empirically true that "manufacturing" as an aggregate systematically offers levels and growth potential of revealed productivity, or degrees of tradability, that are not available in the services sector. There is at least as much variation within manufacturing and services as there is between them. From a policy point of view, therefore, it is important to pay attention to sectoral specificities at the micro-level rather than allowing overly simplified and outdated models that only consider large aggregates to guide decision making. Patterns of specialization of course matter for an economy's growth path, but the level of disaggregation should be as fine as possible. Although this is a challenging task with services, given the state of the international data, it is one that demands analysts' and policy makers' attention.

References

Bamber, P., O. Cattaneo, K. Fernandez-Stark, G. Gereffi, E. van der Marel, and B. Shepherd. 2017. *Diversification Through Servicification*. Washington, DC: World Bank.

Chor, D. 2010. Unpacking Sources of Comparative Advantage: A Quantitative Approach. *Journal of International Economics* 82(2): 152–167.

Costinot, A., D. Donaldson, and I. Komunjer. 2012. What Goods do Countries Trade? A Quantitative Exploration of Ricardo's Ideas. *Review of Economic Studies* 79: 581–608.

Eaton, J., and S. Kortum. 2002. Technology, Geography, and Trade. *Econometrica* 70(5): 1741–1779.

Lemain, E., and G. Orefice. 2013. New Revealed Comparative Advantage Index: Dataset and Empirical Distribution. Working Paper 2013-20. Paris: Centre d'Études Prospectives et d'Informations.

Loungani, P., S. Mishra, C. Papageorgiou, and K. Wang. 2017. World Trade in Services: Evidence from a New Dataset. Working Paper 17/77. Washington, DC: International Monetary Fund.

Organisation for Economic Co-operation and Development-World Trade Organization Trade in Value Added (TIVA) Database. https://stats.oecd.org/index.aspx?queryid=75537 (accessed 1 April 2019).

Rodrik, D. 2016. Premature Deindustrialization. *Journal of Economic Growth* 21(1): 1–33.

van der Marel, E. 2011. Determinants of Comparative Advantage in Services. Working Paper 38933. London: London School of Economics.

van der Marel, E., and B. Shepherd. 2013. International Tradability Indices for Services. Working Paper DTC-2013-3. New York: Developing Trade Consultants.

9

Manufacturing and Services Productivity: The Role of New Technologies and Policy

Erik van der Marel

9.1 Introduction

Manufacturing has traditionally been the primary driver of economic development for many countries around the globe due to its high productivity performance, among other economically beneficial features (Rodrik 2015). In contrast, services are commonly considered secondary, as they often lag behind the manufacturing sector in terms of productivity growth. Despite services' relatively greater size, research has emphasized the manufacturing sector as the source of productivity growth. This is because of the belief that services suffer from a so-called "cost disease," whereby their inability to substitute labor for more productive factors means that the sector acts as a drag on the overall economy over time (Baumol 1967).

However, that notion is appearing increasingly outdated. The belief that services' inherent nature makes them less likely to achieve productivity improvement compared with manufacturing fails to take into account recent developments in services in the area of information and communications technology (ICT). New investments in ICT have overwhelmingly supported service industries, and as a result, services in some countries now match the aggregate productivity trends of the countries or even of the manufacturing sector alone (International Monetary Fund 2018). Early research by Triplett and Bosworth (2003) also showed that productivity in various services in the United States had grown as fast as that in other manufacturing sectors due to the acceleration of total factor productivity (TFP). One of the main factors driving this improvement in TFP was ICT investments in services, which effectively cured Baumol's "cost disease" of low productivity developments in services.

More recently, ICT improvements have affected a number of additional services as a result of the deployment of internet technologies and electronic data across the globe through the internet. Examples of these services include information services, broadcasting services such as digital content services, computer services such as cloud computing services, and electronic publishing services such as software services. The computational power of ICT equipment and the increased use of data, together with the improved digital infrastructure in many countries enabled by deregulated telecommunications networks, have allowed trade in new digital services. These services have contributed to excellent economic performance in many downstream sectors that use these digital services. As a result, it is likely that changes in ICT and internet technology in particular have reduced the productivity gap further between at least some services and manufacturing.

However, the employment of the global internet, in particular the use of electronic data and data services across the internet, has increasingly gained attention from policy makers. For instance, the role of data in the economy has incited governments to regulate the cross-border transfer and domestic use of these data over the internet across many countries. At the same time, the internet is one of the primary economic factors that has improved prospects for economic growth (Hulten and Nakamura 2017). Therefore, the recent policy development of restrictions on internet technology and data would first and foremost have a negative impact on an economy in which manufacturing and services use ICT, software, and data intensively. This in turn constitutes a threat to the massive productivity improvements that some services have recently undergone. It also threatens industries that are willing to take up more internet and data-related services, such as artificial intelligence (AI), to improve productivity.

This chapter discusses the triangular link between productivity in goods and services, data-intensive services, and data regulation. First, we review recent productivity developments in services compared with manufacturing, stressing the positive productivity performance in some digital-intensive services. We then identify the sectors open to potential productivity improvements, as measured through their digital intensity, by investigating which services and manufacturing sectors are the main users of data services. Finally, we discuss recent regulatory policies regarding data that have emerged in recent years, and empirically assesses the detrimental effect on productivity of regulatory restrictions on data services. This section also shows the potential productivity improvements for services and manufacturing in the event that countries implement less costly measures related to data services.

9.2 Total Factor Productivity Developments in Manufacturing and Services

As stated above, services are generally understood to be less productive than manufacturing, an idea first put forward by Baumol (1967). Some services, such as personal services, are less conducive to labor productivity improvements, as labor is not easily substitutable for other, more productive means. As the size of the services sector tends to grow more quickly over time while its relative productivity slows, the sector can become a drag on the overall economic growth performance of a country. This may be true generally if we think about the services sector as whole. For instance, the left-hand panel of Figure 9.1 plots the trend of TFP growth for manufacturing and services together for the Organisation for Economic Co-operation and Development (OECD) countries combined. The trend clearly shows slower productivity growth development when taking stock of services. This suggests that services indeed suffer from a lower productivity trend, weighing down the economy overall.

However, not all services sectors suffer from levels of productivity performance lower than those in manufacturing. Using EU KLEMS data,[1] we show that some parts of the services economy have stable growth patterns in line with those in the manufacturing sector. For instance, information and communications services show a TFP growth rate on par with the manufacturing sector (right-hand panel of Figure 9.1).[2] Van Ark (2016; 2018) also emphasized this pattern of increased productivity performance in ICT, information technology (IT), and other telecommunications services in particular. This development is also consistent with the broader notion of increased productivity growth of the entire ICT sector since the mid-1990s. Some of these sectors are

---

[1]   The EU KLEMS project began in the late 1990s with the objective of developing new productivity measures at the industry level for the European Union (EU). "KLEMS" refers to the decomposition of output growth into contributing factor inputs: capital (K), labor (L), energy (E), materials (M), and service inputs (S).

[2]   The sector of information and communications services contains the following subsectors based on the Statistical Classification of Economic Activities in the European Community (NACE) Revision 2/International Standard Industrial Classification Revision 4: publishing, audio-visual, and broadcasting activities (58–60); telecommunications (61); and IT and other information services (62–63). See Jäger (2017) for further details of this classification.

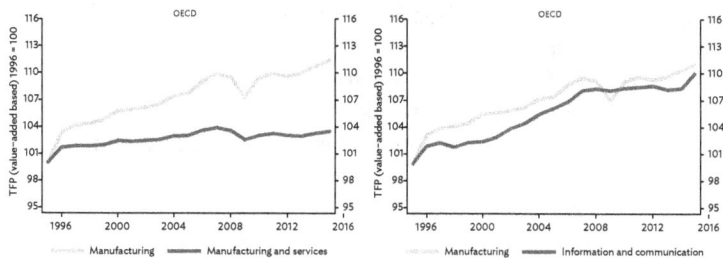

Figure 9.1 Total Factor Productivity in Manufacturing and Services in the OECD (1996–2015)

OECD = Organisation for Economic Co-operation and Development, TFP = total factor productivity.
Note: The EU KLEMS project, from which these data are drawn, began in the late 1990s with the objective of developing new productivity measures at the industry level for the European Union (EU). "KLEMS" refers to the decomposition of output growth into contributing factor inputs: capital (K), labor (L), energy (E), materials (M), and service inputs (S).
Source: Author's calculations using EU KLEMS.

characterized as ICT-producing sectors, as general-purpose technology that provides inputs into many other manufacturing and services sectors to make them more productive.

One important feature of this sector is that it has become increasingly tradable. Due to new technologies, information services, general IT services, data-processing services, publishing, and audio-visual services have become increasingly tradable across borders, particularly over the internet. In fact, digital services, such as computer and information services, as well as other services that use the internet extensively such as finance and retail services, are sectors that have shown a trend of increased cross-border trade since 2000 as opposed to trade through a commercial presence (Andrenelli et al. 2018). This suggests that the internet and ICT technologies have played a crucial role in stimulating trade in services in those sectors that have moved online, thereby increasing their productivity performance in turn. Indeed, technical changes and offerings of new digital services and online financial and retail services have undoubtedly played a part in rendering the entire services sector more productive.

Other services sectors have been less receptive to new digital technologies, which may explain their trailing productivity growth (see Figure A9.1).

Transport and storage have seen a stagnating productivity pattern in which the gap relative to the manufacturing sector has been widening.

Although a large share of cross-border world trade takes place in transport services (around 15%), their estimated *actual* tradability compared with their potential still appears low (van der Marel and Shepherd 2013). A more alarming trend is visible for business services. Although this sector comprises a wide set of sub-categories of services ranging from professional services to marketing and advertising, the downward trend of this sector appears to indicate a real break from the rest of the economy. Business services appear to have not contributed much to the economic performance of many OECD countries. Many business services also suffer from a low uptake of digital inputs in many of these countries' economies (discussed further below).

Financial services, on the other hand, show some positive TFP growth, albeit not at an impressive rate. Nonetheless, compared with manufacturing, the productivity trend in this sector has grown throughout the entire period (1995–2015). The financial services industry is otherwise notable for its digital intensity and operates through the use of many modern internet technologies. Although 10% of world trade takes place in the financial services sector (of which insurance services only account for 3.5%), van der Marel and Shepherd (2013) estimated that the financial sector nevertheless suffers from low tradability across countries. This suggests that there is still great potential for this sector to increase its productivity through technology-induced cross-border trade over the internet, a trend that is gaining pace, as showed by Andrenelli et al. (2018).

The distribution sector (i.e., retail and wholesale services) has experienced yet another impressive productivity growth pattern. Even though the speed of its TFP growth has not been equal to that in manufacturing, the sector has witnessed one of the most impressive productivity improvements in the entire services economy of many OECD countries. Previous analyses, such as that of Triplett and Bosworth (2004), have shown that in the US this pattern had already become established in the early 1990s thanks to the introduction of ICT, which allowed services to introduce novel managerial innovations into distribution.[3] Compared with other factors used by the services sector, this chapter shows that the distribution sector is one of the most ICT-intensive sectors and uses many digital tools, data, and software services.

---

[3]   Moreover, van Ark, Inklaar, and McGuckin (2003) concluded that over half of the economy-wide post-1995 labor productivity growth enjoyed by the US compared with Europe is traceable to strong US performance in the distribution sector. Notwithstanding the statistical challenges that hamper the measurement of productivity in this services sector, Inklaar and Timmer (2008) used alternative productivity measures to confirm the strong productivity performance of retail services in the US.

Furthermore, this sector has experienced a major expansion in terms of cross-border delivery due to e-commerce platforms.

9.2.1 Total Factor Productivity Developments in Non-OECD Countries

All of the countries represented by the EU KLEMS data are OECD countries. Similar to EU KLEMS, World KLEMS provides productivity data for some non-OECD countries for which it can uncover productivity patterns;[4] however, the number of countries in World KLEMS is extremely small. The Russian Federation and India are the only two emerging economies that can be analyzed without any further sector disaggregation.[5]

Figure 9.2 Total Factor Productivity in Manufacturing and Services in Non-OECD Countries (1996–2015)

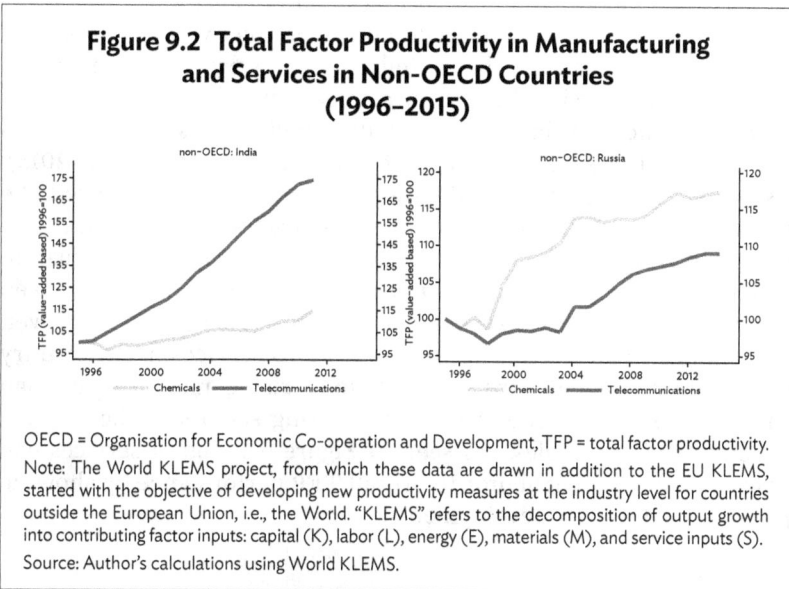

OECD = Organisation for Economic Co-operation and Development, TFP = total factor productivity.
Note: The World KLEMS project, from which these data are drawn in addition to the EU KLEMS, started with the objective of developing new productivity measures at the industry level for countries outside the European Union, i.e., the World. "KLEMS" refers to the decomposition of output growth into contributing factor inputs: capital (K), labor (L), energy (E), materials (M), and service inputs (S).
Source: Author's calculations using World KLEMS.

---

[4] The World KLEMS project, from which these data are drawn in addition to the EU KLEMS, started with the objective of developing new productivity measures at the industry level for countries outside the European Union, i.e., the World. "KLEMS" refers to the decomposition of output growth into contributing factor inputs: capital (K), labor (L), energy (E), materials (M), and service inputs (S).

[5] The only available digital or ICT-producing sector is the telecommunications sector, which falls into information and communications services. The chemicals sector acts as a proxy for the overall manufacturing sector.

As shown in Figure 9.2, India has experienced tremendous productivity growth in telecommunications services since 1995. This is unsurprising, as India has substantially reformed its telecommunications market since 1992, when it provided the first license to a private telecommunications provider. Prior to this, public monopolies controlled the sector. The Government of India introduced further private competition in 2002 and 2003 by opening up to foreign direct investment after equity limits were significantly reduced. The OECD's Foreign Direct Investment (FDI) restrictiveness index records that, particularly after 2012 (not in the chart), the index fell further to the minimum. This effectively means that, together with India's domestic regulatory reform, the number of telecommunications providers was unlimited. This very likely helped boost India's TFP performance in telecommunications compared with the manufacturing sector (for which the chemicals sector proxies in Figure 9.2), as foreign technologies were flowing into the country, creating spillover effects.[6]

In contrast, the Russian Federation's productivity developments in telecommunications have followed a very different route. Although the Russian Federation's telecommunications sector has seen a productivity increase since 1997–1998, it has lagged behind the chemical industry throughout the entire period (1995–2015). As of 2006, the Russian Federation had substantially reduced the remaining establishment restrictions in fixed telecommunications, thereby further opening up for foreign private providers. The Russian Federation's mobile telecommunications market had already been reformed for foreign providers in the pre-1997 period.[7] However, although at lower levels, telecommunications services in the country have followed an upward trend, despite rising more slowly than some of the most productive manufacturing sectors in the Russian Federation. Nevertheless, as seen in Figure 9.2, digital services can at least be a real contributor to overall TFP performance by showing positive productivity developments.

---

[6]   In addition, Arnold et al. (2015) showed that India's reform in telecommunications, which reached the furthest of all of the services sector reforms in India, contributed significantly to downstream manufacturing TFP growth in India over time.

[7]   Despite few remaining equity limits, the two countries may not yet have abolished other types of domestic regulatory restrictions, making it impossible to assess the telecommunications market in both countries as entirely open. In fact, the OECD Services Trade Restrictiveness Index (STRI) reports that other non-discriminatory regulations regarding domestic competition are still in place in the Russian Federation and India, in addition to some restrictions on regulatory transparency.

9.3 Users of Information and Communications Services

The intensive usage of software, data, and ICT services more generally is a real contributor to overall economic development. Although policy analysis has traditionally focused strongly on the productivity-enhancing potential of the ICT-*producing* sector for the overall economy, the ICT-*using* part of the economy should not be neglected, as greater productivity effects for the overall economy are likely to result from downstream industries' and services' intensive use of these digital services.

Digital transformations largely influence long-term productivity gains, such as those experienced by the information and communications services sector. For digital transformations to have a lasting impact on other non-ICT manufacturing and services sectors, companies must embed digital tools, instruments, and software into their operating processes. To improve productivity, it is necessary to infuse into other sectors recently developed digital technologies, such as platforms, the internet, embedded sensors, and AI. With the help of an increasing amount of data, these digital technologies enable firms to make connections between organizations, people, physical assets, and new business models (see van Ark 2018). This latter development, in which the non-digital sector should use digital development intensively, is sometimes known as the "deployment phase," which will benefit growth in more downstream industries and larger segments of society.[8]

Early studies have shown, for example, not only that the productivity gap between the US and European countries was due to a larger ICT-producing sector, but also that faster productivity growth in the US was in large part also caused by the more intensive absorption of ICT services by US industries, especially services industries such as distribution and finance (van Ark, Inklaar, and McGuckin 2003). To a large extent, this productivity gap can be explained by the degree to which the ICT-using sector invested in services from the ICT-producing sectors. Now that the current phase of the digital economy has moved from ICT investments to ICT services, in which data services play a central role (van Ark 2018), the application of data to production and organization processes, services, and other products in particular is likely to mark the difference in productivity between countries further.

---

[8] This "deployment phase" follows the "installation phase" as outlined by van Ark (2018), in which new technologies emerge and advance with new infrastructure. Furthermore, van Ark stated that the productivity gains may not become visible until the "deployment phase," after which digital technologies will diffuse widely and become common practice across organizations.

In recent years, there has been a major increase in the usage of data services, such as data storage and information-processing services (including cloud computing), computer system design, and internet publishing, such as software. These data services are becoming a widespread phenomenon in all sorts of downstream industries and services, as they allow for scaling up and saving on input expenses (such as labor, raw materials, and maintenance), and thereby improve companies' efficiency level and resource allocation. This eventually improves the productivity level of firms in many sectors across the economy (see discussion below). There are currently many intensive users of all of these digital data and software services spread across manufacturing and services (see Figure 9.3).

Figure 9.3 shows the top 25 industries and services sectors that are the most intensive users of digital tools, data, and software services. The ranking is based on non-capital software expenditures, as the 2015 US Census measured for each industry, which act as a proxy for digital, data, and software services (D). The digital usages in each sector are then divided by their labor usage (L), provided by the US Bureau of Labor Statistics (BLS), which gives (D/L). Although a proxy, the intensities presented in this figure correlate strongly with a wider definition of the usage of ICT and data services by each downstream industry

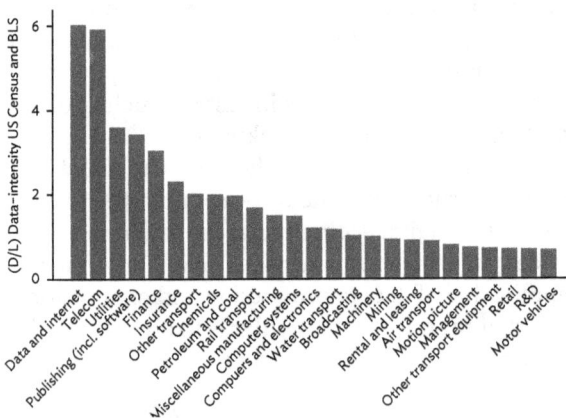

Figure 9.3 Top Users (Intensity) of Data and Software (D/L)

BLS = Bureau of Labor Statistics, D/L = software usage (D) over labor (L), R&D = research and development, US = United States.

Source: Author's calculations using US Census and US BLS data based on the North American Industry Classification System.

and services sector using the US Bureau of Economic Analysis (BEA) input–output tables, following Ferracane, Kren, and van der Marel (2018a). Both digital intensity indicators measure the extent to which each industry and services sector uses all sorts of inputs from all ICT-producing sectors, such as inputs (see Table A9.1). However, the data in Figure 9.3 concern a more recent year.[9]

The most data- and software-intensive sectors are unsurprisingly digital services themselves, such as internet services and telecommunications services, as the ranking shows. Other top users of digital services include publishing services, financial services, and insurance services. Interestingly, together with retail services, these sectors witnessed positive productivity growth after 1995, as shown above. Other notable users of software and data services are advanced manufacturing industries, such as chemicals, computer systems, computers and electronics, machinery, and motor vehicles. These manufacturing sectors are known for their sophisticated supply chains, skill intensity, and large capital shares. The figure suggests that these manufacturing sectors are also at the forefront of the use of digital services developments. Transport services, such as rail, air, and other means of transportation, are also intensive users of digital services.

One unusual services sector that stands out as being very digital and software intensive is management services, which take place between related enterprises. This sector covers firm entities that administer, oversee, and manage establishments of companies (or enterprises) and perform decision making regarding strategic and organizational planning. Given that recent research has shown that intangible inputs, such as management services, represent the majority of intra-firm shipments to foreign affiliates (see Atalay, Hortaçsu, and Syverson 2014), it seems likely that software and other data services have played an important role as input for multinational companies in their transfer of management services across borders.

Figure 9.4 provides a snapshot of the importance of software and data services and their contributing role to the economy. In the figure,

---

[9] In fact, Ferracane, Kren, and van der Marel (2018a) computed the original data intensities that they reported based on input–output data from the US BEA with the selection of sectors in Table A9.1. That is, they computed each downstream industry's and services sector's usage of ICT and data services (as defined in this table) over labor using BLS data. However, the BEA input–output tables are somewhat outdated, and Ferracane, Kren, and van der Marel (2018a) also used data on software expenditures over labor for each sector to provide updated information on the data intensity of each industry and services sector. The two alternative measures for data intensities correlate well, as shown by the two panels in Figure A9.2 based on the North American Industry Classification System and the NACE Revision.

Figure 9.4 Data Users (Intensity) Using Software for D/L and Contribution to Value Added

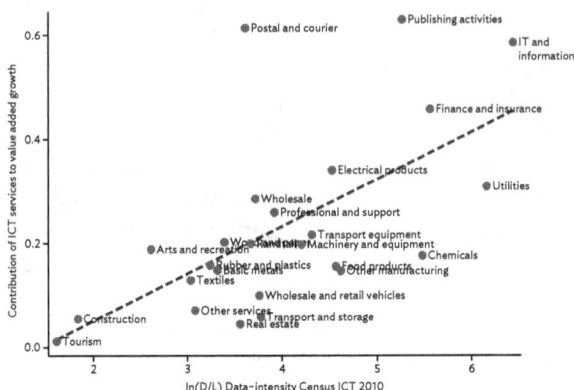

D/L = software usage (D) over labor (L), ICT = information and communications technology, IT = information technology.

Note: The EU KLEMS project, from which these data are drawn, began in the late 1990s with the objective of developing new productivity measures at the industry level for the European Union (EU). "KLEMS" refers to the decomposition of output growth into contributing factor inputs: capital (K), labor (L), energy (E), materials (M), and service inputs (S).

Source: Author's calculations using the United States Census, United States Bureau of Labor Statistics, and EU KLEMS data.

the horizontal axis shows the contribution of total ICT services to value-added growth across the countries present in the EU KLEMS dataset by taking an unweighted average. ICT services consist of telecommunications and computer equipment, computer software and databases (i.e., data services), and other intellectual property services, such as research and development. As such, this variable contains a wider definition than the intensities outlined above, plotted on the vertical axis. This shows our proxy for data services and software intensity, which we take from the US Census and which Ferracane, Kren, and van der Marel (2018a) used (see Figure 9.3). A strong positive correlation appears, meaning that the role of software and data used in each using industry is strongly associated with the extent to which these industries and sectors can contribute to value-added growth across countries. As such, they contribute to the overall productivity.[10]

---

[10] The flip side of this effect of higher productivity growth is a decline in the prices of technologies (see Byrne and Corrado 2017), leading to further diffusion of ICT services into the wider economy.

One area of the digital economy of which the absorption in downstream sectors may generate large productivity gains is AI. Current studies have estimated that the implementation of AI may have large implications for productivity. Sectors receptive to AI developments are those that currently employ a large amount of ICT and data services. Since machine learning uses vast amounts of data to make predictions about what individuals are likely to desire and choose, data constitute a key input for AI (Milgrom and Tadelis 2018). A survey from the Boston Consulting Group and the Massachusetts Institute of Technology Sloan Management Review estimated that sectors such as technology, media, and telecommunications; financial services; and professional support services are likely to feel the greatest impact on processes through AI adoption (Ransbotham et al. 2017). Interestingly, all three sectors are services, and, as seen in Figures 9.3 and 9.4, our proxies in the previous section also assessed the three sectors together as data-intensive.

The intensive use of data services in AI and their absorption into other sectors also has implications for market and trade policy, especially those regulatory policies related to data, as framed by Agrawal, Gans, and Goldfarb (2018) and Goldfarb and Trefler (2018). Policy measures such as data localization and policies regulating the privacy of data have increasingly been a focal point of policy makers considering the future of the ICT-based economy. These policies aim to regulate the collection, storage, transfer, and usage of data. Whether increased usage of ICT, AI, and data services truly translates into sustained economic development growth therefore depends largely on how such policies develop to avoid misallocation of technology. Although numerous productivity studies have pointed out the many factors that determine productivity, trade policy and regulatory market policies in particular have proved to be real sources of plausible productivity-enhancing effects (Sylverson 2011).

Therefore, in the next section we turn to the regulatory policy barriers in data-related services that have arisen in recent years and their impact on productivity developments.

9.4 Regulatory Policies in Information and Communications Technology Services and Their Impact on Productivity

As stated above, greater contributions to value-added growth will have to translate into productive outcomes, ultimately generating greater productivity growth. However, many policy hurdles can inhibit the transformation of productive ICT resources into greater productivity levels for firms, which will eventually forgo a sustainable development path. In recent years, an increasing number of countries have put restrictions on the workings of the internet and digital services. These restrictions are holding back the transfer and usage of electronic data over the internet in particular, and can represent restrictions inhibiting the application of internet technologies (i.e., the optimal allocation of technology resources).

9.4.1 Restrictive Data Policies

Restrictive policies targeting data and the internet exist in various forms, which we can break down into three categories: (i) restrictions targeting data themselves, (ii) intermediate liability restrictions, and (iii) restrictions related to content access. The policies within each of these categories restrict the operations of the internet, data, and ICT services more generally. They all have in common the fact that they increase the operational cost of firms in a disproportionate manner or restrict their entry to markets, often on the basis of discriminatory elements. These restrictions either favor domestic digital companies or domestic users of digital services over their foreign counterparts, or they favor offline companies more than their online competitors. The policy restrictions are often excessively burdensome, and *significantly* increase the costs of digital companies although other, less burdensome alternatives are often available.

Similarly onerous are the policies specifically targeting data. An increasing number of companies, ranging from banks to traditional manufacturing companies, rely heavily on the internet and the free flow of data across the globe to carry out their business activities through of the use of advanced internet technologies. Given the dependence of the economy on data, certain policies concerning data flows can be legitimate and necessary to protect the privacy of individuals or to ensure national security. However, several policies aim not to achieve a legitimate policy objective in the least trade-restrictive manner, but rather to create unnecessary frictions in the movement and usage of data. For example, data localization policies, which have been increasing substantially over time (Figure 9.5), require companies to keep data inside their jurisdiction and not send it abroad. Other such data policies include data retention policies requiring firms to keep data records for a minimum and maximum amount of time, the recruiting of data protection officers, and other burdensome rules on the usage of data.

Intermediate liability restrictions target internet intermediaries, which are those companies that act as an intermediary between content producers and the internet, facilitating its use. Such companies include internet service providers, search engines, and social media platforms.

Figure 9.5 Cumulative Number of Data Localization Measures (1961–2017)

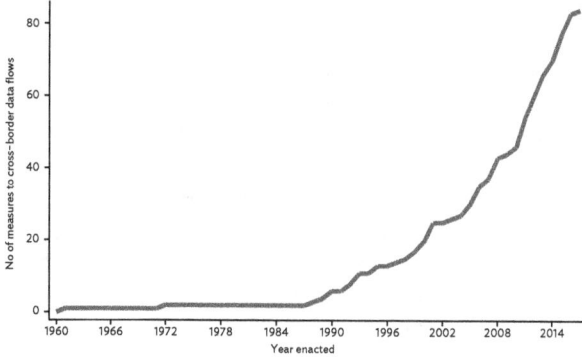

Note: When the year of the law is not available, we consider the year in which the reporting of the measure occurred. The graph does not include measures for which the year was not available.

Source: European Center for International Political Economy; Ferracane, M. F., H. L. Makiyama, and E. van der Marel. 2018. Digital Trade Restrictiveness Index. Brussels: European Center for International Political Economy.

These fall into the sector of information and communications services and in many cases affect the usage of platforms by companies and consumers.

Some jurisdictions provide a so-called safe-harbor mechanism, which shields the intermediary from the responsibility for the user's actions as long as it respects certain conditions and acts promptly when notified of illicit behavior. Conversely, in jurisdictions without a safe-harbor framework, intermediaries bear the legal responsibility, that is, "liability," for illegal or harmful activities that users perform through their services, which can be burdensome. This obliges the intermediaries to prevent the occurrence of unlawful or harmful activity on the part of users of their services. It is therefore possible to consider the existence of a safe harbor as a strategic factor: it provides intermediaries with sufficient legal certainty to conduct a wide range of activities, free from the threat of potential liability and the chilling effect of potential litigation. The lack of a safe harbor is arguably a restriction. Other restrictions related to intermediate liability are burdensome user identity and monitoring requirements, or onerous terms for the noticing and taking down of infringing content.

Restrictions related to content access inhibit companies from using new channels to reach potential customers and users from making informed purchases of new services. These restrictions prevent access to certain online content, potentially increasing the cost of offering services online and, in some cases, even making this impossible. These restrictions exist in various forms, ranging from governments' blocking and filtering activities to discriminatory bandwidth restrictions. The latter includes the issue of net neutrality, which is the principle that internet service providers should enable access to all content and applications, regardless of the source and without favoring or blocking particular products or websites. The measures refer to restrictions on content that companies provide on a commercial basis. All of these measures increase the cost of offering services online, or in some cases even render it impossible. These restrictions therefore limit the opportunities for consumers to access these services.

Figure 9.6 summarizes these restrictions on data by scoring and weighting their importance in the digital economy, following the methodology of Ferracane, Kren, and van der Marel (2018). The figure uses a ranking based on a score between zero (completely open) and one (virtually restricted).

Countries that appear more restrictive with respect to internet technologies and data usage are often larger emerging countries, such as the People's Republic of China, the Russian Federation, and Turkey. However, it is not only non-OECD countries that are more restricted concerning data; Germany and France, and to a lesser extent Denmark and Italy, are also relatively restricted, and lie above the average level of data restrictions indicated by the grey dashed line in Figure 9.6. Countries that are generally less restricted are small open economies, such as the Netherlands, Iceland, and Belgium. These countries, which are open to the internet and data, are often very services-oriented and dependent on global markets. Other countries, such as the US and Japan, also appear to be less restricted. The US in particular is home to some digital giants that operate with high data usage. An open regime regarding the transfer and usage of data as well as access to platforms and content will help these countries expand their economies further with the aid of data.

Ferracane, Lee-Makiyama, and van der Marel (2018) provided some suggestive evidence on the reduced effect of this trade-off between greater levels of data restrictions and an economy based on data. The authors showed that the countries with a greater level of restrictions in the three categories of data restrictions shown in Figure 9.6 also exhibit lower levels of per capita data traffic, using internet provider traffic per month as a proxy. This suggests that higher levels of data restrictions across countries are associated with a lower capability of generating data in the economy, which in turn could have a detrimental effect on

Figure 9.6 Digital Trade Restrictiveness Index for Policies Related to Data

DTRI = Digital Trade Restrictiveness Index.

Note: The country abbreviations used are the International Organization for Standardization 3-digit country codes.

Source: European Center for International Political Economy; Ferracane, M. F., H. L. Makiyama, and E. van der Marel. 2018. Digital Trade Restrictiveness Index. Brussels: European Center for International Political Economy. The index represents the DTRI Cluster C sub-index.

economic performance and productivity of the downstream using sector. The expectation is therefore that industries and services in countries with high data policy restrictions and that rely heavily on data and ICT services will generate lower levels of data activity in their production process, leading to lower productivity performance. The next section will analyze that effect more thoroughly.

9.4.2 Economic Impact of Restrictions on Data

To investigate whether regulatory policies related to data really do have an important economic impact on productivity in sectors that use data and software services more intensively, we estimate the following regression equation, defined by Ferracane, Kren, and van der Marel (2018):

$$\ln TFP_{icjt} = \Phi + \theta_1 DL_{cjt-1} + \theta_2 C_{icjt} + \delta_{ct} + \varsigma_{jt} + \varepsilon_{icjt} \quad (1)$$

Equation (1) uses TFP as a proxy for productivity and computes it using firm-level information from ORBIS AMADEUS for both the services and manufacturing sectors. We also perform robustness regressions using EU KLEMS data (the results of which are provided in the annex and discussed below). The DL term refers to the data linkage variable, which represents the extent to which each individual industry and sector uses data and software services intensively, following the ranking in Figure 9.3. We then interact this intensity measure by sector with a country-wide measure of data policy regulations. In all, therefore, we define the DL term as:

$$Data\ Linkage\ (DL)_{cjt} = \ln\frac{\Sigma_d\ \varphi_{jd}}{LAB_j} * data\ policy\ index_{ct} \quad (2)$$

in which we multiply each of the country-specific regulatory indexes on data specifically with the data intensities that Figure 9.3 shows for country c for each downstream service and manufacturing sector j.[11] φ_{jd} denotes this proxy for data usage, which we define as an intensity by taking this usage value as a ratio over labor (LAB_j) while putting it in logs. The DL variable combines the information on data intensity

---

[11] The ranking of data policy restrictions alone does not therefore follow the one presented in Figure 9.6, as this ranking comprises *all* policy restrictions related to data, including intermediate liability and content access measures.

and data policy by linking to the variables in a weighted manner. The data on data usage come from the US Census, which records software usage by four-digit sectors; we obtain the data on labor from the US BLS for each similar disaggregated sector. In addition, in equation (1), the C_{icjt} term refers to all of the control variables at the level of firm, sector, country, and time, while the terms δ_{ct} and ς_{jt} refer to the fixed effects by country–year and sector–year, respectively. We apply sector fixed effects at the four-digit Statistical Classification of Economic Activities in the European Community (NACE) level, which is stricter than the two-digit level at which we compute our productivity variable.[12]

The expected results are that the countries with greater levels of restrictions on data are also those in which industries and services that rely heavily on data experience lower levels of productivity development. Conversely, countries with lower levels of restrictions on data are likely to show higher productivity development in sectors that are more data driven. This identification strategy relies on the assumption that sectors that are more reliant on data are also proportionately more affected by changes in data policies implemented over time. This empirical estimation strategy follows the one pioneered by Arnold, Javorcik, and Mattoo (2011) and Arnold et al. (2015), who developed a service linkage variable to take stock of this effect. In our case, we develop a *data* linkage index. This weighted approach to data policy regulation that relies on data intensities is, in our view, a more just approach to measure the impact of data policies on TFP than an unweighted one.

In Table 9.1, which shows the results of this regression, each column represents a separate regression for the various TFP measures following the literature (see the note to this table). We divide the regulatory data policies into those regulations that target the cross-border movement of data, such as data localization measures (which we denote using *CB*), and those regulations that target the domestic usage of data, such as the privacy of the data subject or data retention policies, the requirement to establish a data protection officer, or other burdensome administrative requirements for the usage of data. We denote these policies with *DOM*, that is, domestic regulations (see Table A9.2 for the exact distinction). The results clearly show that, across the various firm-level TFP measures, data policies have a negative and significant effect. Table A9.2 provides a robustness check that uses data from EU KLEMS for a similar regression analysis. The results are consistent in the sense

---

[12]   For the sake of brevity, we provide only a succinct explanation of the estimation strategy. For more information on the methodology, identification strategy, estimation strategy, and results, see Ferracane, Kren, and van der Marel (2018).

Table 9.1 Baseline Regression Results with Alternative Total Factor Productivity Measures, Including Labor Productivity

	(1)	(2)	(3)	(4)	(5)	(6)
	ACF	L&P	O&P	TFPR	TFPQ	LabPr
ln(D/L) * data policy CB	−0.305***	−0.311***	0.139	0.047	−0.240***	−0.039
	(0.000)	(0.000)	(0.270)	(0.115)	(0.000)	(0.262)
ln(D/L) * data policy DOM	−0.340***	−0.506***	−0.385***	−0.015	−0.100***	−0.149***
	(0.000)	(0.000)	(0.000)	(0.158)	(0.000)	(0.000)
FE country–year	Yes	Yes	Yes	Yes	Yes	Yes
FE sector–year	Yes	Yes	Yes	Yes	Yes	Yes
Firm controls	Yes	Yes	Yes	Yes	Yes	Yes
Observations	3,516,012	3,521,289	3,521,289	3,521,289	3,521,289	3,521,724
R²A	0.866	0.702	0.615	0.131	0.322	0.569
R²W	0.023	0.191	0.008	0.010	0.242	0.022
RMSE	0.444	0.702	1.017	0.776	1.014	0.670

ACF = Ackerberg, Caves, and Frazer; CB = cross-border; D/L = software usage (D) over labor (L); DOM = domestic; FE = fixed effects; L&P = Levinsohn and Petrin; LabPr = labor productivity; O&P = Olley and Pakes; R²A = adjusted R-squared; R²W = weighted R-squared; RMSE = root mean square error; TFPQ = physical total factor productivity; TFPR = revenue total factor productivity.

Note: * p<0.10; ** p<0.05; *** p<0.01. The dependent variable represents different productivity measures, namely Ackerberg, Caves, and Frazer (2015) for ACF; Levinsohn and Petrin (2003) for L&P; Olley and Pakes (1996) for O&P; Hsieh and Klenow (2009; 2014) for TFPR and TFPQ; and value added per employee for LabPr. All the productivity measures are in logs. Robust standard errors are two-way clustered at the country–industry–year and firm levels. We apply fixed effects for sectors at the NACE Rev. 2 four-digit level. CB denotes cross-border and covers all policies that Ferracane, Kren, and van der Marel (2018) outlined under 1.1 in their Annex A. DOM denotes cross-border and covers all the policies that Ferracane, Kren, and van der Marel (2018) outlined under 1.2–1.6 in their Annex A.

Source: Ferracane, M. F., J. Kren, and E. van der Marel. 2018a. Do Data Policy Restrictions Impact the Productivity Performance of Firms? European Center for International Political Economy Digital Trade Estimates Working Paper 1. Brussels: European Center for International Political Economy.

that most domestic regulatory policies regarding data are now negative and significant.[13]

The above regression analysis takes both the services and manufacturing sectors into account, as both sectors have specific services and industries that are data intensive. However, we can make some predictions regarding how reforms in regulatory data policies may affect the services and manufacturing sectors separately. Using marginal

---

[13] The number of observations reduces significantly when using EU KLEMS data, which should therefore be taken into account when looking at the insignificance of the policy index related to the cross-border flow of data (CB).

effects, Figure 9.7 shows the potential TFP gains resulting from policy reform in data using a scenario in which all countries reduce their level of data restrictions to the average of the three least restricted countries. The figure shows that the TFP gains are greatest in services, making this sector the main beneficiary of reform in data policies. However, both sectors would gain from reforms in data, although the percentage change in TFP for services is 1.4 percentage points higher than that for manufacturing. This result is largely due to the fact that services are generally very data- and software-intense, and high TFP gains naturally occur in many data-intensive services, such as information services activities (6%), telecommunications (7%), and retail (11%).

That does not mean that TFP gains from data reform can be high for individual manufacturing industries: industries such as chemicals, pharmaceuticals, and machinery and equipment would generate TFP gains from around 2%. Most of these manufacturing sectors are considered advanced industries with complex production processes, high skill intensity, and generally higher levels of digitalization. Although it is estimated that these sectors will be more sensitive to future AI developments, a greater productivity effect would be expected from AI for services (Ransbotham et al. 2017), which is an additional factor in explaining its higher TFP gain. Yet, several industries also involve advanced supply chains. Given the geographical dispersion of these industries' production stages, it is expected that digital and data services will play an important role in coordinating the fragmented stages of production.

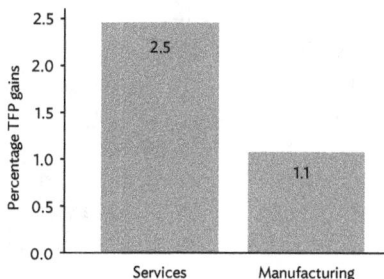

Figure 9.7 Potential Total Factor Productivity Gains from Reducing Restrictions on Data by Sector

TFP = total factor productivity.
Source: Author's calculations using data input from Table 9.1.

9.5 Conclusion

It is often claimed in the international economic policy debate that services do not contribute much to the overall productive performance of an economy. In fact, it is commonly stated that services lag behind manufacturing in terms of productivity and, as a result, act as a drag on the overall economy as the sector grows in size parallel to development (the so-called Baumol "cost disease"). Moreover, coupled with the fact that services cannot "absorb" as many people as manufacturing due to the required high skill level, it is hard to imagine any services sector playing the role of an engine for prospective economic development in poorer countries—something that the manufacturing sector has always been in the past.

However, both of these assertions appear ill-informed of certain factual developments. Firstly, some parts of the services sector have experienced great productivity increases over the years. This is particularly true for information and communications services, which comprise computer, information, and telecommunications services. These digital services have witnessed productivity trends (using TFP as a proxy) that at least keep up with the overall manufacturing sector. In addition, some digital-intensive services, such as distribution (i.e., retail and wholesale) and financial services, have experienced significant upward trends in productivity growth, albeit at lower rates than manufacturing. Overall, these and various other services are therefore real drivers of overall positive productivity development in countries. Hence, it is clear that services would allow countries to grow further and need not be a drag on the economy.

In addition, many digital-intensive services (i.e., those that "use" many internet technologies along with software and data) also show long-term trends of contributing to value-added growth across countries. In fact, most digital-intensive services, such as information services, finance, utilities, and, to a lesser extent, courier services, are precisely those that have contributed the most to the overall growth of value added in many OECD countries. As economies around the globe are becoming increasingly digitalized, nothing precludes less developed countries from tapping into this source of prospective growth. A third often-heard claim is that these sectors together are not substantial enough and indeed are rather "petty." Yet, services sectors are usually big. For instance, in the US, the four most digital-intensive sectors (excluding the large business services sector) in terms of output appear to be as large as the entire US manufacturing sector. Therefore, even small increases in productivity in these services are likely to result in huge overall gains.

Ultimately, however, the extent to which greater contributors to growth can really have a lasting effect on a country's long-term productivity growth (and therefore economic growth) depends on many factors. Of these, a consistent focal point is regulatory policies; such policies targeting the internet and internet technologies have recently been rampant. Some examples include policies that target the cross-border movement and usage of data or regulations for software and cloud computing, all of which have a significant effect on long-term productivity development, as this chapter has shown. Therefore, keeping these policies to a minimum by removing their restrictive nature would help in further increasing the positive productivity effects of this sector, in both developed and developing countries around the world.

References

Ackerberg, D., K. Caves, and G. Frazer. 2015. Identification Properties of Recent Production Function Estimators. *Econometrica* 83(6): 2411–2451.

Agrawal, A., J. Gans, and A. Goldfarb (eds). 2018. *The Economics of Artificial Intelligence: An Agenda*. Chicago: University of Chicago Press.

Agrawal, A. K., J. S. Gans, and A. Goldfarb. 2018. Economic Policy for Artificial Intelligence. National Bureau of Economic Research (NBER) Working Paper 24690. Cambridge, MA: National Bureau of Economic Analysis.

Andrenelli, A., C. Cadestin, K. de Backer, S. Miroudot, D. Rigo, and M. Ye. 2018. Multinational Production and Trade in Services. Organisation for Economic Co-operation and Development Trade Policy Paper 212. Paris: Organisation for Economic Co-operation and Development Publishing.

Arnold, J., B. Javorcik, and A. Mattoo. 2011. The Productivity Effects of Services Liberalization: Evidence from the Czech Republic. *Journal of International Economics* 85(1): 136–146.

Arnold, J., B. Javorcik, M. Lipscomb, and A. Mattoo. 2015. Services Reform and Manufacturing Performance: Evidence from India. *Economic Journal* 126(590): 1–39.

Atalay, E., A. Hortaçsu, and C. Syverson. 2014. Vertical Integration and Input Flows. *American Economic Review* 104(4): 1120–1148.

Baumol, W.J. 1967. Macroeconomics of Unbalanced Growth: The Anatomy of Urban Crises. *American Economic Review* 57(3): 415–426.

Byrne, D., and C. Corrado. 2017. ICT Prices and ICT Services: What Do They Tell Us About Productivity and Technology. *International Productivity Monitor* 33: 150–181.

Ferracane, M. F., J. Kren, and E. van der Marel. 2018a. Do Data Policy Restrictions Impact the Productivity Performance of Firms? European Center for International Political Economy (ECIPE) Digital Trade Estimates Working Paper 1. Brussels: ECIPE.

Ferracane, M. F., H. L. Makiyama, and E. van der Marel. 2018b. *Digital Trade Restrictiveness Index*. Brussels: ECIPE.

Goldfarb, A., and D. Trefler. 2018. Artificial Intelligence and International Trade. NBER Working Paper 24254. Cambridge, MA: NBER.

Hsieh, C.-T., and P. Klenow. 2009. Misallocation and Manufacturing TFP in China and India. *Quarterly Journal of Economics* 124(4): 1403–1448.

Hsieh, C.-T., and P. Klenow. 2014. The Life Cycle of Plants in India and Mexico. *Quarterly Journal of Economics* 129(3): 1035–1084.

Hulten, C. R., and L. I. Nakamura. 2017. Accounting for Growth in the Age of the Internet: The Importance of Output-Saving Technical

Change. NBER Working Paper 23315. Cambridge, MA: National Bureau of Economic Analysis.

International Monetary Fund (IMF). 2018. Manufacturing Jobs: Implications for Productivity and Inequality. In *IMF World Economic Outlook*. Washington, DC: IMF.

Inklaar, R., and M. P. Timmer. 2008. Accounting for Growth in Retail Trade: An International Productivity Comparison. *Journal of Productivity Analysis* 29(1): 23–31.

Jäger, K. 2017. *EU KLEMS Growth and Productivity Accounts 2017 Release—Description of Methodology and General Notes*. New York: The Conference Board.

Levinsohn, J., and A. Petrin. 2003. Estimating Production Functions Using Input Control for Unobservables. *Review of Economic Studies* 70(2): 317–341.

Milgrom, P. R., and S. Tadelis. 2018. How Artificial Intelligence and Machine Learning can Impact Market Design. NBER Working Paper 24282. Cambridge, MA: National Bureau of Economic Analysis.

Olley, S., and A. Pakes. 1996. The Dynamics of Productivity in the Telecommunications Equipment Industry. *Econometrica* 64(6): 1263–1295.

Ransbotham, S., D. Kiron, P. Gerbert, and M. Reeves. 2017. Reshaping Business with Artificial Intelligence. Massachusetts Institute of Technology Sloan Management Review and Boston Consultancy Group Research Report.

Rodrik, D. 2015. Premature Deindustrialization. NBER Working Paper 20935. Cambridge, MA: National Bureau of Economic Analysis.

Syverson, C. 2011. What Determines Productivity? *Journal of Economic Literature* 49(2): 326–365.

Triplett, J. E., and B. P. Bosworth. 2003. "Baumol's Disease" Has Been Cured: IT and Multifactor Productivity in U.S. Services Industries. In D. Hansen (ed.), *The New Economy: How New? How Resilient?*, Chicago: University of Chicago Press; Brookings Institution.

Triplett, J. E., and B. P. Bosworth. 2004. *Productivity in the US Services Sector: New Sources of Economic Growth*. Washington, DC: The Brookings Institution.

van Ark, B., R. Inklaar, and R. H. McGuckin. 2003. ICT and Productivity in Europe and the United States: Where Do the Differences Come From? *CESifo Economics Studies* 49(3): 295–318.

van Ark, B. 2016. The Productivity Paradox of the New Digital Economy. *International Productivity Monitor* 31: 3–18. (also published by the Conference Board).

van der Marel, E., and B. Shepherd. 2013. International Tradability Indices for Services. World Bank Policy Research Working Paper 6712. Washington, DC: World Bank.

Annex

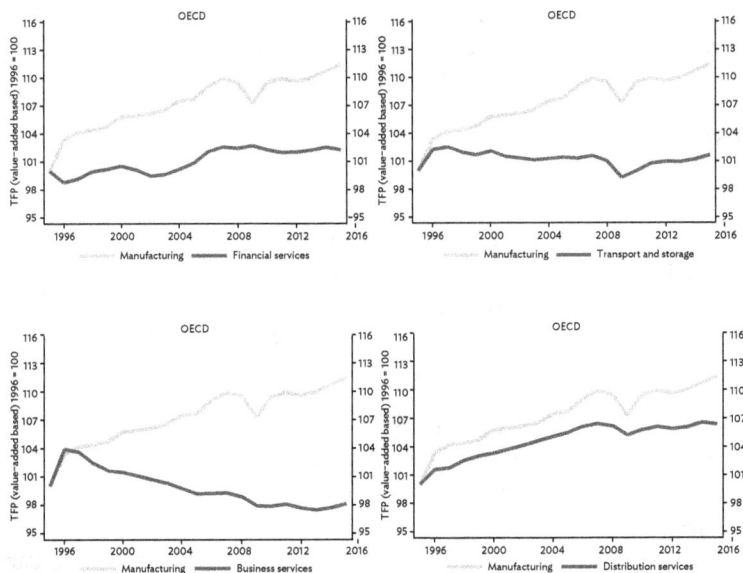

Figure A9.1 Total Factor Productivity in Manufacturing and Other Services in the OECD (1996–2015)

OECD = Organisation for Economic Co-operation and Development, TFP = total factor productivity.

Note: The EU KLEMS project, from which these data are drawn, began in the late 1990s with the objective of developing new productivity measures at the industry level for the European Union (EU). "KLEMS" refers to the decomposition of output growth into contributing factor inputs: capital (K), labor (L), energy (E), materials (M), and service inputs (S).

Source: Author's calculations using EU KLEMS.

Table A9.1 Data Producers in Information and Communications (2007)

NAICS Code	Sector Description
511200	Software publishers
517110	Wired telecommunications carriers
517210	Wireless telecommunications carriers (except satellite)
518200	Data processing, hosting, and related services
519130	Internet publishing and broadcasting and web search portals
541511	Custom computer programming services
541512	Computer systems design services
541513	Other computer-related services, including facilities management

NAICS = North American Industry Classification System.

Source: United States Bureau of Economic Analysis, 2007 Input–Output Use Table. https://www.bea.gov/industry/input-output-accounts-data (accessed 19 April 2019).

Figure A9.2 Correlation between the United States Bureau of Economic Analysis Data Intensity and United States Census Data Intensity over Labor (D/L)

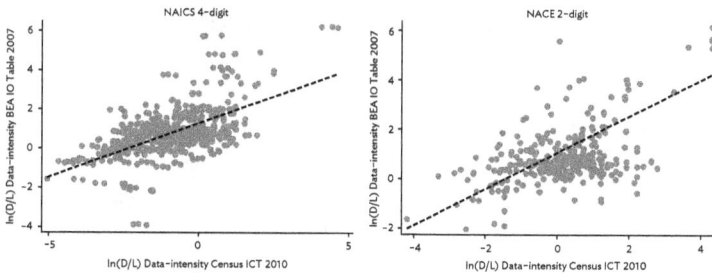

BEA = United States Bureau of Economic Analysis, D/L = software usage (D) over labor (L), ICT = information and communications technology, IO = input–output, NACE = Statistical Classification of Economic Activities in the European Community, NAICS = North American Industry Classification System.

Source: Author's calculations using the BEA 2007 Input–Output Use Tablehttps://www.bea.gov/industry/input-output-accounts-data (accessed 19 April 2019); United States Census, and United States Bureau of Labor Statistics.

Table A9.2 Categories of the Data Policy Index and Weights

Categories		Types of Measures	Weighting
1.		Cross-border data flow measures	0.5
	1.1	Ban on transfer or local processing requirement	0.5
	1.2	Local storage requirement	0.25
	1.3	Conditional flow regime	0.25
2.		Domestic regulatory measures	0.5
2.1		Data retention	0.15
	2.1.1	Minimum period	0.7
	2.1.2	Maximum period	0.3
2.2		Subject rights on data privacy	0.10
	2.2.1	Burdensome consent requirement	0.5
	2.2.2	Right to be forgotten	0.5
2.3		Administrative requirements on data privacy	0.15
	2.3.1	Data protection impact assessment	0.3
	2.3.2	Data protection officer	0.3
	2.3.3	Data breach notification	0.1
	2.3.4	Government access to personal data	0.3
2.4		Sanctions for non-compliance	0.05
	2.4.1	Monetary fine above €250.000 or set as a percentage of revenue	0.5
	2.4.2	Jail time	0.5
2.5		Other restrictive practices related to data policies	0.05
	2.5.1	Other restrictive practices related to data policies	1

Source: Ferracane, M. F., H. L. Makiyama, and E. van der Marel. 2018. Digital Trade Restrictiveness Index. Brussels: European Center for International Political Economy.

Table A9.3 Baseline Regression Results with Sector-Level Productivity Measures from EU KLEMS[a]

	(1) TFPva_i	(2) TFPlp1_i	(3) TFPlp2_i	(4) LP_i	(5) LP1_q	(6) LP2_q
ln(D/L) * data policy CB	−0.002	−0.010	−0.013	0.013	0.300	0.160
	(0.856)	(0.487)	(0.383)	(0.378)	(0.281)	(0.556)
ln(D/L) * data policy DOM	−0.035**	−0.032**	−0.026*	−0.053***	−0.165	−0.128
	(0.018)	(0.035)	(0.092)	(0.001)	(0.498)	(0.562)
FE country–year	Yes	Yes	Yes	Yes	Yes	Yes
FE sector–year	Yes	Yes	Yes	Yes	Yes	Yes
Observations	3,506	3,416	3,416	6,669	3,564	3,747
R^2A	0.170	0.171	0.188	0.105	0.257	0.256
R^2W	0.001	0.001	0.001	0.001	0.000	0.000
RMSE	0.095	0.096	0.098	0.151	1.107	1.105

CB = cross-border, D/L = software usage (D) over labor (L), DOM = domestic, FE = fixed effects, LP_i = gross value added per hours worked, LP1_q = growth rate of value added per hours worked, LP2_q = growth rate of value added per person employed, R^2A = adjusted R-squared, R^2W = weighted R-squared, RMSE = root mean square error, TFPva_i = total factor productivity (TFP) value added based growth, TFPlp1_i = TFP value added per hour worked based growth, TFPlp2_i = TFP value added per person employed based growth.

[a] The EU KLEMS project began in the late 1990s with the objective of developing new productivity measures at the industry level for the European Union (EU). "KLEMS" refers to the decomposition of output growth into contributing factor inputs: capital (K), labor (L), energy (E), materials (M), and service inputs (S).

Note: * $p<0.10$; ** $p<0.05$; *** $p<0.01$. The dependent variable represents different productivity measures from EU KLEMs. All productivity measures are in logs. Robust standard errors are clustered at the country-industry–year level. (D/L) denotes the ratio of total *capitalized* computer software expenditures over labor by the Statistical Classification of Economic Activities in the European Community Revision 2 two-digit sector level, both taken from the United States Census. We apply fixed effects for sectors at this level. CB covers all policies outlined by Ferracane, Kren, and van der Marel (2018: A1.1); and DOM covers all policies outlined by Ferracane, Kren, and van der Marel (2018: A1.2–1.6).

Source: Ferracane, M. F., J. Kren, and E. van der Marel. 2018a. Do Data Policy Restrictions Impact the Productivity Performance of Firms? European Center for International Political Economy Digital Trade Estimates Working Paper 1. Brussels: European Center for International Political Economy.

PART IV

Services and Labor Markets in Developing Countries

10

What are the Prospects for Decent Work in Services?

Sameer Khatiwada and John Paul Flaminiano

10.1 Introduction

The current development paradigm in developing Asia is characterized by vibrant economic growth. However, despite the increase in the number of people in the working middle class holding higher productivity jobs, some reports suggest that the region is still home to more than 800 million workers living on less than $2.00 a day (Martinez, Molato, and Flaminiano 2016). If left unaddressed, this situation will have adverse consequences on the region's long-term growth prospects. Since employment and job quality play a pivotal role in shaping the standard of living in developing Asia, it is crucial for policy makers to design regulatory systems that encourage the creation of good jobs. Moreover, the provision of good jobs would also help sustain the growth trajectory of developing Asia.

Developing Asia contains half of the world's population and half of the world's labor force (World Bank 2018b). Furthermore, the labor force in the region has increased by half a billion from 1990 to 2015, and is projected to grow at an annual rate of 0.49% from 1.9 billion in 2015 to 2.13 billion in 2030 and 2.25 billion by 2050. The current labor market trend is a shift in employment away from agriculture and into higher productivity sectors such as trade services and business services, which also pay higher wages. Previous editions of Key Indicators for Asia and the Pacific published by the Asian Development Bank [ADB] (from 2013 and 2015 in particular) examined many of the issues relevant to the creation of good jobs. In 2013, the Key Indicators looked at structural transformation and industrialization, while in 2015, it looked at the role of education and skills development. This chapter compliments these studies by looking at a few targeted subsets of factors important for good job creation.

Unfortunately, the concept of "decent jobs" lacks a standardized definition. Various organizations employ different characterizations of good jobs that focus on various dimensions. Although the terminologies and elements that characterize good jobs may differ, some of these dimensions are consistent among various international organizations. The definitions of "decent work" and "quality jobs" used by the International Labour Organization (ILO) and Organization for Economic Co-operation and Development (OECD) can help us construct a definition of "good jobs." The ILO's "decent work" framework provides a good reference for understanding what a decent job is. Although the framework spans 10 themes believed to be core elements of a decent job, the framework can be classified into four major themes. These include (i) international labor standards and rights at work, (ii) employment creation (adequate earnings and productive work), (iii) social protection, and (iv) social dialogue and tripartism (voice and representation) (ILO 2013).

Another reference that can help characterize a good job is the OECD's "quality jobs" framework. The OECD highlights three main elements that comprise quality jobs: (i) earnings quality, (ii) labor market security, and (iii) quality of working environment (OECD 2016). Although the terminologies and elements that characterize good jobs may differ, certain dimensions appear consistently among various international organizations. The definitions of "decent work" and "quality jobs" used by the ILO and OECD can help in constructing a definition of good jobs.

Economies that have successfully moved workers from low- to high-productivity sectors have done relatively better in terms of job creation accompanied by improved productivity, higher wages, and large reductions in poverty (ADB 2018: 49). The longstanding challenge for developing economies today is to provide new and gainful employment to the large supply of low-productivity and informal sector workers. Services, which now account for more than two-thirds of the world's gross domestic product (GDP) and more than half of the world's employment (as of 2015) (World Bank 2018a), promises to be a significant driver in generating decent jobs.

10.2 Defining Good Jobs

This chapter defines a good job based on the living wage rates, that is, the level of wages that a worker needs to earn to be able to support a family at a minimum standard of living (Anker 2006). Living wage rates for developing Asia were estimated at $254.28 per month for Option 1 (i.e., anchored on the absolute poverty line) and $414.88 per month for Option 2 (i.e., anchored on the moderate poverty line). The poverty lines are from the thresholds set by the World Bank, of $1.90 per day for absolute poverty and $3.20 per day for moderate poverty (World Bank 2018).

10.2.1 Deriving Living Wages

The derivation of living wage rates is summarized as follows: first, a minimum cost of living is specified. Values are anchored on the poverty line ($1.90 for absolute poverty and $3.20 for moderate poverty) and inflated by 10% to allow for savings and discretionary income. In general, the living wage is based on a specified poverty line or cost of basic living, both of which consist of two basic components: (i) food cost, and (ii) cost of other basic needs. Food cost is usually based on a model diet that follows a certain nutrition standard (e.g., 2,100 calories per day). This model diet is then priced using relevant information about prices and consumption patterns in each country. Non-food cost is commonly estimated by extrapolating from household expenditure survey data. Conceptually, the living wage in a specific area should be higher than its corresponding poverty line, since the former should allow a small margin for savings to provide for unexpected events and for discretionary income.

Table 10.1 Average Household Size, by Country

Country	AHS
Bangladesh	4.7
Cambodia	4.6
India	4.7
Indonesia	4.5
Malaysia	4.2
Nepal	4.9
Pakistan	6.7
Philippines	4.6
Thailand	3.8
Viet Nam	3.8
Sri Lanka	3.9

AHS = average household size.
Sources: 2010 Household Income and Expenditure Survey (Bangladesh); 2013 Cambodia Socio-Economic Survey (Cambodia); 2012 Employment and Unemployment Survey (India); 2014 National Labour Force Survey (Indonesia); 2008 Labor Force Survey (Nepal); 2013 Labor Force Survey (Pakistan); 2013 Labor Force Survey (Philippines); 2014 Labor Force Survey (Sri Lanka); 2010 Labor Force Survey (Thailand); 2013 Labor and Employment Survey (Viet Nam).

Second, the cost of living is multiplied by the size of the family to be supported. The average household size in Asian countries is 3.5–7.0 people (Table 10.1). This chapter assumes an average family size of four. This implicitly assumes that the living wage should be enough to support a family of four (two adults and two children), and should thus be determined by multiplying the cost of basic living by four (Anker 2006).

Third, the maximum number of work hours per week is set at 48 to leave the worker with time for leisure. A good job should pay a living wage while providing a worker with adequate time for leisure and relaxation. Table 10.2 summarizes the average work hours of various Asian countries based on the latest available household surveys.

Table 10.2 Number of Working Hours, by Country

| Country | Hours worked | | |
	Year of latest available data	Average	Statutory hours
Bangladesh	2010	46.0	48
Cambodia	2010	47.0	48
India	2006	46.9	48
Indonesia	2013	37.0	40
Malaysia	2014	46.0	48
Nepal	2008	38.7	48
Pakistan	2015	47.4	48
Philippines	2014	40.8	48
Sri Lanka	2014	41.6	45
Thailand	2014	44.9	48
Viet Nam	2014	43.0	48

Sources: International Labour Organization Working Conditions Laws Database. Geneva. http://www.ilo.org/dyn/travail (accessed 26 April 2019).

Fourth, spatial price differences across regions or provinces within a country are accounted for by adjusting the national living wage rate based on the ratio of the regional or provincial poverty line to the national poverty line. Spatial adjustments to the national-level wage rate are calculated by specifying the length of work hours using the following formula:

$$Living\ wage_j = Living\ wage_{national} * \frac{z_j}{z_{national}}$$

where z_j is the poverty line of the jth province for a specific time period, and $z_{national}$ is the national poverty line.

10.1.1 Good Jobs in Services

This section examines the possibility of securing good jobs in the services sector using the concept of living wage rates as a reference point. Although living wage rates may appear to be a bare minimum criterion, they are nonetheless a benchmark for determining what a good job is, especially given the lack of a formal, universally agreed-upon definition in the existing literature. Thus, a job that pays at least the living wage rate could be viewed as a lower bound standard of what a good job is.

Employment distribution is very diverse across Asia. In 2010, a large proportion of the workforce in developing Asian economies is still employed in agriculture (Figure 10.1). More than half of India's workforce, and more than one-third of the workforces in Indonesia, the Philippines, the People's Republic of China (PRC), and Thailand are still employed in agriculture. On the other hand, in industrialized Asian economies such as Hong Kong, China; the Republic of Korea; Singapore; and Taipei,China more than half of the workforce is employed in services; this figure is close to 70% in Singapore, and almost 90% in Hong Kong, China.

Although a significant portion of the workforce in developing Asian economies is still employed in agriculture, services now accounts for a sizable share of total employment. Although the composition of employment in services may be diverse, some trends in terms of employment type are observable. With the exception of Bangladesh (2010), business services comprise mostly wage workers, while trade services largely comprise self-employed workers (Figure 10.2).

Most workers in agriculture do not earn a living wage; only 28% of wage workers in agriculture earn at least the Option 1 living wage, based on the absolute poverty threshold of $1.90 per day. The issue of inadequate pay in agriculture is further amplified when we refer to Option 2, which is based on the moderate poverty threshold of $3.20 per day: only 4% of wage workers in agriculture earn Option 2. In contrast, manufacturing, and to a larger extent, services, provide their workforces with good jobs, as measured by the living wage threshold (Figure 10.3). More than half of all wage workers in manufacturing, construction, mining, and public utilities earn at least living wage Option 1; however, the services sector, which accounts for almost 40% of total employment, provides its workers with by far a greater share of good jobs.

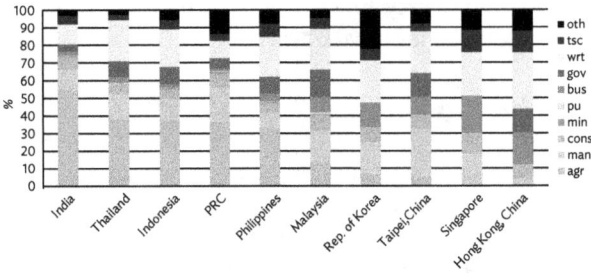

Figure 10.1 Employment Distribution in Some Asian Economies, by Sector, 2010

agr = agriculture, PRC = People's Republic of China, man = manufacturing, cons = construction, min = mining, pu = public utilities, bus = business services, gov = government services, wrt = trade services, tsc = transport and communication services, oth = other services.

Source: Authors' calculations based on M. P. Timmer, G. J. de Vries, and K. de Vries. 2015. Patterns of Structural Change in Developing Countries. In *Routledge Handbook of Industry and Development*, edited J. Weiss and M. Tribe. pp. 65–83. Abdingdon; New York: Routledge; Groningen Growth and Development Centre 10-Sector Database https://www.rug.nl/ggdc/productivity/10-sector/ (accessed 29 April 2019).

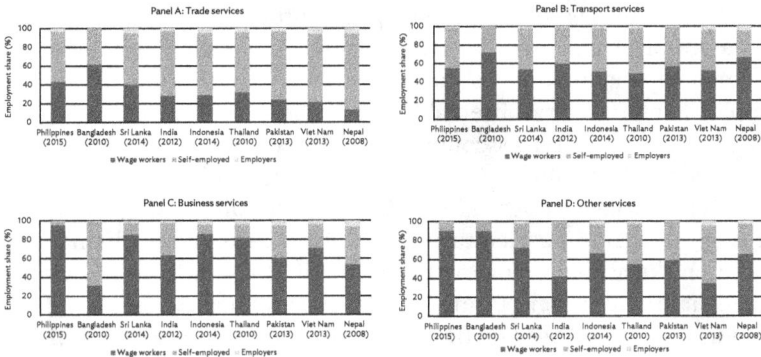

Figure 10.2 Employment Type Within Services in Some Asian Countries, by Sector, Collected from Various Years

Sources: 2010 Household Income and Expenditure Survey (Bangladesh); 2013 Cambodia Socio-Economic Survey (Cambodia); 2012 Employment and Unemployment Survey (India); 2014 National Labour Force Survey (Indonesia); 2008 Labor Force Survey (Nepal); 2013 Labor Force Survey (Pakistan); 2013 Labor Force Survey (Philippines); 2014 Labor Force Survey (Sri Lanka); 2010 Labor Force Survey (Thailand); 2013 Labor and Employment Survey (Viet Nam).

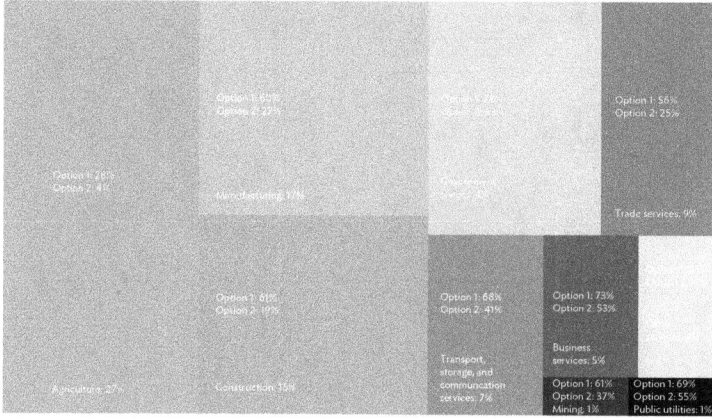

Figure 10.3 Share of Wage Earners Earning a Living Wage in Some Asian Countries, by Sector, Collected from Various Years

Notes: Figures next to the sector labels represent the employment share of a particular sector. The data refer to the following countries, with the year in parentheses: Bangladesh (2010), India (2012), Indonesia (2014), Nepal (2008), Pakistan (2013), the Philippines (2013), Sri Lanka (2014), Thailand (2010), and Viet Nam (2013). Calculations were made using each country's Labour Force Survey data (and Household Income and Expenditure Survey data for Bangladesh).

Source: Authors' calculations based on 2010 Household Income and Expenditure Survey (Bangladesh); 2013 Cambodia Socio-Economic Survey (Cambodia); 2012 Employment and Unemployment Survey (India); 2014 National Labour Force Survey (Indonesia); 2008 Labor Force Survey (Nepal); 2013 Labor Force Survey (Pakistan); 2013 Labor Force Survey (Philippines); 2014 Labor Force Survey (Sri Lanka); 2010 Labor Force Survey (Thailand); 2013 Labor and Employment Survey (Viet Nam).

Among the services subsectors, good jobs are predominantly concentrated in government and business services. About 78% of wage workers in government services earn at least living wage Option 1, and 63% earn at least living wage Option 2; meanwhile, 73% of wage workers in business services earn at least Option 1, and 53% earn at least Option 2. An adequate percentage of wage workers in other services subsectors, such as transport and communication, and trade services earn the living wage; however, these two subsectors only account for a combined 16% of total employment. Fewer wage workers earn a living wage in other services (mostly consisting of personal services) than in manufacturing.

In general, government services, business services, and to some extent, transportation and communication services have the highest proportion of wage workers earning the living wage. In contrast, far fewer wage workers earn the living wage in trade services and other services (Figure 10.4).

Figure 10.4 Share of Living Wage Earners by Services Sector, per Country, Collected from Various Years

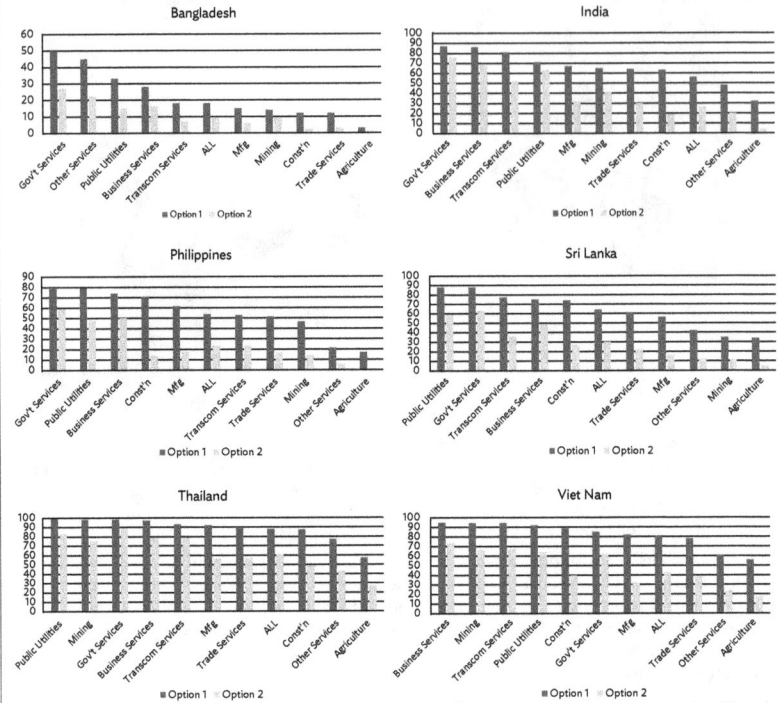

Const'n = construction, Gov't = government, Mfg = manufacturing, Transcom = transcommunication.

Sources: Authors' calculations based on 2010 Household Income and Expenditure Survey (Bangladesh); 2013 Cambodia Socio-Economic Survey (Cambodia); 2012 Employment and Unemployment Survey (India); 2014 National Labour Force Survey (Indonesia); 2008 Labor Force Survey (Nepal); 2013 Labor Force Survey (Pakistan); 2013 Labor Force Survey (Philippines); 2014 Labor Force Survey (Sri Lanka); 2010 Labor Force Survey (Thailand); 2013 Labor and Employment Survey (Viet Nam).

10.3 The Role of Services in the Creation of Decent Jobs

Services-led growth is increasingly being seen as an alternative to the traditional path from agriculture to manufacturing, with services emerging only in the later stages. A review of the recent literature on services describes mechanisms through which the sector can create better and more favorable employment opportunities. These can be broadly summarized as tradability and technology.

10.3.1 Tradability of Modern Services

Services have been long regarded as non-tradable because many require personal interaction and are difficult to transport or provide across distances.[1] However, a better understanding of the sector reveals that services consist of a diverse set of industries, rendering generalizations difficult. Eichengreen and Gupta (2011) differentiate between two waves of services: traditional services (such as lodging, housecleaning, and meal preparation); and modern services (such as financial, communication, computer, technical, legal, advertising, and business services). Modern services are more receptive to the adaptation of new technology and are increasingly becoming tradable across borders (Eichengreen and Gupta 2011: 18). Productivity growth is highest for modern services consumed by households and corporate sectors (Eichengreen and Gupta 2011: 17). One important factor explaining the wage premium in tradable business services is skills intensity. Modern services occupations are often offered to medium- to high-skilled workers, with corresponding secondary or tertiary educational attainment requirements.

Jensen (2013) focused on business services[2] (which closely resembles Eichengreen and Gupta's modern services), and found that the sector's tradability makes it a key player in expanding export growth and is associated with higher levels of average earnings (Jensen 2013: 3–4). Workers in tradable activities earn over 30% more, on average, than do workers in non-tradable activities (Jensen 2013: 16). However, because business services are skill-intensive, the relatively low levels of educational attainment in developing Asia play a crucial role in the development of the business services sector in the region (Jensen 2013: 5). Increasing productivity in the business services sector requires investment in educational development.

The growing significance of tradable services is observed in a related study by Ghani (2010) on economies in South Asia where the modern services sector created jobs faster than did the traditional sector

---

[1]   Tradability of services is a recently-studied concept. Prior to the creation of a services tradability index by van der Marel and Shepherd in 2013, previous studies of which the authors were aware that sought to quantify the tradability of services are Jensen and Kletzer (2005), Gervais and Jensen (2013), and Borchsenius et al. (2010) (van der Marel and Shepherd 2013: 4).

[2]   Jensen (2013) follows the definition of business services activities as categorized in the North American Industrial Classification System categories. These activities, which closely resemble modern services as defined by Eichengreen and Gupta (2011: 3), include the information sector, finance and insurance, real estate, professional, scientific and technical services, management and administrative support, and waste remediation services.

over the past 2 decades. This may help absorb a larger proportion of the region's growing workforce (Ghani 2010: 76–77). Gonzales et al. (2012) report similar trends with a larger share of employment and higher wage returns than manufacturing in their sample economies: Chile, France, India, United Kingdom (UK), and United States (US). Business services have the highest wage rates of all of our sample countries; the wage premium is highest in Chile (followed by India), and lowest in France and the UK (Gonzales et al. (2012: 180–181). An empirical analysis by Gervais and Jensen (2013) of US services and manufacturing industries reports that 20% of aggregate value added is produced in industries classified as tradable, of which the services sector accounts for almost half of tradable value added. Furthermore, workers in tradable industries are about 30% more productive and receive 30% higher wages compared to workers in non-tradable industries, on average (Gervais and Jensen 2013: 27, 30–31).

Policy makers, especially from developing economies, must therefore pay attention to business services as a source of well-paid jobs, as well as export earnings. Citing the case of India, Ghani (2010: 82) attributes India's emergence as an exporter of modern tradable services to a combination of factors: market integration, availability of education and a skilled labor force, better institutions that impact the day-to-day running of service businesses, and improved availability and quality of infrastructure supportive of services growth. Focusing on education, Gupta notes:

> Limitations to growth in modern impersonal service are mostly on the supply side, and in particular the availability of employees with education and skills that meet the requirements of the global service market. The globalizing market for skills, however, allows developing countries to take advantage of their cost advantage in terms of labor and to make investments in expanding the skills of their labor forces in order to make them suitable for employment in the fast-growing global IT [information technology] and ITES [information technology-enabled service] industries. (Ghani 2010: 83)

As cited in Bosworth and Maertens (2010), educational requirements are substantially higher in the services sector. In South Asia, the services sector required roughly 50% more years of schooling than the economy as a whole, and more than twice that required in agriculture. In the modern services industries in particular, employment requires a secondary level certificate at minimum, and often a university-level degree.

In support of Gupta's argument, the authors posit that, although India has a low general level of educational attainment, it has a small minority of persons with unusually high levels of schooling. The availability of such workers has been an important contributor to the expansion of business services in India, but their relative scarcity is beginning to be reflected in the widening of wage premiums for secondary-and university-level graduates (as cited in Bosworth, Collins, and Virmani 2007). There is also an average return to additional schooling across countries of about 10% both overall and for the sub-group of Asian economies (as cited from Psacharopoulus and Patrinos 2004: 116). A series of papers on returns to education in Pakistan and Bangladesh suggest returns in the range of 7%. These results indicate that improvements in educational attainment is an important prerequisite of growth in some services-producing industries.

10.3.2 Technology and Tradability

Advancing technology increases the facilitation of more tradable and productive services. Gonzales et al. (2012) posit that the provision of modern services requires state-of-the-art technology to continue on a path of rapid development. In the case of developing economies, services are needed both as an engine of job creation and as a facilitator of job creation in other sectors. Manufacturing firms need state-of-the-art services to connect to global value chains and further enhance the tradability of skill-intensive activities along the value chain (Gonzales et al. 2012: 176–177).

In describing the relationship between tradability and technology, Jensen and Kletzer (2007: 13) state that advancing technology will continue to increase the feasibility of providing services from remote locations. Mishra, Lundstrom, and Anand (2011) propose a two-step mechanism through which services sophistication, or productivity in services exports, can generate gainful employment from tradability and technology:

> Service exports sophistication matters for growth.... The revolution in ICT [information and communication] technologies has, for example, made services more productive. The distinctiveness of higher service export sophistication and growth is twofold: (1) traditional service activities gain in productivity from technology, transportability and tradability; and (2) there is a host of new service activities that have emerged due to unbundling and new technological innovations. (Mishra, Lundstrom, and Anand 2011: 23–24)

Kochhar et al. (2006), and Broadberry and Gupta (2008) have both argued that services-led growth in India might have roots in the country's history of investment in high human capital and good telecommunications policy. Noland, Park, and Estrada (2012) make the case that a productive information and communications technology (ICT) services sector induces positive externalities and host productivities to other sectors of the economy. Efficient ICT infrastructure and transportation can promote productivity across the entire economy. Moreover, a strong modern services sector (especially business services such as design, prototyping, and marketing) can help middle-income Asian economies move up the value chain and thus escape the much-feared middle-income trap (Noland, Park, and Estrada 2012: 22). The authors further report that growth of services output is more highly correlated with poverty reduction (Noland, Park, and Estrada 2012: 27).

Gayá (2017) reported that knowledge-based services (KBS), which use high technology and have the relatively highly skilled workforce required to benefit fully from technological innovations, have gained relevance in the Argentinian economy and become a strategic sector for three main reasons: (i) the creation of high-quality jobs in terms of skills, formality, and higher wages; (ii) good export performance; and (iii) the potential to foster regional development through the decentralization of economic activity to the provinces. Business, professional, and technical services represent 70% of KBS exports, while wages in KBS are 9.3 percentage points higher than the country's average wage (Gayá 2017: 50).

Labor productivity growth in services brings about structural change and more decent work opportunities to developing economies. Foster-McGregor and Verspagen (2016) studied the relationship between structural change and productivity growth in Asia and found that the sectors in which more developed countries tend to allocate more labor than developing countries tend to offer better opportunities for reaching high-productivity levels. Market services sectors (such as trade; transport and communication; and the finance, insurance, real estate, and business services sectors) will be the vehicles of economic growth. This becomes increasingly true as countries progress along the path from middle-income to high-income levels (Foster-McGregor and Verspagen 2016: 21).

Automation and new technology have long been heralds of increased productivity in manufacturing and other capital-intensive sectors; however, with the onset of Industry 4.0 (also known as "4th industrial revolution"), the impact of new technology is being felt across all sectors, including services (ADB 2018). New technology will also create jobs in new growth sectors, and the net job creation will be positive. While most of these jobs will benefit high-skilled workers, medium- and low-skilled jobs will also continue to increase as large parts of Asia develop. Moreover, technology will affect workers and countries differently: the main challenge going forward will be ensuring that workers are engaged in productive employment while harnessing opportunities from new technology and innovations in management practices to generate good earnings.

Jobs in services have been growing across developing Asia. The highest growth has been in the services and sales worker occupation categories. Some of the highest growth rates of employment share across all occupation categories are seen in Viet Nam and Nepal, while the overall growth of employment shares in the Philippines has been dampened by employment share declines in the trades and plant operator

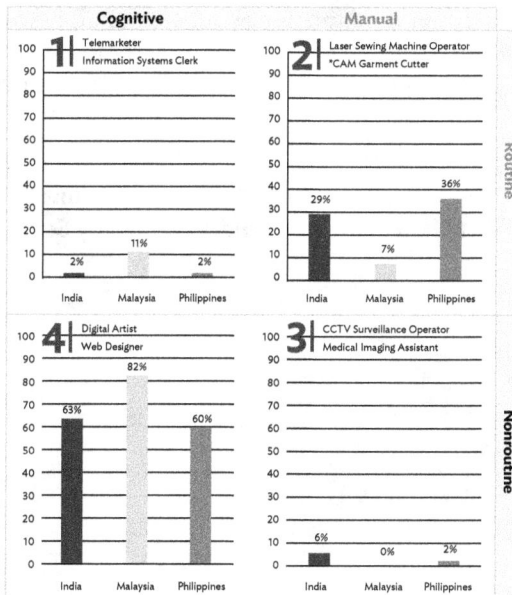

Figure 10.5 Distribution of New Occupations by Job Type, Various Years

* Computer Aided Manufacturing

CAM = computer-aided manufacturing, CCTV = closed-circuit television.

Source: Asian Development Bank. 2018. *Asian Development Outlook 2018: How Technology Affects Jobs.* Mandaluyong City: Asian Development Bank. http://dx.doi.org/10.22617/FLS189310-3 (29 April 2019).

occupation categories. Nevertheless, the overall trend in developing Asian economies is that of job growth in services. Technology leads to new occupations and these tend to be in the non-routine cognitive category, which includes managers, researchers, digital artists, and web designers. Tasks performed in non-routine cognitive occupations include managing others and applying expertise.

A comparison of the National Classification of Occupation codes of India, the Philippines, and Malaysia reveals that new job titles have emerged in each of these three developing Asian economies over two different time periods. Most new job titles in developing Asia are in nonroutine cognitive occupations (Figure 10.5): these accounted for 60% of new job titles in India from 2004 to 2015, and 60% of new titles in the Philippines from 1990 to 2012. Among the sample of developing Asian economies, the highest proportion (82%) of new job titles in the nonroutine cognitive category has been in Malaysia.

A more systematic analysis using the National Classification of Occupations in conjunction with Labor Force Surveys for India and Viet Nam reveals that a majority of new occupations are in services (Figure 10.6). An interesting case is that of Viet Nam, where an astonishing share of all new occupations (close to 86%) are in the services sector (manufacturing accounts for about 13% of all new occupations, with the remaining 1% in agriculture). The sectoral distribution of new occupations is a bit more spread out in India, although services also

Figure 10.6 Share of New Occupations in Viet Nam (2013) and India (2012), by Sector

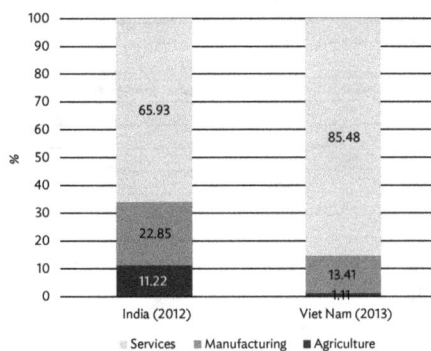

Notes: The number of people employed in new occupations is 5.2 million in India, and slightly less than 1 million in Viet Nam.

Source: Khatiwada, S., and M. K. Veloso. 2019. New Technology and Emerging Occupations: Evidence from Asia. ADB Economics Working Paper Series. No 576.

account for a majority of new occupations (about two-thirds), while manufacturing accounts for 23%. Unlike in Viet Nam, where only 1% of new occupations are in agriculture, India's agriculture sector still accounts for about 10% of new occupations.

The probabilities that workers will enter emerging occupations can be predicted by going beyond industry trends and taking the analysis a step further by using logit regressions. Preliminary results indicate that workers in services have a higher probability of entering emerging occupations (Figure 10.7). In Viet Nam, estimates indicate that the predicted probability of entering an emerging occupation is much higher for a single, male, college-educated, urban worker aged 25–34 employed in services, than for his counterpart in manufacturing or agriculture. These results hold for both 2009 and 2013 in Viet Nam. Similar trends persist in India over the three time periods analyzed: 1994, 2000, and 2012. In India, the predicted probability of entering an emerging occupation is highest for a single, male, college-educated, urban worker aged 35–44 in the services sector.

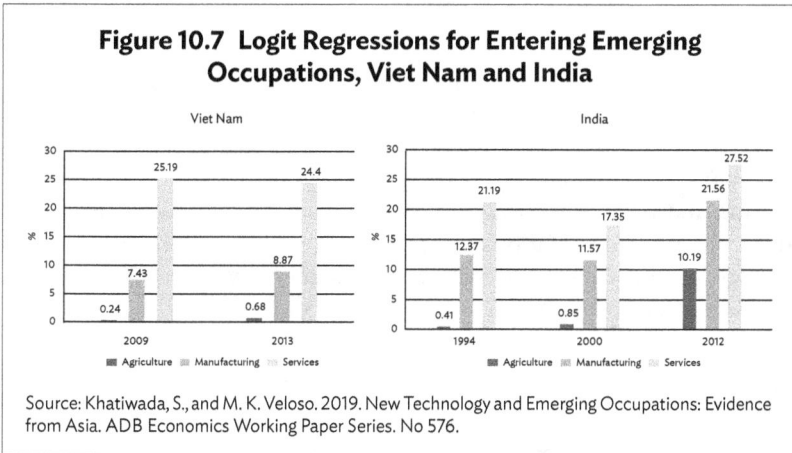

Figure 10.7 Logit Regressions for Entering Emerging Occupations, Viet Nam and India

Source: Khatiwada, S., and M. K. Veloso. 2019. New Technology and Emerging Occupations: Evidence from Asia. ADB Economics Working Paper Series. No 576.

Evidence from Viet Nam further suggests that new jobs pay better than old jobs (Figure 10.8). Across all industries, average monthly wages are higher in new jobs than in old jobs. The wage gap is most apparent in mining, manufacturing, and construction. Even in agriculture where wages have been persistently low, new jobs pay much better than old jobs. On average, new jobs pay 1.5 times more than old jobs in Viet Nam.

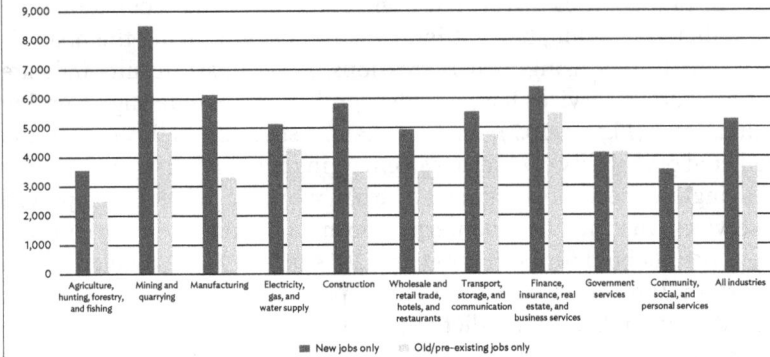

Figure 10.8 Average Monthly Wages in New Versus Old Work in Viet Nam (D)

Source: Khatiwada, S., and M. K. Veloso. 2019. New Technology and Emerging Occupations: Evidence from Asia. ADB Economics Working Paper Series. No 576.

The positive impacts of new technology on the labor market in Asia are undeniable. The vast majority of emerging occupations are in services, where productivity is higher than in other sectors. These emerging occupations are predominantly nonroutine cognitive in nature, and pay higher wages than do existing occupations. However, these emerging occupations are not equally accessible to workers in all sectors. Workers in services have a much higher chance of being selected into emerging occupations.

Table 10.3 Review of Recent Literature on the Role of Services in Generating Decent Jobs

Author	Factor in/ Contributor to the Creation of Decent Jobs	Relevant Findings	Methodology	Coverage
Jensen, B. J. (2013)	Tradability	There appears to be a positive relationship between living standards and the services sector's share of economic activity (p. 2). Workers in tradable services activities are, on average, more educated and skilled. Moreover, workers in tradable activities earn significantly more, on average, than do workers in non-tradable activities.	Follows the methodology by Jensen (2011) who developed the concept of "tradability," then applied it to select services sectors (p. 10).	United States (US), following the results of Jensen (2011) (p. 16); the People's Republic of China (PRC), 2008 (pp. 17–18)
Noland, M., D. Park, and G. Estrada (2012)	Technology	Services account for a large share of output, growth, and jobs. Complementary investments in physical infrastructure and human capital will also be necessary to achieve a strong services sector (p. vi).	Multivariate regression (p. 25); controlling for initial conditions, poverty change is regressed against growth in services, agricultural, and manufacturing outputs.	56 Asian countries (of which 17 are developing Asian economies) covering the period 1990–2010 (p. 25).
Mishra, S., S. Lundstrom, and R. Anand (2011)	Tradability	Service exports sophistication matters for growth and is a good predictor of more gainful employment and subsequent growth, particularly in low- and middle-income economies (pp. 23–24).	Services export sophistication is a measure constructed using the productivity of services exports. A panel regression analyzes the relationship between commercial services productivity and economic growth (p. 11).	The data include dynamic commercial services of up to 103 countries during 1990–2007 (p. 17).

continued on next page

Table 10.3 *continued*

Author	Factor in/Contributor to the Creation of Decent Jobs	Relevant Findings	Methodology	Coverage
Ghani, E. (2010)	Tradability	Over the past 2 decades, the modern services sector created jobs more quickly than did the traditional sector. In recent years wage growth has been higher in the services sector than in manufacturing and agriculture (pp. 76–77).	Cross-section regression of employment shares of industry and services in total employment in India and the PRC in 1991, 2005 (pp. 72–75)	India and the PRC, in 1991 and 2005 (p. 73)
Bosworth, B., and A. Maertens (2010)	Tradability	Growth in services contributes to improvements in productivity and job creation. Services contributed the largest share of growth in overall output per worker during 2000–2006. On the employment side, services have been the major source of job growth since 1990 in both India and Pakistan (p. 100).	Cross-section analysis of sources of growth in output per worker, labor productivity levels, and educational attainment by sector of employment (pp. 108, 110, 112, 116)	South Asian economies (Bangladesh, Bhutan, India, Maldives, Nepal, Pakistan, and Sri vLanka), 1980–2006 (p. 108)
Gayá, R. E. (2017)	Technology	Knowledge-based services that use high technology and/or have the relatively high-skilled workforce required to benefit fully from technological innovations have gained relevance in the Argentinian economy.	Policy analysis (pp. 50–51)	Argentina, 1996–2006 (pp. 50–51)

continued on next page

Table 10.3 *continued*

Author	Factor in/ Contributor to the Creation of Decent Jobs	Relevant Findings	Methodology	Coverage
Eichergreen, B., and P. Gupta (2009)	Tradability, technology	There is evidence of an increase in the share of services in gross domestic product at all levels of income after 1970, and a further increase in the share of services in countries with relatively high per capita incomes (p. 18).	Regression analysis (pp. 39–40, 43–44, 46–49)	Shares of agriculture, industry, and services in gross domestic product covering the period 1950–2005, with country-specific case studies for Japan, Germany, the United Kingdom, and the Republic of Korea (pp. 13–15)
Foster-McGregor, N., and B. Verspagen (2016)	Tradability, technology	The transition from a low-income to high-income developed country involves a process of deep structural transformation in which the productive structure of an economy changes (p. 1).	Sectoral decomposition (p. 9)	This analysis is based on a broad global sample of countries for the period 1950–2011, including many developing countries. Most recent estimates make use of Asian economy statistics, 1990–2011 (pp. 11–13).
Gervais, A., and B. J. Jensen (2013)	Tradability	Accounting for tradable services industries nearly doubles the international exposure of the US economy. Labor productivity and wages are higher, on average, for tradable industries, and potential welfare gains from trade liberalization in the services sector are sizable (p. 1).	Gravity model of international trade, following the Anderson and Van Wincoop (2003) model of trade to include multiple industries and increasing returns in production (p. 8)	Dataset on the distribution of output and demand across regions of the US to estimate trade costs for 969 services and manufacturing industries (p. 15)

continued on next page

Table 10.3 *continued*

Author	Factor in/Contributor to the Creation of Decent Jobs	Relevant Findings	Methodology	Coverage
Gonzales, F., B. J. Jensen, Y. Kim, and H. K. Nordås (2012)	Tradability, technology	Tradable business services employ mainly high- to medium-skilled workers who earn higher wages than those in non-tradable services. However, state-of-the-art business services are essential to ensure the competitiveness of high- to medium-technology manufacturing. Access to such services through imports would help middle-income countries strengthen their comparative advantage in these manufacturing industries and move up the value chain (p. 175).	Statistical analyses (pp. 180–182)	Labour force surveys in Chile, France, India, the United Kingdom and the US, as well as the Organisation for Economic Co-operation and Development input–output database (p. 184)

Source: Authors.

10.3.3 Case Study: Decent Jobs in Information Technology-Business Process Management Services Sector

Although international outsourcing of services has only emerged as a business model in the last couple of decades, it has become a significant source of income for developing countries such as India and the Philippines. Information technology-enabled services (ITES) such as business process outsourcing (BPO) and business process management (BPM) grew out of enhanced and more affordable internet connectivity, technological advancement, and the need of businesses to reduce the cost of delivering services to customers. Developing countries, which are home to a majority of the global labor force, emerged as service providers to European and North American firms. These countries have the attractiveness of cost-effective labor, favorable labor market conditions, and government policies backed by tax incentives. It can be posited that the growing ITES-BPO industries in developing countries such as India and the Philippines played a key role in weathering the economic crises in these countries.

Figure 10.9 Information Technology-Business Process Outsourcing/Business Process Management Industry Revenue Share, 2006–2016 (% of GDP)

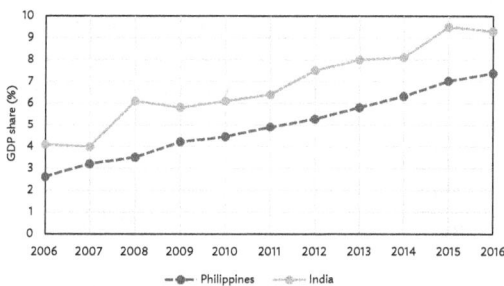

GDP = gross domestic product.
Sources: Philippine Statistics Authority. 2016. 2013/2014 Industry Profile: Business Process Outsourcing. Labstat updates 20(13). Quezon City, Philippines. https://psa.gov.ph/sites/default/files/attachments/ird/pressrelease/vol20_13.pdf (accessed 26 April 2019); Information on India's IT-BPM revenue shares from the National Association of Software and Services Companies for India (NASSCOM) Strategic reviews, referenced in India Brand Equity Foundation. January 2017. IT & ITeS Presentation. https://www.ibef.org/download/IT-and-ITeS-January-2017.pdf (accessed 26 April 2019); T. Gomes. 2012. The Impact of IT Services and ITeS-BPO on India's Growth. ISCTE Business School, Instituto Universitario Lisboa. https://repositorio.iscte-iul.pt/bitstream/10071/6383/1/Tese%20MBA%20Tiago%20Gomes%20FINAL.pdf (accessed 26 April 2019).

In the Philippines, the information technology (IT)-BPO sector began in the early 1990s, enabled by initiatives such as the passing of the Republic Act 7916, also known as the Special Economic Zone Act of 1995. This allowed floors in buildings where BPO companies operates to be considered special economic zones that are exempt from paying national and local taxes. In the following decade, IT-BPO industry revenue increased seven-fold from $3.2 billion or 2.7% of the Philippines' GDP in 2006, to an estimated $22.9 billion or approximately 7.5% of GDP in 2016 (Figure 10.9). This has more than doubled the country's share in the business offshoring market, from 9% in 2004 to 19% in 2013. Industry roadmaps envision that the industry will grow 9.2 percentage points from 2016 to 2022, with revenues reaching $38.9 billion.

The IT sector began to grow in India in around the same decade as in the Philippines, when US-based companies began to outsource work to India's low-cost and skilled talent pool. The industry's revenue grew from $37.4 billion in 2006 to $143 billion in 2016, comprising around 9% of its GDP. The sector has remained a key player in the country's economy and the global IT community, representing more than 30% of the global offshore market share since 2004. Trade Council India projects that the industry will grow to $225 billion by 2020 while the National Association of Software and Services Companies envisions it will reach $350 billion by 2025.

Software development is the highest paying sector in the Philippines' IT-BPO industry, as observed in the 2013 Survey of IT-BPO Services conducted by the Bangko Sentral ng Pilipinas (BSP). Software development has a monthly average compensation of ₱65,272, followed by contact center operations at ₱30,309. Nevertheless, all sectors pay more than the national average. In 2013, software development paid more than seven times the national average[3] while contact centers pay more than three times the national average (Figure 10.10). This wage premium remains high, but has decreased over the years.

The Occupational Wages Survey conducted by the Philippine Statistics Authority reports that computer engineers and programmers earn the highest wages in the IT-BPO industry. In 2016, engineers earned ₱49,335 in the call center sector and ₱18,305 in the medical transcription sector, while programmers earn ₱17,423 and ₱37,865, respectively. In both sectors, wages are still higher than the national average, even for relatively unskilled occupations. However, the premium has

---

[3] The average monthly wage rate in the Philippines and India was collected from the ILO Global Wage Report 2016/2017, with the most recent estimates available for 2015 (ILO 2015). For the Philippines, average rates for the succeeding years are projected assuming an annual growth rate of 5% in average wages.

Figure 10.10 Wage Premium of Information Technology-Business Process Outsourcing Sectors in the Philippines, 2009 and 2013

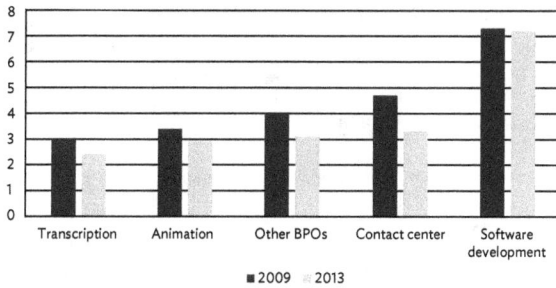

BPO = business process outsourcing.

Note: Wage premium is determined as the average annual age in BPOs over the average annual wage in the Philippines.

Source: Bangko Sentral ng Pilipinas. 2013. Results of the 2013 Survey of Information Technology-Business Process Outsourcing (IT-BPO) Services. Manila: Bangko Sentral ng Pilipinas http://www .bsp.gov.ph/downloads/Publications/2013/ICT_2013.pdf (accessed 26 April 2019).

decreased over the years. Computer engineers, who earned more than seven times the national average under software development in 2013, earned four times the national average in 2016, while customer service representatives earn almost twice the national average (compared to more than triple in 2013).

Despite the observed decrease in the wage premium, IT-BPO jobs in the Philippines remain among the highest paid. According to the 2016 Occupational Wages Survey, computer programmers, system analysts and designers, and computer engineers, belong to the top 10 highly paid occupations (Philippine Statistics Authority 2016). This observation is reinforced by Jobstreet, one of Southeast Asia's largest online employment companies, which likewise reports that IT and technical customer service jobs are among the highest paid at both the junior and managerial levels.[4] In 2015–2017, IT-related work offered, on average, ₱37,000 for junior executives (more than three times the national average), ₱65,000 for junior supervisors, and above ₱85,000 for managerial positions.

---

[4] JobStreet's Annual Salary Reports are determined through the identification of the average salary of all specializations per position level, based on actual salaries posted by employers on their websites. Basic salaries used did not include other forms of compensation such as leave credits, medical benefits, insurance, and incentives.

Figure 10.11 Wage Premium of Information Technology-Business Process Outsourcing Occupations in India, Entry-Level, 2018

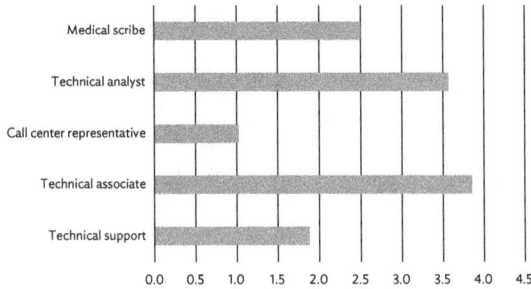

Note: Salary information comes from data points collected directly from employees, users, and past and present job advertisements on Indeed in the past 36 months. The average monthly wage was recorded as ₹19,492 by the Labour Bureau, Ministry of Labour and Trading Economics in March 2017.

Sources: Business Process Outsourcing sector salaries generated from the Indeed Website, Business Process Outsourcing sector salaries. https://www.indeed.co.in/cmp/Bpo-Sector/salaries (accessed 27 August 2018).

The same trends observed in the Philippines' IT-BPO industry can be depicted in India's IT-BPM wage records. Salary records generated from the online job search page Indeed, the most frequently visited job site in the world, report that technical analysts and associates are offered the highest salaries, at more than twice the average national wage. The wage premium for medical transcriptionists (or scribes) in India is comparable to that in the Philippines; however, entry-level wages for call center representatives are lower than the national average (salary information comes from 5,775 data points collected directly from employees, users, and past and present job advertisements on Indeed in the past 36 months) (Figure 10.11).

As expected, premiums increase for senior level positions. A salary-benchmarking study conducted by Emolument in 2016 analyzed and compared 3,071 senior-level salaries and bonuses in India and the UK. The salaries reported for India's IT-BPM occupations show that strategy consulting earned the highest wages (about nine times the national average). Software development premiums vary according to specialization, with the highest observed for finance and telecommunications. BPM earns more than five times the national average (Figure 10.12).

A 2006 study of offshore and nearshore IT-BPO salary reports compared the wages of BPO industries across countries, including

Figure 10.12 Wage Premium of Information Technology-Business Process Management Occupations in India, Senior-Level, 2016

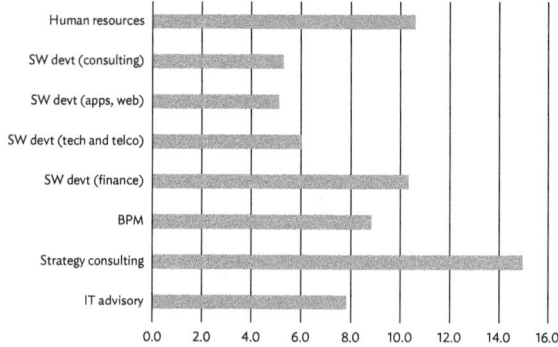

apps = applications, BPM = business process management; SW Devt = software development, IT = information technology, tech = technology, telco = telecommunications, web = websites.

Note: Emolument analyzed and compared 3,071 senior-level salaries and bonuses in India and the United Kingdom. Median salaries from the report are used to determine wage premium values.

Sources: Information technology-business process management total salaries from the 2016 Emolument benchmark study, referenced in M. N. Smith. 2016. Here's How Much Cheaper It Is for Someone in India to Do your Job. Business Insider. June 3. https://www.businessinsider.com /emolument-data-uk-versus-india-salaries-2016-6?r=UK (accessed 27 August 2018); Indeed Website, Business Process Outsourcing Sector Salaries. https://www.indeed.co.in/cmp/Bpo-Sector /salaries (accessed 27 August 2018).

India and the Philippines. The IT outsourcing industry primarily includes application development, maintenance, systems integration, infrastructure management, and IT consulting services. BPO services are broken down into (i) voice-based BPO, which includes call centers, contact centers, customer support, and sales; and (ii) non-voice BPO, which includes transaction processing, human resources, and procurement. The study used data from Tier-1, Tier-2, and Tier-3 cities, at three levels of experience.[5] Compared to the Philippines, India

---

[5]   The rankings Tier-1, Tier-2, and Tier-3 generally pertain to a city's level of competence in delivering IT-BPM services. Tier 1 cities are considered the most ideal for offshoring services. These are highly developed areas with IT infrastructure that readily caters to industry needs, a large labor supply, and a suitable and stable business environment. Tier 2 cities are less developed than Tier 1 cities, but are quickly catching up in terms of competitiveness. These cities are usually regional hubs with industrial parks that offer relatively cheaper rent and labor costs. Lastly, Tier 3 cities are emerging destinations that are in the development stages of providing IT-BPM services.

has higher wage premiums across all work levels, while wages are, on average, higher in the IT outsourcing sector than in the BPO sectors. Comparing the premiums derived in 2006 to more recent statistics reinforces the following observations: (i) wage premiums in the IT-BPO sectors remain higher than national average wages in the Philippines and India, although they have decreased in recent years; (ii) a higher wage premium is observed for IT sector work, which includes software development and management, as well as consulting services, which merit more specialized skills; and (iii) a higher wage premium also comes with longer work experience.

10.4 Challenges

Services-led growth is poised as an alternative mechanism to move workers from low- to high-productivity sectors. This chapter points to two primary challenges facing this strategy: (i) enabling workers to transition from providing traditional services to modern services; and (ii) supporting this transition with the necessary physical and digital infrastructure to facilitate developing economies to move up to higher value services chains.

10.4.1 Upskilling Toward More Highly Valued Services

The previous sections have highlighted that improvements in educational attainment are an important prerequisite of growth in high-value services industries. The recent development of ICT industries, as in the case of India and the Philippines, is a striking example of how developing economies can open up business opportunities through the global outsourcing of tradeable labor. Although the modern services industry is gradually becoming the backbone of inclusive growth, certain prerequisites must be met, such as the availability of high-skilled workers, and the use of a global common language such as English. Further training and upskilling of workers in the traditional services sectors can help generate a more skilled workforce as well as mitigating unemployment. Provisions for technical and vocational education and training programs, for example, can help meet the development aspirations of the country, thereby improving workforce productivity and economic competitiveness in the global economy. Improving the quality of education standards leads to higher wage premiums in the labor market, as well as increased job quality perception and satisfaction for employees and employers alike. Benefits for the sectors mentioned above can thus generate gains for the macroeconomy brought by higher labor productivity in the industries where a more educated labor force will be employed. Highlighting the importance of human capital as a contributor to ICT services growth in India, Goyal (2015: 119) notes:

> Poor human capital in the services-exporting country hinders technology transfer and learning, and has been shown to hamper export growth and diversification in low-income countries (Hausmann, Hwang and Rodrik, 2006; Briggs, Shah and Srivastava, 1996). The empirical literature confirms that services sector performance critically depends on human capital, the quality of the telecommunications network, and the quality of institutions (Shingal 2010).

Upskilling workers in developing Asia can also be seen as a way to deal with the persistence of informal employment, which has been a massive roadblock to the growth of wages and productivity. Despite the structural transformation that has driven the movement of labor from agriculture to manufacturing and services in recent decades, informal employment is still prevalent across developing Asia. According to the latest available data, the share of nonagricultural workers in informal

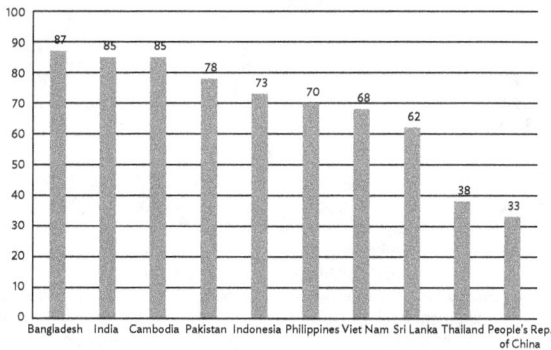

Figure 10.13 Informal Employment as a Share of Total Non-Agricultural Employment in Some Asian Countries (%)

Sources: Latest year available from the International Labour Organization (ILO) statistics, 2018; ILO statistics. 2015 (PRC; based only on six cities); Government of Bangladesh, Bangladesh Bureau of Statistics. 2010 (Bangladesh); ILO statistics. 2006 (Cambodia).

employment is up to 87% in Bangladesh; 85% in India and Cambodia; well over 70% in Pakistan, Indonesia, and the Philippines; and over 60% in Viet Nam and Sri Lanka (Figure 10.13). Among the sample of 10 economies in developing Asia, only Thailand (38%) and the PRC (33%) have less than half of their respective nonagriculture workforces in informal employment.

In Bangladesh, where 87% of workers in non-agriculture sectors are informal, workers in the informal sector earn as little as one-fifth, on average, of what their counterparts earn in the formal sector. The average wages of informal workers in India and Thailand are also less than half that of their counterparts in the formal sector. In a sample of eight developing Asian economies, there was no country in which the average wages of informal workers reached even two-thirds of what their counterparts earned in the formal sector (Figure 10.14).

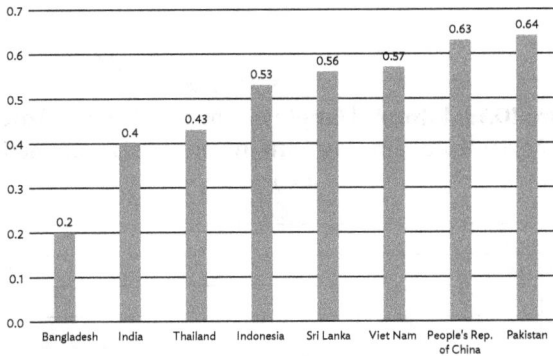

Figure 10.14 Informal to Formal Monthly Wage Ratio in Some Asian Countries, Various Years

Sources: Infran, M. 2008. Pakistan's Wage Structure During 1990/1–2006/7. Islamabad: Pakistan Institute of Development Economics Quaid-E-Azam University Campus (Pakistan); Gifu, C., and H. Shigeyuki. 2009. Formal Employment, Informal Employment and Income Differentials in Urban China. Munich Personal RePEc Archive Paper 17585. Munich: Munich Personal RePEc Archive. (the PRC); Viet (2010) (Viet Nam); Gunatilaka, R. 2008. Informal Employment in Sri Lanka: Nature, Probability of Employment and Determinants of Wages. Colombo: International Labour Organization. (Sri Lanka); Asian Development Bank. 2011. The Informal Sector and Informal Employment in Indonesia. Manila: Asian Development Bank (Indonesia); Dasgupta, S., R. Bhula-or, and T. Fakthong. 2015. Earnings Differentials between Formal and Informal Employment in Thailand. International Labour Organization Working Paper 994896403402676. Geneva: International Labour Organization (Thailand); and J. Unni. 2005. Wages and Incomes in Formal and Informal Sectors in India. Indian Journal of Labour Economics 48(2) (India).

10.4.2 Improving Physical and Digital Infrastructure

Developing economies should also expand their infrastructure investments to increase their capacity to provide modern services. To sustain the rapid growth of services exports, it is necessary to have well-functioning infrastructure, including electric power, road and rail connectivity, telecommunications, air transport, and efficient ports. Infrastructure can further encompass financial and related systems that facilitate the education, training, and export of skilled labor. Similar to human capital, empirical studies also support the positive relationship between infrastructure, development, and services export performance (Eichengreen and Gupta 2011; Shingal 2010; Nasir and Kalirajan, 2014).

The conditions for improved infrastructure are related to the issue of urbanization in developing Asia. Asia is urbanizing rapidly, with almost half of the population living in urban areas in 2015. This is projected to increase to 64% by 2050 (United Nations 2014). As urbanization rises, labor is expected to move from agricultural sectors in rural areas to manufacturing and services sectors in urban areas, where wages are higher. Urbanization is positively correlated with a higher share of employment services around the world, as well as in Asia and the Pacific (Figure 10.15).

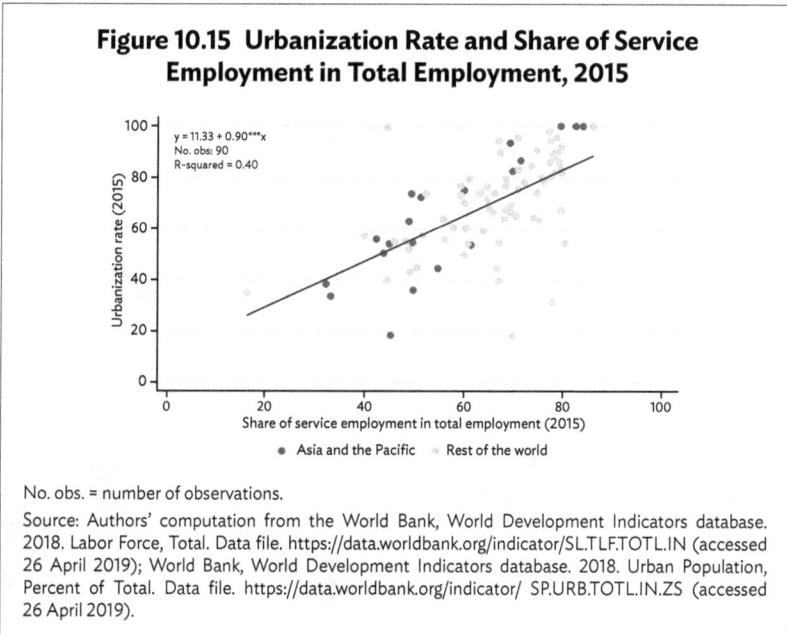

Figure 10.15 Urbanization Rate and Share of Service Employment in Total Employment, 2015

No. obs. = number of observations.
Source: Authors' computation from the World Bank, World Development Indicators database. 2018. Labor Force, Total. Data file. https://data.worldbank.org/indicator/SL.TLF.TOTL.IN (accessed 26 April 2019); World Bank, World Development Indicators database. 2018. Urban Population, Percent of Total. Data file. https://data.worldbank.org/indicator/ SP.URB.TOTL.IN.ZS (accessed 26 April 2019).

10.5 Conclusion

Over the last few decades, developing Asia has made significant progress in moving its workforce from low-productivity, low-wage-paying sectors such as agriculture, toward higher productivity and higher wage-paying sectors such as manufacturing and, more notably, services where good jobs are much more prevalent. This chapter examines how the services sector could provide decent and gainful employment in developing Asia. Using living wages as a reference point, this chapter reports that a significant portion of the workforce in developing Asian economies, the majority of which is employed in the agricultural sector, does not earn a living wage. On the other hand, manufacturing and, to a larger extent, services provide their workforces with good jobs. Recent developments in ICT industries, as in the case of India and the Philippines, offer a striking example of how developing economies can open up business opportunities through the global outsourcing of tradeable labor. This chapter highlights the importance of improving human capital through education and upskilling, as well as investing in physical and digital infrastructure. This is necessary to address the large supply of low-productivity and informal sector workers in developing Asia, and to provide new and gainful employment opportunities.

References

Anderson, J. E. and E. van Wincoop. 2003. Gravity with Gravitas: A Solution to the Border Puzzle. *American Economic Review* 93(1): 170–192.

Anker, R. 2006. A New Methodology for Estimating Internationally Comparable Poverty Lines and Living Wage Rates. Working Paper 72. Geneva: International Labour Office.

Asian Development Bank (ADB). 2018. Asian Development Outlook (ADO) 2018: How Technology Affects Jobs. Mandaluyong City: ADB. http://dx.doi.org/10.22617/FLS189310-3 (accessed 26 April 2019).

ADB. 2011. *The Informal Sector and Informal Employment in Indonesia.* Manila: ADB.

ADB. 2013. Key Indicators for Asia and the Pacific 2013. Mandaluyong City: ADB. http://www.adb.org/publications/key-indicators-asia-and-pacific-2013 (accessed 26 April 2019).

ADB. 2015. Key Indicators for Asia and the Pacific 2015. Mandaluyong City: ADB. https://www.adb.org/publications/key-indicators-asia-and-pacific-2015 (accessed 26 April 2019).

Bangko Sentral ng Pilipinas. 2013. Results of the 2013 Survey of Information Technology-Business Process Outsourcing (IT-BPO) Services. Manila: Bangko Sentral ng Pilipinas http://www.bsp.gov.ph/downloads/Publications/2013/ICT_2013.pdf (accessed 26 April 2019).

Borchsenius, V., et al. 2010. International Trade in Services: Evidence from Danish Micro-Data, *Nationalokonomisk Tidsskrift* 148(1).

Bosworth, B., and A. Maertens. 2010. The Role of the Service Sector in Economic Growth and Employment in South Asia. In E. Ghani, ed. *The Service Revolution in South Asia*, Oxford: Oxford University Press.

Bosworth, B., S. M. Collins, and A. Virmani. 2007. Sources of Growth in the Indian Economy. National Bureau of Economic Research Working Paper 12901. Washington, DC: National Bureau of Economic Research.

Broadberry, S., and B. Gupta. 2008. Historical Roots of India's Service-Led Development: A Sectoral Analysis of Anglo-Indian Productivity Differences, 1870-2000. Warwick Economic Research Papers.

Business Insider. 2018. Median Salaries from Salary-Benchmarking Site Emolument. https://www.businessinsider.com/emolument-data-uk-versus-india-salaries-2016-6?r=UK (accessed 27 August 2018).

Credit Suisse Research. 2017. Philippines Market Strategy. https://research-doc.credit-suisse.com/docView?language

=ENG&format=PDF&sourceid=csplusresearchcp&document_id =1079799301&serialid=SHRD8qOpL7xIvFqtbU8Gv3hjEyd7QHUR 2QBymRNBjGQ%3D (accessed 30 April 2019).

Dasgupta, S., R. Bhula-or, and T. Fakthong. 2015. Earnings Differentials between Formal and Informal Employment in Thailand. International Labour Organization (ILO) Working Paper 994896403402676. Geneva: ILO.

Eichengreen, B., and P. Gupta. 2011. The Service Sector as India's Road to Economic Growth. National Bureau of Economic Research Working Paper 16757. Washington, DC: National Bureau of Economic Research.

Felipe, J., and A. Mehta. 2016. Deindustrialization? A Global Perspective. *Economic Letters* 149, December: 148–151. https://doi.org/10.1016 /j.econlet.2016.10.038 (accessed 26 April 2019).

Foster-McGregor, N., and B. Verspagen. 2016. The Role of Structural Transformation in the Potential of Asian Economic Growth. ADB Economics Working Paper 479. Manila: ADB.

Gayá, R. E. 2017. Policy Approaches for Knowledge-Based Services in Argentina. In *Services and Structural Transformation for Development*, edited by M. Mashayekhi and B. Antunes. Geneva: United Nations Conference on Trade and Development.

Gervais, A., and B. J. Jensen. 2013. Are Services Tradable? Evidence from U.S. Microdata. Cambridge, MA: National Bureau of Economic Research.

Ghani, E. 2010. Is Service-Led Growth a Miracle for South Asia? In *The Service Revolution in South Asia*, edited by E. Ghani. Oxford: Oxford University Press.

Ghani, E. and S. D. O'Connell. 2014. Can Service be a Growth Escalator in Low Income Countries? Policy Research Working Paper 6971. Washington, DC: World Bank.

Gifu, C., and H. Shigeyuki. 2009. Formal Employment, Informal Employment and Income Differentials in Urban China. Munich Personal RePEc Archive Paper 17585. Munich: Munich Personal RePEc Archive.

Gonzales, F., J. B. Jensen, Y. Kim, and H. K. Nordås. 2012. Globalisation of Services and Jobs. Policy Priorities for International Trade and Jobs, International Collaborative Initiative on Trade and Employment. Organisation for Economic Co-operation and Development.

Government of Bangladesh, Bangladesh Bureau of Statistics. Labour Force Survey 2005–2006.

Government of Bangladesh, Bangladesh Bureau of Statistics. 2010. Labour Force Survey 2010.

Government of Bangladesh, Bangladesh Bureau of Statistics. 2013. Labour Force Survey 2013.

Government of Bangladesh, Bangladesh Bureau of Statistics. Quarterly Labour Force Survey 2015–2016.

Government of India. National Sample Survey Office. National Sample Survey—Employment and Unemployment Survey (NSS-EUS) 1999–2000.

Government of India. National Sample Survey—Employment and Unemployment Survey (NSS-EUS) 2004-2005.

Government of India. National Sample Survey—Employment and Unemployment Survey (NSS-EUS) 2011–2012.

Government of Indonesia, Badan Pusat Statistik—Statistics Indonesia. 2000. National Labor Force Survey (SAKERNAS) 2000.

Government of Indonesia, Badan Pusat Statistik—Statistics Indonesia. 2005. National Labor Force Survey (SAKERNAS) 2005.

Government of Indonesia, Badan Pusat Statistik—Statistics Indonesia. 2008. National Labor Force Survey (SAKERNAS) 2008.

Government of Indonesia, Badan Pusat Statistik—Statistics Indonesia. 2010. National Labor Force Survey (SAKERNAS) 2010.

Government of Indonesia, Badan Pusat Statistik—Statistics Indonesia. 2014. National Labor Force Survey (SAKERNAS) 2014.

Government of Nepal, Central Bureau of Statistics. 1999. Labor Force Survey 1998–1999.

Government of Nepal, Central Bureau of Statistics. 2008. Labor Force Survey 2008.

Government of Pakistan, Bureau of Statistics. 2003. Labor Force Survey 2001–2002.

Government of Pakistan, Bureau of Statistics. 2004. Labor Force Survey 2003–2004.

Government of Pakistan, Bureau of Statistics. 2014. Labor Force Survey 2012–2013.

Government of the Philippines, Philippine Statistics Authority. 2001. Labor Force Survey 2001.

Government of the Philippines, Philippine Statistics Authority. 2004. Labor Force Survey 2004.

Government of the Philippines, Philippine Statistics Authority. 2009. Labor Force Survey 2009.

Government of the Philippines, Philippine Statistics Authority. 2013. Labor Force Survey 2013.

Government of the Philippines, Philippine Statistics Authority. 2015. Labor Force Survey 2015.

Government of the Philippines, Philippine Statistics Authority. 2016. Labor Force Survey 2016.

Government of Sri Lanka, Department of Census and Statistics. 2004. Labor Force Survey 2004.

Government of Sri Lanka, Department of Census and Statistics. 2006. Labor Force Survey 2006.

Government of Sri Lanka, Department of Census and Statistics. 2012. Labor Force Survey 2012.

Government of Sri Lanka, Department of Census and Statistics. 2014. Labor Force Survey 2014.

Government of Thailand, National Statistics Office. 2000. Labor Force Survey 2000.

Government of Thailand, National Statistics Office. 2005. Labor Force Survey 2005.

Government of Thailand, National Statistics Office. 2010. Labor Force Survey 2010.

Government of Viet Nam, General Statistics Office. 2007. Labor Force Survey 2007.

Government of Viet Nam, General Statistics Office. 2013. Labor Force Survey 2013.

Government of Viet Nam, General Statistics Office. 2015. Labor Force Survey 2015.

Goyal, A. 2015. Growth Drivers: ICT and Inclusive Innovations. In *Reviving Growth in India*, edited by P. Agrawal. Cambridge: Cambridge University Press.

Groningen Growth and Development Centre database. https://www.rug.nl/ggdc/productivity/10-sector/ (accessed 26 April 2019).

Gunatilaka, R. 2008. *Informal Employment in Sri Lanka: Nature, Probability of Employment and Determinants of Wages*. Colombo: ILO.

Indeed. 2018. Business Process Outsourcing Sector Salaries. https://www.indeed.co.in/cmp/Bpo-Sector/salaries (accessed 27 August 2018).

Information Technology and Business Process Association of the Philippines. Accelerate PH: Future-ready Roadmap 2022. http://itbpm-roadmap2022.ibpap.org/ (accessed 26 April 2019).

Infran, M. 2008. Pakistan's Wage Structure During 1990/1–2006/7. Islamabad: Pakistan Institute of Development Economics Quaid-E -Azam University Campus.

International Labour Organization. 2013. Decent Work Indicators: Guidelines for Producers and Users of Statistical and Legal Framework Indicators. ILO Manual: Second Version. Geneva: ILO. https://www.ilo.org/wcmsp5/groups/public/---dgreports /---integration/documents/publication/wcms_229374.pdf. (accessed 30 April 2019).

International Labour Organization 2015. Global Wage Report, 2014/15: Wages and Income Inequality. Geneva: ILO. https://www.ilo

.org/wcmsp5/groups/public/---dgreports/---dcomm/---publ /documents/publication/wcms_324678.pdf. (accessed 30 April 2019).

International Labour Organization. Hours of Work. Data file. https:// www.ilo.org/ilostat/faces/home/statisticaldata/ContryProfileId ?_adf.ctrlstate=zb7z5im90_401&_afrLoop=1450229264805835 (accessed 26 April 2019).

International Labour Organization. ILO Working Conditions Laws Database. http://www.ilo.org/dyn/travail (accessed 26 April 2019).

LinkedIn Philippines. 2017. Recruiting in the Philippines.

Jensen, J. B. 2011. Global Trade in Services: Fear, Facts, and Offshoring. Washington, DC: Peterson Institute for International Economics.

Jensen, J. B. 2013. Overlooked Opportunity: Tradable Business Services, Developing Asia, and Growth. ADB Economics Working Paper 326. Manila: ADB.

Jensen, J. B., and L. G. Kletzer. 2005. Tradable Services: Understanding the Scope and Impact of Services Outsourcing. Working Paper 05-9. Washington, DC: Peterson Institute for International Economics.

Khatiwada, S., and M. K. Veloso. 2019. New Technology and Emerging Occupations: Evidence from Asia. ADB Economics Working Paper Series. No. 576.

Kochhar, K., U. Kumar, R. Rajan, A. Subramanian, and I. Tokatlidis. 2006. India's Pattern of Development: What Happened, What Follows? Working Paper 22. Washington, DC: International Monetary Fund.

Magtibay-Ramos, N., G. Estrada, and J. Felipe. 2007. An Analysis of the Philippine Business Processing Outsourcing Industry. Economics and Research Department Working Paper 93. ADB. http://hdl .handle.net/11540/1849 (accessed 26 April 2019).

Martinez Jr., A., R. Molato, and J. P. Flaminiano. 2016. ADB Technical Note: Defining Good Jobs. Manila: ADB.

Mishra, S., S. Lundstrom, and R. Anand. 2011. Service Export Sophistication and Economic Growth, World Bank Research Working Paper WPS5606. Washington, DC: World Bank Group.

Nasir S., and K. Kalirajan. Modern Services Export Performances Among Emerging and Developed Asian Economies. ADB Working Paper Series on Regional Economic Integration 143. Manila: ADB.

Noland, M., D. Park, and G. Estrada. 2012. Developing the Service Sector as Engine of Growth for Asia: An Overview. ADB Economics Working Paper 320. Manila: ADB.

Organization for Economic Co-operation and Development (OECD). 2016. How Good Is your Job? Measuring and Assessing Job Quality. http://www.oecd.org/employment/labour-stats/Job-quality -OECD.pdf (accessed 26 April 2019).

Philippine Statistics Authority. 2016. 2013/2014 Industry Profile: Business Process Outsourcing. Labstat updates 20(13). Quezon City, Philippines. https://psa.gov.ph/sites/default/files/attachments/ird/pressrelease/vol20_13.pdf (accessed 26 April 2019).

Psacharopoulus, G., and H. A. Patrinos. 2004. Returns to Investment in Education: A Further Update. *Education Economics* 12(2).

Rodrik, D. 2014. Are Services the New Manufactures? www.project-syndicate.org/commentary/are-services-the-new-manufactures-by-dani-rodrik-2014-10 (accessed 26 April 2019).

Schwab, K. 2017. *The Fourth Industrial Revolution.* Cologny: World Economic Forum.

Shingal, A. 2009. How Much Do Agreements Matter for Services Trade? Munich Personal RePEc Archive Paper 32815. University Library of Munich.

SME Finance Forum. MSME Country Indicators Database. https://www.smefinanceforum.org/data-sites/msme-country-indicators (accessed 26 April 2019).

Timmer, M. P., G. J. de Vries, and K. de Vries. 2015. Patterns of Structural Change in Developing Countries. In *Routledge Handbook of Industry and Development,* edited by J. Weiss and M. Tribe.; Abingdon; New York: Routledge.

United Nations, Department of Economic and Social Affairs, Population Division. 2014. World Urbanization Prospects: The 2014 Revision, Highlights (ST/ESA/SER.A/352).

Unni, J. 2005. Wages and Incomes in Formal and Informal Sectors in India. *Indian Journal of Labour Economics* 48(2).

van der Marel, E., and B. Shepherd. 2013. International Tradability Indices for Services. Policy Research Working Paper 6712. Washington, DC: World Bank.

World Bank. 2018. PovCalNet Methodology. http://iresearch.worldbank.org/Povcalnet/methodology.aspx (accessed 26 April 2019).

World Bank, World Development Indicators database. 2018a. Employment in Services, Percent of Total Employment, Modeled ILO Estimate. Data file. https://data.worldbank.org/indicator/SL.SRV.EMPL.ZS (accessed 26 April 2019).

World Bank, World Development Indicators Database. 2018b. Labor Force, Total. Data file. https://data.worldbank.org/indicator/SL.TLF.TOTL.IN (accessed 26 April 2019).

World Bank, World Development Indicators Database. 2018c. Urban Population, Percent of Total. Data file. https://data.worldbank.org/indicator/ SP.URB.TOTL.IN.ZS (accessed 26 April 2019).

11

Sectoral and Skill Contributions to Labor Productivity in Asia

Matthias Helble, Trinh Q. Long, and Trang T. Le

11.1 Introduction

Economic development has been progressing rapidly in Asia in recent decades, moving many people out of subsistence agriculture into more productive jobs in manufacturing and services. However, this has given rise to concerns in many countries in Asia as to whether enough jobs are being created to absorb new workers entering the labor market as well as existing workers moving across sectors. In India, it is estimated that the labor force is increasing by over 10 million people every year. The challenge is how to bring these workers into jobs, and more particularly into productive jobs.

It is a well-established fact that, during the rapid economic development of today's advanced economies, a large number of jobs were created in these economies' manufacturing sectors. At the manufacturing sector's peak, around one-quarter to one-third of all jobs were typically found in manufacturing industries. In contrast, in many Asian economies the number of jobs in the manufacturing sector peaked at a level well below that. Rodrik (2016) calls this phenomenon "premature deindustrialization." Slow technological progress and other underdeveloped factors, such as trade, limit the potential of the manufacturing sector to create jobs. As a consequence, many developing countries can no longer rely only on the manufacturing sector as a source of new and productive jobs.

Although employment in the agricultural sector is continuously shrinking in many lower income developing countries in Asia, the sector still employs a considerable share of workers. For example, in 2017 agriculture as a share of employment reached 43% in India, 31% in Indonesia, and 26% in the Philippines (World Bank, World Development Indicators). However, the productivity of these workers is typically low. Mechanization and land reform will further reduce the demand for agricultural labor. Therefore, the best strategy is to create new jobs in the services sector, which is already outpacing the manufacturing sector in many Asian economies in terms of share of economic activity as well as growth. Overall, services account for about 60% of the region's economic activity and 45.5% of employment (World Bank, World Development Indicators).

As services continue to replace jobs in agriculture and manufacturing, the important question is, what perspective does this structural transformation offer on growth? The main obstacle when analyzing this question is that we still lack a sound understanding of the productivity of the services sector in developing countries. This chapter therefore aims to provide new evidence on the labor productivity of the services sector in developing Asia. We exploit the data provided by the Asian Productivity Organization (APO) as well as the World Input–Output data for recent years to estimate the contribution of services to aggregate labor productivity.

Our main results show that, in many economies, services are already making a substantial contribution to labor productivity growth. Furthermore, we demonstrate that a major reallocation of labor directly from agriculture to services is taking place, bypassing the manufacturing sector. This finding challenges the traditional view that countries in the process of economic development must first see their workforce employed in manufacturing before switching to services. Lastly, we study how different skill levels contribute to productivity growth. Our findings suggest that medium- to high-skilled workers have been contributing the most to labor productivity growth in general, as well as in services in particular.

This chapter contributes to the literature by providing the first detailed analysis of services labor productivity for a large number of Asian economies. In 2018, the International Monetary Fund (IMF) published new estimates on labor productivity in services for emerging and advanced economies. However, most Asian countries are still at an early stage of structural transformation and do not fall within either category. In this context, having a better understanding of the role of services during the economic development of these countries gives us important clues that can inform the policy discussion and help with the designing of better development strategies.

The second contribution of this chapter is to extend the methodology developed by the IMF in two ways. First, we dissect the contribution of services in a holistic way by studying the contribution of each industry to aggregate labor productivity growth. Second, we provide a detailed analysis of productivity growth accounting by categorizing labor into low-, medium-, and high-skilled labor.

11.2 Data and Methodology

11.2.1 Data

In this chapter we exploit data from two sources. The first of these is the APO database, which contains the contributions of nine sectors to the gross domestic product (GDP), as well as the employment shares (number of jobs) in every sector. These nine sectors, which correspond to the EU KLEMS,[1] are as follows:

- (i) agriculture, hunting, forestry, and fishing;
- (ii) mining and quarrying;
- (iii) manufacturing;
- (iv) electricity, gas, and water supply;
- (v) construction;
- (vi) retail;
- (vii) transport and storage;
- (viii) financial intermediation, real estate, renting, and business; and
- (ix) other services.

The data are based on national accounts and were made comparable by the APO in a joint research effort together with the Keio Economic Observatory, at Keio University, Tokyo. The United Nations (UN) System of National Accounts 2008, the latest version of the international statistical standard for national accounts (UN 2009), has been introduced in 21 countries in Asia. However, some countries, such as Cambodia, the Lao People's Democratic Republic, and Nepal, are still working with earlier versions of national accounts, making it necessary to harmonize the data before carrying out comparative productivity analyses. More details about the GDP harmonization process, including the capitalization of software and research and development (R&D), can be found in the APO Productivity Databook (APO 2018).

The APO database covers around 30 economies in the Asia and Pacific region for the period 1970–2015. In our analysis, below, we only use 19 economies (we decided to drop Australia and New Zealand as they do not fall under the category of developing or emerging economies in the Asia and Pacific region). We also ignored several small

---

[1] The EU KLEMS project began in the late 1990s with the objective of developing new productivity measures at the industry level for the European Union (EU). "KLEMS" refers to the decomposition of output growth into contributing factor inputs: capital (K), labor (L), energy (E), materials (M), and service inputs (S).

economies because their data were incomplete during the period under consideration. We use the APO data to estimate the contribution of each sector to aggregate labor productivity in Asia in sections 11.3 and 11.4.

Our second data source is the World Input–Output Database (WIOD). Specifically, we use the World Input–Output Tables (July 2014 version), which cover 40 economies, divide each economy into 35 sectors (Timmer et al. 2015), and cover the period 1995–2009. The industry classification follows the International Standard Industrial Classification (ISIC) revision 3.[2] The database contains industry-level data on employment, skill levels, capital stocks, gross output, and value added at current and constant prices. Although the data for some economies run up to 2011, we only use data from 1995 to 2009 for the sake of comparability. We use this dataset for our analysis in section 5.

11.2.2 Methodology

The main objective of this chapter is to estimate the contribution of services to labor productivity growth. We therefore apply decomposition methods that separate the growth of aggregate productivity into sectoral contributions.

First, we follow Fernández and Palazuelos (2018) who use the following approach:

$$
q = \sum_{j=1}^{N} \left[q_j \frac{V_j}{V} + e_j \left(\frac{V_j}{V} - \frac{E_j}{E} \right) \right]
$$

where q stands for the growth rate of aggregate productivity, q_j is the productivity growth of sector j, e_j measures the employment growth of sector j, V captures the aggregate value added (VA), V_j is the value added in sector j, E captures the total employment, and E_j is the employment in sector j.

The growth in productivity is the aggregation of productivity changes across N sectors in the economy. In each sector j the change in productivity can have two sources: (i) the sector productivity growth rate weighted by the contribution of the sector to total value added, and (ii) the change in employment in sector j weighted by the difference of the contribution of sector j and employment in the whole economy. If that difference is positive, the productivity level of the sector is higher than the average for the entire economy. This then implies that an

---

[2]   Please refer to the Appendix for the list of industries and industry categories.

increase in employment in this sector makes a positive contribution to aggregate productivity growth.

11.3 Results: Decomposition of Aggregate Labor Productivity Growth

Applying the method used by Fernández and Palazuelos (2018) for the selected Asian economies', we obtain the results summarized in Figure 11.1, which shows the contribution of both labor productivity growth and employment growth to aggregate labor productivity across 15 Asian economies from 1990 to 2015. We see that in all economies, except Nepal, the increase in labor productivity was higher than the increase due to the reallocation of labor across sectors. The strongest increase in labor productivity is observed in Japan. Other high performers with labor productivity growth rates above 80% are India; Pakistan; Malaysia; the People's Republic of China (PRC); Taipei,China; and the Republic of Korea. Overall, there seems to be a tendency for more developed economies to experience higher increases in labor productivity and small changes in productivity due to employment changes. In contrast, in the developing countries of Southeast Asia the reallocation of jobs helped to increase productivity significantly. For example, Indonesia, Thailand, and Viet Nam had high rates of productivity growth due to the reallocation of labor across sectors.

More relevant for our chapter is the question of the contribution by industry. To answer this, we divide all of the sectors into four industries: (i) agriculture and mining; (ii) manufacturing; (iii) construction,

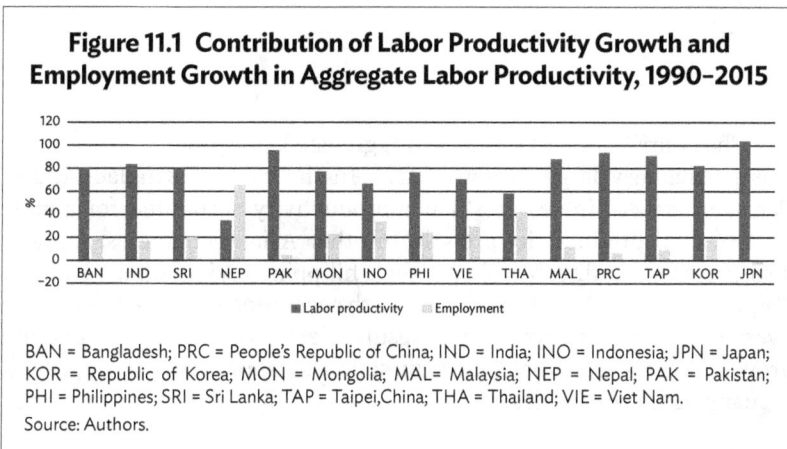

Figure 11.1 Contribution of Labor Productivity Growth and Employment Growth in Aggregate Labor Productivity, 1990–2015

BAN = Bangladesh; PRC = People's Republic of China; IND = India; INO = Indonesia; JPN = Japan; KOR = Republic of Korea; MON = Mongolia; MAL= Malaysia; NEP = Nepal; PAK = Pakistan; PHI = Philippines; SRI = Sri Lanka; TAP = Taipei,China; THA = Thailand; VIE = Viet Nam.
Source: Authors.

electricity, and water supply; and (iv) services. Services include the sectors vi–ix in the EU-KLEMS classification (listed above). Although productivity can be rather different within the four services sectors, as we will see later, we first use the division into four industries for the sake of simplicity.

The results for all 15 economies and the same time period are summarized in Figure 11.2. As we can easily observe, services made the largest contribution to productivity growth in Asia, except in the case of Malaysia and Mongolia, where the mining sector accounts for a large share of national GDP and has developed strongly over the period covered in our analysis.

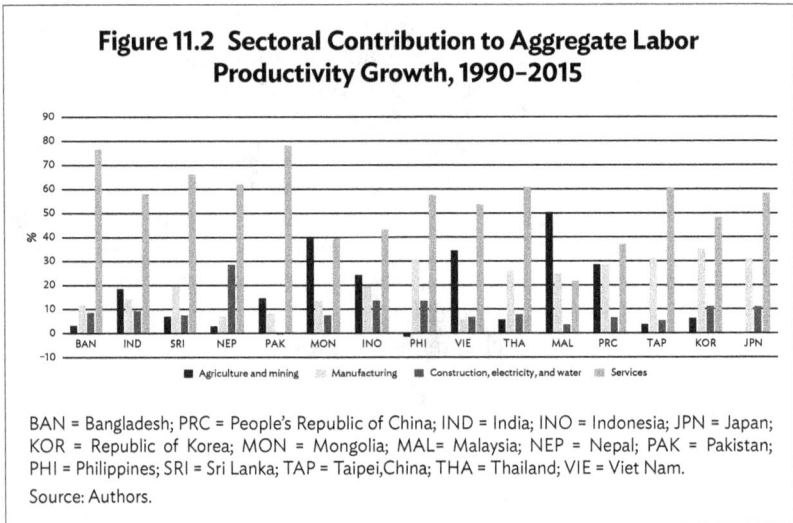

Figure 11.2 Sectoral Contribution to Aggregate Labor Productivity Growth, 1990–2015

BAN = Bangladesh; PRC = People's Republic of China; IND = India; INO = Indonesia; JPN = Japan; KOR = Republic of Korea; MON = Mongolia; MAL= Malaysia; NEP = Nepal; PAK = Pakistan; PHI = Philippines; SRI = Sri Lanka; TAP = Taipei,China; THA = Thailand; VIE = Viet Nam.
Source: Authors.

The contribution of services to aggregate labor productivity growth was particularly large in South Asia. In the case of Bangladesh and Pakistan, growth in services' labor productivity accounted for almost 80% of total productivity growth. In other Asian economies, services also played a significant role. In the Philippines; Viet Nam; Thailand; Taipei,China; and Japan, services growth accounted for more than half of overall productivity growth. The results clearly show that productivity growth in services has been the main source of labor productivity growth in many Asian economies.

Increases in manufacturing productivity were particularly high (above 30%) in the Philippines; Taipei,China; the Republic of Korea; and Japan; and 20%–30% in Thailand, Malaysia, and the PRC. Labor productivity growth in manufacturing in Viet Nam was surprisingly small (6%), and manufacturing productivity increased equally slowly in some South Asian economies (e.g., Nepal, at 7%; and Pakistan, at 8%).

The method used above requires us to calculate the employment component in aggregate labor productivity separately. Figure 11.3 depicts how the employment shares have changed and thereby contributed to aggregate labor productivity. We see that, throughout South Asia, agriculture and mining saw a fall in their labor share contribution, except for Malaysia and Mongolia where the mining sector is strong. At the same time, the employment component in services increased. In other words, we observe a reallocation of labor away from agriculture and mining toward services. We see similar pattern in the Philippines, Viet Nam, and Thailand. East Asia behaves somewhat differently. The employment change in the primary sector was negligible. The employment changes in services (except for Japan) were the main drivers of higher aggregate labor productivity. One interpretation of this could be that the expansion of services was not accompanied by an equal contraction of employment in the primary sector.

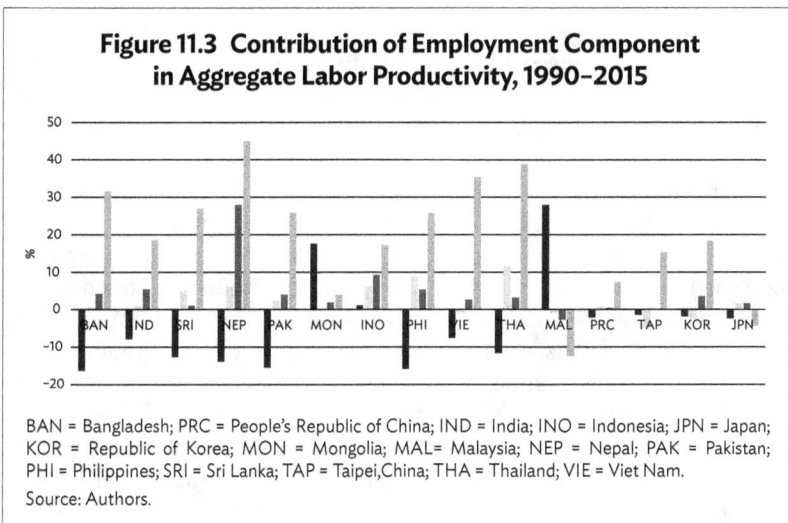

Figure 11.3 Contribution of Employment Component in Aggregate Labor Productivity, 1990–2015

BAN = Bangladesh; PRC = People's Republic of China; IND = India; INO = Indonesia; JPN = Japan; KOR = Republic of Korea; MON = Mongolia; MAL= Malaysia; NEP = Nepal; PAK = Pakistan; PHI = Philippines; SRI = Sri Lanka; TAP = Taipei,China; THA = Thailand; VIE = Viet Nam.
Source: Authors.

11.4 Industrial Structure and Aggregate Labor Productivity in Asia

Another way to gauge productivity growth is the method proposed by Tang and Wang (2004) and Zhao and Tang (2015):

$$\Delta X = \frac{X_t - X_s}{X_s} = \sum_i w_{is}\Delta x_i + \sum_i w_{is}[(1 + \Delta x_i)\Delta \tilde{s}_i]$$

where w_{is} stands for the nominal value-added share in total GDP; Δx_i is the labor productivity growth of industry i between year t and year t-1, and $\Delta \tilde{s}_i$ is the percentage of change in relative size of industry i between year t and t-1.

The first term captures the industry's contribution to the improvement of labor productivity. It can therefore also be called the "pure productivity effect." The second term reflects the change in the economic significance of the industry in terms of employment and the ability to create economic value. This can be labelled the "shift effect," as the sum of the shift effects is positive if the economy shifts toward industries with relatively high value-added shares or relatively high labor productivity growth.

The results in Figure 11.4 show that, in all economies except Japan, the productivity effect and shift effect were both positive. In the case of Japan, the productivity effect was largely positive and indicates that the productivity of Japanese industry has improved substantially. However, Japan's economy shifted to less productive sectors and the value of the shift effect became negative, implying that, in Japan, labor shifted from higher productivity sectors to lower productivity ones.

In three countries—Malaysia, Pakistan, and the Republic of Korea— we observe almost no shift effect, but instead a pure productivity effect. In these three economies, productivity increased mainly due to the increased productivity of existing sectors. Almost no shift from low to high productivity sectors can be observed. Singapore and Taipei,China also show high levels of the pure productivity effect. Notable cases on the other end include Nepal and Thailand, where productivity grew predominately due to the "shift effect." Sectors with relatively high productivity were able to attract labor and therefore boosted the overall productivity of the economy. In all other economies the "pure productivity effect" dominated and the "shift effect" played a relatively smaller role in explaining productivity growth.

Figure 11.4   Contribution of Productivity Effects and Shift Effects to Aggregate Labor Productivity, 1990–2015

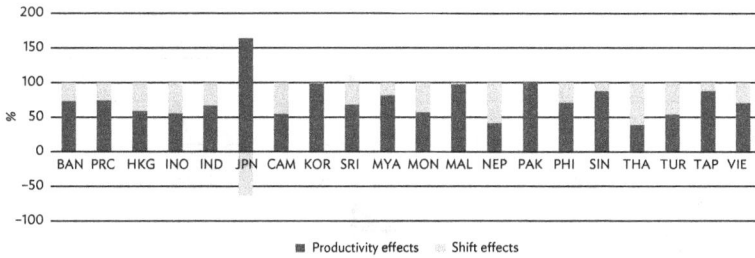

BAN = Bangladesh; PRC = People's Republic of China; HKG = Hong Kong, China; IND = India; INO = Indonesia; JPN = Japan; KOR = Republic of Korea; MON = Mongolia; MAL= Malaysia; MYA = Myanmar; NEP = Nepal; PAK = Pakistan; PHI = Philippines; SIN = Singapore; SRI = Sri Lanka; TAP = Taipei,China; THA = Thailand; TUR = Turkey; VIE = Viet Nam.

Source: Authors.

When we calculate the sectoral contribution to aggregate labor productivity growth, a more nuanced picture emerges (see Figure 11.5). We observe that agriculture accounted for more than 50% of aggregate labor productivity growth in only four countries: Cambodia, Nepal, Thailand, and Viet Nam. In nine out of 20 economies, productivity growth was mainly generated by productivity growth in services. The economy with the highest growth in services productivity is Hong Kong, China, where almost 74% of productivity growth stems from services, while growth of 50% or higher was seen in India, Japan, Singapore, and Sri Lanka. These economies (with the exception of Sri Lanka) are well known to have shifted toward the services industries in recent years. It is interesting that services have been the main driver of services growth even in countries with a relatively low per capita income, such as Bangladesh, Indonesia, and Pakistan.

The contribution of services only remained below 20% in Cambodia, Nepal, the Philippines, and Viet Nam. The case of the Philippines might be explained by the fact that the shift toward a services industry is relatively recent. As we will see in the section below (where the time period under study is shorter and more recent), the services sector in the Philippines has strongly helped boost productivity.

Figure 11.6 shows the results of this method when the study period is restricted to 1990–2015. During this timeframe, the contribution of services increased overall in most economies relative to the longer

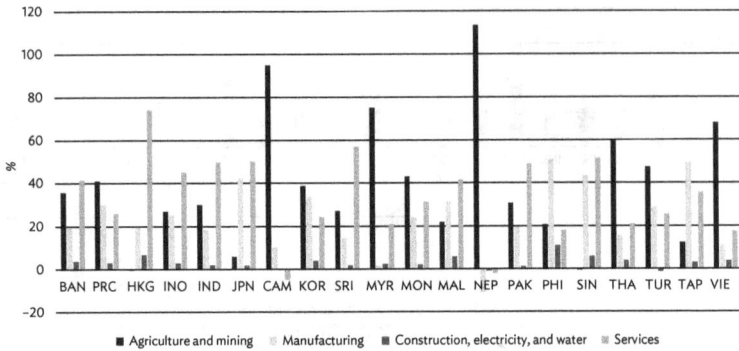

Figure 11.5 Sectoral Contribution to Aggregate Labor Productivity Growth, 1970–2015

■ Agriculture and mining   Manufacturing   ■ Construction, electricity, and water   ■ Services

BAN = Bangladesh; PRC = People's Republic of China; IND = India; INO = Indonesia; JPN = Japan; KOR = Republic of Korea; MON = Mongolia; MAL = Malaysia; MYA = Myanmar; NEP = Nepal; PAK = Pakistan; PHI = Philippines; SIN = Singapore; SRI = Sri Lanka; TAP = Taipei,China; THA = Thailand; TUR = Turkey; VIE = Viet Nam.

Source: Authors.

timeframe. This indicates that productivity in services has grown more quickly in recent years. A comparison of Figures 11.5 and 11.6 reveals that the contribution of agriculture has been declining. This again indicates a structural transformation from agriculture to services-based growth.

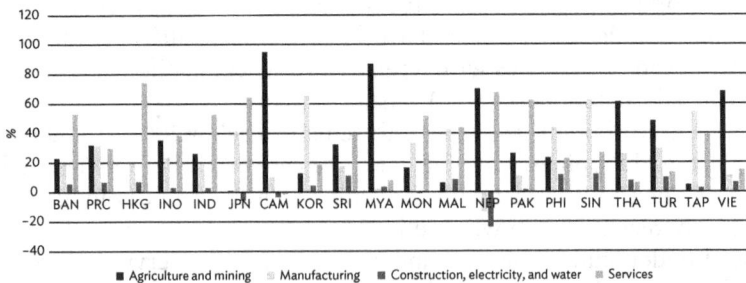

Figure 11.6 Sectoral Contribution to Aggregate Labor Productivity Growth, 1990–2015

■ Agriculture and mining   Manufacturing   ■ Construction, electricity, and water   ■ Services

BAN = Bangladesh; PRC = People's Republic of China; HKG = Hong Kong, China; IND = India; INO = Indonesia; JPN = Japan; KOR = Republic of Korea; MON = Mongolia; MAL = Malaysia; MYA = Myanmar; NEP = Nepal; PAK = Pakistan; PHI = Philippines; SIN = Singapore; SRI = Sri Lanka; TAP = Taipei,China; THA = Thailand; TUR = Turkey; VIE = Viet Nam.

Source: Authors.

11.5 Role of Skills and Skills Distribution

In the sections above we have shown that services have been one of the major sources of labor productivity growth in Asia. An interesting question to ask is whether this growth was mainly generated by low- or high-skilled workers. Unfortunately, data on productivity by skill level are not available in the APO database and are only available in the WIOD database for a handful of Asian economies, namely the PRC, India, Japan, the Republic of Korea, and Taipei,China. As a benchmark, we also include data for the United States (US).

The first two columns of Table 11.1 list the change in overall labor productivity (across all sectors) as well as in employment from 1995 to 2009. Labor productivity growth was strongest in the PRC and India, an intuitive result, since both countries were the furthest from the international productivity frontier. Labor productivity increased by 24 percentage points in Japan and 34 percentage points in the US, while the Republic of Korea and Taipei,China fall in between. Thus, a trend toward convergence of labor productivity is observable in the six economies included in the sample.

Table 11.1 Labor Productivity Growth, Employment Growth, and Skill Groups, 1995–2009

	Labor productivity growth	Employment growth	Low-skilled workers		Medium- and high-skilled workers	
			1995	2009	1995	2009
	(1)	(2)	(3)	(4)	(5)	(6)
People's Republic of China	192%	28%	72%	62%	27%	37%
India	139%	13%	71%	63%	29%	36%
Japan	24%	-13%	16%	8%	84%	92%
Republic of Korea	78%	13%	22%	9%	78%	91%
Taipei,China	39%	11%	50%	30%	50%	70%
United States	34%	8%	11%	9%	89%	91%

Source: Authors.

The country with the highest employment growth is the PRC, whereas Japan saw its labor force shrink by 13 percentage points. Interestingly, India, despite its high population growth rate, experienced a relatively modest increase in its labor force, by a mere 13 percentage points. One reason for this might be that the WIOD data are based on formal employment, while the overwhelming majority of India's workforce is still in the informal sector and relatively few formal jobs have been added.

Columns (3)–(6) in Table 11.1 list the percentage of workers classified as low- or medium- and high-skilled in 1995 and 2009. In this study, we adopt the skills classification of the WIOD Socio-Economic Accounts, which defines skills based on educational attainment levels (Erumban et al. 2012) and divides skills into three groups: (i) low-skilled workers, having a lower secondary or secondary stage of basic education; (ii) medium-skilled workers, having an (upper) secondary education and post-secondary, non-tertiary education; and (iii) high-skilled workers, having a tertiary education. In all economies, we observe a shift from low-skilled workers to medium- and high-skilled workers over time. As education and vocational training have improved, more and more workers have moved out of the low-skilled category. Interestingly, the PRC and India show very similar patterns. In 1995, low-skilled workers accounted for 70% of the labor force, but by 2009 this figure had fallen by about 10 percentage points. The number of medium- and high-skilled workers increased respectively.

Taipei,China has been the most successful in raising the skill level of its workers, with the percentage of low-skilled workers as a share of the labor force dropping from 50% of the labor force in 1995 to 30% in 2009. The Republic of Korea also achieved a rapid upskilling of its workforce, with its share of medium- and high-skilled workers increasing from 78% of the labor force in 1995 to 91% in 2009, the same level as the US. Japan already had a highly qualified workforce in 1995, but its share of medium- and high skilled workers rose further to 92%.

11.6 Methodology

In light of this information on the different skill levels, we next analyze how labor productivity growth and employment growth differ across the following four sectors: (i) agriculture and mining, (ii) manufacturing, (iii) electricity supply and construction, and (iv) services. In this we follow Tang (2016) who proposed a decomposition method to estimate the impact of an improvement in skills and productivity by skill level on overall productivity. We decompose the labor productivity growth as follows:

$$g = \sum_i [\bar{\theta}_i(\tilde{s}_i^1 - \tilde{s}_i^0)] +$$

$$+\left\{ \sum_i [\bar{\phi}_i^L (w_{i,L}^1 - w_{i,L}^0)] + \sum_i [\bar{\phi}_i^H (w_{i,H}^1 - w_{i,H}^0)] \right\}$$

$$+ \sum_i [\bar{\varphi}_{i,L} (\tilde{q}_{i,L}^1 - \tilde{q}_{i,L}^0)] + \sum_i [\bar{\varphi}_{i,H}(\tilde{q}_{i,H}^1 - \tilde{q}_{i,H}^0)]$$

The three components on the right-hand side reflect four different factors determining the labor productivity growth from year 0 (1995) to 1 (2009). The first term measures the change in industry composition and is called the "industry composition effect." The second term, consisting of two sub-terms in { } captures the changes in skill distribution over time and is called the "skill distribution effect." Finally, the remaining terms gauge the change in the productivity of low-skilled workers (the third term) and medium- and high-skilled workers (the fourth term, from years 0 to 1). They capture an improvement or deterioration in the productivity of the two skill groups.

Please note, $\bar{\theta}_i$ is the pseudo average labor productivity:

$$\bar{\theta}_i = \left[\frac{1}{2} (w_{iL}^1 \tilde{q}_{iL}^0 + w_{iL}^1 \tilde{q}_{iH}^0 + w_{iL}^0 \tilde{q}_{iL}^1 + w_{iL}^0 \tilde{q}_{iH}^1) \right]$$

$\bar{\varphi}_{i,L}$ and $\bar{\varphi}_{i,H}$ are the average employment shares of low- and high-skilled employees:

$$\bar{\varphi}_{iL} = \frac{1}{2} (\tilde{s}_i^1 w_{iL}^1 + \tilde{s}_i^0 w_{iL}^0)$$

$$\bar{\varphi}_{iH} = \frac{1}{2} (\tilde{s}_i^1 w_{iH}^1 + \tilde{s}_i^0 w_{iH}^0)$$

11.6.1 Empirical Results

Applying the method described above to the six economies for which we have detailed information by skill level, we obtain the results summarized in Tables 11.4 and 11.5. Table 11.4 shows the results for the four elements included in the decomposition. We observe that industrial restructuring accounted for 28% of labor productivity growth in India, and almost 20% of this growth in the Republic of Korea and Taipei,China (in the remaining economies it was much lower). In terms of skill

Table 11.4 Decomposition of Labor Productivity Growth by Industrial Structure, Skill Distribution, and Skill Levels (1995–2009)

	Industrial structure	Skill distribution	Low-skilled workers	Medium- and high-skilled workers	Total
PRC	10%	3%	36%	51%	100%
India	28%	8%	21%	44%	100%
Japan	7%	20%	5%	68%	100%
Republic of Korea	19%	14%	9%	58%	101%
Taipei,China	19%	21%	16%	43%	100%
US	-2%	15%	3%	83%	100%

PRC = People's Republic of China, US = United States.
Source: Authors.

distribution, investments in education and retraining in Taipei,China and Japan helped these economies increase labor productivity significantly. Finally, when we analyze contributions by skill level, we find that low-skilled workers in the PRC and India made an important contribution to labor productivity growth; however, as we move up in terms of level of economic development, the contribution of low-skilled workers declines (5% in Japan and 3% in the US). We also see clearly that medium- to high-skilled workers made the largest contribution to labor productivity growth across all economies in the sample. The more advanced the economy, the larger the contribution of this skill group (reaching 83% in the US).

In Table 11.5, we go one level deeper and decompose the contributions at the industry level. In column 1 we list the contributions of a change in the industrial structure to a change in labor productivity. In all six economies, the structural transformation toward services has driven labor productivity growth. In the PRC, which is widely known to have become the world powerhouse for the manufacturing industry, the contribution of manufacturing to labor productivity growth was surprisingly small, accounting for only 1.1%. In contrast, services helped to increase labor productivity by almost 20 percentage points. Although a similar pattern can also be seen in the other economies, the contribution of the manufacturing sector in the industrial structure was always negative, implying that industrial restructuring has lowered the labor productivity growth.

Table 11.5 Decomposition of Labor Productivity Growth by Sector, Industrial Structure, Skill Distribution, and Skill Levels (1995–2009)

Economy	Sector	Industrial structure	Skill composition	Low-skilled	Medium- and high- skilled
People's Republic of China	Agriculture and mining	-8.8%	0.2%	20.7%	6.9%
	Manufacturing	1.1%	0.6%	29.4%	29.6%
	Electricity and water	4.0%	0.3%	6.1%	8.7%
	Services	19.9%	0.8%	14.4%	58.8%
India	Agriculture and mining	-1.8%	0.9%	13.6%	5.6%
	Manufacturing	-3.0%	0.8%	4.9%	16.0%
	Electricity and water	9.8%	0.4%	2.5%	3.4%
	Services	35.1%	1.7%	8.5%	40.4%
Taipei,China	Agriculture and mining	-1.1%	0.1%	0.0%	1.2%
	Manufacturing	-1.0%	1.4%	1.6%	1.8%
	Electricity and water	-0.9%	0.2%	-0.7%	-1.4%
	Services	10.8%	2.1%	5.6%	19.1%
Republic of Korea	Agriculture and mining	-3.9%	0.3%	0.6%	1.6%
	Manufacturing	-25.5%	1.4%	6.7%	39.6%
	Electricity and water	0.2%	0.1%	0.0%	3.4%
	Services	43.1%	2.1%	0.1%	7.9%
Japan	Agriculture and mining	-0.4%	0.0%	0.1%	0.1%
	Manufacturing	-10.4%	0.2%	1.1%	7.9%
	Electricity and water	-0.8%	0.2%	0.0%	0.1%
	Services	13.1%	1.0%	0.0%	11.3%
United States	Agriculture and mining	1.0%	0.1%	0.0%	0.2%
	Manufacturing	-11.4%	0.2%	0.3%	10.6%
	Electricity and water	2.8%	0.0%	-0.2%	-1.1%
	Services	6.7%	0.6%	1.1%	23.2%

Source: Authors.

The second component of the decomposition captures the effect of differences in skill composition over time. This effect of changes in the skill composition of the labor force played a minor role in raising labor productivity across sector. With regard to services it only surpasses 1% for services in certain economies.

Our analysis focuses on the last two columns, which summarize how much low-, medium-, and high-skilled workers contribute to labor productivity growth across the four industries. In the PRC, low-skilled workers were mainly responsible for productivity growth in agriculture and mining (20.7%), and manufacturing (29.4%). In contrast, medium- and high-skilled workers drove productivity primarily in services (58.8%), but also in manufacturing (29.6%). Thus, medium- and high-skilled workers make the largest difference in the services sector.

In India, low-skilled workers helped increase productivity most in agriculture and mining (13.6%), followed by services (8.5%). Similar to the PRC, in India medium- and high-skilled workers contributed the most to productivity growth in services (40.4%), followed by manufacturing (16.0%). In Taipei,China, sectors i–iii recorded very modest labor productivity growth; productivity only increased in services, driven mainly by medium- and high-skilled workers.

In the Republic of Korea, Japan, and the US, low-skilled workers contribute little to labor productivity growth across all sectors. This might be explained by the fact that low-skilled workers have been systematically replaced by technological advances, as documented for the US by Autor and Dorn (2013). Medium- and high-skilled workers manage the machines and production processes, as reflected in their relatively high contribution to productivity growth, especially in the case of the Republic of Korea. Medium- and high-skilled workers have made a significant contribution to labor productivity growth in Japan (11.3%) and the US (23.3%). In a recent paper, Trinh (2019) differentiates between medium- and high-skilled workers in the US and finds that medium-skilled workers made the highest contribution to labor productivity growth.

In summary, looking across the six economies, we find robust evidence that the high labor productivity growth of services has been mainly driven by industrial restructuring and the higher productivity of high-skilled workers. The observed effect of industrial restructuring underscores the earlier finding of this chapter, namely, that the structural transformation toward services does not lead to lower overall productivity, but achieves the opposite. Our analysis further demonstrates that labor productivity growth in services is driven to a large extent by high-skilled workers. This highlights the need for governments to support the corresponding increase in skills that a successful move toward services requires.

11.7 Conclusion

The first objective of this chapter was to estimate the contribution of services to labor productivity growth in Asia. By applying different decomposition methods, we found strong evidence that services have contributed substantially to labor productivity growth in Asia. Our analysis also shows that most Asian economies are seeing a major reallocation from agriculture to services, skipping the manufacturing phase. This switch is not necessarily leading to a fall in productivity. Instead, we found that the labor reallocation from agriculture to services has helped increase labor productivity.

The second objective of the chapter was to study contributions to labor productivity growth by skill level. Given the data constraints, we limited the analysis to five major economies. We first found that skill levels in these economies increased substantially from 1995 to 2009. When we decomposed the labor productivity growth, we found that in all economies, high-skilled workers made the biggest contribution to increased labor productivity. The numbers are especially high in Japan, the Republic of Korea, and the US (a rather intuitive result). Technological progress raises the necessary skill level, that is to say, higher skilled workers can make better use of existing technology to boost productivity. When we dissect the growth by industry, we observe that labor productivity has grown fastest in the services sector in all economies in our sample. This growth is mainly driven by two factors: (i) the change in industrial structure, and (ii) the increased labor productivity of high-skilled workers.

Overall, our results provide evidence that the services sector has become one of the main sources of labor productivity growth in Asia. Our results ran counter to the argument put forth by Rodrik (2013) that premature deindustrialization cannot generate sustained growth. In the Asian economies in our sample, the services sector has become a driver of sustained growth, exhibiting high growth rates in labor productivity. The trend toward services is thus not a worrying development and does not necessarily imply that economic growth is slowing. On the contrary, this chapter shows that moving toward services can become an engine of sustained growth.

At the same time, our results indicate that labor productivity growth largely stems from an increase in skills. Governments need to increase their investment in the education and training of their workforce, as low-skilled labor will be stuck in low-productivity jobs irrespective of the sector. Manufacturing no longer absorbs large number of low-skilled workers, as technological advances are making them increasingly redundant.

One question that deserves future research is which services sectors are particularly likely to have high labor productivity growth. In this chapter we aggregated across all services sectors; however, we know from studies in other countries that the differences in labor productivity within services can be large. Another important research question concerns the compensation of services workers across skill levels. Evidence is emerging that high-skilled workers earn a higher premium in services than in manufacturing (IMF 2018). To ensure that services-led development generates inclusive growth, we need to better understand how the gains in labor productivity are distributed across skill levels. The list of open questions is long and calls for new efforts by scholars.

Governments in the region can no longer choose between manufacturing-led or services-led development, as technological progress and trade have put most economies on the path of services-led development. It would be extremely costly and inefficient to reverse this and artificially engineer a development process led by manufacturing. The question that we must answer is how to embrace services-led development and transform it into a process that leads to sustained, inclusive, and sustainable economic growth.

References

Asian Productivity Organization. 2018. *APO Productivity Databook.* Tokyo: Keio University Press.

Autor, D.H., and D. Dorn. 2013. The Growth of Low-Skill Service Jobs and the Polarization of the US Labor Market. *American Economic Review* 103(5): 1553–1597.

Erumban, A., R. Gouma, G. de Vries, K. de Vries, and M. Timmer. 2012. WIOD Socio-Economic Accounts (SEA): Sources and Methods. http://www.wiod.org/publications/source_docs/sea_sources.pdf (accessed 22 November 2018).

Fernández, R., and E. Palazuelos. 2018. Measuring the Role of Manufacturing in the Productivity Growth of the European Economies (1993–2007). *Structural Change and Economic Dynamics* 46: 1–12.

International Monetary Fund (IMF). 2018. Manufacturing Jobs: Implications for Productivity and Inequality. *IMF World Economic Outlook 2018.* Washington, DC: IMF.

Rodrik, D. 2016. Premature Deindustrialization, *Journal of Economic Growth* 21: 1–33.

Tang, J. 2016. Industrial Structure Change and the Widening Canada-US Labor Productivity Gap in the Post-2000 Period. *Industrial and Corporate Change* 26(2): 259–278.

Tang, J., and W. Wang. 2004. Sources of Aggregate Labour Productivity Growth in Canada and the United States. *Canadian Journal of Economics* 37(2): 421–444.

Timmer, M. P., E. Dietzenbacher, B. Los, R. Stehrer, and G. J. de Vries. 2015. An Illustrated User Guide to the World Input–Output Database: The Case of Global Automotive Production. *Review of International Economics* 23: 575–605.

Trinh, L. 2019. Role of Workers' Skills and Skill Distributions in Labor Productivity Catch-Up. Unpublished paper.

United Nations. 2009. *System of National Accounts 2008.* New York: United Nations.

United Nation Statistical Commission 2002. *International Standard Industrial Classification of All Economic Activities, ISIC Revision 3.1.* https://unstats.un.org/unsd/statcom/doc02/isic.pdf (accessed 22 November 2018).

World Bank, World Development Indicators. http://wdi.worldbank.org/ (accessed 22 November 2018).

Zhao, J., and J. Tang. 2015. Industrial Structural Change and Economic Growth in China, 1987–2008. *China & World Economy* 23(2): 1–21.

Appendix: List of Industries by International Standard Industrial Classification Code (Revision 3)

ISIC Section	ISIC Division	Industry	Sector
A, B	01, 02, 05	Agriculture, hunting, forestry, and fishing	Agriculture
C	10–14	Mining and quarrying	Mining
D	15–16	Food, beverages, and tobacco	Manufacturing
D	17–18	Textiles and textile	Manufacturing
D	19	Leather, leather, and footwear	Manufacturing
D	20	Wood and of wood and cork	Manufacturing
D	21–22	Pulp, paper, printing, and publishing	Manufacturing
D	23	Coke, refined petroleum, and nuclear fuel	Manufacturing
D	24	Chemicals and chemical	Manufacturing
D	25	Rubber and plastics	Manufacturing
D	26	Other non-metallic mineral	Manufacturing
D	27–28	Basic metals and fabricated metal	Manufacturing
D	29	Machinery, not elsewhere classified	Manufacturing
D	30–33	Electrical and optical equipment	Manufacturing
D	34	Transport equipment	Manufacturing
D	35–37	Manufacturing, not elsewhere classified; recycling	Manufacturing
E	37–41	Electricity, gas, and water supply	Electricity, water
F	45	Construction	Electricity, water
G	50	Sale, maintenance, and repair of motor vehicles and motorcycles; retail sale of fuel	Services
G	51	Wholesale trade and commission trade, except of motor vehicles and motorcycles	Services
G	52	Retail trade, except of motor vehicles and motorcycles; repair of household goods	Services
H	55	Hotels and restaurants	Services
I	60	Other inland transport	Services
I	61	Other water transport	Services
I	62	Other air transport	Services
I	63	Other supporting and auxiliary transport activities; activities of travel agencies	Services

continued on next page

Appendix *continued*

ISIC Section	ISIC Division	Industry	Sector
I	64	Post and communications	Services
J	65–67	Financial intermediation	Services
K	70	Real estate activities	Services
K	71–74	Renting of machines and equipment and other business activities	Services
L	75	Public administration and defense; compulsory social security	Services
M	80	Education	Services
N	85	Health and social works	Services
O	90–93	Other community, social, and personal services	Services

ISIC = International Standard Industrial Classification.

Source: United Nation Statistical Commission (2002), *International Standard Industrial Classification of All Economic Activities, ISIC Revision 3.1.* https://unstats.un.org/unsd/statcom/doc02/isic.pdf (accessed 22 November 2018).

12

Women and the Services Sector

Justine Lan and Ben Shepherd

12.1 Introduction

Women's employment plays a vital role in reducing poverty as it increases household income and saving, raises the economic status of women, and drives higher education. Women tend to invest more in the education and health of children than men do. They also tend to employ more women, reinforcing this virtuous cycle and promoting a higher female labor participation rate. According to McKinsey, tapping into the economic potential of women entrepreneurs could add up to $28 trillion to the world's gross domestic product (GDP) by 2025 (McKinsey 2015).

As economies grow, consumers tend to shift their spending toward services. In higher income economies, spending on services related to human capital, such as education and healthcare, is higher. Historically, most countries have developed through a period in which the importance of agriculture has decreased relative to total output, with major increases in manufacturing and a slower rate of increase in services. At some point, manufacturing output relative to the size of the economy peaks, and the economy shifts to be predominantly services-based. In more recent times, economies appear to have been shifting toward services relatively earlier. As such, the potential for services to be a positive force in terms of gender equity should be considered at an earlier stage in the development process.

This chapter attempts to cast some light on the impact of structural transformation on the gender aspect of employment, with a particular focus on Asia. While social norms ascribing gender roles in some economies still contribute to socioeconomic disadvantages for women and limit their involvement in certain industries, the shift toward services may provide a promising channel for unlocking women's potential and driving their engagement in the workforce, as well as in management and entrepreneurship.

Previous studies suggest that occupations in services have traditionally been perceived as more respectable for women as they involve cleaner working conditions and shorter working hours than those in manufacturing (Goldin 2006). The reallocation of labor from brawn-intensive (physical skills) manufacturing to brain-intensive (intellectual abilities) services has been associated with the rise in female labor participation (Rendall 2010).

Against this background, the purpose of this chapter is to provide insights into some of these questions by comparing female engagement in manufacturing and in services, in order to better understand whether structural transformation can provide a channel to narrow the gender gap and alleviate discrimination against women. The chapter further investigates the gender aspect of structural transformation by examining the variation within sectors, as women's expanded role in the labor market is sometimes not matched by a higher quality of employment. In the past, women's opportunities were concentrated in light manufacturing sectors and unskilled manufacturing jobs, which were thought to require less physical strength. Although technological advancement is associated with greater automation of manual work in physically demanding sectors, women are believed to still have a comparative advantage in the services sectors, in which interpersonal skills are more useful than in manufacturing as services are often produced and consumed simultaneously. Women also traditionally worked disproportionately in home production, as the labor market did not provide enough social benefits for working women (e.g., subsidized childcare) to incentivize them to enter the labor market (Buera, Kaboski, and Zhao 2013).

Structural transformation could bring about an improvement in the services sector in which women have comparative advantage, which in turn could have important implications for women's economic opportunities and their involvement in the labor and entrepreneurship markets. This structural shift may give rise to the question as to whether women are better represented in the services sector. This chapter tries to bring some perspective to some of these questions by comparing various aspects of gender disparity in manufacturing and services to better understand the implications of services sector growth from a gender point of view.

12.2 Country-level Data Analysis

As countries develop and shift to become more services-oriented, this change could potentially generate more employment opportunities for women, based on the assumption that services sectors are less closed to women than manufacturing, and that more resources will be invested in education, including female education. In Asia, the average share of young females in the population (aged 15–24) attending tertiary school is increasing steadily (see Figure 12.1).

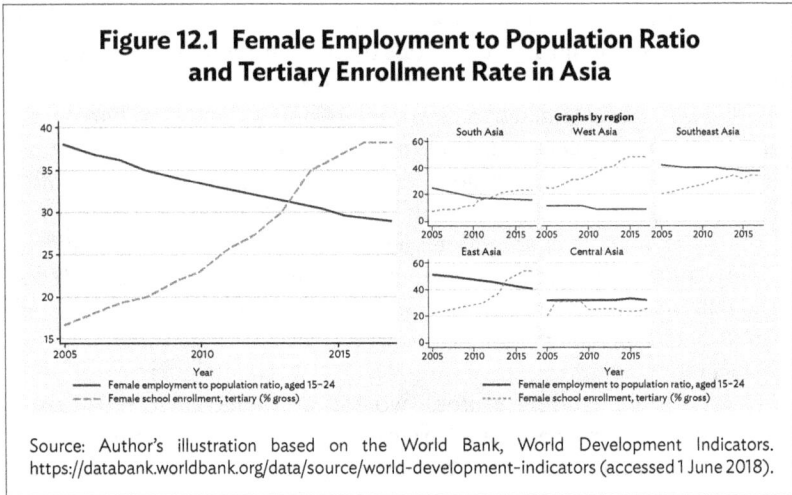

Figure 12.1 Female Employment to Population Ratio and Tertiary Enrollment Rate in Asia

Source: Author's illustration based on the World Bank, World Development Indicators. https://databank.worldbank.org/data/source/world-development-indicators (accessed 1 June 2018).

Despite the growing momentum around female education in Asia, the proportion of young women going on to tertiary studies and the rate of increase over time vary across all five Asian regions (i.e., Central, East, South, Southeast, and West Asia). For instance, South Asia registered the lowest share of women attaining higher education to begin with, as well as a rate of increase that is fairly low compared to other regions. This may reflect differences in cultural norms, quality of education, and gender-related policies. A reduction in female youth employment over time can be interpreted as a positive sign if it is correlated to the rising share of young females attending tertiary school (as is the case in Figure 12.1). This indicates that, in recent decades, more women in that age category have attained higher education than have worked. It is vital to ensure equal access to educational and skill development for women as a way to maximize their employability and generate greater accumulation of the skills needed for inclusive growth in today's economy. Despite similar patterns of female tertiary education in East and West Asia, female youth employment in West Asia settles at a much lower rate than in East Asia, demonstrating that women's educational progress cannot translate into economic benefits without overcoming a complex set of social and legal barriers. Female educational attainment complemented by the right set of policies leads to greater female participation in the labor market and increased productivity. As service sectors tend to be more skill-intensive than manufacturing and employ more women, gender equality in educational attainment is needed to enhance competitiveness among services and better adapt to changing economic realities.

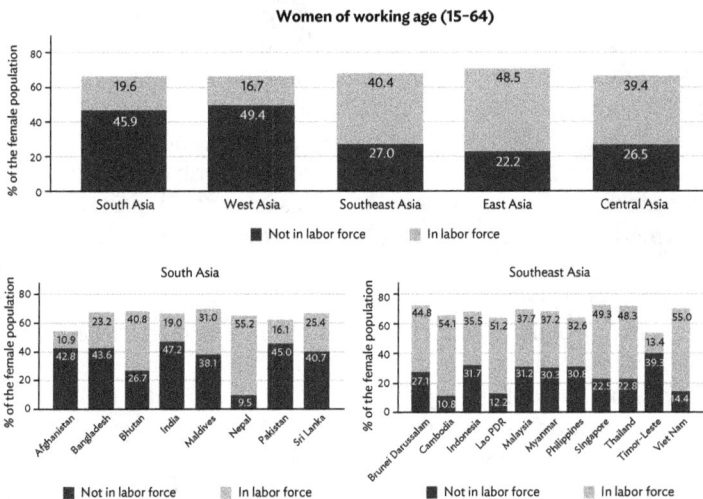

Figure 12.2 Share of Working-Age Individuals in the Female Population in Asia, 2017

Lao PDR = Lao People's Democratic Republic.
Source: Author's illustration based on the World Bank, World Development Indicators. https://databank.worldbank.org/data/source/world-development-indicators (accessed 1 June 2018).

Even though 60%–70% of the female population in Asia is of working age, the female labor force participation rate remains low in some regions, particularly in South and West Asia. This indicates the underrepresentation and untapped potential of women in the workforce. The proportion of women engaging in the labor market varies greatly across regions, hovering around 19.6% in South Asia and 40.4% in Southeast Asia, for example. Within each region, variations in female labor force participation across economies are also apparent.

325

For instance, despite the low share of females active in the workforce in South Asia, Nepal employs a large proportion of working-age women. Similarly, gender disparity is not equally distributed in South Asia, with a higher gap in economies like Afghanistan and Pakistan and a lower gap in Nepal (World Economic Forum 2016).

Nevertheless, a high female labor force participation rate does not necessarily imply gender equality, as the quality of employment remains unevenly distributed between males and females. Cambodia, for example, employs the largest share of women workers in Southeast Asia, accounting for 54.1% of the female population, but these workers are largely concentrated in the garment or informal sector. The overall picture shows that there is significant untapped potential for women's employment in Asia in general.

Services have the potential to provide opportunities for women, who are heading into services sector jobs at a faster rate than they are into manufacturing. Structural transformation enlarges the sector in which women have a comparative advantage and the marketization of services is driving the rise of female work (Ngai and Petrongolo 2017). The share of people employed in the services sector has risen over the last few decades globally as well as in Asia; this is a natural part of structural transformation. As countries develop, they produce and consume more services while technological advancement contributes to labor savings, especially in manufacturing. Expansion in services is often accompanied by the shrinking of the agriculture sector. While this tends to be the case in general, there are observable differences in the shifts in sector allocation between female and male employment in Asia (see Figure 12.3).

The distribution of female employment in the three major sectors has continuously shifted away from agriculture and industry and toward services in all regions in Asia. The share of services in female employment is generally larger than that in male employment, with the exception of South Asia where agriculture remains the main source of female employment. The difference in the shifts between female and male employment is particularly apparent in Southeast Asia and East Asia where services absorb women at a faster rate than men. In Southeast Asia from 2003 to 2017, the contribution of services to female employment rose by 15 percentage points, while the contribution to male employment rose by 9 percentage points. Similarly, the share of services in employment in East Asia rose by 28 percentage points for females and 17 percentage points for males. While the agriculture share in employment for both males and females has declined steadily over time, the industry share in employment seems to have slightly risen for males and dropped for females in East Asia. For women, structural change is driven to an important extent by services: female employment in Southeast, East, and Central Asia has changed

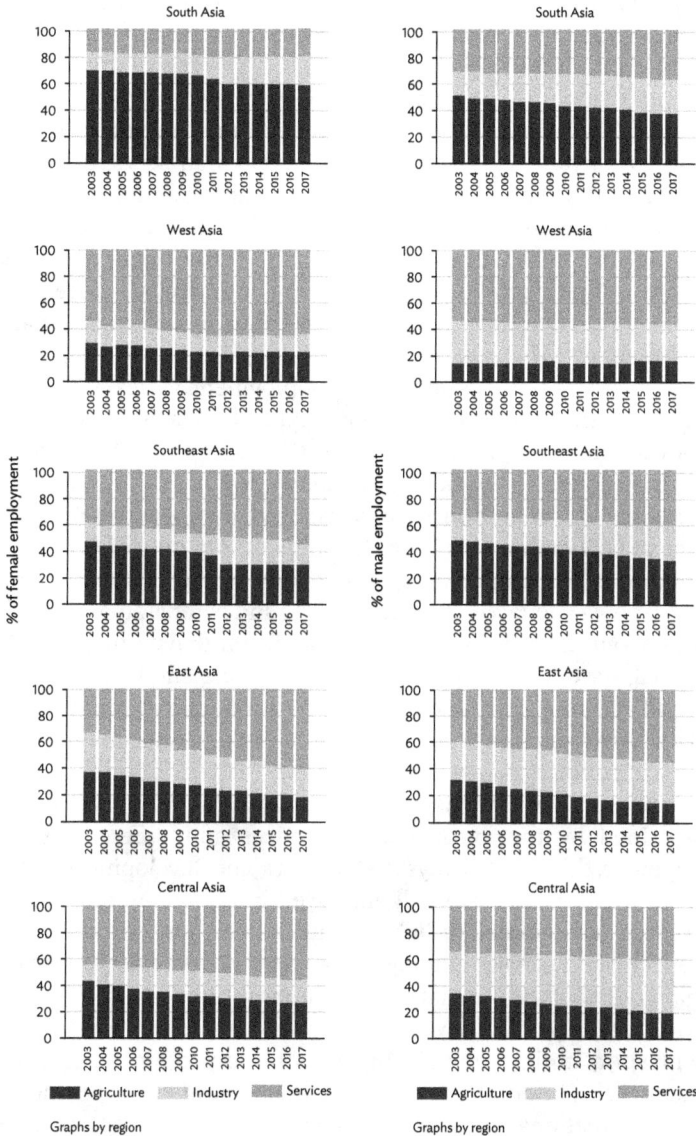

Figure 12.3 Female and Male Employment in Asia, 2003-2017

Source: Author's calculation based on the World Bank, World Development Indicators. https://databank.worldbank.org/data/source/world-development-indicators (accessed 1 June 2018).

from being predominantly in agriculture (in 2003) to services. A similar pattern is observed for male employment in the region, although the shift toward services seems to be moving at a slower pace. The relatively quick absorption of women into the services sector can be explained by the increasing relative importance of services, the comparative advantage women have in services, and/or the inadequate demand for female labor in industry. The existing literature shows that in some cases the growth of services mirrors the growth of female labor in services (Ngai and Petrongolo 2017). This expansion of services does not necessarily imply the disappearance of manufacturing given the interdependence of the two. It may simply depict the increasing role that services play in other sectors as the production of goods requires numerous services inputs. The share of services in employment has generally grown faster among females than males in Asia.

The share of services in female employment varies among Asian economies, with developed economies typically having a higher share than developing economies. Hong Kong, China; Japan; and Singapore are among the economies in the region that score a percentage share close to that of the global high-income average, which hovers around 87%. A number of economies, including the People's Republic of China (PRC) and Indonesia, attain a percentage share that is fairly close to the average in the East Asia Pacific (EAP) region (58%) and comparable to the global middle-income average (54%). Economies in South Asia, including India and Nepal, have lower services shares in female employment (26% in India and 11% in Nepal) since women are predominantly concentrated in agriculture, which accounts for 83% of female employment in Nepal and 56% in India.

While some variations in gender equality in Asia can partly be explained by the expansion of services and different stages of development, this is not always the case. In some developing economies, the majority of women are still employed in the agriculture sector. In other cases, labor-intensive light manufacturing such as garments and textiles remain the major employers for women in economies that have a comparative advantage in that sector. The large representation of women in agriculture is particularly prominent in South Asia, while the female concentration in light manufacturing is more prominent in East and Southeast Asia (International Labour Organization 2017). Furthermore, there is occupational segregation reflecting gender stereotypes, which results in women being represented in a less diversified range of occupations than men. These are typically occupations that are informal, poorly remunerated, or temporary. Women also work longer than men on average when taking both paid and unpaid work into account (Chaudhary and Verick 2014).

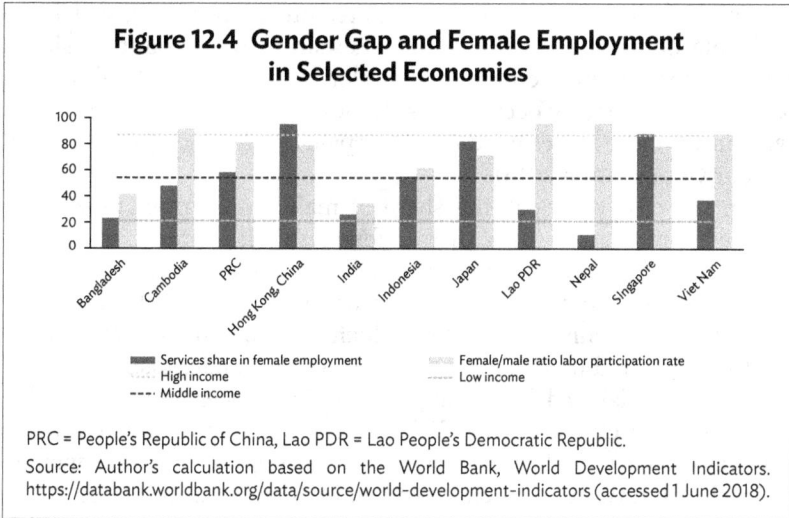

Figure 12.4 Gender Gap and Female Employment in Selected Economies

PRC = People's Republic of China, Lao PDR = Lao People's Democratic Republic.
Source: Author's calculation based on the World Bank, World Development Indicators. https://databank.worldbank.org/data/source/world-development-indicators (accessed 1 June 2018).

Figure 12.4 above reveals that a narrower gender gap in the workforce in general does not necessarily mean gender equality and it may not necessarily be attributed to the growth of the services sector. In Singapore and Hong Kong, China, for instance, the high female–male labor participation ratio is accompanied by a higher share of female employment in services. While female engagement in services does not always translate into female representation in leadership or senior roles, where persistent gender segregation exists, the opportunities for women to attain higher roles are more promising in services than in manufacturing. In Hong Kong, China, the proportion of women occupying managerial roles in 2014 was a quarter of that of men in manufacturing, and a third of that of men in financing, insurance, real estate, and professional and business services (Women's Commission 2015).

Women may seem to be roughly on par with men in some labor markets in terms of their share of employment; however, this is not the same as gender equality. In some economies, such as the Lao People's Democratic Republic and Nepal, a large share of female employment is concentrated in non-services sectors despite a high female–male labor participation ratio. In Nepal, for instance, agriculture still accounts for the majority (83%) of total female employment, compared to 60% for male employment. Further, when women work in the informal economy, they are prevented from accessing decently paid work, which therefore does not translate into economic gains. The share of women occupied in other sectors is largely clustered in low-skilled jobs and is negligible in high-skilled jobs such as technician positions, which are still male-dominated (Acharya 2014). Research on 142 countries shows that women are overrepresented in clerical, service, and sales work as well as elementary occupations. In developed economies, however, women are more represented in higher paid occupations (International Labour Organization 2016).

In the case of Nepal, the share of male employment in services is three times higher than that of females. With limited absorption capacity in the services sector, especially for females in Nepal, a large majority of the female working population is still involved in low-productivity agricultural activities, which contributed only 33% of GDP in 2016 compared to 52% for services. In India, gender disparity in the labor force is high and female employment in services is low. According to recent research, the gender-differentiated wage gap is much lower in services than in manufacturing, with men earning 5% more than women in services but twice as much as women in manufacturing (Epod 2016). This last point is important, as it highlights that the services sector is potentially more accommodating to women than is manufacturing.

There is untapped potential for women to enter the services market where gender discrimination appears less severe. To attain sustainable growth, a structural transformation from low to higher levels of female productivity is needed.

Figure 12.5 shows that an increase in the manufacturing share in male employment is correlated with higher labor productivity, while an increase in the share of female employment is correlated with lower labor productivity (value added per worker). In contrast to manufacturing, an increase in the share of services in employment is correlated with higher labor productivity for both females and males. However, the impact is slightly more prominent for males than females, indicating the need to invest in education and skills to help women move into higher productivity sectors in services.

Although correlation does not imply causation, these figures portray the real opportunities that services offer for women's economic transformation compared to manufacturing. In other words, gender-based discrimination seems to be less apparent in services than it is in manufacturing. The graph, however, captures the picture at an aggregated level and does not reveal occupational segregation. Encouraging female employment in services can bring about positive repercussions for labor productivity as a whole. Achieving meaningful economic transformation may require facilitation of the movement of female labor, not only between sectors (transitioning from non-services to services sectors), but also within sectors (from low-productivity to high-productivity occupations).

Figure 12.5 Share in Employment and Labor Productivity, by Sector and Gender, 2016

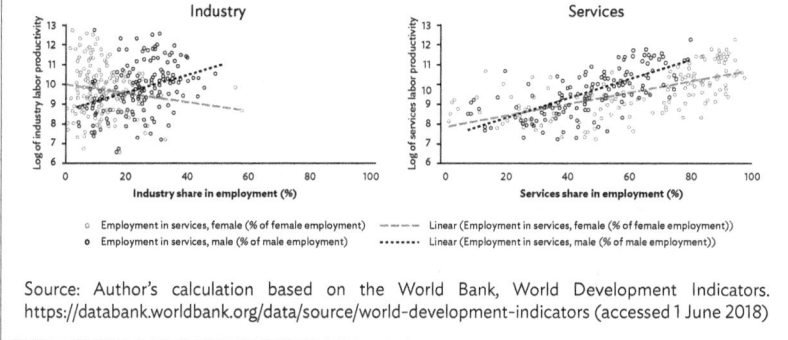

Source: Author's calculation based on the World Bank, World Development Indicators. https://databank.worldbank.org/data/source/world-development-indicators (accessed 1 June 2018)

While deindustrialization provides new economic opportunities for women, there are also risks of increased poverty for women left behind by the restructuring. As countries develop, the relative demand for higher skilled labor is likely to increase, and opportunities for those lacking the required skills are likely to become relatively less abundant (Shepherd and Stone 2017). This poses a risk especially in economies where women tend to enter the labor market with a relatively lower level of education than men. Policy formulations that incorporate gender considerations to help women achieve higher skills will increase the number of opportunities for women to secure emerging high-skilled and better paid jobs as countries develop. These policies therefore play an important role in achieving inclusive growth and an equitable outcome.

In many economies in Asia, the services sector exhibits a better gender balance than does manufacturing (Figure 12.6). It may be counterintuitive at first to observe larger differences between manufacturing and services in developed economies such as Japan and smaller differences in developing economies such as Viet Nam and Thailand. This can be explained by the fact that the female–male ratio in employment in services exceeds that in manufacturing in most cases, except in economies that still rely on agriculture or manufacturing sectors. For instance, the textile and apparel industry in Viet Nam is a vital high-growth, labor-intensive industry that employs largely low-skilled workers, mostly women with few employment alternatives. Similarly, the expansion of employment arising from the garment industry in Bangladesh plays an important role in providing opportunities for women, resulting in a much higher gender ratio in manufacturing than in services.

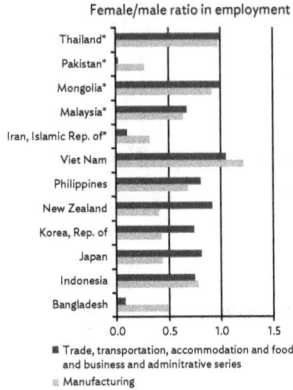

**Figure 12.6 Gender Employment Ratio
in Selected Economies in Asia, by Sector, 2017**

Iran, Islamic Rep. of = Islamic Republic of Iran; Korea, Rep. of = Republic of Korea.

* 2016 data are used because 2017 data are unavailable.

Source: Author's calculation based on the World Bank, World Development Indicators. https://databank.worldbank.org/data/source/world-development-indicators (accessed 1 June 2018).

Women often do not have the same footing as men due to gender-based legal impediments that continue to exist and perpetuate the gender gap in many economies in Asia. These impediments effectively crystallize and legalize historical discrimination, and drive gender gaps that tend to undermine GDP growth (Gonzales et al. 2015). Legal restrictions may affect the kinds of work women can perform, the sectors they are allowed to work in, and the conditions under which they can work. The figure shows that gender restrictions based on types of work are prevalent in Central Asia. The pervasive gender disparity in employment revolves around a range of issues from perception to legal restrictions, which vary across regions. A World Bank study reveals that labor market laws not only encourage women to enter the formal labor force but also increase their earning potential (World Bank 2018).

Women typically face gender-based restrictions on the types of work or working conditions, and these are more prevalent in manufacturing than in services (see Figure 12.7). Gender biases may exist in certain services sectors, such as construction, owing to the nature of the work being similar to that found in heavy industries.

Figure 12.7 reveals that gender-based legal restrictions vary across all five regions in Asia. For instance, gender inequality or restrictions

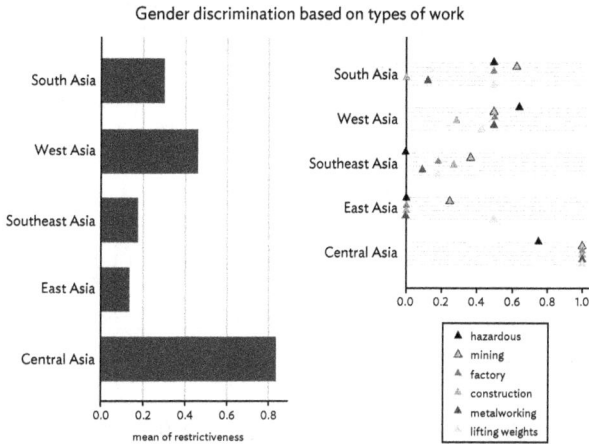

Figure 12.7 Women, Business, and the Law Indicators, Asia

Gender discrimination based on types of work

Note: The graph on the left averages out the restrictiveness across 15 variables related to gender-based discrimination in different types of work.

Source: Author's calculation based on the World Bank, Women, Business and the Law Data. https://datacatalog.worldbank.org/dataset/women-business-and-law (accessed 1 June 2018).

on jobs deemed hazardous is rated at 0% in East and Southeast Asia compared to 50% in South Asia. Socially constructed beliefs that women need protection from high-risk work, especially in South Asia, can partly explain the low female engagement in heavy industries. A large number of economies in South and West Asia deem women to be unable to work in the same industries as men, when in fact it has been found that eliminating barriers preventing women from working in certain sectors or occupations can increase labor productivity by as much as 25% in some economies (World Bank 2012). The notion that men are stronger than women and therefore better suited to certain jobs is deeply entrenched in some societies, which may partly explain the restrictions women face in manufacturing or certain services sectors deemed more physically demanding, such as construction. While women face fairly low restrictions in East Asia, gender-based discrimination still exists in occupations that involve mining or lifting heavy objects. Meanwhile, women in Central Asia face legal impediments in most types of work perceived as more suitable for men. Such restrictions limit women's employment opportunities in sectors available to men and exacerbate gender segregation in labor markets. Perhaps implicit in restrictions on working hours is the belief that women need to undertake (unpaid) domestic labor during evening and night hours, such as preparing meals and childcare. Restrictions like this explain the historical patterns of discrimination against women, with corresponding negative economic impacts. Biased gender perceptions along with legal gender differences tend to cluster women in certain sectors. Services, complemented by proper policies and sectoral development strategies, can contribute to gender equity by providing equal opportunities for women and encouraging their economic independence. Policies enabling a level playing field between women and men should be central to the nexus of deindustrialization and gender employment trends.

12.3 Firm-level Data Analysis

The World Bank Enterprise Survey compiles firm-level data covering more than 130,000 firms in a large range of economies across the different regions in different years. The survey covers a cross-section of firms for a single year of data in a particular country. While some countries are surveyed more than once, they may not be the same set of firms. The survey employs stratified random sampling in which all population units are grouped within homogeneous groups and simple random samples are selected within each group.

The dataset contains gender-specific information on the firms, including indicators of whether or not the senior manager is female, whether or not there is a female owner, and the number of female employees. Other relevant gender variables may or may not be used depending on the number of observations available. It also contains other information on output, employment, and wages, among others. Data points deemed unreliable by the surveyor are dropped. Data points for manufacturing are found to be more complete than those for services. Therefore, variables that do not capture enough observations for services are omitted from this analysis. Total factor productivity estimates produced by the World Bank based on sales are used to capture data from manufacturing and services firms; the reason for this is that measuring value added is problematic for services firms. Data are transformed into a common currency and deflated to 2009 using the GDP deflator for the United States from the relevant fiscal year. Similarly, data on female production and nonproduction workers are only available for firms that responded to the manufacturing survey; thus, we cannot investigate this from a services perspective. Table 12.1 lists the variables we use and their definitions.

Table 12.1 Variable Definitions

Variable	Definition
Female manager	Dummy variable equal to 1 for firms that have a female top manager
Female owner	Dummy variable equal to 1 for firms that have at least 1 female owner
% female ownership	Share of female ownership in a firm
Log (female employees)	Logarithm of the number of female employees
Log (employees)	Logarithm of the number of total full-time employees
Log (sales)	Logarithm of total sales for the last fiscal year, deflated to 2009 US dollars
Log (labor productivity)	Logarithm of output per worker, deflated to 2009 US dollars
Log (capital per worker)	Logarithm of estimated capital per worker calculated using the perpetual inventory method and investment in the last fiscal year (in 2009 US dollars)
Log (wage per worker)	Logarithm of wage per worker, deflated to 2009 US dollars
Firm's age	Number of years elapsed since the year the firm was established
Level of education	Share of workers who completed high school
% skilled production workers	Share of skilled workers among total production workers

US = United States.
Source: Authors.

12.3.1 Preliminary Analysis

This section analyzes the gender aspect of firms in manufacturing compared to services. A preliminary analysis is conducted using descriptive statistics without implying any causal relationship. The associations between female variables and other characteristics of the firm can be examined using graphical methods. The descriptive statistics part of the analysis is simply aimed at shedding light on observed differences and correlations.

The kernel density chart below examines whether female-managed firms tend to have higher labor productivity and if there is any difference between manufacturing and services in this regard. Female-managed firms are compared with nonfemale-managed firms in the case of manufacturing as well as services. The density for female-managed firms is shifted slightly to the right compared to nonfemale-managed firms in the case of services. This shows preliminary evidence that female-managed firms tend to have higher labor productivity than nonfemale-managed firms in services.

Unlike in manufacturing, female- and male-managed firms perform relatively equally in terms of generating productivity in services. This shows that female leadership and its relationship with productivity (measured by sales per worker) is more pronounced in services than it is in manufacturing, indicating better opportunities for female managers in services than in manufacturing.

A similar analysis is conducted to examine any association between the same female variable and the size of the firms for services as well as manufacturing. Services firms tend to be smaller than manufacturing firms in general. Unlike manufacturing firms, services firms tend to have lower capital requirements and can operate on a small scale without facing a cost disadvantage. Manufacturing firms invest in machinery, which pressures the firms to grow and operate on a larger scale to drive down average costs. Services, on the other hand, generally do not require large production facilities. This should be interpreted with caution as there may be variation within services themselves, with smaller firms clustering in certain sectors such as restaurants and business services, for instance.

Female-managed firms tend to be smaller in size in both sectors, but more so in manufacturing. This may reflect higher self-employment among women or women entrepreneurship in services, where they typically face less gender-based discrimination than in manufacturing.

Figure 12.8 Kernel Density of Labor Productivity, by Sector

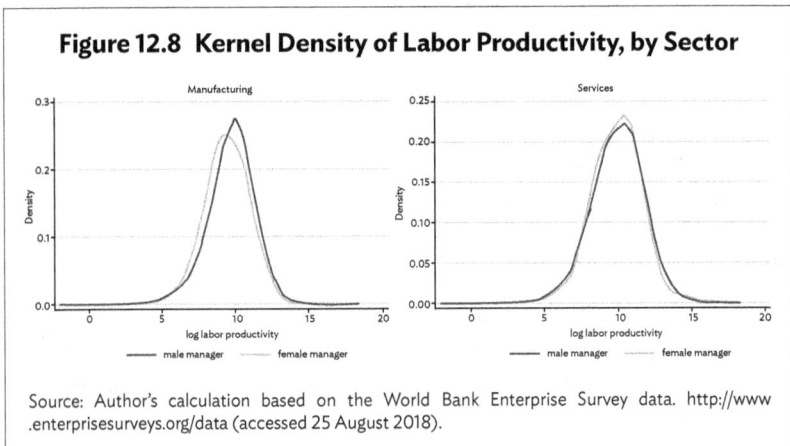

Source: Author's calculation based on the World Bank Enterprise Survey data. http://www .enterprisesurveys.org/data (accessed 25 August 2018).

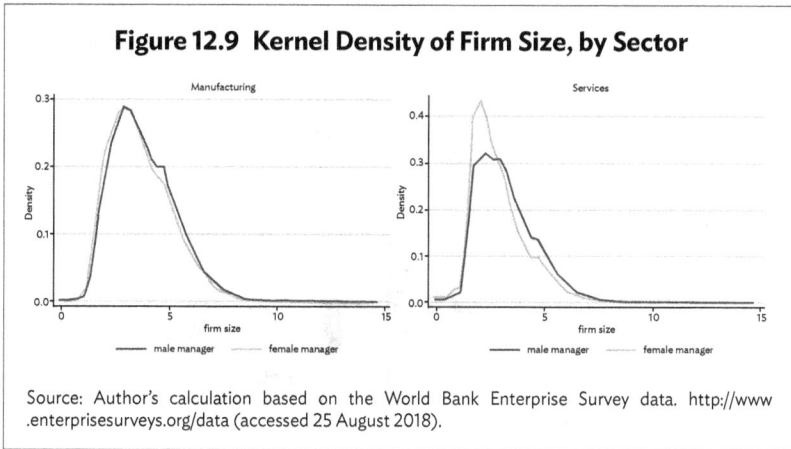

Figure 12.9 Kernel Density of Firm Size, by Sector

Source: Author's calculation based on the World Bank Enterprise Survey data. http://www
.enterprisesurveys.org/data (accessed 25 August 2018).

It is easier for women to start and operate a small-scale business in services than it is in manufacturing.

While simple averages only reveal observed differences without controlling for other factors, the survey data show that labor productivity is slightly higher in services than it is in manufacturing, except in South Asia and Africa. The same pattern is observed for female-managed and nonfemale-managed firms. However, this should be interpreted with care as there may be variation across sectors in services with higher productivity in knowledge-intensive business sectors, for example. In addition, the interlinkages between manufacturing and services must be taken into account as manufacturing firms that integrate more and better services inputs tend to have higher productivity than those who do not.

Although labor productivity in South Asia appears slightly lower in services than in manufacturing, there is variation within the region. In India, the rapid growth in services and rather stagnant state of manufacturing are likely to result in higher labor productivity in services than in manufacturing. Other economies may still be relying largely on agriculture and caught in low-productivity jobs in services. Sectoral shifts happening around the globe imply that resources are gradually being reallocated to the services sector as the services share of employment grows.

The decline in manufacturing's share in employment may give rise to concerns based on the belief that manufacturing plays a key role as a driver of productivity growth. As shown above, female employment in Asia is generally shifting away from agriculture (largely) and from

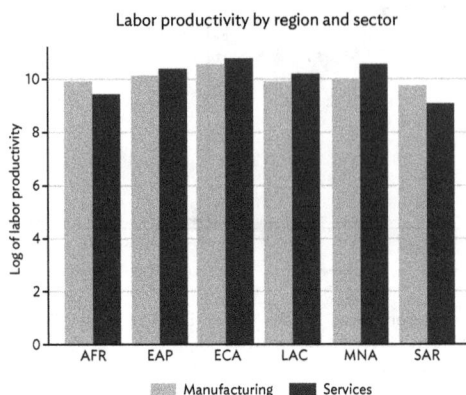

Figure 12.10 Labor Productivity, by Region and Sector

Labor productivity by region and sector

AFR = Africa, EAP = East Asia and the Pacific, ECA = Eastern Europe and Central Asia, LAC = Latin America and the Caribbean, MNA = Middle East and North Africa, SAR = South Asian Region.

Source: Author's calculation based on the World Bank Enterprise Survey data and Total Factor Productivity estimates. http://www.enterprisesurveys.org/data (accessed 25 August 2018).

manufacturing (partly) toward services. The case for men is different, with employment shifting away from agriculture toward both manufacturing and services. Therefore, concerns over bypassing the traditional manufacturing sector may be more prominent among female workers in this case. It may be questioned whether displaced female workers in agriculture could be equally or more productive in services than they would have been in manufacturing. This largely depends on human capital accumulation to boost absorption in high-end services as well as tradable services. For instance, the large mobility cost associated with switching sectors negatively affects output (Lee and Wolpin 2006).

Female leadership in firms is generally low around the world, and this may be attributed to discriminatory practices in hiring women for higher positions. However, the picture looks more promising in services than in manufacturing. The share of female-managed firms is, on average, higher in services than in manufacturing in all of the regions under consideration (Figure 12.11). This difference is particularly profound in the EAP region, where women manage one in four services firms, surpassing the shares in all of the other regions. For instance, this share is nearly halved in South Asia where the role of women in leadership is still limited, but it is still higher in services than in manufacturing, on average.

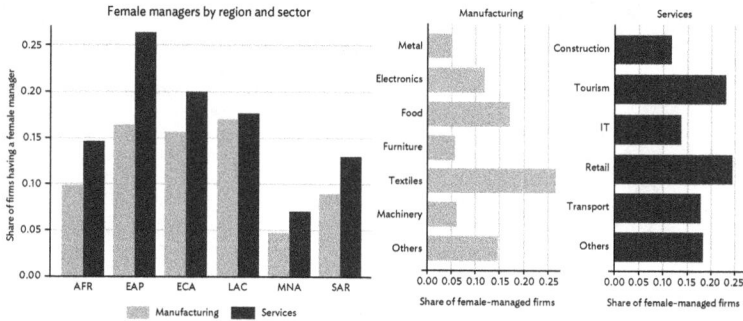

Figure 12.11 Female-Managed Firms, by Region

AFR = Africa, EAP = East Asia and the Pacific, ECA = Eastern Europe and Central Asia, IT = information technology, LAC = Latin America and the Caribbean, MNA = Middle East and North Africa, SAR = South Asian Region.

Source: Author's calculation based on the World Bank Enterprise Survey data. http://www .enterprisesurveys.org/data (accessed 25 August 2018).

The variation within sectors is then examined to provide better insights into the opportunities for women in managerial roles (Figure 12.11). In manufacturing, the share of female-managed firms is highest in food and textiles, showing that the opportunities for women to acquire higher positions are still limited to light manufacturing, which employs a relatively high share of female labor.

Heterogeneity also exists in services, with certain sectors, including tourism and retail, having relatively higher shares of female-managed firms. Tourism is a top foreign exchange earner in many developing economies, and is typically labor-intensive, enabling quick entry of women into the workforce. Compared to other sectors, tourism generally requires a lower level of education and less financing, thereby allowing more women to run their own businesses in this sector. As digital technology revolutionizes the tourism industry through the emergence of sharing platforms, it offers a flexible employment model for women, who often cannot commit to a full-time job due to family responsibilities when their male partners do not share burdens equally. This time limitation may contribute to the clustering of women in occupations in which they are typically paid less. While it may be easier for women to reach higher positions in female-dominated sectors where they face less competition from men, there may still be disparity in women's ability to take up senior roles. In addition, female-managed firms in these areas may still be largely in the informal sector.

Table 12.2 Descriptive Regressions, Female Manager

Manufacturing	ln_sales	ln_employees	ln_lab_prod	ln_cap_empl	ln_wage_empl	ln_female_employees
female_manager	−0.295***	−0.177***	−0.150***	−0.205***	−0.064**	−0.036
	(0.000)	(0.000)	(0.000)	(0.002)	(0.030)	(0.328)
_cons	13.236***	3.742***	9.496***	9.571***	7.535***	2.376***
	(0.000)	(0.000)	(0.000)	(0.000)	(0.000)	(0.000)
N	23,297.000	29,199.000	23,246.000	11,315.000	23,045.000	18,336.000
Services						
female_manager	−0.366***	−0.330***	−0.059*	−0.128*	−0.072**	−0.003
	(0.000)	(0.000)	(0.057)	(0.056)	(0.024)	(0.892)
_cons	13.034***	3.175***	9.877***	9.943***	7.723***	1.839***
	(0.000)	(0.000)	(0.000)	(0.000)	(0.000)	(0.000)
N	20,540.000	25,818.000	20,407.000	9,486.000	20,056.000	21,104.000

Statistical significance is indicated as follows: * (10%), ** (5%), and *** (1%).
Source: Author's calculation based on the World Bank Enterprise Survey data. http://www.enterprisesurveys .org/data (accessed 25 August 2018).

The descriptive regressions below attempt to analyze the associations between female leadership roles (e.g., female managers) and other basic information on firm performance, including sales, firm size, labor productivity, capital intensity, wages, and the number of female employees. The labor productivity variable used here is defined as output per worker, instead of value added per worker as defined in the kernel density chart above, so as to capture more observations.

Female-managed firms are associated with lower sales, more so in services than in manufacturing (Table 12.2). As female-managed firms tend to be smaller in size, especially in services, the sales generated and the wages paid may be lower than is the case for larger firms, although no causal relationship can be drawn at this stage. The association between having a female manager and a smaller firm size is stronger in services than in manufacturing. In other words, female-managed firms tend to run smaller operations in services than do non-female-managed firms. It is generally harder for women to access the financing and resources needed to expand or formalize their businesses. Female-managed firms tend to have lower productivity than non-female-managed firms, especially in manufacturing; this may indicate higher barriers for women in leadership roles in manufacturing. Duke (2017) finds that the representation of women in leadership roles is particularly low in certain fields, such as energy, mining, and manufacturing. Female-managed firms also tend to have lower capital intensity in both sectors, but this is more apparent in manufacturing than in services. This may suggest that women tend to cluster around less capital-intensive sectors and/or have more limited access to capital. There is no obvious association between the number of female employees and that of female managers.

It is important to benchmark female participation, not only in managerial positions, but also in ownership. The dataset used in this study includes an indicator of female ownership, which takes the value of 1 for the presence of at least one female owner. While another indicator would make it possible to disentangle different levels of female ownership, the observations captured would be limited.

Women's share in firm ownership has been on the rise as the world moves toward narrowing gender inequality. Figure 12.12 uses the percentage share of female ownership in a firm and compares the situation between manufacturing and services. Women's share of ownership has been, on average, higher in services than in manufacturing, indicating lower initial barriers for women in services than manufacturing. Moreover, among younger firms, the share of women's ownership is higher and the difference between manufacturing and services is narrower. There are more women in managerial and ownership positions than there were a few decades ago. Over time, increasingly more economies have been adopting reforms to address discriminatory legal provisions—such as laws discriminating against

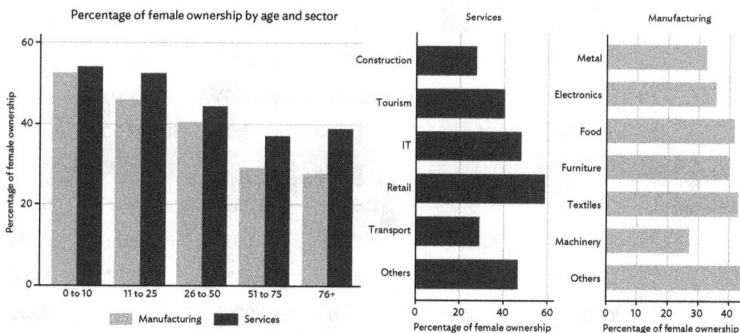

Figure 12.12 Share of Female Ownership, by Firm's Age and Sector

IT = information technology.

Source: Author's calculation based on the World Bank Enterprise Survey data. http://www.enterprisesurveys.org/data (accessed 25 August 2018).

women opening a bank accounts and registering their businesses, among others—that discourage females from participating in ownership or entrepreneurship. As such measures become less prevalent, women's ownership naturally increases.

The patterns in the variations in the share of female ownership across different subsectors are similar to those observed for women in leadership roles, reflecting persistent occupational segregation. In services, the largest average share of female ownership is found to be highest in retail and lowest in construction. In manufacturing, the largest average share of female ownership is found to be highest in textiles and lowest in machinery. Overall, the average share of female ownership is relatively low in the male-dominated sectors.

Firms that report gender diversity in their ownership tend to be larger and have higher sales; this is especially true in manufacturing. However, female-owned firms generally employ more female workers; this association is stronger in services than in manufacturing. Similar to our previous observations of female-managed firms, female-owned firms tend to have lower capital intensity. This may indicate that women can more easily acquire ownership in less capital-intensive sectors. There is no clear association between gender diversity in ownership and labor productivity.

Table 12.3 Descriptive Regressions, Female Owner

Manufacturing	ln_sales	ln_employees	ln_lab_prod	ln_cap_empl	ln_wage_empl	ln_female_employees
female_owner	0.103***	0.150***	-0.035	-0.068*	-0.015	0.121***
	(0.007)	(0.000)	(0.110)	(0.050)	(0.381)	(0.000)
_cons	13.026***	3.569***	9.471***	9.643***	7.588***	2.204***
	(0.000)	(0.000)	(0.000)	(0.000)	(0.000)	(0.000)
N	30,718.000	38,006.000	30,670.000	15,506.000	30,423.000	24,908.000
Services						
female_owner	-0.005	0.022	-0.037	-0.069*	-0.028	0.142***
	(0.875)	(0.314)	(0.103)	(0.091)	(0.182)	(0.000)
_cons	12.874***	3.052***	9.830***	9.983***	7.719***	1.782***
	(0.000)	(0.000)	(0.000)	(0.000)	(0.000)	(0.000)
N	25,314.000	30,793.000	25,187.000	11,826.000	24,846.000	19,980.000

Statistical significance is indicated as follows: * (10%), ** (5%), and *** (1%).

Source: Author's calculation based on the World Bank Enterprise Survey data. http://www.enterprisesurveys .org/data (accessed 25 August 2018).

Structural transformation implies a change in the composition of jobs and skills. In addition, the potential jobs lost due to automation can be offset by jobs gained from products and services enabled by technologies only if they are complemented by an appropriate level of skills. The rise of services is likely to be increasingly dominated by highly skill-intensive sectors, and skill-biased technological change will increase the need for human capital accumulation and higher skills.

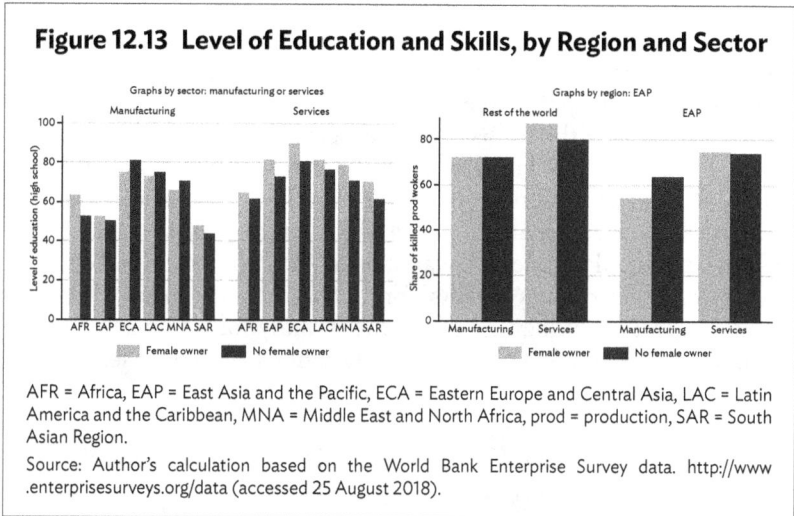

Figure 12.13 Level of Education and Skills, by Region and Sector

AFR = Africa, EAP = East Asia and the Pacific, ECA = Eastern Europe and Central Asia, LAC = Latin America and the Caribbean, MNA = Middle East and North Africa, prod = production, SAR = South Asian Region.

Source: Author's calculation based on the World Bank Enterprise Survey data. http://www.enterprisesurveys.org/data (accessed 25 August 2018).

Figure 12.13 reveals that the level of education of workers is generally higher in services than in manufacturing. The level of education is measured by the share of workers with a high school education. From a gender perspective, it is interesting to observe that services firms with diversified ownership tend to be slightly higher skilled than purely male-owned firms across all regions. This is not the case for manufacturing firms, for which the results are mixed. The difference in educational levels between services and manufacturing is particularly prominent in the EAP and South Asian regions. While this chart presents preliminary observations from which a solid conclusion cannot be derived, it shows the importance of investing in education to facilitate the transition of displaced workers from manufacturing to services. While it cannot be assumed that higher educational attainment is synonymous with higher skills, a similar pattern is observed when looking at the difference between the share of skilled workers in manufacturing and services.

Services firms are typically characterized by a larger share of skilled workers than are manufacturing firms. From a gender perspective, services firms with diversified ownership have an equal (in the EAP region) or higher (rest of the world) share of skilled workers than do male-owned services firms. The opposite is true for manufacturing, where firms with diversified ownership tend to have an equal or lower share of skilled workers than do male-owned firms.

12.3.2 Econometric Models

The following section uses econometric modeling to examine women's prospects in services relative to manufacturing, focusing on managerial responsibility, entrepreneurship (ownership), and labor. Specifically, we estimate models of the probability of observing female management or female ownership based on firm-level characteristics. Then we estimate conditional labor-demand models for female labor. In all cases, we distinguish between manufacturing and services firms to determine how the impact of firm-level covariates varies according to sector.

Table 12.4 presents results for a conditional (fixed effects by country-sector-year) logit model of the dummy for a female manager. Column 1 uses manufacturing firms only, while Column 2 uses services

Table 12.4 Regression Results for Female Management

	Manufacturing	Services
ln_sales	−0.103***	−0.190***
	(0.002)	(0.000)
ln_wage_empl	0.002	−0.029
	(0.964)	(0.320)
ln_lab_prod	0.001	0.171***
	(0.982)	(0.000)
ln_cap_empl	−0.039*	−0.036*
	(0.052)	(0.068)
N	8,471.000	7,434.000
Pseudo R^2	0.008	0.011
Fixed Effects	Country-sector-year	Country-sector-year

Note: All models are estimated by conditional (fixed effects) logit with female management as the dependent variable. Samples are indicated at the top of each column. P-values based on robust standard errors adjusted for clustering by country-sector-year are presented in parentheses underneath the parameter estimates. Statistical significance is indicated as follows: * (10%), ** (5%), and *** (1%).

Source: Authors' calculation.

firms only. Larger firms are less likely to have female managers, and the effect is stronger in services than in manufacturing, which is consistent with the kernel density figures presented in the previous section. More productive firms are more likely to have a female senior manager in services, but not in manufacturing. The result for services is statistically significant. The relationship between labor productivity and female manager indicates that women have better prospects in services. More capital-intensive firms are less likely to have a female manager in both manufacturing and services. We conclude that the services sector offers opportunities for female managers, but it is difficult to assess those opportunities relative to manufacturing, as the size and productivity relationships move in opposite directions. Based on productivity, there is evidence that the services sector is more open to female managers than is manufacturing, but we do not draw a strong conclusion based on these results.

Table 12.5 presents results from similar models for female ownership. The variable takes a value of 1 if the firm has at least one female owner. The relationship between firm size and the probability of having a female owner is the reverse of what was seen for a female manager: there is a positive association between firm size and the probability of having a

Table 12.5 Regression Results for Female Ownership

	Manufacturing	Services
ln_sales	0.071***	0.036
	(0.000)	(0.116)
ln_wage_empl	0.007	0.024
	(0.792)	(0.259)
ln_lab_prod	-0.106***	-0.071**
	(0.000)	(0.015)
ln_cap_empl	-0.007	-0.016
	(0.558)	(0.235)
N	13,326.000	10,145.000
Pseudo R²	0.002	0.001
Fixed Effects	Country-sector-year	Country-sector-year

Note: All models are estimated by conditional (fixed effects) logit with female ownership as the dependent variable. Samples are indicated at the top of each column. P-values based on robust standard errors adjusted for clustering by country-sector-year are presented in parentheses underneath the parameter estimates. Statistical significance is indicated as follows: * (10%), ** (5%), and *** (1%).
Source: Authors' calculation.

female owner, but the relationship is significant only in manufacturing. In contrast, more productive firms are less likely to have a female owner, and that effect is stronger in manufacturing than in services. The results for labor productivity are the reverse of what was observed for a female manager, but they again indicate better prospects for women in services. There is no clear relationship between wages or capital intensity and female ownership. The results from the regression models confirm that services offer prospects for female entrepreneurship, but there is only weak evidence that the environment is more conducive to female ownership in services than in manufacturing, based on the fact that the negative relationship between productivity and female ownership is stronger in manufacturing than in services.

Finally, Table 12.6 presents the results from the conditional labor-demand models for female workers. These models fit the data much better than do the two conditional logit models, since most of the independent variables have coefficients that are statistically significant

Table 12.6 Regression Results for Conditional Labor Demand Models for Women

	Manufacturing	Services
ln_sales	0.926***	0.816***
	(0.000)	(0.000)
ln_wage_empl	0.069***	0.041***
	(0.000)	(0.000)
ln_lab_prod	-1.000***	-0.780***
	(0.000)	(0.000)
ln_cap_empl	-0.020***	-0.027***
	(0.001)	(0.000)
_cons	-0.878***	-1.209***
	(0.000)	(0.000)
N	10,562.000	6,943.000
Pseudo R^2	0.609	0.571
Fixed Effects	Country-sector-year	Country-sector-year

Note: All models are estimated by ordinary least squares with the logarithm of the number of female employees as the dependent variable. Samples are indicated at the top of each column. P-values based on robust standard errors adjusted for clustering by country-sector-year are presented in parentheses underneath the parameter estimates. Statistical significance is indicated as follows: * (10%), ** (5%), and *** (1%).

Source: Authors' calculation.

at the 5% level or better. In terms of the relationship between these variables and female labor demand, we see a positive impact of size in both sub-samples, with a stronger coefficient for manufacturing. Labor productivity has negative coefficients, but it is stronger in the case of manufacturing than services. Capital intensity also has a negative coefficient in both manufacturing and services. Although the pattern of signs is ambiguous, these results provide evidence that the services sector offers opportunities for women workers, and in particular that the negative effect of productivity is lower than in the case of manufacturing. Although we do not draw any strong conclusions, as noted above, we believe the data are consistent with superior labor market conditions for women in services relative to manufacturing.

While the relationship between labor productivity and all three female variables varies, the results consistently indicate that women have better prospects in services. For instance, the observation that more productive firms tend to have lower gender diversity in ownership and fewer female workers is more apparent in the case of manufacturing than in services. Similarly, more productive firms are likely to have a female manager in services, but this is not necessarily the case for manufacturing.

12.4 Conclusion

Using both country-level and firm-level data, this chapter provides some evidence that the sectoral shift toward services is in fact not gender-neutral. While women are still largely clustered in lower order services such as retail and tourism, evidence from this chapter indicates that services generally provide better prospects for women in the labor market than does manufacturing. Formal legal barriers and cultural norms confine women to a narrow range of sectors perceived by society as more suitable or appropriate for women, particularly sectors that require fewer physical skills or provide a safer environment. This partly explains the limited involvement of women in heavy industries and the overrepresentation of women in light manufacturing, driving occupational segregation. Services sectors are typically characterized by occupations that require less manpower and more interpersonal or intellectual skills. Our findings reveal that services firms, especially those with gender diversity in ownership, generally employ workers with a higher level of education and skills. Therefore, a shift toward a sector in which women have a comparative advantage such as services has the potential to promote gender equality in the labor market. For instance, the share of services in employment is rising relatively faster for women than for men in Asia, particularly in East Asia.

Gender differences in terms of entrepreneurship or leadership are also more apparent in manufacturing than services. The gender-based barriers faced by women are lower in services than in manufacturing. For instance, while women's share of firm ownership has increased in recent decades, women's share of ownership has on average always been higher in services than in manufacturing. In addition, the share of female-managed firms is higher in services than in manufacturing, particularly in the EAP region. The descriptive regressions in this chapter indicate that women are also likely to occupy managerial positions or participate in the ownership of firms that are smaller, have lower capital intensity, and require a lower entry cost, traits more commonly found in services than in manufacturing.

Globally, the share of services in employment is positively correlated with labor productivity for both men and women. However, this is not the case for female employment in industry. Observations from the enterprise survey indicate that, unlike in manufacturing, female- and male-managed firms perform more equally in terms of generating productivity in services. Similarly, our regression results show that women have better prospects in services, not only in terms of employment, but also leadership. More productive firms are likely to have a female manager in services.

Several policy implications can be drawn from these findings. The rise of services has the potential to promote gender equality in the labor market, contributing to the fifth Sustainable Development Goal. However, structural transformation will only translate into real economic opportunities for women when other factors affecting occupational segregation are addressed, including through legal reforms, promoting women's education, and facilitating women's access to capital. Additionally, institutional changes can address gender differences in carrying family responsibilities by providing more flexible employment and better working conditions for women. Achieving meaningful economic transformation may require facilitating the movement of female labor not only between sectors (transitioning from non-services to services sectors) but also within sectors (from low-productivity to high-productivity occupations). While structural transformation provides economic opportunities for women, it also creates risks for the women left behind by the restructuring. The ability to absorb female labor into higher skilled and more productive services sectors is key to women's empowerment and largely depends on investment in skills and education for women. Services can serve as a powerful avenue toward achieving gender equality if the proper policies are put in place.

References

Acharya, S. 2014. *Gender, Jobs and Education: Prospects and Realities in Nepal*. Kathmandu: United Nations Educational, Scientific and Cultural Organization.

Buera, F. J., J. P. Kaboski, and M. Q. Zhao. 2013. The Rise of Services: The Role of Skills, Scale, and Female Labor Supply. National Bureau of Economic Research Working Paper 19372. Cambridge, MA: National Bureau of Economic Research.

Chaudhary, R., and S. Verick. 2014. Female Labour Force Participation in India and Beyond. International Labour Organization (ILO) Working Papers. Geneva: International Labour Organization.

Duke, S. 2017. *The Key to Closing the Gender Gap? Putting More Women in Charge*. 2 November. https://www.weforum.org/agenda/2017/11/women-leaders-key-to-workplace-equality/ (accessed 1 June 2018).

Epod. 2016. *BCURE Case: Skills Training Programmes in South Asia*. September. https://skills-case2.herokuapp.com/index.html (accessed 1 June 2018).

Goldin, C. 2006. The Quiet Revolution that Transformed Women's Employment, Education, and Family. *American Economic Review* 96: 1–21.

Gonzales, C., S. Jain-Chandra, K. Kochhar, and M. Newiak. 2015. Fair Play: More Equal Laws Boost Female Labor Force Participation. *IMF Staff Discussion Notes*.

ILO. 2016. *Women at Work 2016*. Geneva: ILO.

ILO. 2017. *World Employment and Social Outlook: Trends for Women 2017*. ILO.

Lee, D., and K. I. Wolpin. 2006. Intersectoral Labor Mobility and the Growth of the Service Sector. *Econometrica* 74(1): 1–46.

McKinsey. 2015. *How Advancing Women's Equality Can Add $12 Trillion to Global Growth*. McKinsey Global Institute.

Ngai, R. L., and B. Petrongolo. 2017. Gender Gaps and the Rise of the Service Economy. *American Economic Journal: Macroeconomics* 9(4): 1–44.

Rendall, M. 2010. Brain Versus Brawn: The Realization of Women's Comparative Advantage. *Institute for Empirical Research in Economics Working Paper 491*.

Shepherd, B., and S. Stone. 2017. Trade and Women. Tokyo: Asian Development Bank Institute Working Paper 648.

World Economic Forum. 2016. *The Global Gender Gap Report 2016*. Geneva: World Economic Forum.

Women's Commission. 2015. *Hong Kong Women in Figures 2015*. Hong Kong, China: Women's Commission.

World Bank. 2012. *World Development Report 2012: Gender Equality and Development*. Washington, DC: World Bank.

World Bank. 2018. *Women, Business and the Law*. Washington, DC: World Bank.

Appendix

	Figure 2	Figure 3	Figure 7
South Asia			
Afghanistan	X	X	X
Bangladesh	X	X	X
Bhutan	X	X	X
India	X	X	X
Maldives	X	X	X
Nepal	X	X	X
Pakistan	X	X	X
Sri Lanka	X	X	X
West Asia			
Armenia	X	X	X
Azerbaijan	X	X	X
Bahrain	X	X	X
Georgia	X	X	X
Iran, Islamic Republic of	X	X	X
Iraq	X	X	X
Israel	X	X	
Jordan	X	X	X
Kuwait	X	X	
Lebanon	X	X	X
Oman	X	X	X
Qatar	X	X	X
Saudi Arabia	X	X	X
Syrian Arab Republic	X	X	X
United Arab Emirates	X	X	X
Yemen, Republic of	X	X	X
Southeast Asia			
Myanmar	X	X	X
Brunei Darussalam	X	X	X
Cambodia	X	X	X
Indonesia	X	X	X
Lao People's Democratic Republic	X	X	X

continued on next page

Appendix *continued*

	Figure 2	Figure 3	Figure 7
Malaysia	X	X	X
Philippines	X	X	X
Singapore	X	X	X
Thailand	X	X	X
Timor-Leste	X	X	X
Viet Nam	X	X	X
East Asia			
People's Republic of China	X	X	X
Taipei,China			X
Hong Kong, China	X	X	X
Japan	X	X	
Korea, Democratic People's Republic of	X	X	
Korea, Republic of	X	X	
Macau, China	X	X	
Mongolia	X	X	X
Central Asia			
Kazakhstan	X	X	X
Kyrgyz Republic	X	X	X
Tajikistan	X	X	X
Turkmenistan	X	X	
Uzbekistan	X	X	X

Source: Authors.

13

Conclusion

Matthias Helble and Ben Shepherd

13.1 Introduction

According to Rodrik (2016), premature deindustrialization refers to the fact that "[d]eveloping countries are turning into service economies without having gone through a proper experience of industrialization." He argues that this process has negative implications for developing countries' growth trajectories because manufacturing has three unique characteristics: (i) it is technologically dynamic; (ii) it has historically absorbed large quantities of unskilled labor; and (iii) it is tradable, so demand is not limited by the size of the domestic market.

The approach of the contributors to this book has been to examine each of these claims from the reverse angle, namely, the ability of services to contribute to development in the same way that manufacturing historically has. Our point of view is forward-looking and policy-oriented. Concretely, we aim to provide decision makers and analysts with information that can help them support rapid economic growth and poverty reduction in a very different economic and technological context from that faced by, for example, the Asian Tigers when they developed.

Although Rodrik (2016) is not a normative paper—its aim is primarily descriptive—the danger of calling a shift to a services economy in much of the developing world "premature" is that it could be read as recommending that governments use policies and incentives to keep resources in the manufacturing sector. If governments should wish to do so, there are many available measures to this end, although they have varying degrees of World Trade Organization (WTO) legality. However, whenever interventions aim to change the relative sizes of different sectors of the economy there is a need for caution. At a minimum, policymakers must be aware of what the two macro-sectors—manufacturing and services—actually involve. To the extent that intervention is warranted, it seems unlikely a priori that it would be at such a broad and general level, instead of at a more focused, micro-level. Yet, the premature deindustrialization argument does not delve into sectoral detail, but focuses primarily on the two aggregates. A subsidiary aim of this book has been to unpack these aggregates to look at them in greater detail and, to some extent, to expand upon what is presented as a simple descriptive framework.

In this chapter, we summarize the insights of the various contributions from the perspective of the four issues referred to above, which we distill into the following questions and provide some tentative answers:

(i)   Can services and manufacturing be meaningfully separated?

(ii) What are the links between services and technological dynamism?

(iii) How tradable are services?

(iv) Can services provide large numbers of good jobs?

13.2 Can Services and Manufacturing be Meaningfully Separated?

As an approach to a "whiteboard model" of the economy, it traditionally made sense to assume a separation between manufacturing and services. On the one hand, these aggregates reflect two of the three macro-sectors recognized by the national accounts (the other being agriculture). On the other hand, manufacturing was seen as the engine of global trade relations while services were seen as being produced and consumed locally and traded internationally relatively little.

How much sense does that distinction make now? Clearly, there are still important differences in the ways that services and manufactured goods are produced and consumed. Yet, as the chapters by Nayyar and Cruz, Miroudot, and Mercer-Blackman and Ablaza (Chapters 2, 4, and 5) make clear, the linkages between the two sectors are in fact extremely close, and only growing closer over time. Most manufacturing firms rely to a considerable extent on services inputs to produce and trade their goods, and this is reflected in trade in value added data when the transactions are at arm's length. However, many firms also provide services in-house. For instance, a factory with a design department, engineering department, maintenance workers, and sales associates is in fact engaged simultaneously in the production of manufactured goods and commercial services.

The ever closer association between manufacturing and services has implications for the data analysis used to develop the thesis of premature deindustrialization. The key issue is that some proportion of what appears in statistics as manufacturing value added, employment, and exports is in fact services activities that are embodied in the final product. From a measurement perspective, this development means that it is increasingly difficult to divorce trends in manufacturing value added, employment, and trade from similar trends in services. Although this statistical artifact is unlikely to drive the results that underlie the thesis of premature deindustrialization fully, it is clearly an area that requires further attention from statisticians and policy researchers.

The trends just referred to come together under the heading of the "servicification" or "servitization" of the economy. They are only accentuated when we consider the rise of the digital sector, which is discussed in van der Marel's chapter. Information and communications technologies (ICTs) are increasingly being used by manufacturing and services firms alike to reach customers in distant locations. These technologies tend to reduce trade costs for goods, while making it possible to trade in immaterial form services that previously required physical presence. Again, these developments complicate trade statistics, and make it increasingly difficult to maintain a strict separation between manufacturing and services. Of course, from a purely statistical point of view, there are major differences in the extent and details of the data available to analyze manufacturing and services; however, it is increasingly important for analysts to question the extent to which this reflects genuine characteristics of each aggregate, and the extent to which it is a historical hangover from a time when different technologies predominated. For instance, analysts, statisticians, and policymakers need to question how it is that, while there are numerous product categories devoted to a single manufactured good, like shirts, most countries do not adequately distinguish computer services from management consultancy services in their trade statistics.

All of these aspects come together in an empirical sense in the two chapters by Shepherd. In Chapter 6, on comparative advantage, he shows that the trade boom in manufactured goods in "Factory Asia" in the early 2000s was in fact accompanied by a remarkably similar boom in services trade. Even with respect to the data, it is difficult to disaggregate the two and speak of them completely independently. For example, it seems highly unlikely that Factory Asia could have developed without high quality transport services as inputs. This is reflected in Shepherd's second chapter (Chapter 8), in which he shows that there is a direct linkage between applied services policies and trade in manufactured goods, likely because manufacturers need to access high-quality services inputs. Indeed, manufacturing likely gains more from liberalizing services barriers than from the elimination of remaining tariffs, reflecting the fact that services sectors remain relatively restricted globally.

Thus, it seems that, unlike in the past, the reality of the current global economy is that manufacturing and services are closely intertwined. As a result, it is difficult to divorce them analytically and talk about secular trends in one sector that differ radically from secular trends in the other. Rather, we need to recognize—as Section 1.2 makes clear—that both are extremely heterogeneous aggregates. As a result, broad generalizations are unlikely to hold at a micro-level. While many would agree that an economy's pattern of specialization matters for its growth path, it does not follow that it makes sense to examine specialization at such a macro-level. Indeed, in the era of value chain-based development, it is more likely that patterns of comparative advantage and specialization are in fact narrowing, not broadening. Hence, it makes sense to look at the data in as disaggregated a form as possible, and to allow for significant differences across sectors within aggregates, rather than looking for secular differences between aggregates.

13.3 What Are the Links Between Services and Technological Dynamism?

Since the 1980s, with the rise of endogenous growth theories, services have been at the center of the analysis of economic growth, even if not explicitly named as such. Romer (1990), for example, looks at the production of "usable technology" in the sense of designs that can be combined with labor and capital to produce outputs, such as manufactured goods. Clearly, research and development of this type, as well as the engineering activity that converts the design into a product, are all services, not manufacturing as such. If the activity is outsourced, it appears in national accounts and input–output tables as services value added. If done in-house in a manufacturing firm, by contrast, it is not directly accounted for. However, many countries encourage this kind of activity through subsidies like tax credits for research and development, as they are convinced that the increasingly efficient production of research and engineering services can help sustain rapid economic growth, particularly close to the technology frontier.

Against this background, it is somewhat striking that the premature deindustrialization thesis sees services as inherently low productivity and low growth, but sees manufacturing as the opposite. The expectation from growth theory is that manufacturing cannot be high growth (i.e., technologically dynamic) without key services inputs. In standard economic theory, the causal link clearly runs from services to manufacturing in terms of the generation of growth and technological development. Indeed, even within manufacturing firms, when learning by doing or learning by exporting occurs, resulting in technological progress, this is typically the result of efforts by engineers, managers, and other service providers rather than those directly involved in the production of goods. Indeed, the chapter by van der Marel (Chapter 9) shows that an important piece of technological process in the current economic context, namely the use of digital technologies, is robustly associated with higher manufacturing productivity. This demonstrates the kind of link expected in the growth literature, but not dealt with in the premature deindustrialization literature.

Of course, it is not obvious where to draw the line between manufacturers and service providers (exactly the point made in Section 1.1 above). If the reality of technological change is complex, as this analysis suggests, how can it be useful for policy purposes to apply a rigid distinction between the two aggregates and assert that one is linked to technological progress and development, while the other is associated with stagnation?

A more challenging question relates to the growth potential and technological dynamism of services sectors themselves, on a more micro basis. It is very challenging to measure total factor productivity in services sectors, and all the more so since the literature in this area typically comes from the manufacturing sector. As a result, most analyses use simpler measures of productivity, like labor productivity. In her chapter (Chapter 7), Winkler shows that an important dimension of technological progress—the ability to generate positive externalities (i.e., spillovers external to the firm)—is present within services in the same way that it is commonly thought to be within manufacturing. Specifically, she uses data from developing countries to show that there are positive spillovers from services firms to manufacturing firms in the same geographical area. Importantly, she goes on to lay bare the complex mechanisms that mediate the ability to create and absorb spillovers—a vital policy question from the perspective of harnessing services to support growth and development in a comprehensive sense.

In his chapter on comparative advantage (Chapter 6), Shepherd takes a different approach. In a Ricardian model, trade is driven by differences in relative productivity, leading to an analytical possibility of inferring patterns of relative productivity in manufacturing and services alike from patterns of bilateral trade. Using disaggregated data, he shows that there is no simple dichotomy between manufacturing and services in terms of the level of productivity and its change over time (dynamism); instead, there are high-productivity, high-growth manufacturing subsectors, just as there are high-productivity, high-growth services subsectors (of course, the reverse is also true). Services is often caricatured as "burger flipping" in rich countries, and as household or personal services in poor countries. Yet, the reality is much more complex: the trade data demonstrate that a proper understanding of the growth potential of manufacturing and services requires a detailed analysis at the subsector level. Although this should not be surprising, such an analysis is not offered by the premature deindustrialization thesis.

13.4 How Tradable are Services?

The General Agreement on Tariffs and Trade Uruguay Round saw the negotiation of the General Agreement on Trade in Services (GATS), a partner to the former agreement but specifically for services trade. The GATS is now a key part of the WTO legal system. From a legal perspective, very few services cannot be traded at all under the GATS because the agreement adopts a broad definition of "trade," encompassing four modes of supply: (i) pure cross-border services trade, (ii) movement of the consumer, (iii) commercial establishment, (iv) and temporary movement of the service provider. Historically, economics textbooks referred to a haircut as an example of a non-tradable service, as it requires physical proximity between producer and consumer. However, under the GATS, these types of services are indeed tradable under Mode 4, and such trade does occur, albeit to a small extent: for example, professional hairdressers move back and forth to cater for fashion events and film production. Similarly, trade in haircuts can take place under Mode 3, when a salon chain establishes a subsidiary in another country. Again, this kind of trade is not only conceptually possible, but actually happens, albeit on a limited basis. Thus, in the modern services economy with its international legal basis, it is clearly untenable to describe services as "non-tradable" in a broad-based sense.

Of course, when economists claim that services are non-tradable they typically mean that they cannot be traded by Mode 1. However, although this is true of haircuts, it is less and less true of other services thanks to the rise of ICTs and associated changes in business practices. Even university professors who may see their services as non-tradable in fact provide educational services via Mode 1 themselves whenever a foreign student signs up for an online course. In sectors like legal services and financial services, cross-border trade is very substantial, and is expanding all the time in both volume and scope. Baldwin's "second unbundling" (Baldwin 2013) shows how tradable services are used to power further disaggregation of manufacturing activities across borders: offshoring is only possible if coordination costs can be kept down through the use of ICTs, and if management and headquarters services can be supplied reliably and cost-effectively at distance. His "third unbundling" (Baldwin 2016) leaves open the prospect of an even greater role for services, as technology makes it possible to limit the types of services where physical presence is in fact required, shifting more and more cross-border activity toward Mode 1 and away from Modes 3 and 4.

Shepherd's chapter on comparative advantage makes the point well using data for Factory Asia. As mentioned above, the boom in manufactured goods exports from that region during the 2000s was accompanied by growth of trade in services that was nearly as rapid. "Services" in this sense essentially captures Mode 1 trade, through balance of payments statistics. The policy takeaway is clear: changes in law and technology are rendering the tradability distinction between manufactures and services less and less relevant. Again, to make meaningful analytical headway, it is important to drill down to a much finer level of detail, looking at subsectors rather than aggregates. From a services perspective, some subsectors are highly tradable via Mode 1, and others are still difficult to trade in that way, although they are legally tradable under other modes of supply. Similarly, some manufactured goods tend to be traded intensively, and others less so. The insight in both cases is that it is really an issue of trade costs that determines the extent to which a particular product or service is in fact traded. The available evidence suggests that trade costs are higher in services than in goods (Miroudot, Sauvage, and Shepherd 2013), but a downward trend is apparent in some subsectors. This area is one where policy could make a large impact in terms of increasing the intensity of services trade, a point to which we return below.

13.5 Can Services Provide Large Numbers of Good Jobs?

In developed countries, especially the United States (US), core manufacturing activities like the metal and automotive sectors have historically been seen as providing large numbers of "good jobs" for low- and medium-skilled workers. The term "good jobs" has a particular sense in the US, where benefits like health insurance have historically been tied to employment relationships, and agreements with unions have historically been strong in large manufacturing sectors.[1] This can

---

[1] It is not clear that factory workers in low-income countries share the view of some US commentators that manufacturing offers "good jobs": Blattman and Dercon (2018) provide experimental evidence that workers in Ethiopia showed a strong disinclination to remain tied to employment in manufacturing, and that those with exposure experienced greater health problems.

also be operationalized more broadly in terms of "decent work", that is, the idea that what matters from a development perspective is not only the creation of jobs, but also the conditions under which people work, from salary to environmental features such as health and safety, as well as rights at work.

There is a clear tension between a sector's technological dynamism and its ability to provide decent work for large numbers of low- and medium-skilled workers. As technology progresses, it typically leads to some degree of substitution between capital and labor, and between different types of labor (e.g., skilled for unskilled). This is true in manufacturing and services alike. Although the relative importance of technology versus trade in driving losses in manufacturing employment in the US is a question on which there is no consensus as yet, estimates suggest that technological change accounted for perhaps 60% of total US job losses in manufacturing in the early 2000s (Autor, Dorn, and Hanson 2016). However, during that period, manufacturing value added continued to grow, suggesting that technological change was to some extent labor-substituting. This development brings out the clear tension between technological dynamism and job creation, and there is no reason to expect that the situation would be any different in services than it is in goods.

An important coda to the "China shock" research in the US comes from Feenstra and Sasahara (2018), who show that there are indeed net job losses due to trade when only merchandise is considered.[2] However, when services are included in the equation, the same period saw substantial net growth in US jobs thanks to trade integration. This result suggests that, at least in a developed economy, services trade is capable of generating very substantial job growth.

However, as shown by Helble, Long, and Trang (Chapter 11), the skill composition of jobs growth in services is not the same as in manufacturing. They show that while recent job growth in services has been rapid in Asia, even in an environment of rapidly increasing labor productivity, it has been skewed more toward high-skilled workers than has manufacturing. This finding is important from a labor market point of view, because it lends credence to one part of the premature deindustrialization thesis, namely that job creation for poor people in developing countries may be more limited under a services economy than in one where manufacturing plays a larger role. Having said this, the appropriate policy response to such a finding is open for debate: the orthodox view would be that it reinforces the already strong arguments

---

[2] The term "China shock" refers to the surge in exports from the People's Republic of China after the country joined the WTO in 2001.

for investing in education and training in low- and middle-income countries. We return to this point when we consider policy implications below.

In Chapter 10, Khatiwada looks at the issue more broadly, through the lens of decent work as understood in the international community. He shows that, from the perspective of job creation and earnings, some services subsectors in fact perform quite well in comparison with manufacturing. However, as discussed in a different context above, heterogeneity is a major issue: skill profiles, labor intensity, and wages differ significantly across services subsectors; and the same is likely true of manufacturing. Thus, although the labor market aspects of premature deindustrialization seem to be the part of the thesis with the strongest empirical support, the point remains that, in order to craft effective policy responses, it is necessary to move beyond analyzing large economic aggregates to look at subsectors. In doing so, it is important to recognize that it is not a sector's classification as "manufacturing" or "services" that matters most for its labor market characteristics, but instead its combination of technology, skill intensity, labor intensity, and growth potential. Nonetheless, Khatiwada makes the important point that the tradable (in a Mode 1 sense) services sector is still growing in most developing countries, and it is unclear whether it has the same immediate potential as manufacturing to access worldwide demand and thereby realize scale economies. Although this stance should be somewhat nuanced, as discussed above, an important issue for government policy is identifying the extent to which different sectors can access world markets, either immediately or in the short- to medium-term. Technological change is key in this regard: for example, most developing countries strongly resisted the inclusion of services in the Uruguay Round, but with technological change making business process outsourcing possible, countries like India and the Philippines have ended up seeing major export-side benefits from the expansion of services trade, in a way completely unforeseen only a short time earlier.

Lan and Shepherd explore the issue from a different angle, namely gender. Labor markets are, of course, highly gendered: women face barriers to entry that men do not, sometimes explicit legal prohibitions on working in particular sectors, and sometimes cultural norms that privilege "masculine" attributes for the performance of certain tasks. However, the evidence suggests that legal prohibitions are less of an issue in services than in manufacturing, particularly heavy manufacturing. This means that labor market opportunities for women may be relatively better following a trade-led expansion of services relative to an expansion of manufacturing. The point is an important one, as it suggests that in the current legal environment in many developing countries, the rise of the services economy may have fundamentally different implications for good jobs depending on whether it is men or women who are being considered. Given that women have historically been marginalized from labor markets, and that issues with access and equity continue around the world, there is an argument for allowing growth in sectors, like services, that are relatively favorable to female employment.

13.6 Policy Implications

The contributions brought together here are rich in policy implications for governments and decision makers in developing countries. We restate some of the most important in summary form here:

(i) Focus on disaggregated data rather than macroeconomic aggregates. As development economics has shifted focus from macroeconomic stabilization to the microeconomics of development, it has become necessary for policy makers to take a much more focused and nuanced view of economic behavior. The premature deindustrialization thesis breaks down in important respects when brought to the data at a disaggregated level. As a result, policy makers should avoid industrial policies that favor manufacturing at the expense of services; where vertical policies are necessary, they should be highly specific and time-bound, and could equally well be directed at dynamic services subsectors as manufacturing subsectors.

(ii) Recognize the interdependence of manufacturing and services. Manufacturers cannot be competitive without access to high-quality, reasonably priced services inputs, whether supplied in-house or at arm's length. These relationships are poorly understood because they are not well reflected in data. Firm-level surveys could usefully examine the connections between services and manufacturing activities at a highly disaggregated level, taking full account of in-house service provision. Policy makers need to be aware of the interdependence between services and manufacturing to avoid incentivizing manufacturers at the expense of service providers.

(iii) Services trade policies matter just as much, if not more, than tariffs. Given the high levels of restrictiveness of applied services policies in much of the world, there is a strong argument for focusing on reducing trade costs in services as a primary aim of international economic policy. As in other areas of trade, countries can either achieve most of the gains from liberalization through unilateral measures, or they can coordinate with partners. As multilateral negotiations on services have proved difficult, there is scope for countries to work creatively to reduce services trade costs, perhaps by adopting a quantitative target similar to what was done for goods under the Asia-Pacific Economic Cooperation's Trade Facilitation Action Plans.

(iv) Trade policies need to integrate the digital dimension. The rise of the digital economy is profoundly changing the dynamics of trade in manufacturing and services alike. Although adapting to rapidly changing technologies is challenging from a policy point of view, the evidence suggests that an overly restrictive stance can have economic costs. Although further work is needed in this area, there is an argument for privileging relatively liberal policies on data and digital trade, so as to allow industries that use these technologies to grow as quickly as possible.

(v) Deindustrialization is not gender-neutral. The shift in economic activity from manufacturing to services can potentially benefit women given historical patterns of discrimination in manufacturing. However, the policy priority for governments should be removing legal restrictions that prevent women from freely choosing their sector of employment, in the same way men do. Similarly, policies to address the gender wage gap are an important part of the policy agenda in all countries, developed and developing alike.

(vi) In a services economy, education and training are more important than ever. Given that the skill composition of services jobs is different from that in manufacturing, governments need to ensure the right match between skills and growing sectors. Investing in primary and secondary education is a key policy priority for developing country governments, and facilitating access to tertiary studies is also important, particularly in middle-income countries. Similarly, active labor market policies to enable workers to move to expanding sectors, including services, are important in an environment of significant economic shifts.

Underlying each of these policy priorities is a need for more data and research. Data on services are much less detailed than data on manufacturing, particularly when it comes to trade data.[3] International

---

[3] An overview of existing databases covering statistics of international trade in service at different international organizations is available at: https://unstats.un.org/unsd/tradeserv/TFSITS/matrix.htm

agencies can usefully work with national statistics agencies to build capacity in terms of collecting data on all modes of supply of services trade at a disaggregated level. Similarly, researchers who have traditionally focused on measuring total factor productivity in manufacturing sectors could turn their attention to services: there is a need for new and innovative methodologies to measure productivity at a disaggregated level, and better understand its dynamics and determinants. Similarly, the rise of the services economy, and its gendered nature, makes clear the need for gender-disaggregated statistics in all areas of economic life.

The contributions brought together here have taken some first steps in each of these directions. Our aim is to stimulate further policy and academic discussion of the development implications of the shift toward services. It is important that that discussion move beyond an analysis based on aggregates that are of less and less concrete meaning in the current economic context. Focusing on detailed data and mechanisms will make it possible for governments to design policies that will help support the next generation of growth and development.

References

Autor, D., D. Dorn, and G. Hanson. 2016. The China Shock: Learning from Labor Market Adjustment to Large Changes in Trade. *Annual Review of Economics* 8: 205–240.

Baldwin, R. 2013. Trade and Industrialization after Globalization's Second Unbundling: How Building and Joining a Supply Chain are Different and Why it Matters. In *Globalization in an Age of Crisis: Competition in the Twenty-First Century*, edited by R. Feenstra and A. Taylor. Cambridge, MA: National Bureau of Economic Research.

Baldwin, R. 2016. *The Great Convergence: Information Technology and the New Globalization*. Boston: Harvard University Press.

Blattman, C., and S. Dercon. 2018. The Impacts of Industrial and Entrepreneurial Work on Income and Health: Experimental Evidence from Ethiopia. *American Economic Journal: Applied Economics* 10(3): 1–38.

Feenstra, R., and A. Sasahara. 2018. The China Shock, Exports, and US Employment: A Global Input–Output Analysis. *Review of International Economics* 26(5): 1053–1083.

Miroudot, S., J. Sauvage, and B. Shepherd. 2013. Measuring the Cost of International Trade in Services. *World Trade Review* 12(4): 719–735.

Rodrik, D. 2016. Premature Deindustrialization. *Journal of Economic Growth* 21(1): 1–33.

Romer, P. 1990. Endogenous Technological Change. *Journal of Political Economy* 98(5): S71–S102.

Index

Figures, notes, and tables are indicated by f, n, and t following the page number.

www.ingramcontent.com/pod-product-compliance
Lightning Source LLC
Chambersburg PA
CBHW061232220326
41599CB00028B/5406